Space Regulations Library

Volume 13

The *Space Regulations Library* is a long-standing series of cutting-edge research written by practitioners and academics and addressing novel and emerging issues relating to the national and international regulation of space activities. The series covers key topics relating to, among other topics of significance, various approaches to the regulation of national space activities, the privatisation and commercialisation of space activities, NewSpace applications and developments, the role of cybersecurity and Artificial Intelligence in space activities, military uses of outer space, the exploration, exploitation and utilisation of space natural resources, and the settlement of space disputes. Through a rigorous selection and peer-review process, the *Space Regulations Library* aims to publish innovative works that highlight legal and policies issues of interest and concern for actors and stakeholders in the competitive and congested domain of outer space. In a shared global commons where various socio-economic, scientific, security, and commercial interests intersect, it is vital for industry professionals, government officials and academics worldwide to take note of existing rules as well as the challenges and trends in the formulation and implementation of regulations and policies governing space activities. With the practical insights and recommendations offered by the authors on a variety of topics in a domain where developments often outpace existing rules and policies, the *Space Regulations Library* aims to contribute to the continued dialogue on how to safeguard and promote the long-term sustainability, safety and security of outer space.

Stefan-Michael Wedenig

The International Responsibility of States for AI-enabled Space Activities

Springer

Stefan-Michael Wedenig
Institute of Air and Space Law
McGill University
Montreal, QC, Canada

ISSN 1572-6134 ISSN 2542-9558 (electronic)
Space Regulations Library
ISBN 978-3-032-09505-3 ISBN 978-3-032-09506-0 (eBook)
https://doi.org/10.1007/978-3-032-09506-0

This Springer imprint is published by the registered company Springer Nature Switzerland AG
The registered company address is: Gewerbestrasse 11, 6330 Cham, Switzerland

Acknowledgements

How foolish it might appear to express my gratitude to everybody who has contributed to this research within the meagre space of one page and a half. This research work is not mine alone, it belongs to everybody who encouraged me, who nudged me in the right direction, who talked me through different ideas and who endured my constant ramblings about AI and public international law.

To my family, whose support I could always rely on. Particularly, my mother, who, in every sense of the word, is a role-model to me.

To my best friend, Jürgen, whose weekly calls became a welcome distraction from every-day academia.

To my close friends, Jack Wright Nelson, Sandrine Ampleman-Tremblay and Miroslaw Michal Sadowski.

To my fellow DCL candidates, particularly Federico Suarez Ricaurte, Yuri Alexander Romana Rivas, Giusto Amadeo Boccheni, Jose Saldaña, Tanya Oberoi, Kaito Suzuki, Clarisse Delaville, Ihsan Ibrahim Daldaban and Ajey Sangai.

To my colleagues at the McGill Institute of Air and Space Law. Professor Donal Hanley, for giving me the opportunity to serve as the IASL's Executive Director.

To Arnold Agaba, Martina Elia Vitoloni and Judith Jahnke, for kindly lending their time to help me prepare for my second DCL Seminar and providing me with valuable feedback.

To Maria D'Amico whose support has been crucial in the first two years of my doctorate. She was not only a great IASL institution but also became a great colleague and good friend.

To Kuan-Wei (David) Chen for providing editorial feedback prior to publication.

To my wonderful supervisory committee chaired by my supervisor Prof. Ram Jakhu. His constant guidance, thoughtful comments and vast knowledge of space and public international law were crucial for my DCL journey and my work would not have been possible without his guidance. To Professor Fabien Gélinas and Professor Peer Zumbansen who opened my eyes to different perspectives and encouraged me to look at things differently. Their valuable feedback and comments were paramount for the success of this endeavour.

Finally, as I believed in the beginning of my academic journey and maintained throughout: *In Domino Confido.*

Competing Interests The author has no competing interests to declare that are relevant to the content of this manuscript.

Contents

Abbreviations

AI	Artificial Intelligence
ANN	Artificial Neural Network
BBP	Black Box Problem
COPUOS	Committee on the Peaceful Uses of Outer Space
DNN	Deep Neural Network
EU	European Union
GNSS	Global Navigation Satellite System
ICJ	International Court of Justice
IGA	Intergovernmental Agreement
ILC	International Law Commission
IoT	Internet of Things
ISO	International Organization for Standardization
ITU	International Telecommunication Union
ML	Machine Learning
OECD	Organization for Economic Co-Operation and Development
PCIJ	Permanent Court of International Justice
PPWT	Treaty on Prevention of the Placement of Weapons in Outer Space and of the Threat or Use of Force against Outer Space Objects
TCBM	Transparency and Confidence Building Measures
UN	United Nations
UNESCO	United Nations Educational, Scientific and Cultural Organization
UNOOSA	United Nations Office for Outer Space Affairs
US	United States
USSR	Union of Soviet Socialist Republics
VCLT	Vienna Convention on the Law of Treaties

Chapter 1
Introduction

1.1 Introductory Note

Imagine a computer so advanced that it can fully autonomously operate without human input and successfully accomplish missions in outer space. This is the notion upon which Stanley Kubrick builds his idea of HAL 9000 for his famous 1968 classic "2001: A Space Odyssey".[1] In the story the main character Dave and his partner Frank are sent on a secret mission to Jupiter accompanied by HAL 9000, an all-knowing highly advanced computer system which controls most of the spaceship's operations with only minimal input from the astronauts. The system is so highly developed that the HAL "9000 series is the most reliable computer ever made [and] has never made a mistake or distorted information" and is "by any practical definition of the word foolproof and incapable of errors".[2]

Once the mission commences, tension between the astronauts and HAL 9000 quickly begins to arise as the computer wants the astronauts to share more details about the secret mission, which they refuse to do. Soon, HAL 9000 warns the crew of a failure in an antenna system on the outside of the ship. Dave and Frank, wary of HAL 9000, try to conceal their conversation by locking themselves into the evacuation chamber, where the computer system cannot hear them. However, HAL 9000 reads their lips and learns of their suspicions. They eventually decide to replace the antenna but to shut HAL 9000 down, in case the computer made an error. When Frank leaves the spacecraft, HAL 9000 cuts his oxygen supply, locks Dave, who tried to help Frank, out of the space craft and shuts down life support for the other

[1] Stanley Kubrick, "2001: a Space Odyssey", DVD (Burbank, Cal: Warner Brothers, 2001).

[2] Khan Mata (2016) Hal 9000s interview. In: https://www.youtube.com/watch?v=BDha7nj4s10. Accessed 11 July 2025.

S.-M. Wedenig, *The International Responsibility of States for AI-enabled Space Activities*, Space Regulations Library 13,
https://doi.org/10.1007/978-3-032-09506-0_1

crew members. HAL 9000 justifies these steps by claiming that its deactivation would jeopardize the success of the mission.

As dystopian and dark as Kubrick's vision of a supercomputer might be, it directly reaches towards the very heart of the matter, namely unexpected outcomes produced by a machine that operates autonomously.

Artificial Intelligence (AI) has undoubtedly been a major driving force behind the industrial revolution of the twenty-first century. Within a relatively short period of time, this technology has expanded to many industries while developing at such a pace that it poses a challenge to lawmakers and legal experts alike.

Outer space, historically always one of the most technologically developed domains, is certainly no exception. The outer space environment is becoming increasingly accessible to private entities and educational institutions rather than purely being a "state domain".[3] Space activities, which were once solely the domain of rich space-faring nations, are now increasingly carried out by private enterprises for purely commercial purposes.[4]

From a legal point of view this poses some challenges. Space law is primarily founded upon the five UN space treaties, namely the Outer Space Treaty,[5] the Liability Convention,[6] the Registration Convention,[7] the Return and Rescue Agreement[8] and the Moon Agreement.[9] These international treaties were drafted, negotiated and concluded at a time when States were the main actors in outer space and thus commercial activities of private entities were not the main focal point of the negotiations.[10] The ambiguous wording of various treaty provisions and their applicability to private non-State actors in outer space has been the subject of vivid academic discussion since their inception, as will be highlighted throughout this book.[11]

[3] Hameed (2018); Baiocchi and Welser (2015); Welser WI (2016) The Democratization of Space. In: The Democratization of Space: New Actors Need New Rules. https://www.rand.org/pubs/commentary/2016/03/the-democratization-of-space.html. Accessed 16 July 2025.

[4] Farsaiya and Sharma (2014); de Zwaart (2017); Manoli (2017); Masson-Zwaan and Hofmann (2019); Dempsey (2017).

[5] Treaty on Principles Governing the Activities of States in the Exploration and Use of Outer Space, including the Moon and Other Celestial Bodies, (27 January 1967) 610 UNTS 205 [Outer Space Treaty].

[6] Convention on the international liability for damage caused by space objects (29 March 1972) 961 UNTS 187 [Liability Convnetion].

[7] Convention on Registration of Objects Launched into Outer Space (12 November 1974) 1023 UNTS 15 [Registration Convention].

[8] Agreement on the Rescue of Astronauts, the Return of Astronauts and the Return of Objects Launched into Outer Space, 22 April 1968, 672 UNTS 119.

[9] Agreement Governing the Activities of States on the Moon and Other Celestial Bodies, 05 December 1979, 1363 UNTS 3 [Moon Agreement].

[10] Rapp (2015); Freeland (2017); Dempsey (2017), pp. 754–755.

[11] See generally Palkovitz (2020), p. 63ff.

The introduction of AI adds an additional layer of complexity to the task of correctly assigning responsibility and liability in the outer space domain.[12]

The development of AI for outer space applications is rapidly evolving and investment in this developing area of technology is steadily increasing.[13] Indeed, AI is uniquely suited for the outer space environment, as it can be utilised for a wide variety of different space applications, especially those that are too hazardous or impossible for humans to conduct. Such applications include, *inter alia*, remote sensing, space communications, data collection and analysing, satellite navigation, cloud computing, asteroid mining, assisting astronauts, supporting deep-space exploration and facilitating space transportation.[14] AI is, without doubt, firmly part of humanity's future in outer space. Likewise, future space activities may predominately be conducted in outer space rather than on Earth. The outer space domain will become an even more important arena for commercial and State activities and the majority of future space applications will take place in outer space rather than on the surface of the Earth. Major investments and future planned missions are evidence of this.[15]

Despite all this, little attention in legal literature has been devoted to this emerging technology in the realm of international law, particularly in space law. The five UN Space Treaties are built around human interaction, and the advancement in AI technology may reach a point where the human is taken out of the equation entirely. This has direct implications for ascertaining the fault of the launching State for damage caused by a space object in outer space. A critical analysis of the

[12] Soroka and Kurkova (2019); Gal et al. (2020); Bratu et al. (2021); Vladeck (2014); Chatzipanagiotis (2020).

[13] Hameed (2018); Global AI in Space Market Outlook and Growth Forecast Report. https://www.bccresearch.com/market-research/information-technology/ai-in-space-market.html. Accessed 8 July 2025.

[14] Martin and Freeland (2021), sec. 4; Shekhtman L (2019) NASA Applying AI Technologies to Problems in Space Science. NASA. http://www.nasa.gov/feature/goddard/2019/nasa-takes-a-cue-from-silicon-valley-to-hatch-artificial-intelligence-technologies. Accessed 11 July 2025; Russek H et al. Automation, AI and Outer Space: Tech and the Future of Work in Canada. https://brookfieldinstitute.ca/new-technologies-future-of-work-in-canada-covid19. Accessed 11 July 2025; Artificial Intelligence in Space - Our Planet. https://ourplnt.com/artificial-intelligence-space/. Accessed 11 July 2025; Artificial Intelligence and your space business: A guide for the smart navigation of the challenges ahead. https://www.hoganlovells.com/~/media/hogan-lovells/pdf/2018/ai_article_space_02_01_2018.pdf?la=en. Accessed 11 July 2025; ESA Φ-lab. https://philab.phi.esa.int. Accessed 11 July 2025; Schmelzer R How Is AI Helping To Commercialize Space? In: Forbes. https://www.forbes.com/sites/cognitiveworld/2020/03/21/how-is-ai-helping-to-commercialize-space/. Accessed 11 July 2025; Saarela O (2022) A Promising Future for AI and Autonomy in Space. https://www.electronicdesign.com/technologies/embedded/article/21212499/mathworks-a-promising-future-for-ai-and-autonomy-in-space. Accessed 11 July 2025; Fowler G Council Post: AI's Role In Space Exploration. https://www.forbes.com/sites/forbesbusinessdevelopmentcouncil/2020/07/20/ais-role-in-space-exploration/. Accessed 11 July 2025.

[15] For example, the Artemis programme, under the leadership of the United States, intends to establish a permanent lunar base, a gateway in lunar orbit to launch future deep space mission, and to make first steps towards commercial resource exploitation. Artemis - NASA. https://www.nasa.gov/feature/artemis/. Accessed 11 July 2025.

fundamental principles relating to responsibility and liability of States for their AI-enabled space activities under the Outer Space Treaty and the Liability Convention is largely absent in contemporary space law literature. The question of whether the Outer Space Treaty and the Liability Convention are still adequate to govern highly-advanced AI applications, or whether the solution should rather be sought within the *lex lata* of general international law, needs to be urgently discussed in order to assess the rules that will be applicable once AI will predominantly be used in the space industry. This inquiry becomes especially important, if we consider that the Liability Convention requires the fault of the launching State for damage caused by a space object in outer space.[16] On the other hand, the Articles on State Responsibility, which are widely considered to be a codification of the rules of State responsibility in general international law, are silent on the question of subjective fault of the State and only seem to require objective fault.[17] These issues need to be considered because space law, as mentioned below, is embedded in general international law.

1.2 Outline and Theory

1.2.1 A Closer Theoretical Look at Responsibility

At the very outset of this book, it is necessary to briefly write a few words about the theory that informs the present research, in particular what this research, from a more theoretical perspective, understands under the term responsibility, and what it sees as the theoretical foundation of public international law, of which space law is a part.

Responsibility is a vague and broad concept, subject to a multitude of debates ranging from the political theoretical and moral philosophical to the normative. These debates often create "responsibility gaps" leading many to call for better or more regulation to address a specific challenge.[18] The difficulty in assessing responsibility lies in the fact that "different definitions of responsibility emphasize different aspects, depending on what the concept of responsibility is used for, such as addressing injustices, past or future challenges, taking care and so on".[19] Therefore, it is necessary that we carve out right at the beginning the boundaries of our understanding of responsibility. Responsibility may be understood as "the result of social relations and a dialogue between political actors intended to find a policy solution

[16] The Liability Convention establishes a two-tiered liability regime. For damage on the surface of the Earth the launching State is strictly liable, while for damage in outer space, fault is required. We will look at this more in detail in Chaps. 2 and 3.

[17] For the differentiation between objective and subjective fault see Chap. 2, Sect. 2.2, Footnote 10.

[18] Sienknecht and Vetterlein (2023), p. 1.

[19] Ibid, p. 2.

for problems",[20] and, regardless of what exact concept we emphasise, it is generally based on the relationship between a subject of responsibility, an object of responsibility and a normative authority.[21] Following this understanding, Sienknecht and Vetterlein argue that the responsibility relationships are not always clear and pose difficulties in determining how responsibility is established. These difficulties can range from a direct relationship between the subject and object of responsibility to a diffuse relationship which does not allow for a direct attribution to one or several specific actors. This can also encompass the specificity of the regulatory framework. In this regard the authors distinguish between situations with a fixed regulatory framework "where the question is one of applying the rules, and situations characterized by an unspecified, that is fragmented, contested or absent regulatory framework".[22] By combining these aspects, Sienknecht and Vetterlein argue that we arrive at four different types of responsibility, namely obligatory, prescribed, structural and discursive responsibility.[23]

Obligatory responsibility is a type of responsibility that has a clear fixed normative framework alongside clear relations between subject and object.[24]

Prescribed responsibility arises in situations in which we have a clear normative framework, but the responsibility relations are unclear thus making it difficult to allocate responsibility to specific actors.[25]

Structural responsibility describes a situation where the relation between subject and object is clear, but the normative framework does not exist or is insufficiently clear.[26]

Finally, discursive responsibility has been defined as a situation in which both the subject-object relations are unclear, and the normative framework is missing.

It is within the last category that debates regarding emerging and new technologies, such as AI or more broadly the Internet of Things (IoT), are often contained, which leads many authors to propose new regulatory frameworks to determine the subject and object of responsibility alongside the normative authority (usually a new legal regime). The present research aims to show that we can primarily assess the responsibility of States for AI-enabled space activities under obligatory responsibility, and the currently available normative framework, *the lex lata*, is adequate to govern these claims under space law and general international law because, in this author's view, subject, object and normative authority are sufficiently clear. In other

[20] Ibid, p. 6.

[21] Ibid. The subject, object and normative authority relationship is best illustrated with a legal example: A subject A has caused harm to object B, which entitles object B to claim "justice" based on the normative authority of the law. To bring it into the realm of space law, imagine the following example: A rocket of State A explodes during launch and destroys a government facility of State B. State B is entitled to claim compensation based on the Liability Convention.

[22] Ibid, p. 3.

[23] Ibid, p. 3.

[24] Ibid, p. 9.

[25] Ibid, p. 10.

[26] Ibid, pp. 10–11.

words, this research will work on the theoretical assumption that the normative framework of general international law provides a viable and preferred solution to govern AI applications in space activities, and that both subject and object relations are determined.[27]

1.2.2 State Consent in Public International Law

This understanding of State responsibility is further rooted in a more general understanding that all norms of public international law are based on the consent of States. "International law governs relations between independent States. The rules of law binding upon States therefore emanate from their own free will",[28] and therefore State consent plays a pivotal role in the creation of international law. This positivist-voluntarist point of view sees the consent of States as a pre-requisite for international obligations. It rests upon the belief that "all obligations are human created [and] that all obligations rest upon the consent of the obligated parties".[29] Therefore, any obligation under international law flows only from the consent-to-be-bound by a State.[30] This point of view finds its origin in the assumption that States are sovereign.[31]

This perspective stands in contradiction to the naturalist school of thought that assumes that there are certain universal laws and acknowledges these unwritten behavioural standards as primary sources of law which are binding upon States even without their consent.[32] In this regard, the positivist-voluntarist approach has often been criticized in the wake of the debate over *ius cogens*, that is norms States cannot contradict or opt-out from and are binding on the legal community as a whole. The Vienna Convention on the Law of Treaties (VCLT) in Article 53 for example references *ius cogens* and declares that any "treaty is void if, at the time of its conclusion, it conflicts with a peremptory norm of general international law".[33]

Voluntarism is often criticized for being incompatible with the *ius cogens* doctrine and its very acceptance in public international law is seen as the nail in the coffin of the voluntarist theory.[34] In this author's opinion, this view is fundamentally

[27] Space Law, as will be shown later, is distinctively clear as to whom responsibility is attributed by making States directly internationally responsible for the activities of non-governmental entities.

[28] The Steamship Lotus (Fance v Turkey) (1927), PCIJ (Seri A) No 10 at 18, p. 18.

[29] Gould (2011), p. 255.

[30] Ibid, p. 261.

[31] Ibid, pp. 261–262.

[32] Parker and Neylon, pp. 419–420; Paul (1971), p. 20; Gould (2011), p. 268.

[33] Art. 53 Vienna Convention on the Law of Treaties, 23 May 1969, 1155 UNTS 331 [VCLT].

[34] Gould (2011), p. 264. It must be noted that the concept of *ius cogens* is contentious and debated on the international level. For example, France has been critical of the concept of *ius cogens* and has not signed the VCLT due to the inclusion of the concept. However, during the negotiation of the VCLT, France did not seem to be opposed to the concept itself but rather pointed towards the

misconceived as it neglects to further examine how *ius cogens* itself comes into being. The author does not share the view that *ius cogens* derives from a source that is outside of State consent. Indeed, the author believes that *ius cogens* is equally founded upon the consent of States, namely the consent of States to declare certain norms as not being subject to modification, to elevate them above the other sources of international law. Consequently, the obligation upon States to adhere to these preemptory norms of international law is equally anchored in the consent to be bound to them. A rather clear example of this is the matter of slavery. There once was a time when States accepted slavery as valid and in accordance with international law. One only needs to look towards the US, which declared it illegal over 160 years ago. In the past, States regulated the slave trade and passed laws and other legislative acts.[35] This means that international law permitted slavery because State consented to the practice of it.[36] We have since evolved and it is nowadays undisputed that slavery is prohibited. This absolute prohibition is accepted to be *ius cogens* and considered an obligation *erga omnes*.[37] Accordingly, States cannot validly conclude treaties legalising slavery and regulating the slave trade. But to make illegal what once was legal under public international law requires a certain will. This will, in this author's view, manifests in the consent of States. In the case of *ius cogens* the consent can be seen in the acceptance of States that certain norms are preemptory.

Customary international law, which is generally binding upon all States, similarly finds its origin in State consent. One might raise the argument that customary law binds all States, regardless of whether they consented to the rule or not. Therefore, voluntarism might come to its limits when confronted with customary international law. However, what is neglected in this argument is the element of State practice and *opinio iuris*.[38] The latter describes the subjective belief of a State that a rule has normative character, the former requires consistent State practice adhering to the rule. While the temporal element of consistent State practice over a

danger of its application and the imprecise nature of the concept. See United Nations Conference on the Law of Treaties, 54th Mtg, UN Doc A/CONF.39/11 (1968) at 309 ["His country could hardly formulate an objection to such an attempt, but it was a difficult undertaking. (…) Accordingly, article 50 in its present form presented serious defects which should be remedied by inserting, if not a satisfactory definition of jus cogens, at least a method of defining that notion. Several delegations had made an effort in that direction, which showed that such a step was necessary and no doubt feasible."]

[35] See e.g. Slave Trade Act, 1788 (UK), 28 Geo III, c 54; Act Prohibiting Importation of Slaves, Pub L No 9-22, 2 Stat 426 (1807); Slave Trade Act, 1807 (UK) 47 Geo III, c 36.

[36] Indeed, the very fact that States subsequently abolished slave trade by statute and treaties is evidence that there was once consent which was then no longer given.

[37] See e.g. Frowein JA (2007) Ius Cogens. Max Planck Encyclopedia of International Law; Brownlie (2008), p. 511; Case concerning the Barcelona Traction, Light and Power Company, Limited (Belgium v Spain), [1970] ICJ Rep 3, para. 34 ["Such obligations [erga omnes] derive, for example, (…) also from the principles and rules concerning the basic rights of the human person, including protection from slavery and racial discrimination."].

[38] North Sea Continental Shelf Cases, [1969] ICJ Rep 3, paras 74ff.

long period of time has been questioned, most notably by Bing Cheng,[39] the element of State practice itself has not. Once a rule has crystallised into customary law, not only do the States acting in compliance consider it valid, but other State do too.[40] As Professor Watson aptly explains,

> States that could have objected or attempted to stop the practice will have been acquiescing, consenting to the evolving rule. Custom is thus more than just practice; it is tolerated practice, practice with the consent of other [S]tates. Seen in this light, custom is as much dependent on [S]tate consent as are treaties. In the latter the consent is expressed openly, while in the former it is tacit. Without an authoritative institutional structure, any concept of legal validity not based on [S]tate consent would be hopelessly subjective and relativistic.[41]

Therefore, State consent is necessary for norms to crystallise into customary law. The consent is two-fold and is not only reflected in *opinio iuris* but also in State practice itself, may it be by actively adhering to norms or tacitly consenting to them in the form of non-objection. The well-recognised principle of the "persistent objector" can, in this author's view, be seen as support of the positivist-voluntarist theory. According to this principle, if a State consistently objects to an emerging norm of customary law, that State will be exempt from the rule once it crystallises into customary law.[42] A State persistently objecting to an emerging norm of customary international law, does not consent to the norm.

The element of State consent is also present in the other sources of international law. International conventions are perhaps the clearest example of the necessity of State consent. A treaty relationship can only arise when a State has given its consent to be bound to the respective treaty.[43]The general principles of law recognised by nations is but another example of State consent. To find general principles of law one ought to look towards municipal legal systems and municipal law is created by the States themselves and thus dependent on their consent.[44]

Another example that lends support to this view is the succession of States. When one State succeeds another, the government of the newly formed State ordinarily makes a declaration to be bound to the treaties of the old State (or not to be bound, as the case may be). For example, when Ghana gained independence from the UK, the newly formed State declared that all obligations and responsibilities of the UK arising from a validly concluded instrument, as far as they are applicable to Ghana, are assumed by the government of Ghana.[45] In other words, Ghana as a State gave

---

[39] Cheng (1965).

[40] Watson (1992), p. 111.

[41] Ibid.

[42] See e.g. Olufemi E (2007) Persistent Objector. Max Planck Encyclopedia of International Law. https://opil.ouplaw.com/display/10.1093/law:epil/9780199231690/law-9780199231690-e1455. Accessed 11 July 2025.

[43] Art. 11 VCLT.

[44] Brownlie (2008), p. 16.

[45] United Nations (1967), p. 30; Another example would be that of the Russian Federation which succeeded the Soviet Union. For instance, Russia declared to continue to perform its rights and fulfil its obligations under the Hague Conference on Private International Law. See Netherlands

consent to be bound to obligations and responsibilities originally assumed by the UK.[46]

In conclusion, to use the words of Louis Henkin, "State consent is the foundation of international law. The principle that law is binding on a State only by its consent remains an axiom of the political system, an implication of state autonomy".[47]

This theoretical view is complemented by a traditional doctrinal research methodology. This research will examine court decisions from domestic and international courts, arbitrational awards, treaties, government policies and existing legal principles, both domestic and international. Doctrinal research is research into the law and its legal concepts and has been described as synthesis of different rules, principles, norms, interpretive guidelines and values. It further explains and brings clarity to segments of the law as part of a larger system of law. Doctrines can either be binding or non-binding.[48] This research looks at all these existing legal doctrines to propose a viable way forward in the *lex lata* to address the international responsibility of States for their AI-enabled space activities. It attempts to bring clarity to the existing *lex lata* by looking to decisions of courts and interpreting legal principles.

This positivist-voluntarist understanding that State consent is required to give rise to public international law, is what informs the present research and underlies every argument. In this author's view, this is necessary because the present research attempts to show how the currently available legal system (i.e., the norms States have consented to) is capable of addressing the challenges highly advanced next generation AI can bring. Below, we will argue that a pragmatic view requires us to look towards the *lex lata* because States, in the current political environment, are unwilling to create new binding rules States will not reach consensus on such rules, and State consent for new rules is missing. This theoretical view is complemented by a traditional doctrinal research methodology that examines the existing legal principles, the *lex lata*.

With this theoretical ground clearing out of the way, let us know turn towards one of the subjects of the present research, AI.

e-V nl The HCCH | Declaration/reservation/notification. https://www.hcch.net/en/instruments/conventions/status-table/notifications/?csid=341&disp=resdn. Accessed 11 July 2025.

[46] The requirement of consent is also present in the Vienna Convention on Succession of States in respect of treaties. For example, Article 17 states that, "a newly independent State may, by a notification of succession, establish its status as a party to any multilateral treaty which at the date of the succession of States was in force in respect of the territory to which the succession of States relates." See Vienna Convention on Succession of States in Respect of Treaties, 23 August 1978, 1946 UNTS 3.

[47] Henkin (1995), p. 27.

[48] Hutchison and Duncan, pp. 84–85.

1.3 Artificial Intelligence: Basic Terminology and Overview

At the outset of this book, it is necessary to clearly set out the basic terminology and provide the reader with an overview of what the present research understands when it speaks of AI. This is important because (1) AI is an emerging technology and it is continuously developing and in constant flux, and (2) the term AI is very broad and not defined (something this author will come back to further below). A simple Roomba vacuum cleaner or trading algorithm, which automatically buys and sells stocks, is as much part of this emerging field as an autonomous car or a highly advanced computer system built on machine learning.

AI has slowly started to place itself in our every-day lives. Tasks such as financial and credit card transactions, online trading or home assistance systems have been utilising AI. Further, AI is used, for example, to unlock your phone with your face, to make newsfeed suggestions on social media based on past behaviour and interests, to deploy and operate autonomous flying unmanned aerial vehicles and to support powerful writing software, such as ChatGPT.[49] AI has sparked a movement away from an industry principally directed towards manufacturing to one oriented to the accumulation, production and processing of information.[50] Even in traditional industries AI "assumes an increasingly prominent role in the control of industrial production and in the management of all kinds of enterprises".[51]

Unsurprisingly, AI has generated substantial interest in recent history. A substantial body of literature in technology and legal journals has started to emerge but legal academic discussions pertaining to space law are scarce, perhaps because AI has not received much attention in the realm of general international law. However, as has been pointed out above, AI can be used for a wide variety of different space

[49] See e.g. Banerjee P (2022) AI-based advanced analytics is making credit, debit cards smarter. https://www.livemint.com/technology/aibased-advanced-analytics-is-making-credit-debit-cards-smarter-11649003838074.html. Accessed 11 July 2025; Harris M (2021) Impact Of Artificial Intelligence And Machine Learning on Trading And Investing. https://towardsdatascience.com/impact-of-artificial-intelligence-and-machine-learning-on-trading-and-investing-7175ef2ad64e. Accessed 11 July 2025; Powers J (2024) AI Trading: How AI Is Used in Stock Trading. https://builtin.com/artificial-intelligence/ai-trading-stock-market-tech. Accessed 15 July 2025; Baker W (2021) Using AI for Smart Homes. https://canterbury.ai/using-ai-for-smart-homes/. Accessed 11 July 2025; Eliaçik E (2023) Best Usages Of Artificial Intelligence In Everyday Life (2022) - Dataconomy. https://dataconomy.com/2022/05/09/artificial-intelligence-in-everyday-life/. Accessed 11 July 2025; Marr B (2019) The 10 Best Examples Of How AI Is Already Used In Our Everyday Life. https://www.forbes.com/sites/bernardmarr/2019/12/16/the-10-best-examples-of-how-ai-is-already-used-in-our-everyday-life/. Accessed 11 July 2025; Hughes A (2023) ChatGPT: Everything you need to know about OpenAI's GPT-4 tool. https://www.sciencefocus.com/future-technology/gpt-3/. Accessed 11 July 2025.

[50] Cohen (2016), p. 371.

[51] Ibid, p. 371.

applications and investment in this technology in the space sector is rapidly increasing.[52]

Therefore, this section will provide an overview of AI and the terminology used throughout this book. This section aims to familiarise the reader with the subject of AI, explain how it relates to the broader discussion and establish the groundwork upon which the subsequent research will be placed.

The author is aware that he is not an expert in software engineering and the overview provided will naturally be quite simplistic, more general and geared towards the subsequent legal analysis contained in this book. This chapter was completed in 2023 and does not take subsequent AI development into account. However, important legal developments until the end of 2024 have been considered.

1.3.1 Artificial Intelligence: The Search for a Definition

Although AI research is not new, the first attempts to explore this developing area of modern technology having been made shortly after World War II, it only started to receive widespread attention recently, and to date there has not been any consensus on a definition of the term "artificial intelligence".[53]

The word AI consists of an explicit reference to the notion of intelligence. However, intelligence, be it in humans or machines, is a very vague concept, the study of which shall be left to the more capable hands of psychologists, biologists, theologists and neuroscientists. Researchers in AI typically refer to the notion of rationality when addressing AI systems.[54]

Alan Turing, who is widely considered to be the first to discuss AI in recent history, argued that if a machine could successfully pretend to be a human to a knowledgeable observer, then such a machine could be considered intelligent.[55] However, what we now consider very simple computer programs can successfully fool a real human and thus Turing's definition is nowadays too simplistic in its nature.[56]

[52] Taylor D (2020) The Impact of Artificial Intelligence on Space Investment. https://www.geospatialworld.net/prime/the-impact-of-artificial-intelligence-on-space-investment/. Accessed 11 July 2025; Artificial intelligence in space. https://www.esa.int/Enabling_Support/Preparing_for_the_Future/Discovery_and_Preparation/Artificial_intelligence_in_space. Accessed 11 July 2025; Aerospace Artificial Intelligence Market Size, Growth, Research - 2028. In: Allied Market Research. https://www.alliedmarketresearch.com/aerospace-artificial-intelligence-market-A11337. Accessed 11 July 2025.

[53] See Abbott (2020), p. 22; Castelvecchi (2016), p. 22; Hohman et al. (2018), sect. 1.

[54] Russell et al. (2010), p. 1; High-Level Expert Group on Artificial Intelligence (2019) A Definition of Artificial Intelligence: Main Capabilities and Scientific disciplines. https://digital-strategy.ec.europa.eu/en/library/definition-artificial-intelligence-main-capabilities-and-scientific-disciplines. Accessed 11 July 2025.

[55] Cf Turing (1950).

[56] See McCarthy J What is AI?/ Basic Questions. In: What is AI?/ Basic Questions. http://jmc.stanford.edu/artificial-intelligence/what-is-ai/index.html. Accessed 11 July 2021; Cf Dennett

Professor John McCarthy, often called the father of modern AI, defined AI as "the science and engineering of making intelligent machines, especially intelligent computer programs" and explained intelligence in this regard as "the computational part of the ability to achieve goals in the world".[57] It appears that it is upon this understanding that most subsequent definitions are built. The International Organization for Standardization (ISO) understands AI as a "branch of computer science devoted to developing data processing systems that perform functions normally associated with human intelligence, such as reasoning, learning, and self-improvement".[58] The European Union's (EU) High-Level Expert Group on Artificial Intelligence similarly provides an expanded definition of AI and states that,

> [a]rtificial intelligence (AI) systems are software (and possibly also hardware) systems designed by humans that, given a complex goal, act in the physical or digital dimension by perceiving their environment through data acquisition, interpreting the collected structured or unstructured data, reasoning on the knowledge, or processing the information, derived from this data and deciding the best action(s) to take to achieve the given goal. AI systems can either use symbolic rules or learn a numeric model, and they can also adapt their behaviour by analysing how the environment is affected by their previous actions.[59]

EU Regulation 2024/1689 (AI Act) which recently entered into force explains that,

> AI system' means a machine-based system that is designed to operate with varying levels of autonomy and that may exhibit adaptiveness after deployment, and that, for explicit or implicit objectives, infers, from the input it receives, how to generate outputs such as predictions, content, recommendations, or decisions that can influence physical or virtual environments.[60]

Put differently, AI can be considered to refer to "a class of computer programs designed to solve problems requiring inferential reasoning, decision-making based on incomplete or uncertain information, classification, optimization, and perception".[61]

Many authors agree with this classification and generally understand AI to have the elements of self-learning, autonomy, intelligence and a certain degree of

(1998); Abbott (2020), p. 26.

[57] McCarthy J What is AI?/ Basic Questions. In: What is AI?/ Basic Questions. http://jmc.stanford.edu/artificial-intelligence/what-is-ai/index.html. Accessed 11 July 2025.

[58] Artificial Intelligence. In: International Organization for Standardization. https://www.iso.org/obp/ui/#iso:std:iso-iec:2382:ed-1:v1:en. Accessed 11 July 2025.

[59] High-Level Expert Group on Artificial Intelligence (2019) A Definition of Artificial Intelligence: Main Capabilities and Scientific disciplines. https://digital-strategy.ec.europa.eu/en/library/definition-artificial-intelligence-main-capabilities-and-scientific-disciplines. Accessed 11 July 2025.

[60] EU, Regulation (EU) 2024/1689 of the European Parliament and of the Council of 13 June 2024 laying down harmonised rules on artificial intelligence and amending Regulations (EC) No 300/2008, (EU) No 167/2013, (EU) No 168/2013, (EU) 2018/858, (EU) 2018/1139 and (EU) 2019/2144 and Directives 2014/90/EU, (EU) 2016/797 and (EU) 2020/1828, [2024] OJ, L 2024/1689 [EU AI Act].

[61] Bathaee (2018a), p. 898.

independence.[62] This understanding also reflects the literal meaning of the word AI, which generally defines AI as the study and development of systems that are able to copy human behaviour.[63]

However, the definition of AI as such is just one side of the coin. The term AI is a broad term and is also a scientific discipline which includes various approaches and techniques. Terms, such as machine learning (ML), of which deep learning and neural networks are specific examples, and robotics are usually found in this realm.[64] These disciplines form part of the overall phenomenon we call AI, but they need to be explained separately.[65] Let us therefore work our way from the outside of the machine to its insides.

1.3.2 Robotics

The European Union's Expert Group on Artificial Intelligence elegantly defines robotics as "AI in action in the physical world".[66] A robot is something we can touch, see and interact with. It is a physical machine that copes with the complexities of the physical world.[67] It is robots that people usually have in mind when they talk about the future of highly advanced AI. Works of fiction, such as Azimov's famous iRobot, are evidence of this.

---

[62] See e.g. Giuffrida (2019), p. 441; Heiss (2021), p. 5; Chatzipanagiotis (2020); Bratu et al. (2021), p. 425; Čerka et al. (2015), p. 378; Long (2018); Butcher and Beridze (2019), p. 88; Martin and Freeland (2021), p. 101408; Soroka and Kurkova (2019), p. 132; Powell (2020), pp. 312–313; Cofone (2021).

[63] The Oxfords Learner's Dictionary defines AI as "the study and development of computer systems that can copy intelligent human behaviour". The Cambridge dictionary understands AI as "the study of how to produce machines that have some of the qualities that the human mind has, such as the ability to understand language, recognize pictures, solve problems, and learn". Merriam-Webster sees AI as "a branch of computer science dealing with the intelligent behaviour in computers" and "the capability of a machine to imitate intelligent human behaviour". Artificial Intelligence. https://www.oxfordlearnersdictionaries.com/definition/english/artificial-intelligence?q=artificial+intelligence. Accessed 11 July 2026; Artificial Intelligence. https://dictionary.cambridge.org/dictionary/english/artificial-intelligence. Accessed 11 July 2025; Artificial Intelligence. https://www.merriam-webster.com/dictionary/artificial%20intelligence. Accessed 11 July 2025.

[64] High-Level Expert Group on Artificial Intelligence (2019) A Definition of Artificial Intelligence: Main Capabilities and Scientific disciplines. https://digital-strategy.ec.europa.eu/en/library/definition-artificial-intelligence-main-capabilities-and-scientific-disciplines. Accessed 11 July 2025.

[65] The following analogy may serve as clarification. If the AI were the human, machine learning and reasoning, robotics et cetera would be the organs the body needs to function.

[66] High-Level Expert Group on Artificial Intelligence (2019) A Definition of Artificial Intelligence: Main Capabilities and Scientific disciplines. https://digital-strategy.ec.europa.eu/en/library/definition-artificial-intelligence-main-capabilities-and-scientific-disciplines. Accessed 11 July 2025. Robotics are therefore also often referred to as embodied AI to emphasize the physical properties.

[67] Ibid.

Indeed, robotics is part of the overall discipline of AI. However, it needs to be addressed separately as the discipline of robotics bridges the gap between the AI, its machine learning and reasoning, and the physical world. Robotics is thus a science which "studies the intelligent connection between perception and action".[68] Although there is not an accepted definition of the term "robotics" there seems to be some degree of consensus around the idea that robots are mechanical objects that sense the world around them, process what they sense and act upon it accordingly.[69] However, as Calo points out, "[e]ach of these characteristics of sensing, processing, and acting exists on a spectrum" and one needs to exercise a certain degree of flexibility in this regard.[70] Thus there is a wide range of robots and examples include, *inter alia*, autonomous cars, drones, automated vacuum cleaners or an autonomous space object.[71]

In the realm of outer space, the Mars rover Perseverance is a good example of a robot powered by AI. Perseverance utilises AI to search for evidence of life and navigate the planet. The rover is equipped with sensors, arms and is built to adapt to and explore the hostile environment of Mars.[72] The rover itself is what we would refer to as a robot, its brain is the AI built into the machine.

1.3.3 Machine Learning

In very simple terms a machine "is learning if it improves its performance on future tasks after making observations about the world".[73] Machine learning is therefore a way for the AI to become more accurate at predicting outcomes and gives it the

---

[68] Siciliano and Khatib (2016), p. 3.

[69] See Calo (2015), p. 529; Barfoot et al. (2020), sec. 2.1; Texts adopted - Civil Law Rules on Robotics - Thursday, 16 February 2017. https://www.europarl.europa.eu/doceo/document/TA-8-2017-0051_EN.html. Accessed 11 July 2025; European Parliament resolution of 16 February 2017 with recommendations to the Commission on Civil Law Rules on Robotics (2015/2103(INL)), [2019] OJ/C 252/239, Annex [EU Parliament Resolution]; Robotics: What Are Robots? Robotics Definition & Uses. | Built In. https://builtin.com/robotics. Accessed 11 July 2025; What is robotics? In: WhatIs.com. https://www.techtarget.com/whatis/definition/robotics. Accessed 11 July 2025.

[70] Calo (2015), p. 530; In his famous article, Calo proposes three characteristics to define a robot and place it within the existing legal system, namely embodiment, emergence and social valence. Embodiment means that the robot acts upon the world, emergence captures the unpredictability of the actions of the robot and social valence is concerned with the perception of the robot as human being by real people. See ibid., p. 532ff.

[71] A robot is distinguished from other technologies via the so-called "sense-think-act" paradigm. A mobile phone with a camera may sense and process the external world but it does not act upon in. Calo (2015), p. 529; Pfeifer and Scheier (2001), pp. 55, 201–202, 307.

[72] NASA (2021).

[73] Russell et al. (2010), p. 693; Cohen (2021), p. 5.

ability to learn without being explicitly programmed to do so.[74] In their often-cited book, Russell, Norvig and Davis identify three reasons why we would want a machine to learn, namely that (1) the software designers cannot predict all possible scenarios in which an AI might find itself, (2) the programmer cannot anticipate all changes over time and (3) that the designers are not able to program the solution themselves.[75]

All of these considerations are applicable to the outer space environment.

First, space is largely an unexplored domain and the knowledge we have is presently very limited to our own Solar System. This is ultimately the reason why we send unmanned probes to Mars or utilise the James Webb Space Telescope. We stretch toward and aim to explore this "final frontier".

Second, how should a programme designer anticipate all the changes that might be encountered by the AI while traversing outer space if not even space scientists are entirely sure what is out there?

Third, the unexplored nature of outer space will make it difficult, if not impossible, for software designers to programme a solution themselves. How would they programme a solution to a problem they do not know?

The multitude of these unknowns will make it impossible, or at the very least incredibly hard, to programme foreseeable solutions that might be suitable for the hostile environment of outer space. Machine learning can therefore be an integral building block for next-generation AI used in outer space.

Generally, there are three ways an AI can learn: supervised learning, unsupervised learning, and reinforcement learning.[76]

In supervised learning the AI is provided with as set of input data (i.e., known variables) and is tasked to make predictions. For example, the AI receives camera images, and a "teacher" would tell the AI what the imagine is (e.g., a bus, a car, a chair etc.- these are the known input variables).[77] For example, let us assume that we wish to train an AI to recognise the image of a dog or a cat. The AI would be provided with a set of known input data, such as notable features of a cat or dog (e.g., tail, ears, fur, nose, claws etc.) and a set of class designations that correspond to these features (i.e., cat or dog).[78] A teacher would tell the system what features pertain to a cat and what features to a dog.[79] The more the system learns the more

[74] Brown S (2021) Machine learning, explained. https://mitsloan.mit.edu/ideas-made-to-matter/machine-learning-explained. Accessed 11 July 2025; IBM Cloud Education (2020) What is Machine Learning? https://www.ibm.com/cloud/learn/machine-learning. Accessed 11 July 2025; Samuel (1959). A L Samuel, often seen as one of the first researchers to focus on ML, seems to lean in his 1959 article towards this understanding.

[75] Russell et al. (2010), p. 693.

[76] Ibid., pp. 695–696; Hervey and Lavy (2021), ch. 2.

[77] Russell et al. (2010), p. 695; Hervey and Lavy (2021), sect. 2/013.

[78] Hervey and Lavy (2021), sect. 2/013.

[79] Ibid., sect. 2/013.

accurate it will become in predicting unknown data, that is input data which was not labelled by the teacher previously.[80]

In unsupervised learning the AI learns without any feedback provided from the "teacher" and more closely resembles how humans naturally learn.[81] We are usually not told what is what but simply observe and draw our own conclusions which will either be confirmed or rejected.[82] For example, an autonomous taxi may be able to recognise on its own times of increased traffic (rush-hour).

In reinforced learning the AI learns from a host of reinforcements, that is rewards and punishments.[83] For example the lack of tip at the end of a journey might tell an autonomous taxi that it did something wrong, or a win in a chess game might indicate to the AI that it did something right while a loss conversely might tell the AI that it did something wrong.[84] It will be up to the AI to determine what led to the win or loss (or lack of tip).[85]

Supervised, unsupervised and reinforced learning may be seen as indications of an AI systems' ability to independently develop from human input to achieve complex and multilayered goals.[86]

Different learning techniques are used within supervised, unsupervised, and reinforced machine learning. One such learning technique used by the AI is the neural network.[87] However, the reader ought to be aware that the neural network is but one of many different machine learning techniques.[88]

Neural networks have gained a lot of attention in recent years as they are among the best performing machine learning techniques currently employed. Therefore, it is this type of machine learning technique that the present book will pay closer attention to. It seems therefore beneficial to provide the reader with a brief simplified explanation as to what "neural network" exactly means for the purposes of the present research.

---

[80] We are already participating in this form of supervised learning in every-day life. Google's verification system ("prove you are human") is used to train Google's AI. When we select all pictures that contain certain elements (e.g., stairs), we train the AI to recognise stairs in the future. The algorithm learns.

[81] Hervey and Lavy (2021), sect. 2/014; Russell et al. (2010), p. 695.

[82] Russell, Norvig & Davis, *supra* note 51 at 695.

[83] Russell et al. (2010), p. 695; Hervey and Lavy (2021), sect. 2/014.

[84] Russell et al. (2010), p. 695; Hervey and Lavy (2021), sect. 2/033.

[85] Russell et al. (2010), p. 695.

[86] See e.g. Bertolini (2013), pp. 235–35. See also Turner (2019), p. 74.

[87] Russell et al. (2010), p. 695.

[88] Other machine learning techniques include, inter alia, actuarial tables, simple linear regression, complex linear regression, logistic regression and classification, ranking algorithms and decision trees. See e.g. Hervey and Lavy (2021), pp. 17–20.

1.3.3.1 Neural Networks

The term "neural network" refers to a type of machine learning that is inspired by, and loosely based on, the human brain.[89] The human brain has over 80 billion neurones that are all connected in a highly complex network consisting of trillions of connections, which change based on learning and experience.[90] It is this structure that inspired artificial neural networks (ANNs), which are "an aspect of AI that is focused on emulating the learning approach that humans use to gain certain types of knowledge".[91] Like a human brain, an ANN contains a certain amount of neurones (in the case of AI, artificial neurones) which are used to identify and store information.[92] The neurones are linked, pass information along and form layers. These layers transmit data to each other and "can be trained to complete tasks by altering the relevance of data as they pass between layers (…) until the network produces the desired output".[93] Consequently, an ANN consists of input and output layers, as well as hidden layers which transform the input data into something the output layer can use.[94]

A deep neural network (DNN), simply put, consists of a number of stacked individual neural networks, which enable deep learning.[95]

In a training scenario, we provide the AI with input data and specify a desired output (i.e., the desired result).[96] The behaviour of the different layers, other than the output layer, is not determined by the input data but rather the learning algorithm must determine on its own how to produce the desired outcome and how to use the

[89] See e.g. Das and Roy (2019), sec. 5.5; Koul and Manvi (2021), sec. 6.3.3; Phillips-Wren (2013), sec. 2.4.1; Pfeifer and Scheier (2001), p. 140; High-Level Expert Group on Artificial Intelligence (2019) A Definition of Artificial Intelligence: Main Capabilities and Scientific disciplines. https://digital-strategy.ec.europa.eu/en/library/definition-artificial-intelligence-main-capabilities-and-scientific-disciplines. Accessed 11 July 2025; Abbott (2020), p. 30; Castelvecchi (2016).

[90] Abbott (2020), p. 30; Newman T (2017) All you need to know about neurons. https://www.medicalnewstoday.com/articles/320289. Accessed 11 July 2025; Woodruff A What is a neuron? https://qbi.uq.edu.au/brain/brain-anatomy/what-neuron. Accessed 11 July 2025 (2022); Ludwig M (2017) How Your Brain Cells Talk to Each Other—Whispered Secrets and Public Announcements. https://kids.frontiersin.org/articles/10.3389/frym.2017.00039. Accessed 11 July 2025; Pfeifer and Scheier (2001), p. 141.

[91] Das and Roy (2019), sect. 5.6.

[92] Ibid, sect. 5.6.

[93] Abbott (2020), p. 30; See also Phillips-Wren (2013), sect. 2.4.1.

[94] See Goodfellow et al. (2016), sec. 5.7, 5.8; High-Level Expert Group on Artificial Intelligence (2019) A Definition of Artificial Intelligence: Main Capabilities and Scientific disciplines. https://digital-strategy.ec.europa.eu/en/library/definition-artificial-intelligence-main-capabilities-and-scientific-disciplines. Accessed 11 July 2025.

[95] Das and Roy (2019), sec. 5.5; High-Level Expert Group on Artificial Intelligence (2019) A Definition of Artificial Intelligence: Main Capabilities and Scientific disciplines. https://digital-strategy.ec.europa.eu/en/library/definition-artificial-intelligence-main-capabilities-and-scientific-disciplines. Accessed 11 July 2025.

[96] Goodfellow et al. (2016), pp. 164–165.

layers, which is why they are called hidden layers.[97] DNN and artificial neurones have been, *inter alia*, utilised to recognise images and detect cancer cells.[98] In a DNN "thousands or hundreds of thousands of neurons work together to arrive at a decision".[99]

DNNs analyse a tremendous amount of data within seconds utilising a multitude of hidden layers.[100] However, what each hidden layer does, is often not intelligible to humans. As Bathaee accurately puts it,

> [t]he net result is akin to the way one "knows" how to ride a bike. Although one can explain the process descriptively or even provide detailed steps, that information is unlikely to help someone who has never ridden a bike before (…) [o]ne learns to ride a bike by attempting to do so over and over again and develops an intuitive understanding.[101]

An ANN learns from experience and therefore its decision-making processes are equally intuitive.[102] As mentioned above, the algorithm decides on its own how to utilise each layer to reach the desired outcome. Thus, it becomes increasingly difficult to reduce the "knowledge" of the AI to a set of instructions and in most cases it is hard to determine what each hidden layer did or what parameters the AI used in each layer to reach a specific conclusion.[103] We cannot have a look at the information that is stored in the network, and particularly we are unable to ascertain what information is not represented in the DNN.[104] As Gillespie succinctly puts it "there may be something (…) impenetrable about algorithms".[105] We give up control for the benefit of machine learning and automation and "[i]n the same degree as the influence of the creator over the machine decreases, the influence of the operating environment increases".[106] This is what gives rise to the so-called Black-Box Problem.

---

[97] Ibid.

[98] Stumpe M, Peng L (2017) Assisting Pathologists in Detecting Cancer with Deep Learning. http://ai.googleblog.com/2017/03/assisting-pathologists-in-detecting.html. Accessed 22 August 2022; Bathaee (2018a), p. 902.

[99] Bathaee (2018a), p. 902.

[100] Cf Mitchell (2021), p. 43.

[101] Bathaee (2018a), p. 902.

[102] Ibid, p. 902.

[103] Ibid, p. 903; Cohen (2021), p. 7.

[104] Matthias (2004), pp. 178–179.

[105] Gillespie (2014), p. 192.

[106] Matthias (2004), p. 182.

1.3.4 The Black-Box Problem

In general, the Black-Box Problem (BBP) refers to the inability to fully understand the decision-making process of the AI or predict its output.[107] As mentioned earlier, in a scenario in which a DNN is utilised by the AI, a human might only know the input data and the actual generated output (i.e., the result). What exactly led to a specific output, that is how the AI utilised each hidden layer, may be entirely obscure. In other words, the AI becomes opaque. This can lead to a myriad of problems not only from a legal but also from a practical or theoretical standpoint.[108]

For example, from a practical standpoint, the trust of the end-user in machines they do not fully understand might be limited and they could be less likely to hand control over to them.[109] Further, software developers and engineers might not be able to intervene or quickly re-programme to improve performance.[110]

On the theoretical plane, the BBP raises various questions, such as whether and to what extent machines using machine learning can be considered intelligent or have feelings.[111]

Legally, the BBP could cause significant obstacles in the realm of foreseeability, which has a direct impact on fault and thus the determination of liability for AI, due to the nature of machine-learning algorithms on which modern AI is frequently built. While this is a problematique the present research will reference and engage with in detail later, in this section, we shall be content with only briefly outlining the challenges.

As previously mentioned, an AI utilising a neural network is capable of learning from and adapting to tremendous amounts of data and attempting to reach decisions "intuitively" like humans.[112] This means that the AI is no longer only executing a pre-written set of code but is able to reach dynamic solutions based on patterns in a data stream that humans might not be able to perceive.[113] Thus, it might be difficult, maybe even impossible, to ascertain the elements the AI considered to reach its decision and how it was able to arrive at a specific conclusion.[114]

This in turn could have implications for our traditional conceptions to establish liability, which usually rely on the ability to ascertain what is foreseeable, what is causally related and what was planned or expected.[115]

---

107 Bathaee (2018a), p. 905; See also Zednik (2021), p. 265; Wadden (2021), p. 1.

108 Zednik (2021), p. 266.

109 Ribeiro et al. (2016); Zednik (2021).

110 Hohman et al. (2018), sect. 4.2; Zednik (2021), p. 266.

111 Zednik (2018); For an excellent collection of articles on the philosophy and theory of Artificial Intelligence see Müller (2018).

112 Bathaee (2018a), p. 892; Cofone (2021), p. 21; Munakata (2008), pp. 1–3.

113 Bathaee (2018a), p. 892; Zednik (2018), p. 226; Castelvecchi (2016).

114 Bathaee (2018a), p. 892; Bathaee (2018b), pp. 140–141; Burrell (2026), p. 1; Wadden (2021).

115 Bathaee (2018a), p. 892.

Under normal circumstances humans can be examined, or at the very least leave some trail of evidence behind that can aid a court to reach a decision.[116] This is not necessarily the case for advanced AI using machine learning.

Thus, many authors agree that this may cause problems in the realm of assigning liability correctly and support a system of strict liability. Some favour a system in which AI is granted legal personhood, similar to corporations, to make them strictly liable for damage either directly or via the vehicle of agency law.[117] Others point towards a strict products liability regime, especially in the realm of autonomous driving.[118] There are also proposals for a "robot common sense" standard, similar to the reasonable person standard that is currently used in legal systems to measure behaviour against, and establish fault.[119] Such a standard should adapt to the nuances brought in by AI. There are further those who suggest developing a new approach and adapt the current legal framework to include AI in its scope.[120]

Finally, some point towards reversing the regulatory approach, imposing legal duties on the developers of AI and placing the use of AI under a licensing regime. For example, Malgieri and Pasquale propose ex-ante accountability for AI and suggest that AI developers must perform a preliminary risk assessment followed by a self-certification before their AI product enters the market and, should the assessment reveal that the system is high-risk, then an approval request to a public authority should follow.[121] In this regard it has been suggested that the robot should always indicate the identity of its creator controller or owner.[122]

All these arguments were discussed in the context of national legislation and using them in the realm of space law and public international law, which a sizable part of this book will focus on, might be challenging. The question of legal personhood does not necessarily arise in space law because it places responsibility directly

---

[116] Ibid, p. 892.

[117] Bayern (2015); Allain (2013); Powell (2020); Vladeck (2014) propose two ways to solve the liability issue, either by establishing a 'common enterprise' liability or establish legal personhood for the autonomous vehicle itself; Giuffrida (2019); Heiss (2021) propose a strict liability regime in which losses are paid to the state; Čerka et al. (2015); Wagner (2018).

[118] LeValley (2013) who favours product liability but also proposes to hold the vehicle manufacturer strictly liable as a common carrier; See also Lohmann (2016), p. 335.

[119] Abbott (2018); Giuffrida (2019), pp. 449–450. The author primarily bases her assessment on a US Case (State v Loomis) to show how robot common sense makes its way into the US legal system.

[120] Lemley and Casey (2019); Goodrich (2013).

[121] Malgieri and Pasquale (2022); see also Pasquale (2019); This seems to be the approach the European Union has taken with the adoption of the Artificial Intelligence Act which divides AI in unacceptable risk (banned), high-risk (require assessment before being put onto the market) and non-high-risk AI (needs to fulfill certain transparency requirements). See EU, Regulation (EU) 2024/1689 of the European Parliament and of the Council of 13 June 2024 laying down harmonised rules on artificial intelligence and amending Regulations (EC) No 300/2008, (EU) No 167/2013, (EU) No 168/2013, (EU) 2018/858, (EU) 2018/1139 and (EU) 2019/2144 and Directives 2014/90/EU, (EU) 2016/797 and (EU) 2020/1828, [2024] OJ, L 2024/1689 [EU AI Act].

[122] Pasquale (2017), p. 4.

on States and liability on the launching State.[123] Similarly, a common-sense standard would only find narrow application within Article VI of the Liability Convention which grants exoneration of the launching State in case the claimant State is, *inter alia*, guilty of gross negligence.

On its face, the argument to develop new rules for AI is an intriguing solution. A desirable outcome for the *lex ferenda* in general would undoubtedly be an amendment to existing treaties or the creation of an entirely new binding international agreement to reflect better the technological development. However, such an argument does not consider the inherent difficulty in creating new binding agreements. States in the twenty-first century show an increasing unwillingness to subject themselves to new binding legal regimes.[124] Recent empirical studies have shown that treaties seem no longer be very effective.[125] Additionally, in the realm of technology, a new legal or licensing regime might also not be the most suitable solution and would come with its own set of problems. "Technology is capable of leaving the law behind at any phase of the regulatory cycle-before regulators have anything resembling an agreed position",[126] even more so in the international legal arena where many varying State interests and policy issues are at play. The legal system will always reflect a certain tension between the need to draft legislation flexibly and the demand for consistency and predictability.[127] "[T]he more that regulators (…) try to establish an initial set of standards that are clear, detailed, and precise, the more likely it is that the regulation will lose connection with its technological target".[128]

Although different authors propose different solutions on how to handle liability involving AI, their common denominator seems to be the fact that in accidents fault (and causation) might be difficult to prove. Our current laws are mostly "built on legal doctrines that are focused on human conduct, which when applied to AI may not function".[129] This brings us again back to the BBP discussed above.

To what degree the AI's lack of transparency will challenge our existing legal rules will depend on the extent of the lack of transparency. Bathaee therefore divides the BBP into two sub-categories, namely a "strong black box" and a "weak black box".[130] The former describes an AI where the decision-making process is not transparent and cannot be examined or reverse engineered ex-post, the latter an AI that, even though it is opaque to the ordinary user, can be ex-post examined and therefore afford a limited insight into the decision making process.[131]

[123] Arts VI-VII Outer Space Treaty; Liability Convention.

[124] Jakhu and Pelton (2017), p. 37.

[125] See e.g. Hoffman et al. (2022).

[126] Brownsword (2008), p. 162.

[127] Ibid, p. 287.

[128] Ibid, p. 288.

[129] Bathaee (2018a), p. 891.

[130] Ibid, p. 906.

[131] Ibid, p. 906.

It must be noted that the BBP also impacts other legal issues, such as the inability of regulatory bodies to determine whether the AI processes data fairly and securely or problems under data protection legislation, to name a few.[132]

1.3.5 Autonomy

The term "autonomy" or "autonomous" will be frequently employed throughout the present research. It seems therefore beneficial to discuss briefly this fuzzy and imprecise word. As is the case with many areas of AI, there is no clear-cut definition of the term "autonomous" and many authors employ varying definitions for this term. The central idea of the term "autonomy" can be found in the etymological origins of this word. It originated from the Greek terms of *autós* (meaning self) and *nomos* (meaning law or custom).[133] Thus, autonomy is nowadays often defined as the ability to make one's own decision independently without control by anyone else.[134]

It appears that a number of authors base their own definitions on this understanding. Russel, Norvig and Davis understand autonomy in AI as the ability to learn in order to compensate for incorrect or incomplete prior knowledge and thus becoming independent from prior knowledge.[135] Other authors similarly see autonomy as the AI's capacity to form and adapt its principles of behaviour while operating in the environment. In other words, autonomy implies some degree of adaptability.[136] To adapt to changing circumstances and act independently to realise the goals the AI was designed to accomplish.

The autonomy of AI overlaps with the different levels of human oversight under which the AI can be operated. Generally, there are three levels of human oversight, namely human-in-the-loop (human has control over the AI), human-on-the-loop (AI acts autonomously but human has oversight and can intervene) and finally

[132] See generally Rieder and Simon (2017), sect. 3.4; Goodman and Flaxman (2017); Wachter et al. (2017).

[133] Steels (2018), pp. 84–85 citing T Smithers; Nomos. www.britannica.com/topic/nomos-Greek-philosophy. Accessed 11 July 2025; Autos. www.perseus.tufts.edu/hopper/text?doc=Perseus:text:1999.04.0057:entry=au)to/s. Accessed 11 July 2025.

[134] The Cambridge Dictionary defines "autonomy" as "the ability to make your own decisions without being controlled by anyone else". Autonomy. https://dictionary.cambridge.org/dictionary/english/autonomy. Accessed 11 July 2025; Miriam Webster understand autonomy as the right of self-government. Autonomy. https://www.merriam-webster.com/dictionary/autonomy. Accessed 11 July 2025; The Oxford Dictionary explains the term "autonomy" as "the fact or quality of being unrelated to anything else, self-containedness; independence from external influence or control, self-sufficiency". Autonomy. https://www.oed.com/dictionary/autonomy_n. Accessed 11 July 2025.

[135] Russell et al. (2010), p. 39.

[136] Steels (2018), p. 85; Maes (1995), p. 108; Hengstler et al. (2016), p. 105; Lee and See (2004), p. 50.

human-out-of-the-loop (action is carried out without human supervision).[137] The present research will mainly be concerned with human-out-of-the-loop, and to a certain extend with human-on-the-loop, operations as these will be the modes mainly employed in the outer space environment once AI has matured enough.[138]

1.3.6 Working Definition for AI

After having introduced the reader to the basic terminology as it relates to AI, we now must conclude with our working definition for AI in the light of the issues discussed thus far. However, unlike other academic works produced in the realm of AI, this research does not seek a universal definition which can be applied in multiple contexts. The purpose of our definition is much less ambitious: the present research is concerned with the responsibility of States under international law for their AI-enabled space activities. As Jacob Turner aptly points out, "[o]ne of the main principles of legal interpretation is to find out the purpose of the speaker".[139] Our purpose is to find a way to regulate the responsibility of States for AI within the *lex lata* of public international law. Therefore, we must ask ourselves: what is the unique factor of AI that needs regulation or, put differently, what aspects of AI challenge our understanding of current legal principles?[140] Throughout this book we will refer continuously to the ability of the machine to act and make decisions autonomously. These decisions and their impact on the real world are the focus of the present research. For the purposes of this research, we will therefore adopt and build upon the definition of AI brought forward by Jacob Turner, namely "Artificial Intelligence Is the Ability of a Non-natural Entity to Make Choices by an Evaluative Process."[141]

However, to highlight the autonomous nature of AI, and to differentiate it from cases in which we can anchor the liability in the human actor, this author proposes to make a small addition to Turner's definition and submits the following wording:

> Artificial Intelligence is the ability of a non-natural entity to make choices *autonomously* by an evaluative process.

---

137 Vilmer (2013), p. 129; Martin and Freeland (2021), p. 3; Tomaszewski (2021), p. 245; Verney and Vinçotte (2021).

138 This is due to the nature and vast distances in outer space. For example, under optimal weather conditions a command signal from Earth to Mars could take up to 24 minutes one-way. A human-in-the-loop approach would therefore not be optimal and could hinder exploration. See e.g. Katherine Schauer (2020) Space Communication: 7 Things you need to know. https://www.nasa.gov/missions/tech-demonstration/space-communications-7-things-you-need-to-know/#:~:text=NASA%20/%20JPL%2DCaltech-,6.,interference%20for%20space%20communications%20transmissions. Accessed 11 July 2025.

139 Turner (2019), p. 15.

140 Ibid, p. 15.

141 Ibid, p. 16.

This definition seems to reflect adequately the issues discussed throughout this research. The author prefers 'non-natural' to 'man-made' as AI could eventually develop the ability to create other AI and humans might, at some point, drop out of the picture.[142] Autonomy, as described above, refers to the ability to make decisions independently and an evaluative process is a process in which the machine weighs principles against each other.[143]

Principles ought to be contrasted with rules. Rules are applicable in an "all for nothing fashion" and once the facts stipulated by a rule are given then the rule either applies, in which case the answer it mandates must be accepted, or not, in which case it does not contribute to the decision.[144] If two rules stand in conflict, only one can apply. Which rules ought to be rejected must be made by taking considerations beyond the conflicting rules into account. Legal systems might resolve such conflict by other rules, such as giving the rule enacted by the higher authority precedence, rules enacted later supersede older rules or more specialised rules override more general rules (for example the well-known *lex specialis* principle).[145]

Principles, on the other hand, have a dimension that is absent in rules, namely that of weight and importance.[146] They give support to multiple courses of action, but they may not be necessarily conclusive.[147] When two valid principles conflict they are not invalid but rather such a conflict has to be resolved by weighing principles against each other and choosing the position that is supported by the principle with the most weight.[148] In other words, principles require evaluation while rules do not.[149]

To illustrate this difference in the context of modern AI technology let us look briefly into two types of "intelligent" systems, AI utilising a decision tree and AI utilising a neural network.

In simple terms, a decision tree consists of a set of rules to tell the AI what to do with a given input. In this scenario the AI uses deductive reasoning through yes or

---

142 Turner shares this view. See ibid., p. 16.

143 This is what we described above as ML by using different learning systems, such as a ANN. See also ibid., p. 16.

144 See Dworkin (1967), p. 25. Dworkin further explains:

This all-or-nothing is seen most plainly if we look at the way rules operate, not in law, but in some enterprise they dominate-a game, for example. In baseball a rule provides that if the batter has had three strikes, he is out. An official cannot consistently acknowledge that this is an accurate statement of a baseball rule, and decide that a batter who has had three strikes is not out. Of course, a rule may have exceptions (the batter who has taken three strikes is not out if the catcher drops the third strike). However, an accurate statement of the rule would take this exception into account, and any that did not would be incomplete. If the list of exceptions is very large, it would be too clumsy to repeat them each time the rule is cited; there is, however, no reason in theory why they could not all be added on, and the more that are, the more accurate is the statement of the rule.

145 Ibid., p. 27.

146 Ibid, p. 27.

147 Turner (2019), p. 18.

148 Dworkin (1967), p. 27; Turner (2019), p. 18.

149 See Turner (2019), p. 18.

no answers to follow the decision tree to reach a pre-determined output.[150] The decision-making process is deterministic, that is each step can be traced back to the programmer no matter how large the decision tree is.[151] It becomes evident, that the decision tree is a "rules-based" system in which only one answer (i.e., either yes or no) can be valid.

In contrast, neural networks use weights to determine the connectivity between inputs and outputs.[152] As mentioned above, an ANN consists of different artificial neurones. ANNs can be programmed to alter themselves by changing the weight on the connections to make the activity in one neurone more or less likely to excite an activity in another neurone. In a ML scenario, the AI can be given the ability to re-calibrate the weights over time to optimise outcomes.[153]

Any intelligence seen in a decision tree is that of the programmer and not the system itself. This is different in neural networks. The ability of ANNs to "determine weights between connections is an evaluative function characteristic of intelligence".[154] ANNs and ML are methods that fall within Turner's definition and the definition of this book. ANNs and ML, which are themselves based on an evaluative process, are also the basis upon which this research will discuss the challenges that it causes within the ambit of the responsibility of States for their AI-enabled space activities. It must be noted, again, that AI is an emerging technology and there is no "clear-cut" approach to a definition, nor does this research intend to conclusively define AI. The author bases his definition on Turner's understanding of AI because it seems broad and flexible enough to cover the problematique set out in the present research as well as to encompass other technologies which might become important in the future, such as whole brain emulation.[155]

1.3.7 The Use of AI

As mentioned previously, AI has started to firmly become part of our everyday lives. Modern devices, such as smartphones, smart TVs and computers, give the average end-user access to AI enabled programmes. A powerful example of this is the wide host of virtual personal assistants such as Amazon's Alexa, Apple's Siri, Google's Google Assistant, Microsoft's Cortana as well as automated phone answering machines, which sometimes test the patience of the caller, and companies direct

[150] Russell et al. (2010), sect. 18.3.
[151] Ibid., sect. 18.3; Turner (2019), p. 18.
[152] Cai et al. (2022).
[153] Wischmeyer (2020), pp. 81–82; Turner (2019), p. 19; Rumelhart et al. (1986).
[154] Turner (2019), p. 19.
[155] See Hilton B (2022) Whole brain emulation. In: 80,000 Hours. https://80000hours.org/problem-profiles/whole-brain-emulation/. Accessed 11 July 2025; Turner (2019), p. 19.

significant amounts of funding towards these applications.[156] This is connected to the wider growth of the "Internet of Things" (IoT) where everyday devices are connected to the Internet.[157] These systems take over mundane tasks, be it automatically brewing a fresh cup of coffee in the morning or vacuum cleaning the floor. The use of AI "as an aid to or even as a replacement for human judgement and decision-making can go from the immaterial (…) to the highly consequential".[158] For example, AI has started to find its way into day-to-day email communications. Canary Mail, a privacy-oriented email client for iOS, Android, Microsoft and Mac, has introduced an AI powered software. The software is meant to make daily email conversations quick and easy thus saving professionals valuable time. The programme is remarkably accurate, successfully drafting a variety of emails, from personal to professional.[159] On the other end of the spectrum we can find autonomous (i.e., self-driving) cars which are currently being tested by companies such as Tesla and Google. Autonomous weapon systems are another example of how AI is being developed for use in highly consequential, indeed life or death, situations.[160] AI is also being utilised to assist medical professionals in reaching a diagnosis and suggest subsequent treatment for various illnesses.[161]

It comes therefore as no surprise, that the potential of AI is also highly sought after in the space industry. As mentioned at the outset of the present research, outer space is a hostile environment and AI has the potential to take over many activities that are too hazardous for humans and enable further deep-space exploration, especially because, as mentioned, the future of space activities will mostly take place in outer space. At the date of writing, AI is already being used in a wide range of space applications. For example, the Crew Interactive Mobile Companion (CIMON), which was introduced onboard the International Space Station in 2018, was the first free-flying AI assistant in outer space. It was the successful result of a partnership between IBM, Airbus and the German Aerospace Agency (DLR).[162] CIMON is a small, 11-pound robot that can converse with astronauts, uses facial recognition to know to whom it talks, and has basic facial expressions.[163] CIMON uses as its AI

---

[156] AI Virtual Assistants Revolutionizing Industries | Market Set for 16.5% CAGR Growth - Valuates Reports. https://www.prnewswire.com/news-releases/ai-virtual-assistants-revolutionizing-industries%2D%2Dmarket-set-for-16-5-cagr-growth%2D%2D-valuates-reports-302403357.html. Accessed 10 July 2025.

[157] Turner (2019), p. 23.

[158] Ibid, p. 24.

[159] How AI Email Assistants Can Drive Customer Service Excellence - Canary Mail Blog. https://canarymail.io/blog/ai-email-assistants-for-customer-service. Accessed 11 July 2025. This assessment is based on the author's own use of Canary mail and its Co-Pilot system.

[160] ICRC (2022) What you need to know about autonomous weapons | ICRC. https://www.icrc.org/en/document/what-you-need-know-about-autonomous-weapons. Accessed 11 July 2025.

[161] Artificial Intelligence in Medicine | IBM. https://www.ibm.com/topics/artificial-intelligence-medicine. Accessed 11 July 2025.

[162] IBM (2022) IBM CIMON AI in space. https://web.archive.org/web/20230929105115/www.ibm.com/thought-leadership/innovation-explanations/cimon-ai-in-space. Accessed 11 July 2025.

[163] Ibid.

technology IBM's famous WATSON Assistant and is able to act as a "floating brain" for astronauts. As Matthias Biniok, the IBM project lead explains,

> [i]magine you're an astronaut in space, and you're at your station working on an experiment. Your hands are busy, and you have a question about the project you're working on. Normally, you would have to float over to your laptop to get the answer, then back to the experiment station. With CIMON, you can just say, 'CIMON, what's the next step?' and you don't have to interrupt your workflow. Another way CIMON provides assistance is in helping to document the experiments as they're being done. Astronauts need to record and film everything that they do. With CIMON, they can just tell him, 'CIMON, come here. Turn your camera 30 degrees to the right and record.[164]

Space debris removal is another area in which AI can be suitably employed. Plans are already well underway. The European Space Agency (ESA) announced in 2020 that it had signed a contract with Swiss start-up Clear Space to launch its first active debris removal mission.[165] Clear-Space One will be equipped with advanced guidance software, control systems and navigation using vision-based AI to capture and remove debris successfully.[166]

SpaceX is another company that utilises AI. Their rockets are equipped with an AI-driven autopilot that calculates optimal trajectories to reduce stress on the rocket, as well as an AI-powered emergency abort system.[167]

Further, AI can be effectively used in satellite data processing. It has been used to monitor the health of satellites and help analysing smartly the sheer number of images and data received via satellite imagery.[168]

Finally, AI plays a vital part in robotics used in outer space. A good example is the already mentioned Mars rover Perseverance which is currently exploring and mapping the surface of Mars. It uses an AI component to navigate safely, analyse the surrounding environment and execute mission parameters efficiently.[169] These are but a few examples of how AI is already being used, and will be used in future for activities in outer space. This shows that future space activities will, as

[164] IBM (2022) IBM CIMON AI in space. https://web.archive.org/web/20230929105115/www.ibm.com/thought-leadership/innovation-explanations/cimon-ai-in-space. Accessed 11 July 2025.

[165] ESA (2020) ESA purchases world-first debris removal mission from start-up. https://www.esa.int/Newsroom/Press_Releases/ESA_purchases_world-first_debris_removal_mission_from_start-up. Accessed 11 July 2025.

[166] Ibid.

[167] Gray C (2022) Three ways AI is being used to help with space exploration. https://aimagazine.com/technology/three-ways-ai-is-being-used-to-help-with-space-exploration. Accessed 11 July 2025; Lian R Community AI - AI on SpaceX. https://www.thecommunityai.org/ai-blog/ai-on-spacex. Accessed 11 July 2025.

[168] Berquand A, Bandivadekar D (2021) Five ways artificial intelligence can help space exploration. In: The Conversation. http://theconversation.com/five-ways-artificial-intelligence-can-help-space-exploration-153664. Accessed 11 July 2025.

[169] Good A et al. (2021) You Can Help Train NASA's Rovers to Better Explore Mars. In: NASA. http://www.nasa.gov/feature/jpl/you-can-help-train-nasa-s-rovers-to-better-explore-mars. Accessed 10 February 2023; Gupta S (2023) 7 Incredible Ways AI Is Being Used in Space Exploration. https://www.springboard.com/blog/data-science/ai-space-exploration/. Accessed 11 July 2025.

previously mentioned, largely be conducted in outer space rather than from Earth. Talking about these various applications, and the implications it can have under space law, makes it necessary to turn our attention more towards this area of the law.

1.4 Space Law: A General Overview

The title of the book—the International Responsibility of States for AI-enabled Space Activities—indicates that there are three major subjects this book will look at, namely AI, international law and space law. While this book has already established a foundation for AI, we now need to turn our attention towards space law. In particular, we need to provide a basic overview of what the present research means when it speaks of space law, briefly how space law is unique and its relationship to general international law. This general overview will naturally be more simplified, compact and focus on the main areas that will subsequently be expanded upon in the course of the writing.

1.4.1 The "Uniqueness" of Space Law

At the beginning of any research into the discipline of space law, it is worthwhile to briefly discuss the uniqueness of this specialised legal regime and describe its overall position in, and relationship to, the broader regime of public international law.

Such a discourse, however, would not be complete without at least a short glimpse back into the pages of history and shed some more light onto how the specialised norms pertaining to outer space came into being.

While many authors see the beginning of space law in the late 1950s, it appeared on the mind of authors far earlier than that. In 1903, Konstantin Tsiolkovsky had published a paper concerning the expansion of humanity in outer space by using rockets.[170] Seven years later, in 1910, Belgian legal expert Emilie Laude indicated that, [u]n droit nouveau régira des relations juridiques nouvelles. Ce ne sera plus du *Droit Aérien*. (…) Mais, à coup sûr, il s'agit du *Droit de l'Espace*"[171] and thus already expressed the necessity for a dedicated legal regime governing outer space. In the years that followed such writings became more numerous. Prominent academic experts, such as John Cobb Cooper, Nicolas Matte and Eugene Pépin, all of whom would go on to serve as Director of the McGill Institute of Air and Space Law, argued for a dedicated regime to deal with these legal issues.[172] Their efforts

[170] See Diederiks-Verschoor and Kopal (2008), p. 2.

[171] Laude (1910), p. 18 ["A new law will govern the new legal relations. It will no longer be air law but surely it is space law"].

[172] See e.g. Jankowitsch (2015), p. 2; Matte (1969), ch. 1; Cooper (1968), pp. 287–293; Pepin (1956).

eventually paid off and outer space was put into the focus of the international community.

Just like the first flight of 36 meters of the Wright Brothers propelled the international community to draft legal rules that eventually culminated in the Paris Convention of 1918[173] the precursor to the Chicago Convention of 1944,[174] so did the launch of Sputnik I force States, especially the United States and Union of Soviet Socialist Republics (USSR), to the bargaining table as the need for a specialised legal regime for outer space became apparent.[175] In, for international law, remarkably quick fashion, States negotiated and concluded over a period of roughly 20 years five major treaties, which went on to become better known as the five UN space treaties. For example, as Professor Bin Cheng noted "the [Outer Space] [T]reaty was drawn up not only in some haste within the space of less than 12 months but also less than ten years after the launch of the earth's first artificial satellite".[176] The Outer Space Treaty is interesting insofar as it is shaped by the political landscape of the time, many provisions being a political compromise between the United States and the USSR, and is innovative in its nature.[177] The Outer Space Treaty introduced some remarkable concepts, such as subjecting the exercise of sovereign rights in outer space to new rules, making outer space, including the moon and other celestial bodies, free from national appropriation by any means,[178] setting out new rules for State responsibility and liability[179] (see more below), making space the province of all mankind[180] and mandating that all activities are to be carried out in the interest of "maintaining international peace and security and promoting international co-operation and understanding".[181] The Treaty "is innovative also in the sense that to this day it has attempted, albeit not always successfully, to move ahead of technological developments and to try to create a secure legal environment for future scientific or economic activities".[182]

---

[173] Convention Relating to the Regulation of Aerial Navigation, 13 October 1919.

[174] Convention on International Civil Aviation, 7 December 1944, 15 UNTS 295 (entered into force 4 April 1947).

[175] Report of the Ad Hoc Committee on the Peaceful Uses of Outer Space, 1959, UN Doc A/4141.

[176] Cheng (1997a), p. 203.

[177] Jankowitsch (2015), p. 5.

[178] Art. II, Outer Space Treaty.

[179] Ibid, arts VI–VII.

[180] Ibid, art I.

[181] Ibid, arts III.

[182] Jankowitsch (2015), p. 5. The Outer Space Treaty was quite future oriented insofar as it accounted for private non-State actors in Article VI by making States directly responsible for the activities of non-governmental entities. This shows the awareness by States of the potential commercial uses of outer space. Additionally, the principle of free exploration and scientific investigation of outer space as well as declaring it "the province of all [hu]mankind was undoubtedly worked into the treaty to ensure that outer space remains accessible to future generations and all nations. However, the author doubts that the intentions of the negotiators were entirely selfless but rather coined by the political climate of the time and perhaps the US and Soviet Union were trying to make sure that outer space remains accessible primarily to them.

One unique, indeed remarkable, legal principle introduced by the Outer Space Treaty can be found in Articles VI and VII concerning responsibility and liability aspects of activities in outer space, something with which this book will mostly be concerned. The present research will talk in greater detail about these legal aspects in Chap. 3 but suffice it to say at this point that the Outer Space Treaty introduced a unique way of governing the responsibility of States for their national space activities.

It is a well-established principle of international law that a State can only be responsible for its own behaviour and therefore international responsibility only arises when the breach of an international obligation is attributable to the State.[183] Since a State cannot act on its own, international law regards the act of an organ,[184] actions of persons or entities empowered to exercise governmental authority[185] as well as private actors acting under the instruction or control of the State, without them being state organ or empowered to exercise governmental authority, as being attributable to the State.[186] Provided that none of these circumstances are present, a State is generally not internationally responsible for the conduct of foreign nationals or private individuals, unless the State fails to act upon an international obligation to prevent a certain conduct of private individuals.[187]

Article VI changes this dynamic. It states that "State parties shall bear international responsibility for national activities in outer space whether such activities are carried on by governmental agencies or *by non-governmental entities* [emphasis added]" and the "activities of non-governmental entities (…) shall require the authorization and continuing supervision of the appropriate State Party".[188] In other words, Article VI does away with the attribution problem and makes States directly internationally responsible for the conduct of private parties. To use the words of Judge Manfred Lachs, "[t]his is intended to ensure that any outer space activity, no matter by whom conducted, shall be carried on in accordance with the relevant rules of international law, and to bring the consequences of such activity within its ambit. The acceptance of this principle removes all doubts concerning imputability."[189]

---

[183] See e.g. Momtaz (2010); Shaw (2008); Abass (2012); Cassese (2001); Aust (2010).

[184] See Question relating to Settles of German Origin in Poland (1931), Advisory Opinion, PCIJ (Ser B) No 6; Anzilotti (1929); Cassese (2001); Momtaz (2010).

[185] Cassese (2001); Momtaz (2010); James Crawford (2006) State Responsibility. Max Planck Encyclopedia of International Law.

[186] Case Concerning Military And Paramilitary Activities in and Against Nicaragua (Nicaragua v United States) [1986], ICJ Rep 14; De Frouville (2010); Brownlie (2008); Abass (2012); Aust (2010); Cassese (2001); Shaw (2008).

[187] See generally Koivurova (2003); Mazzeschi (2004); De Frouville (2010); Cassese (2001); Case Concerning United States Diplomatic and Consular Staff in Tehran (United States v Iran [1980] ICJ Rep 3.

[188] Art. VI, Outer Space Treaty.

[189] Lachs (2010), p. 114.

This is certainly a unique feature and to date there is only one other international regime that contains a similar provision.[190]

Article VI of the Outer Space Treaty is a clear example of the "Realpolitik" of the time and constitutes a political compromise between the United States and the Soviet Union. The former wanted outer space to be accessible to private entities, the latter preferred outer space to remain solely a State domain.[191] Article VI finally reconciled the opposing views by opening the legal regime to private entities but requiring States to accept direct international responsibility for these private entities.

Whereas Article VI of the Outer Space Treaty deals with international responsibility of States for their national activities in outer space, Article VII addresses liability. A State Party to the Outer Space Treaty "that launches or procures the launching of an object into outer space" or "from whose territory or facility an object is launched" is internationally liable for damage caused by "[a space] object or its component parts on Earth, in air space or in outer space, including the moon and other celestial bodies".[192] Article VII introduces the concept of launching State, which can be different from the responsible State, and addresses the liability aspect separately from the responsibility aspect contained in Article VI of the Outer Space Treaty. Within general international law there is a vivid academic discussion as to whether it is necessary to separate responsibility from liability, something the present research will investigate in detail at a later stage.[193]

The Outer Space Treaty defines launching State as the "State which launches or procures the launching of a space object" or "from whose territory or facility a space object is launched".[194] This leaves room for interpretation and there can be more than one launching State, in addition to the responsible State, which could

---

[190] The ITU Constitution and its corresponding Radio Regulations require that Member States assure that stations do not cause harmful interference. Constitution and Convention of the International Telecommunication Union, 22 December 1992, 1825, 1826 UNTS; Radio Regulations Edition of 2024, WRC-23 (Dubai, 2023) art. 18.

[191] For example, the Soviet Union repeatedly proposed that "[a]ll activities of any kind pertaining to the exploration and use of outer space shall be carried our solely by State" while the United States avoided such formulation. See e.g. UNCOPUOS, Union of Soviet Socialist Republics: Draft Declaration of the Basic Principles Governing the Activities of States Pertaining to the Exploration and Use of Outer Space, UN Doc A/AC.105/L.2 (1962); Report of the Committee on the Peaceful Uses of Outer Space, UNCOPUOS, 18th Sess, Annex III, Agenda Item 28, UN Doc A/5549 Add.1, (1963); LSC, Report of the Legal Sub-Committee on the Work of its Second Session (16 April–3 May 1963) to the Committee on the Peaceful Uses of Outer Space, UNCOPUOS, 1963, UN Doc A/AC.105/12.

[192] Art. VII, Outer Space Treaty.

[193] Professor Brownlie, for example, expresses 'total opposition to this particular enterprise'. See Brownlie (2008), pp. 49–50 His view is thus contrary to the ILC which considers liability and responsibility to be based on different concepts. While responsibility necessitates a wrongful act, liability does not. In the ILC's view liability can arise even though the activity was perfectly legal. Like Professor Brownlie, we remain critical of this particular view and discuss this in more detail later (see Sect. 4.4).

[194] Art. I, Liability Convention.

cause some problems in the context of our multinational space industry of the twenty-first century.[195]

Article VII of the Outer Space Treaty established the framework which required a more precise elaboration to determine the obligations that arise from damage caused by a space object.[196] Thus States, parallel to the Outer Space Treaty, negotiated a dedicated treaty concerned solely with the liability for damage caused by space objects as an additional avenue to the more general rules of the Outer Space Treaty, the Liability Convention.[197]

The Liability Convention is particularly interesting from a legal point of view as it introduced some quite unique features.

First, the Liability Convention is based on two different liability principles. For damage caused by a space object on the surface of the Earth or to an aircraft in flight, the launching State is absolutely liable whereas for damage elsewhere than on the surface of the Earth (i.e., in outer space) the launching State is only liable if it is at fault, which was a novel concept at the time of inception.[198]

Second, under general international law, a State can generally only present claims against another State if the damage was suffered by the State or one of its nationals.[199] The Liability Convention relaxes this in Article VIII and states:

> 1. A State which suffers damage, or whose natural or juridical persons suffer damage, may present to a launching State a claim for compensation for such damage.
> 2. If the State of nationality has not presented a claim, another State may, in respect of damage sustained in its territory by any natural or juridical person, present a claim to a launching State.
> 3. If neither the State of nationality nor the State in whose territory the damage was sustained has presented a claim or notified its intention of presenting a claim, another State may, in respect of damage sustained by its permanent residents, present a claim to a launching State.

This provision seems to establish a hierarchy as to who can make a claim, namely the (1) national State, (2) territorial State and (3) the State of permanent residence.[200]

Third, subject to certain conditions, the Liability Convention allows international organisations to participate without becoming a State Party.[201]

Besides the Liability Convention there are three other dedicated space law treaties that elaborate provisions of the Outer Space Treaty. The Return and Rescue

[195] See e.g. Lee (2012); Awford (1995); Kerrest and Thro (2017); Schrogl and Davies (2002); Kerrest (1997); Hurwitz (1992); Matte (1984); Von der Dunk (2015); Kayser (2001).

[196] Lachs (2010), p. 114.

[197] Ibid, p. 114.

[198] The liability for surface damage and damage to an aircraft in flight is legally speaking a strict rather than an absolute liability as the Liability Convention allows for exoneration under certain circumstances. See more in Sect. 1.5.

[199] Mavrommatis Palestine Concessions (Greece v. U.K.) (1924), PCIJ (Ser A) No 3, p. 21; Muse (1997); This is of course again not as clear-cut as presented. If, for example, an obligation erga omnes is breached then other States can invoke responsibility too. See Case concerning the Barcelona Traction, Light and Power Company, Limited (Belgium v Spain), [1964] ICJ Rep 6, para 33; Kindred et al. (2014), p. 453.

[200] For an excellent detailed analysis see Cheng (1997b), pp. 306ff.

[201] Art. XXII Liability Convention; Cheng (1997b), p. 313ff; Lachs (2010), p. 115.

Agreement,[202] the Registration Convention[203] and, finally, the Moon Agreement.[204] These instruments equally constitute dedicated separate avenues to the more general provisions of the Outer Space Treaty. Since the present research will mainly be concerned with responsibility and liability issues arising from the use of AI in outer space, the focus will mainly be on the Outer Space Treaty and the Liability Convention and reference to the other space treaties will only be made when appropriate. The author will therefore not delve into a more detailed analysis of these instruments.

As mentioned at the very beginning, while in the past the actors in outer space were primarily States, space activities are now increasingly carried out by private entities for purely commercial purposes.[205] This shift in focus from old to new space actors also meant that the development of space law did not end in the late 1970s.

---

[202] Return and Rescue Agreement.

[203] Registration Convention.

[204] Moon Agreement.

[205] Farsaiya and Sharma (2014); de Zwaart (2017); Manoli (2017); Masson-Zwaan and Hofmann (2019); Dempsey (2017); Space activities are, for now, still mainly driven by governments with private actors predominantly acting as contractors for public programmes and relying on large government funding. While in the past those private actors were not directly in the position to make political decisions on behalf of a government, this has notably changed in recent months, particularly in the United States. Elon Musk, billionaire and owner of Space X, is heading a newly formed government agency, the Department of Government Efficiency or DOGE. Although DOGE was "only" charged with terminating government waste, Elon Musk's own companies interestingly seem to have gained a market advantage with an increase in the number of potential government contracts for vital systems. For example, Elon Musk, while conducting a "review" of the FAAs air navigation system, proposed an upgrade to the FAAs air traffic control system and argued to replace Verizon with Space X, a contract worth USD 2.4 billion. Testing of Starlink terminals for the FAA is already underway. This marks a departure from the traditional modes of offering public contracts and shows the direct influence billionaires start to exhibit in the space domain. The space component needed to provide air navigation services is critical, control over such system puts a company in the position to be able to directly impact air traffic, potentially leading to catastrophic outcomes. Further, Starlink is used in the Russian-Ukrainian war giving Elon Musk the ability to interfere and withdraw the satellite-based infrastructure if he so chooses. Another example is the push towards going back to the Moon. Space X launched a private Moon lander to find traces of water. In other words, private for-profit companies led by their CEOs, are in positions like never before to directly influence governments and politics, some, like Elon Musk even going so far as heading a government agency without a vote ever being cast in their name. Given this climate, it becomes even more important to adhere to the rules-based international legal order and the existing lex lata. See e.g. Isidore C (2025) Elon Musk says upgrade of FAA's air traffic control system is failing and SpaceX needs to take over Verizon's contract | CNN Business. https://www.cnn.com/2025/02/27/business/elon-musk-faa-air-traffic-control-failing-spacex. Accessed 11 July 2025; Dinner J (2025) SpaceX rocket launches private moon lander and NASA 'trailblazer' to hunt for lunar water (video). https://www.space.com/space-exploration/launches-spacecraft/spacex-rocket-launches-private-moon-lander-and-nasa-trailblazer-to-hunt-for-lunar-water. Accessed 11 July 2025; Denisova K (2025) Ukrainian front line 'would collapse' if Starlink is turned off, Musk claims. https://kyivindependent.com/ukrainian-front-line-would-collapse-if-starlink-is-turned-off-musk-claims/. Accessed 11 July 2025; ESPI (2017) The Rise of Private Actors in the Space Sector. https://www.espi.or.at/wp-content/uploads/2022/06/ESPI-report-The-rise-of-private-actors-Executive-Summary-1.pdf. Accessed 16 July 2025.

Quite the contrary, new rules to govern the increasing number of private actors started to emerge and the development of space law has not stopped. Peter Jankowitsch aptly calls it an "unfinished history", and this author agrees.[206]

The five UN space treaties serve merely as a foundational framework, but the shift from a focus on political and military uses of outer space during the early years of space exploration to broader applications necessitates the ongoing development and adaptation of the legal framework governing outer space activities.[207] One important aspect of this development is the creation of a high number of bi- and multilateral agreements between States and governmental agencies. As of 2022, the United States alone signed over 3000 space agreements with international and domestic entities.[208] This development is further driven by the wide variety of intergovernmental organisations, such as INTELSAT[209] (now privatised), INMARSAT[210] (now privatised), INTERSPUTNIK,[211] ARABSAT and the European Space Agency,[212] to name a few.[213] Further, the International Telecommunication Union (ITU) played, and continues to play, an important part in the development of rules governing specific activities in outer space.[214]

Thus, "international intergovernmental organizations such as the European Space Agency, the International Telecommunication Union (ITU) and, more recently, the European Union play an important regulatory, administrative and legal role at the international level"[215] and the development of space law also includes in its scope private non-governmental entities and individuals.[216]

This regulatory process is now mainly driven by the development of non-binding measures, such as codes of conduct or soft law. As previously pointed out, States seem to be increasingly unwilling to subject themselves to binding measures but rather look towards non-binding instruments.[217] A very prominent example of this

---

[206] Jankowitsch (2015), p. 20.

[207] Ibid, p. 21.

[208] A detailed, and up-to-date list, of all agreements can be found on NASA's website. For more information see Current Space Act Agreements - NASA. https://www.nasa.gov/partnerships/current-space-act-agreements/. Accessed 11 July 2025.

[209] Our Story | Intelsat. https://www.intelsat.com/about-us/our-story/. Accessed 11 July 2025; Lyall' (2000).

[210] Celebrating 35 years of aeronautical satellite communications. https://www.inmarsat.com/en/news/latest-news/aviation/2020/celebrating-35-years-of-aeronautical-satellite-communications.html. Accessed 11 July 2025; Who we are. https://www.inmarsat.com/en/about/who-we-are.html. Accessed 11 January 2023.

[211] Intersputnik, Home page. In: Intersputnik. https://intersputnik.int/. Accessed 11 July 2025.

[212] European Space Agency (2025) This is ESA. https://esamultimedia.esa.int/docs/corporate/This_is_ESA_EN_LR.pdf. Accessed 16 July 2025.

[213] Cf Jakhu et al. (2020).

[214] The main objectives of the ITU are to eliminate harmful interference as well as allocate spectrums and allot frequencies and orbital positions of satellites. See Jakhu (2016); Henri et al. (2017).

[215] Freeland (2012), p. 11.

[216] Jankowitsch (2015), p. 23. Cf Freeland (2012).

[217] Jakhu and Pelton (2017), p. 101.

development in recent history is the withdrawal of Saudi Arabia from the Moon Agreement in 2024, which remains binding and in force amongst other State Parties.[218]

The Artemis Accords, which are "a non-binding, "political commitment" that operationalizes the bedrock of international space law, the Outer Space Treaty", are another example.[219] In the context of AI, non-binding instruments are also starting to emerge. For example, the United Nations Educational, Scientific and Cultural Organization (UNESCO) published its "Recommendations on the Ethics of Artificial Intelligence" and the Organisation for Economic Co-operation and Development (OECD) adopted AI principles in 2019.[220] This can arguably be seen as the root of the increasing academic interest in the role soft law can play in international law and space law.[221] Soft law is a term that has emerged in legal writings but is hard to define.[222] While it is beyond the scope of this section to engage in a deeper interpretative analysis of the term, it might be worthwhile to just briefly mention that soft law can generally be seen as instruments that are not binding *per se* and can appear in various forms, such as non-binding principles, standards of behaviour, codes of conduct, resolutions, recommendations, and guidelines.[223] This stands in contrast with "hard law", such as treaties, which are legally binding in their nature.

The preceding paragraph shall not be misunderstood as to mean that States have completely stopped creating binding agreements. There are some notable exceptions to the trend, the most recent example being the conclusion of "The Council of Europe Framework Convention on Artificial Intelligence", which, according to the EU is "the first-ever international legally binding treaty in this field".[224]

---

[218] Moon Agreement; Saudi Arabia's official notification to withdraw can be found under <treaties.un.org/doc/Publication/CN/2023/CN.4.2023-Eng.pdf>.

[219] Wedenig S-M, Nelson Wright J (2023) The Moon Agreement: Hanging by a Thread? In: Institute of Air and Space Law. https://www.mcgill.ca/iasl/moon-agreement-hanging-thread. Accessed 14th July 2025. Indeed, the Artemis Accords are a powerful example of the development towards non-binding measures. Concluded in 2020, the number of participants grew to 24 in under two years. In November 2025 the number of signatories stands at 60.

[220] See UNESCO Ethics of Artificial Intelligence. https://www.unesco.org/en/artificial-intelligence/recommendation-ethics. Accessed 11 July 2025; OECD AI AI Principles Overview. oecd.ai/en/principles. Accessed 11 July 2025.

[221] See e.g. Byrd (2022);; Martinez (2020); Blount (2011); Freeland (2011); Freeland (2012); Marboe (2012).

[222] Blount (2011), p. 525.

[223] Martinez (2020), p. 522; Freeland (2011), p. 430; Aust (2010), p. 11; Kindred et al. (2014), p. 60.

[224] EU The Framework Convention on Artificial Intelligence - Artificial Intelligence. https://www.coe.int/en/web/artificial-intelligence/the-framework-convention-on-artificial-intelligence. Accessed 16 July 2025.

1.4.1.1 National Space Law

So far, this section has only discussed the international dimension of space law. However, it must be pointed out that approaching space law from an international perspective is only one side of the coin. Space law also contains a national dimension. States have, in one form or the other, created national space legislation to ensure compliance with their international obligations.[225] The need for the national development of space law has risen as States attempt to establish a framework for the authorisation of governmental and non-governmental space activities.[226] This is important because, as mentioned previously, the outer space environment is not solely a State domain anymore and private activities are on the rise. However, private entities are ordinarily not bound by norms of public international law or international treaties as generally only States (and some international organisations) possess international legal personality.[227] This is where national legislation (e.g., national space law) comes in.

National legal norms fold international rules into the respective national legal order of the State and make them directly applicable and enforceable. It affords the State the ability to control space activities of private, non-governmental entities.[228] Additionally, national space law can serve as a tool for the State to set out its national space agenda, enforce public policy decisions and support the development of a healthy space industry.[229] Therefore, various efforts have been made in academia and practice to raise awareness for the importance of national space legislation and also to define the most pressing issues that should be addressed.[230]

One of these pressing issues, in this author's opinion, is the lack of legislative initiative shown by States in an international law context in recent history considering the increasing use of AI for space activities, and emerging technologies more

---

[225] See e.g. Space (Launches and Returns) Act (Australia), 123/1998, Bundesgesetz über die Genehmigung von Weltraumaktivitäten und die Einrichtung eines Weltraumregisters (Weltraumgesetz) (Austria)[Austrian Space Act]; Law on the Activities of Launching, Flight Operation or Guidance of Space Objects (Belgium) [Belgian Space Law]; Outer Space Act 1986 (UK) [UK Outer Space Act]; Space Development Promotion Act (Republic of South Korea) [South Korean Space Development Act]; 51 USC § 50902; 51 USC § 20103.

[226] Marboe (2015), p. 127; Jankowitsch (2015), p. 27.

[227] The Steamship Lotus (Fance v Turkey) (1927), PCIJ (Seri A) No 10; Marboe (2015), pp. 127–128; Brownlie (2008), p. 58ff.The author admits that this is a very simplistic statement. Indeed, international legal personality is much more nuanced and while States are the prime subjects of international law, there can be various entities and individual who posses some attributes of international legal personality. For an excellent overview of the issue see Kindred et al. (2014), p. 73ff.

[228] A prime example in national space legislation is the various licensing and authorization regimes. This affords the State a dual advantage. On the one hand, it can assert a certain degree of control over private space activities, and on the other hand, it ensures the State complies with its international obligations, especially under Art VI of the Outer Space Treaty.

[229] Marboe (2015), pp. 184–185.

[230] Marboe (2015). See generally Von der Dunk (2011b); Jakhu (2010); Hermida (2004); Bourély (1991).

generally.[231] While States created national space legislation in the past, they do not seem to be particularly motivated to make amendments to take AI and other emerging technologies into account. The increase in the number of private space actors combined with State's increasing preference to rely on private actors to conduct space activities that were once solely a State operated endeavour exacerbates the problem. The utilisation of AI is able to lower the entry barriers to space exploration and enables an even broader category of private actors, such as start-ups, to engage with the outer space environment, making dedicated national space legislation even more important.[232]

However, the rapid development of AI and related technology continues to outpace regulation, making it difficult for regulators to exercise adequately their mandate to authorise and provide continuing supervision as required by Article VI of the Outer Space Treaty. Interestingly, this seems to be a sentiment echoed by the industry itself. In 2022, the Centre for Strategic and International Studies commissioned a research study which included interviews with various companies active in the space sector. Most interviewees cast doubt on the regulators ability to regulate modern space activities effectively and to keep up with the development of new technology.[233] This has led some, most notably the chairman of the Indian Space Research Organisation, to call for "deregulation" of space activities.[234]

However, albeit there are some companies that open-source their base code, there are many others that are not particularly keen to share detailed information about their AI algorithms and are largely operating independently without much regulatory oversight. This already poses hurdles in other legal areas. For example, as Julie Cohen correctly argues, "[t]he institutions we now have were designed around the regulatory problems and competencies of an era in which industrialism was the principal mode of development" and they did not consider the problems caused by a data-driven development and technology.[235] Without initiative of the regulator, AI-enabled space activities could continue, in the context of national

---

[231] This is not only confined to space law but also a problem from a wider public international law perspective and therefore there are calls for the development of new and the adaption of existing legal rules to take the growing use of AI into account. See e.g. Marwala T (2024) Militarization of AI Has Severe Implications for Global Security and Warfare. https://unu.edu/article/militarization-ai-has-severe-implications-global-security-and-warfare. Accessed 14 July 2025; Peterson D, Hoffman S Geopolitical implications of AI and digital surveillance adoption. www.brookings.edu/articles/geopolitical-implications-of-ai-and-digital-surveillance-adoption/. Accessed 11 July 2025.

[232] See e.g. Maguire P (2024) AI at the crossroads of cybersecurity, space and national security in the digital age. In: SpaceNews. https://spacenews.com/ai-crossroads-cybersecurity-space-national-security-digital-age/. Accessed 9 August 2024.

[233] Goessler A (2022) The Private Sector's Assessment of U.S. Space Policy and Law. https://aerospace.csis.org/the-private-sectors-assessment-of-u-s-space-policy-and-law/. Accessed 7 July 2025.

[234] See Deregulation imperative for space sector growth: ISRO chairman Somanath. https://www.business-standard.com/industry/news/deregulation-imperative-for-space-sector-growth-isro-chairman-somanath-123112500564_1.html. Accessed 7 July 2025; Another author advocates for the abolition of licensing in Ukraine. See Semenyaka (2019).

[235] Cohen (2016), p. 370.

space legislation, to develop, as they have already begun, partly in a legal vacuum.[236] This is not solely confined to a lack of regulatory actions, but also encompasses the issue of who is responsible to ensure compliance (if regulation is in place). While the development is still nascent in the space context, a look towards other industries might provide insight as to how regulators could treat this in the outer space domain in future.

Cohen, for example, highlights the apparent mismatch between regulatory goals and methods.[237] In Europe, for instance, the primary responsibility for emissions testing of automobiles lies with private entities that certify compliance.[238] The grounding after two fatal accidents of the Boeing 737-Max is but another example that showed the flaws of the FAAs policy to entrust aviation manufacturers to certify their own systems to comply with US regulations.[239] New institutional forms that would ensure compliance have been slow to develop, and there is no reason to suspect that this might be different in the space industry.[240] Indeed, the apparent lack of new regulation pertaining to AI, even in light of the wider adoption of use of such technology, seems to be an indication that regulators are drifting into the same direction. This could in turn cause a breach of a State's obligation under Article VI Outer Space Treaty, particularly if we consider that the development of AI can give rise to a new responsible State under Article VII (see section 4.3.3.1).

In this author's view, the lack of new national space legislation ensuring proper authorisation and providing continuing supervision, is connected to a wider political problem that is not entirely confined to the issues discussed in the present research, or to space law in general. Indeed, States have shown an increasing willingness to partly ignore their obligations under public international law.

For example, according to Article II of the Registration Convention 1974, States are under the obligation to register in an appropriate registry any space object launched into Earth's orbit or beyond, maintain such registry and inform the Secretary General of the United Nations of the establishment of such registry.[241] However, States have been delinquent in their duty to do so. While civil satellites are generally registered, the information submitted is often so general that it does not create transparency as envisioned under the Registration Convention.[242] Military satellites are often inadequately reported, or not reported at all, which blatantly

[236] It must be noted that this refers to a legal vacuum within a national dimension and is separate from the question of international law. Indeed, as will be argued throughout the present research, public international law is capable of governing AI.

[237] Cohen (2016), p. 373.

[238] Ibid.

[239] See e.g. Davis AC, Lopes M (2019) How the FAA allows jetmakers to 'self certify' that planes meet U.S. safety requirements. www.washingtonpost.com/investigations/how-the-faa-allows-jetmakers-to-self-certify-that-planes-meet-us-safety-requirements/2019/03/15/96d24d4a-46e6-11e9-90f0-0ccfeec87a61_story.html. Accessed 7 July 2025.

[240] Cohen (2016), p. 375.

[241] Art. II, Registration Convention.

[242] Jakhu et al. (2018a).

stands in conflict with States' obligations under the Registration Convention.[243] As of date of writing, the United Nations Office for Outer Space Affairs (UNOOSA) lists over 2222 unregistered in orbit satellites.[244] While part of the non-compliance can be seen as inadvertent, there may also be politically motivated deliberate abuses.[245]

Politically motivated decision-making in the space domain is not a recent phenomenon. For example, as this author pointed out elsewhere, the negotiation of the Moon Agreement was supported by the then Soviet Union and the US only to occupy the time of the Committee on the Peacful Uses of Outer Space (COPUOS) and to stall other meaningful legislative processes.[246] Further, as pointed out above, the Outer Space Treaty as such constitutes in many regards a political compromise between the US and the Soviet Union.

Another example of political influence on the development of space law is the US opposition to the Russian-Chinese proposal for a treaty on the prevention of the placement of weapons in outer space.[247] The US vehemently opposed any treaty that would tie their hands in the field of space security.[248] Politics also seemed to inform the decision of China, the US and India to conduct anti-satellite weapons tests creating additional space debris which could infringe on the rights of other States to freely explore outer space as guaranteed by Article I of the Outer Space Treaty.

Indeed, it becomes increasingly apparent that States adopt a more confrontational stance in the context of space activities. Lunar exploration serves as an example for this development. While the US led Artemis Accords currently have 60 signatories, Russia and China remain notably absent from the list and decided to jointly build a lunar base in response to the Artemis Accords.[249]

---

[243] The Registration Convention makes no differentiation between military or civil use space objects. Indeed, it only speaks of space objects which includes both military and non-military applications. See also Jakhu et al. (2018a), p. 411; Wright Nelson J (2018) Lost in Space? Gaps in the International Space Object Registration Regime. www.ejiltalk.org/lost-in-space-gaps-in-the-international-space-object-registration-regime/. Accessed14 July 2025.

[244] Online Index of Objects Launched into Outer Space. www.unoosa.org/oosa/osoindex/search-ng.jspx?lf_id=. Accessed 7 July 2025.

[245] Jakhu et al. (2018a), p. 417.

[246] Wedenig S-M, Nelson Wright J (2023) The Moon Agreement: Hanging by a Thread? In: Institute of Air & Space Law. https://www.mcgill.ca/iasl/article/moon-agreement-hanging-thread. Accessed 14 July 2025.

[247] Draft Treaty on Prevention of the Placement of Weapons in Outer Space and of the Threat or Use of Force against Outer Space Objects, CD/1985 (2014).

[248] See U.S. National Space Policy (2006). https://obamawhitehouse.archives.gov/sites/default/files/microsites/ostp/national-space-policy-2006.pdf. Accessed 14 July 2025; see also Bracht and Martinez (2021), p. 118.

[249] Artemis Accords - NASA. https://www.nasa.gov/artemis-accords/. Accessed 14 July 2025; Anqi F (2024) Putin signs into law joint building of lunar base with China as Beijing expands circle of friends in Moon exploration - Global Times. www.globaltimes.cn/page/202406/1314079.shtml. Accessed 7 July 2025.

When the Russian Federation made the decision to launch a military attack on Ukraine—in itself a violation of public international law—the war was quickly brought into outer space.[250] On the day of the invasion, the Russian Federation conducted a cyber operation against the KA-SAT network to disrupt communications. The Russian Federation also utilises SpaceX's Starlink satellites for battlefield operations.[251]

It will be but a matter of time until hostile nations start utilising AI in their military operations conducted in outer space or executed through a space-based component. This is by no means confined to States alone. The wider adoption of AI, and the corresponding increase in potential actors in outer space, brings also with it a heightened cybersecurity risk. Hostile parties could utilise AI to circumvent security measures and wreak havoc on vital communications or other important infrastructure, which could pose a risk to national security.[252]

While all these problems are undoubtedly pressing, they deserve their own dedicated research and addressing them would go beyond the limit of the present book. Nevertheless, it is important to point towards this conundrum, especially because outer space can really be seen as a unique composition, a melting pot of different actors and an arena where international law interacts with private actors by making, *inter alia*, States directly internationally responsible and liable for the activities of non-governmental entities.

1.4.1.2 Use of Terminology

Two terms—general (public) international law and space law—will frequently be used throughout this book. This should not indicate that these are two entirely separate legal regimes. Quite the contrary, space law is international law. It is imbedded in international law and all activities in outer space have to be carried out "in

[250] Resolution adopted by the General Assembly on 2 March 2022, UNGA, 11th Sess, UN Doc A/Res/ES-11/1 (2022), Res ES-11/1.

[251] Russian cyber operations against Ukraine: Declaration by the High Representative on behalf of the European Union. https://www.consilium.europa.eu/en/press/press-releases/2022/05/10/russian-cyber-operations-against-ukraine-declaration-by-the-high-representative-on-behalf-of-the-european-union/. Accessed 14 July 2025; Marson J, Grove T (2024) Russia Using Thousands of Musk's Starlink Systems in War, Ukrainian General Says. www.wsj.com/world/russia-using-thousands-of-musks-starlink-systems-in-war-ukrainian-general-says-29303242. Accessed 9 July 2024.

[252] Maguire P (2024) AI at the crossroads of cybersecurity, space and national security in the digital age. https://spacenews.com/ai-crossroads-cybersecurity-space-national-security-digital-age/. Accessed 14 July 2025. For example, bad actors could also use communication satellites to spread false information. "Fake news" already poses a problem exacerbated by AI algorithms used by social media platforms. Artificial Intelligence (AI) Challenges and Opportunities in National Security. onlinewilder.vcu.edu/blog/ai-challenges-and-opportunities-national-security/. Accessed 14 July 2025.

accordance with international law, including the Charter of the United Nations".[253] To quote the words of Professor Bing Cheng,

> [i]n order to avoid any misunderstanding, let it be said at the very outset that space law, as it now exists, is not an independent legal system. It is merely a functional classification of those rules of international law and of municipal law relating to outer space, natural or man-made objects in outer space, space-men, and [humanity's] activities in outer space.[254]

In our present discussion we will be mainly concerned with the international dimension of space law and those rules of public international law that are applicable to outer space and provide the legal framework for the activities of States in outer space.

In this regard, space law norms are international norms dedicated to space activities and complement the other more general norms of public international law.[255] However, space law is still public international law. This is important to point out at the beginning to avoid any misconception or confusion. It follows therefore that the five U.N. space treaties are just that, international treaties. They are level with any other validly concluded international agreement and the Outer Space Treaty is certainly not a "Magna Carta" as some authors erroneously claim.[256]

1.5 Problems & Research Question

This Introduction served two purposes: (1) to provide the reader with a basic understanding of AI and place this AI in the wider legal arena of space law and (2) to introduce the legal framework of space law which is, in turn, embedded in general international law. At the end of this chapter, there is only really one aspect left to discuss, namely how does AI challenge our understanding of the law as it relates to the responsibility of State for their AI-enabled space activities and how do we frame our research questions in this regard? While we cannot answer this question in this part of the book, we can attempt to provide the reader with a short overview of what is to come. Each chapter in turn will discuss each aspect of the research question in detail.

Over the past two decades a trend has emerged, namely a withdrawal of State actors and an increase of private commercial actors in outer space.[257] Although this transformation led a fair number of authors to suggest that the UN Space Treaties should be amended to better reflect the "changing times", the treaties still offered a

[253] Art. III, Outer Space Treaty; See also Jakhu et al. (2018b), p. 113ff; Freeland and Jakhu (2017), p. 46; Jakhu (2006); Jakhu and Freeland (2016); Jakhu et al. (2021).

[254] Cheng (1997b), p. 383.

[255] See e.g Salmeri (2021), p. 203; van Traa-Engelman (1984), p. 140; Von der Dunk (1994), p. 161.

[256] Von der Dunk (2011a), p. 8; Jankowitsch (1998), p. 103; Qizhi (1997); Finch (1980); Von der Dunk (1992); Salmeri (2021), p. 204.

[257] States started to rely on private actors even for their own activities in outer space. An example is the ISS which is re-supplied by SpaceX. See Commercial Resupply - NASA. https://www.nasa.gov/international-space-station/commercial-resupply/. Accessed 14 July 2025.

steady legal framework for these activities.[258] This is because the treaties were drafted, negotiated and eventually adopted with the understanding that humans, whether it is the State acting through its organs or agents, or private individuals, are the sole actors in outer space and anything can, at a minimum, be traced back to humans. This was a fundamental basis upon which the legal framework of responsibility and liability was placed.

This understanding is now being challenged. As discussed above, the development and the introduction of AI has reached a point where our current understanding, and subsequent application of the law, is brought to its limits. This is especially evident in tort law where our current understanding of subjective fault is challenged.[259]

In order to illustrate this point further, we remind the reader again of two aspects, namely (1) AI is an emerging technology, that is it is continuously developing and in constant flux, and (2) the term AI is very broad and not defined. A simple Roomba vacuum cleaner or trading algorithm, which automatically buys and sells stocks, is as much part of this emerging field as an autonomous car or a highly advanced computer system built on machine learning.

Arguably, AI is not the first instance in which the law is confronted with new and emerging technology, and one could argue that our understanding of fault, as it currently exists in our common and civil law systems, might be entirely sufficient to address these issues. Our systems have held persons extra-contractually liable for things in their custody or under their control for a long time.[260] For example, people had been held liable for their horses, before cars were invented, and the same legal principles were generally applied to motor vehicles subsequently.[261] Even within the realm of AI, the law has already found ways to address this new technology. Strict liability regimes, such as product liability, the liability for parents or the liability for owners of animals, have been brought forward to address AI. Similarly, the doctrine of negligence has been seen to be adequate to establish liability for currently available AI and its applications.[262]

One might now rightfully ask the simple question of how the law reaches its limits in the case of AI, when it has thus far been successfully applied? The answer to this question lies in the fact that AI is an emerging technology. AI evolves rapidly; law does not. This is particularly true for public international law which is generally created through lengthy treaty negotiations. Nevertheless, these technologies, however new they seem to be, will be measured against existing legal norms and regulations.[263] As this research will elaborate in Chap. 2, fault in public international law

---

[258] Hameed (2018); Petrovici and Carlo (2018); Smuclerova (2018).

[259] This research rests upon the understanding that fault consists of two sides, objective fault and subjective fault. Cf Barboza (2011), p. 23.

[260] See e.g. Gray (2021), chs 1–2.

[261] Cf Easterbrook (1996) who argues that the best way to study law applicable to specialize regimes is to study general rules of law as they contain the rules needed.

[262] Hervey and Lavy (2021), pp. 193–194.

[263] Ibid, p. 117.

requires either intent or negligence which is a general principle of law recognised by nations.

At this part of the book it will suffice to say that for a plaintiff to establish the subjective fault of the defendant, they must provide, *inter alia*, evidence of negligence to the court.[264] Negligence is based on a breach of duty of care imposed on the community.[265] To evaluate whether a breach of duty occurred, the court employs the reasonable person test. In this regard the court tries to ascertain whether the damage was objectively foreseeable for a reasonable third person under the same circumstances and how that person would have acted.[266] The reasonable person test thus evolves mainly around two elements, namely foreseeability and reasonableness. Evidently, this requires a certain standard of behaviour against which the negligent conduct is measured. This standard of behaviour has developed over time around human behaviour. Unfortunately, an "AI standard" has not been developed yet. In the absence of such an "AI standard", the question we need to ask is whether the human standard of behaviour can be applied to the AI. This will entirely depend on the AI involved.

The wide range of different AI applications, mentioned earlier in this section, serves as a good starting point to illustrate this. A Roomba, whose sole purpose is to follow and execute a cleaning programme, is based on a rather "simple" algorithm and a human (e.g., the owner) can at any time switch off the vacuum cleaner. Should the Roomba cause damage to a third party the question will not be how advanced the AI inside the Roomba was but rather whether the owner of the Roomba had breached a duty of care. The notion of reasonableness and foreseeability will hardly be challenged.[267]

The situation changes, the more advanced the AI becomes. Development in AI is progressing towards fully autonomous machines, which are programmed to learn on their own (machine learning) by utilising a deep neural network. This can create problems in the realm of foreseeability due to, *inter alia*, the following reasons:

(1) As explained earlier, DNNs consist of many hidden layers and are based on the human brain. But because the layers are hidden, only the output (i.e., the result, the action taken by the AI) is known. What happens in between is hidden and cannot be seen, not even ex-post facto. In this regard the AI is opaque.
(2) The AI learns and adapts to tremendous amounts of data and reaches dynamic solutions based on patterns in the data stream that humans are not able to perceive.[268]

---

[264] Crepeau (1962); Dunlop (1962).

[265] Dunlop (1962), p. 241.

[266] Buckley (2011), p. 51.

[267] At least when we focus on the liability aspects of physical damage caused by a Roomba. It needs to be pointed out that even a simple Roomba is not actually quite that simple but there are many other issues that can have a legal impact, such as privacy issues relating to the data collected by the Roomba or location data etc.

[268] Bathaee (2018a), p. 892.

This makes it "practically—not theoretically—impossible to retroactively connect a specific input to a specific output and vice-versa"[269] and causes the undesired outcome that neither the actions of nor the harm caused by the AI are objectively foreseeable anymore. Without this foreseeability, negligence cannot be successfully established.

This problem comes even more to the forefront when we consider the development towards fully autonomous machines. A fully autonomous AI will act without human supervision, oversight or, as is the case in deep-space exploration, the ability of humans to intervene.

This author admits that, at the present, we have not reached this level of technological advancement, at least not yet. Experts in the realm of AI may well remind us that even advanced AI utilising deep learning techniques, such as a DNN, are still far from being independent of human input and are constantly nudged and supervised by humans.[270] Machines that we colloquially call autonomous, such as a Tesla car equipped with an auto-pilot function, may act to a certain degree autonomously but the driver monitors the car and can ultimately intervene at any moment. Should an accident occur, the liability will likely be anchored in the human conduct.[271] Nevertheless, technological development towards full autonomy is rapidly progressing and it is prudent to address these issues *ex-ante* rather than *ex-post*. It is submitted that the further autonomy develops the more human input is likely to decrease and the "more remote that the actual decision-making procedure becomes from the original designer, the clearer it will be that the entity is making choices".[272] Especially in outer space, where the ability of a human to intervene rapidly decreases the further the space object travels from Earth.[273]

If a human is unable to intervene, what can be the reasonable behaviour expected of them? Herein lies the challenge and this might arguably be seen as one reason why we have not established a standard of behaviour for AI. This is not to say that there have not been suggestions in this regard. Some sources advocate for a "robot common sense" standard against which a court can measure the actions of an AI.[274] This might be in principle a good suggestion, but it fails to take the rapid technological development into account. As this author pointed out above, AI is an emerging field, which is constantly changing and developing. Even if we were able to establish a "robot common sense" in time, which, in this author's view, is doubtful, the

[269] Wischmeyer (2020), p. 81.

[270] Turner (2019), p. 21.

[271] For example, let us assume that a Tesla is driving on a highway with the autopilot function enabled. The driver keeps both hands on the steering wheel but at the same time watches a movie on his phone. Due to this distraction the driver is not able to intervene on time and the Tesla hits a car in slow going traffic. In this case, the court will look towards the actions of the driver, who obviously acted differently than a reasonable objective third person, who would have not watched a movie but rather monitored the car and traffic.

[272] Turner (2019), p. 21.

[273] For example, it can take up to 13 minutes for a command signal on Earth to reach the Mars Rover.

[274] Giuffrida (2019), pp. 449–450.

standard would soon be outdated, and we would be faced with the same question as we are at present (*supra*, note 123).

The foregoing paragraphs serve to illustrate that our current understanding of negligence in AI has come to its limits and once highly advanced autonomous AI emerges, the legal doctrine of fault will be challenged.[275]

However, as we have discussed earlier, fault may play part in the question of assigning liability for damages caused by space objects as the Liability Convention establishes a two-tiered liability regime, in which liability is absolute for surface damage and damage to an aircraft in flight but fault-based for damage in outer space.

Unfortunately, the Liability Convention does not define the term fault and is not entirely instructive as to how fault can be established. Article VI allows for exoneration of the launching State if "damage has resulted either wholly or partially from gross negligence or from an act or omission done with intent to cause damage on the part of a claimant State or of natural or juridical persons it represents".[276] This could be seen as indication that the States Parties saw intent and negligence as possible elements to establish fault in international law. An examination of the other space treaties in this regard is not particularly helpful as they do not mention fault.

In the absence of any other provisions in space law that would deal with the notion of fault, a look towards other norms in international law might be instructive. For example, the International Convention on Civil Liability for Oil Pollution Damage, in a similar fashion to the Liability Convention, allows for exoneration of the owner in case of gross negligence or intent of the claimant.[277] Intent and negligence are further mentioned, *inter alia,* in the International Convention on Liability and Compensation for Damage in Connection with the Carriage of Hazardous and Noxious Substances by Sea,[278] the 1999 Basel Protocol on Liability and Compensation for Damage Resulting from Transboundary Movements of Hazardous Wastes and their Disposal,[279] the 1929 Convention for the Unification of certain

[275] As this book discusses in Sects. 1.3 and 2.2.2 highly advanced autonomous AI utilising a DNN will create a black box. The outcome can only be examined ex-post. What led to the outcome and how the AI arrived at that specific result will be impossible to ascertain. A software engineer will be able to point out where the deviation in the code happened, but they will not be able to determine why and how it happened. The code sequence will not make sense to anybody but the AI and we cannot reconstruct the process, find a solution or solve it mathematically.

[276] Art. VI, Liability Convention.

[277] Art. III, International Convention on Civil Liability for Oil Pollution Damage, 29 November 1969, 973 UNTS 3.

[278] International Convention on Liability and Compensation for Damage in Connection with the Carriage of Hazardous and Noxious Substances by Sea, 3 May 1996.

[279] Basel Protocol on Liability and Compensation for Damage Resulting from Transboundary Movements of Hazardous Wastes and their Disposal, 10 December 1999, UNTS.

Rules relating to International Carriage by Air[280] and the 1999 Convention for the Unification of Certain Rules for International Carriage by Air.[281]

Some international judgements and proceedings also deal with the notion of fault and refer to intent and negligence, which will be discussed further below.[282]

Arguably this could be seen as indication that there is some loose understanding in international law that fault can be established via intent or negligence. However, the foregoing should not be understood to mean that there is a definitive international consensus, or a rule of customary law, which would define fault in international law and the elements giving rise to it. Indeed, since reference to intent and negligence is usually made in quite a "self-explanatory" fashion, that is that international agreements and decisions do not define, or further describe, negligence and intent but rather pre-suppose a certain understanding of these terms and treat them as a "matter of fact", this author submits that this should be seen as an indirect reference to the general principles of law recognised by nations.[283]

Regardless of the view taken, it leads us directly back to the same problem namely that our understanding of subjective fault could be challenged by highly advanced AI.

Within the legal framework of space law, this could lead to the undesirable consequence that a claimant State may not be able to prove the fault of the launching State anymore. Even if there was a way to somehow prove fault of the launching State, it would be so difficult that a launching State would be, in practice, shielded from such claims, which would in turn defeat the primary purpose of the Liability Convention, namely, to ensure quick access to compensation for harm suffered.

The author therefore submits the following:

(1) Increasingly advanced AI will challenge our current understanding of fault as the action of and harm caused by AI are not foreseeable anymore and there is no standard of behaviour, apart from the human standard of behaviour, against which the actions of an AI can be measured.
(2) Neither the Liability Convention or the other four UN space treaties nor, at a preliminary view, general international law contains a definition for fault.
(3) These circumstances make it difficult, if not impossible, to bring forward liability claims against the launching State under international space law.

---

280 Convention for the Unification of certain Rules relating to International Carriage by Air, 12 October 1929, 137 UNTS 11.

281 Convention for the Unification of Certain Rules for International Carriage by Air, 28 May 1999, 2242 UNTS 309.

282 See e.g. Case Concerning Application of the Convention on the Prevention and Punishment of the Crime of Genocide (Bosnia and Herzegovina v Serbia and Montenegro), [2007], ICJ Rep 40 [Genocide Case]; Prosecutor v Duško Tadić, IT-94-1-A, Judgement (15 July 1999) at 51ff (International Criminal Tribunal for the former Yugoslavia, Appeals Chamber)[Prosecutor v Tadić]; Prosecutor v Ratko Mladić, IT-09-92-T, Judgement (22 November 2017) (International Criminal Tribunal for the former Yugoslavia).

283 Statute of the International Court of Justice, 18th April 1946, 33 UNTS 993, UKTS 67 (1946), art 38(c).

(4) This would also bring the Outer Space Treaty and the Liability Convention to its limits and could fundamentally change the circumstances under which they were concluded.

Therefore, this book will discuss the following sub-questions throughout the subsequent chapters:

- **How can a possible fault standard under international law be reconciled with the emerging nature of AI?**
- **Should such a fault standard be challenged, how can States be held responsible and liable for their space activities?**
- **Could the norms of State responsibility under general international law be the appropriate avenue to seek recourse for harm caused by AI-enabled space activities?**

These sub-questions will be framed, and give answer to the overall research question of **how can States be held responsible under international law for AI-enabled space activities?**

The reader of the present research may well point out that a scientific discourse in this area is premature, and humanity has still a long way to go before we reach a level of autonomy where we can take the human entirely out of the equation and the AI will be the sole decision-maker. Perhaps our time might be better spent discussing more pressing problems the international and space legal regime is facing at the moment, or at the very least limit our legal research only to AI that is currently available (i.e., narrow AI) rather than take a level of technology into account that might possibly not arrive for a long time. This author respectfully disagrees with the view and finds it overly dismissive. First, this view is an underestimation how much AI has penetrated our day-to-day lives already, even though this technology is arguably still nascent.[284] Venture capital investment has increased more than six times to US$ 266 billion over a period of just five years from 2014 to 2019 and the aerospace artificial intelligence market is estimated to increase from US$ 373 million to US$ 5.8 billion by 2028.[285]

Second, this view seems to rely on the belief that humanity will always be able to address quickly and adequately legal issues raised by AI. Humans tend to not realise small changes and then scramble backwards to put adequate legislation in place. Lawmaking has been, and continues to be, mostly reactive rather than proactive. Why should the regulation of AI be any different? As Jacob Turner pointed out in his book: if we had known the dangers of global warming at the dawn of the Industrial Revolution, we might perhaps have come up with a different system altogether and put measures in place to study climate change and legislate

---

[284] Turner (2019), p. 34. Turner shares the same view.

[285] Aerospace Artificial Intelligence Market Size, Growth, Research - 2028. https://www.alliedmarketresearch.com/aerospace-artificial-intelligence-market-A11337. Accessed 14 July 2024; Taylor D (2020) The Impact of Artificial Intelligence on Space Investment. https://www.geospatialworld.net/prime/the-impact-of-artificial-intelligence-on-space-investment/. Accessed 14 July 2024.

accordingly.[286] But technology is developing at a rapid pace and "[a]s fast as innovation has multiplied and spread in recent years, it is poised to change and grow at an exponential speed beyond the power of human intuition to anticipate".[287] Therefore, an *ex-ante* rather than an *ex-post facto* approach is advisable in this area of the law and any academic work should be future oriented rather than looking at it backwards. However, to reconcile the argument to take only currently available AI into account with the viewpoint of dedicating research to future AI, this book will address both throughout the research. Indeed, it will attempt to show that there is viable way within the *lex lata* of public international law to address both currently available narrow AI and future highly advanced AI. In this author's view, we can only adequately understand responsibility and liability rules for AI when we assess them in light of the existing legal framework. To paraphrase Frank Easterbrook, only by putting the law of AI in the context of broader rules about international responsibility of States for their space activities, can one really understand the law about AI.[288]

Websites and Online Sources

Aerospace Artificial Intelligence Market Size, Growth, Research - 2028. https://www.alliedmarketresearch.com/aerospace-artificial-intelligence-market-A11337. Accessed 11 July 2025.

Aerospace Artificial Intelligence Market Size, Growth, Research - 2028. https://www.alliedmarketresearch.com/aerospace-artificial-intelligence-market-A11337. Accessed 14 July 2024.

AI Virtual Assistants Revolutionizing Industries | Market Set for 16.5% CAGR Growth - Valuates Reports. https://www.prnewswire.com/news-releases/ai-virtual-assistants-revolutionizing-industries%2D%2Dmarket-set-for-16-5-cagr-growth%2D%2D-valuates-reports-302403357.html. Accessed 10 July 2025.

Anqi F (2024) Putin signs into law joint building of lunar base with China as Beijing expands circle of friends in Moon exploration - Global Times. www.globaltimes.cn/page/202406/1314079.shtml. Accessed 7 July 2025.

Artemis - NASA. https://www.nasa.gov/feature/artemis/. Accessed 11 July 2025.

Artemis Accords - NASA. https://www.nasa.gov/artemis-accords/. Accessed 14 July 2025.

Artificial Intelligence (AI) Challenges and Opportunities in National Security. onlinewilder.vcu.edu/blog/ai-challenges-and-opportunities-national-security/. Accessed 14 July 2025.

[286] Turner (2019), p. 35.

[287] Dobbs et al. (2015), p. 6. For an excellent discussion on how technology disrupts see Chap. 2.

[288] Easterbrook (1996), p. 208.

Artificial Intelligence and your space business: A guide for the smart navigation of the challenges ahead. https://www.hoganlovells.com/~/media/hogan-lovells/pdf/2018/ai_article_space_02_01_2018.pdf?la=en. Accessed 11 July 2025.
Artificial Intelligence in Medicine | IBM. https://www.ibm.com/topics/artificial-intelligence-medicine. Accessed 11 July 2025.
Artificial Intelligence in Space - Our Planet. https://ourplnt.com/artificial-intelligence-space/. Accessed 11 July 2025.
Artificial intelligence in space. https://www.esa.int/Enabling_Support/Preparing_for_the_Future/Discovery_and_Preparation/Artificial_intelligence_in_space. Accessed 11 July 2025.
Artificial Intelligence. https://dictionary.cambridge.org/dictionary/english/artificial-intelligence. Accessed 11 July 2025.
Artificial Intelligence. https://www.merriam-webster.com/dictionary/artificial%20intelligence. Accessed 11 July 2025.
Artificial Intelligence. https://www.oxfordlearnersdictionaries.com/definition/english/artificial-intelligence?q=artificial+intelligence. Accessed 11 July 2026.
Artificial Intelligence. In: International Organization for Standardization. https://www.iso.org/obp/ui/#iso:std:iso-iec:2382:ed-1:v1:en. Accessed 11 July 2025.
Autonomy. https://dictionary.cambridge.org/dictionary/english/autonomy. Accessed 11 July 2025.
Autonomy. https://www.merriam-webster.com/dictionary/autonomy. Accessed 11 July 2025.
Autonomy. https://www.oed.com/dictionary/autonomy_n. Accessed 11 July 2025.
Baker W (2021) Using AI for Smart Homes. https://canterbury.ai/using-ai-for-smart-homes/. Accessed 11 July 2025.
Banerjee P (2022) AI-based advanced analytics is making credit, debit cards smarter. https://www.livemint.com/technology/aibased-advanced-analytics-is-making-credit-debit-cards-smarter-11649003838074.html. Accessed 11 July 2025.
Berquand A, Bandivadekar D (2021) Five ways artificial intelligence can help space exploration. In: The Conversation. http://theconversation.com/five-ways-artificial-intelligence-can-help-space-exploration-153664. Accessed 11 July 2025.
Brown S (2021) Machine learning, explained. https://mitsloan.mit.edu/ideas-made-to-matter/machine-learning-explained. Accessed 11 July 2025.
Celebrating 35 years of aeronautical satellite communications. https://www.inmarsat.com/en/news/latest-news/aviation/2020/celebrating-35-years-of-aeronautical-satellite-communications.html. Accessed 11 July 2025.
Who we are. https://www.inmarsat.com/en/about/who-we-are.html. Accessed 11 July 2025.
Commercial Resupply - NASA. https://www.nasa.gov/international-space-station/commercial-resupply/. Accessed 14 July 2025.
Current Space Act Agreements - NASA. https://www.nasa.gov/partnerships/current-space-act-agreements/. Accessed 11 July 2025.
Davis AC, Lopes M (2019) How the FAA allows jetmakers to 'self certify' that planes meet U.S. safety requirements. www.washingtonpost.com/investigations/

how-the-faa-allows-jetmakers-to-self-certify-that-planes-meet-us-safety-requirements/2019/03/15/96d24d4a-46e6-11e9-90f0-0ccfeec87a61_story.html. Accessed 7 July 2025.
Denisova K (2025) Ukrainian front line 'would collapse' if Starlink is turned off, Musk claims. https://kyivindependent.com/ukrainian-front-line-would-collapse-if-starlink-is-turned-off-musk-claims/. Accessed 11 July 2025.
Deregulation imperative for space sector growth: ISRO chairman Somanath. https://www.business-standard.com/industry/news/deregulation-imperative-for-space-sector-growth-isro-chairman-somanath-123112500564_1.html. Accessed 7 July 2025.
Dinner J (2025) SpaceX rocket launches private moon lander and NASA 'trailblazer' to hunt for lunar water (video). https://www.space.com/space-exploration/launches-spacecraft/spacex-rocket-launches-private-moon-lander-and-nasa-trailblazer-to-hunt-for-lunar-water. Accessed 11 July 2025.
Eliaçik E (2023) Best Usages Of Artificial Intelligence In Everyday Life (2022) - Dataconomy. https://dataconomy.com/2022/05/09/artificial-intelligence-in-everyday-life/. Accessed 11 July 2025.
ESA (2020) ESA purchases world-first debris removal mission from start-up. https://www.esa.int/Newsroom/Press_Releases/ESA_purchases_world-first_debris_removal_mission_from_start-up. Accessed 16 July 2025.
ESA Φ-lab. https://philab.phi.esa.int. Accessed 11 July 2025.
Schmelzer R How Is AI Helping To Commercialize Space? https://www.forbes.com/sites/cognitiveworld/2020/03/21/how-is-ai-helping-to-commercialize-space/. Accessed 11 July 2025.
ESPI (2017) The Rise of Private Actors in the Space Sector. https://www.espi.or.at/wp-content/uploads/2022/06/ESPI-report-The-rise-of-private-actors-Executive-Summary-1.pdf. Accessed 16 July 2025.
EU The Framework Convention on Artificial Intelligence - Artificial Intelligence. https://www.coe.int/en/web/artificial-intelligence/the-framework-convention-on-artificial-intelligence. Accessed 16 July 2025.
European Space Agency (2025) This is ESA. https://esamultimedia.esa.int/docs/corporate/This_is_ESA_EN_LR.pdf. Accessed 16 July 2025.
Fowler G Council Post: AI's Role In Space Exploration. https://www.forbes.com/sites/forbesbusinessdevelopmentcouncil/2020/07/20/ais-role-in-space-exploration/. Accessed 11 July 2025.
Frowein JA (2007) Ius Cogens. Max Planck Encyclopedia of International Law.
Global AI in Space Market Outlook and Growth Forecast Report. https://www.bccresearch.com/market-research/information-technology/ai-in-space-market.html. Accessed 8 July 2025.
Goessler A (2022) The Private Sector's Assessment of U.S. Space Policy and Law. https://aerospace.csis.org/the-private-sectors-assessment-of-u-s-space-policy-and-law/. Accessed 7 July 2025.
Good A et al. (2021) You Can Help Train NASA's Rovers to Better Explore Mars. In: NASA. http://www.nasa.gov/feature/jpl/you-can-help-train-nasa-s-rovers-to-better-explore-mars. Accessed 11 July 2025.

Gray C (2022) Three ways AI is being used to help with space exploration. https://aimagazine.com/technology/three-ways-ai-is-being-used-to-help-with-space-exploration. Accessed 11 July 2025.

Gupta S (2023) 7 Incredible Ways AI Is Being Used in Space Exploration. https://www.springboard.com/blog/data-science/ai-space-exploration/. Accessed 11 July 2025.

Harris M (2021) Impact Of Artificial Intelligence And Machine Learning on Trading And Investing.https://towardsdatascience.com/impact-of-artificial-intelligence-and-machine-learning-on-trading-and-investing-7175ef2ad64e. Accessed 11 July 2025.

High-Level Expert Group on Artificial Intelligence (2019) A Definition of Artificial Intelligence: Main Capabilities and Scientific disciplines. https://digital-strategy.ec.europa.eu/en/library/definition-artificial-intelligence-main-capabilities-and-scientific-disciplines. Accessed 11 July 2025.

Hilton B (2022) Whole brain emulation. In: 80,000 Hours. https://80000hours.org/problem-profiles/whole-brain-emulation/. Accessed 11 July 2025.

How AI Email Assistants Can Drive Customer Service Excellence - Canary Mail Blog. https://canarymail.io/blog/ai-email-assistants-for-customer-service. Accessed 11 July 2025.

https://www.europarl.europa.eu/doceo/document/TA-8-2017-0051_EN.html. Accessed 11 July 2025.

Hughes A (2023) ChatGPT: Everything you need to know about OpenAI's GPT-4 tool. https://www.sciencefocus.com/future-technology/gpt-3/. Accessed 11 July 2025.

IBM (2022) IBM CIMON AI in space. https://web.archive.org/web/20230929105115/www.ibm.com/thought-leadership/innovation-explanations/cimon-ai-in-space. Accessed 11 July 2025.

IBM Cloud Education (2020) What is Machine Learning? https://www.ibm.com/cloud/learn/machine-learning. Accessed 11 July 2025.

ICRC (2022) What you need to know about autonomous weapons | ICRC. https://www.icrc.org/en/document/what-you-need-know-about-autonomous-weapons. Accessed 11 July 2025.

Intersputnik, Home page. In: Intersputnik. https://intersputnik.int/. Accessed 11 July 2025.

Isidore C (2025) Elon Musk says upgrade of FAA's air traffic control system is failing and SpaceX needs to take over Verizon's contract | CNN Business. https://www.cnn.com/2025/02/27/business/elon-musk-faa-air-traffic-control-failing-spacex. Accessed 11 July 2025.

Katherine Schauer (2020) Space Communication: 7 Things you need to know. https://www.nasa.gov/missions/tech-demonstration/space-communications-7-things-you-need-to-know/#:~:text=NASA%20/%20JPL%2DCaltech-,6.,interference%20for%20space%20communications%20transmissions. Accessed 11 July 2025.

Khan Mata (2016) Hal 9000s interview. In: https://www.youtube.com/watch?v=BDha7nj4s10. Accessed 11 July 2025.

Lian R Community AI - AI on SpaceX. https://www.thecommunityai.org/ai-blog/ai-on-spacex. Accessed 11 July 2025.

Ludwig M (2017) How Your Brain Cells Talk to Each Other—Whispered Secrets and Public Announcements. https://kids.frontiersin.org/articles/10.3389/frym.2017.00039. Accessed 11 July.

Maguire P (2024) AI at the crossroads of cybersecurity, space and national security in the digital age. In: SpaceNews. https://spacenews.com/ai-crossroads-cybersecurity-space-national-security-digital-age/. Accessed 9 August 2024.

Maguire P (2024) AI at the crossroads of cybersecurity, space and national security in the digital age. https://spacenews.com/ai-crossroads-cybersecurity-space-national-security-digital-age/. Accessed 14 July 2025.

Marr B (2019) The 10 Best Examples Of How AI Is Already Used In Our Everyday Life. https://www.forbes.com/sites/bernardmarr/2019/12/16/the-10-best-examples-of-how-ai-is-already-used-in-our-everyday-life/. Accessed 11 July 2025.

Marson J, Grove T (2024) Russia Using Thousands of Musk's Starlink Systems in War, Ukrainian General Says. www.wsj.com/world/russia-using-thousands-of-musks-starlink-systems-in-war-ukrainian-general-says-29303242. Accessed 9 July 2024.

Marwala T (2024) Militarization of AI Has Severe Implications for Global Security and Warfare. https://unu.edu/article/militarization-ai-has-severe-implications-global-security-and-warfare. Accessed 14 July 2025.

McCarthy J What is AI?/ Basic Questions. In: What is AI?/ Basic Questions. http://jmc.stanford.edu/artificial-intelligence/what-is-ai/index.html. Accessed 11 July 2025.

Netherlands e-V nl The HCCH | Declaration/reservation/notification. https://www.hcch.net/en/instruments/conventions/status-table/notifications/?csid=341&disp=resdn. Accessed 11 July 2025.

Newman T (2017) All you need to know about neurons. https://www.medicalnewstoday.com/articles/320289. Accessed 11 July 2025.

Nomos. www.britannica.com/topic/nomos-Greek-philosophy. Accessed 11 July 2025.

Autos. www.perseus.tufts.edu/hopper/text?doc=Perseus:text:1999.04.0057:entry=au)to/s. Accessed 11 July 2025.

Olufemi E (2007) Persistent Objector. Max Planck Encyclopedia of International Law. https://opil.ouplaw.com/display/10.1093/law:epil/9780199231690/law-9780199231690-e1455. Accessed 11 July 2025.

Online Index of Objects Launched into Outer Space. www.unoosa.org/oosa/osoindex/search-ng.jspx?lf_id=. Accessed 7 July 2025.

Our Story | Intelsat. https://www.intelsat.com/about-us/our-story/. Accessed 11 July 2025.

Peterson D, Hoffman S Geopolitical implications of AI and digital surveillance adoption. www.brookings.edu/articles/geopolitical-implications-of-ai-and-digital-surveillance-adoption/. Accessed 11 July 2025.

Powers J (2024) AI Trading: How AI Is Used in Stock Trading. https://builtin.com/artificial-intelligence/ai-trading-stock-market-tech. Accessed 15 July 2025.

Robotics: What Are Robots? Robotics Definition & Uses. | Built In. https://builtin.com/robotics. Accessed 11 July 2025.

Russek H et al. Automation, AI and Outer Space: Tech and the Future of Work in Canada. https://brookfieldinstitute.ca/new-technologies-future-of-work-in-canada-covid19. Accessed 11 July 2025.

Russian cyber operations against Ukraine: Declaration by the High Representative on behalf of the European Union.https://www.consilium.europa.eu/en/press/press-releases/2022/05/10/russian-cyber-operations-against-ukraine-declaration-by-the-high-representative-on-behalf-of-the-european-union/. Accessed 14 July 2025.

Saarela O (2022) A Promising Future for AI and Autonomy in Space. https://www.electronicdesign.com/technologies/embedded/article/21212499/mathworks-a-promising-future-for-ai-and-autonomy-in-space Accessed 11 July 2025.

See UNESCO Ethics of Artificial Intelligence. https://www.unesco.org/en/artificial-intelligence/recommendation-ethics. Accessed 11 July 2025.

OECD AI AI Principles Overview. oecd.ai/en/principles. Accessed 11 July 2025.

Shekhtman L (2019) NASA Applying AI Technologies to Problems in Space Science. NASA. http://www.nasa.gov/feature/goddard/2019/nasa-takes-a-cue-from-silicon-valley-to-hatch-artificial-intelligence-technologies. Accessed 11 July 2025.

Stanley Kubrick, "2001: a Space Odyssey", DVD (Burbank, Cal: Warner Brothers, 2001).

Stumpe M, Peng L (2017) Assisting Pathologists in Detecting Cancer with Deep Learning. http://ai.googleblog.com/2017/03/assisting-pathologists-in-detecting.html. Accessed 11 July 2025.

Taylor D (2020) The Impact of Artificial Intelligence on Space Investment. https://www.geospatialworld.net/prime/the-impact-of-artificial-intelligence-on-space-investment/. Accessed 11 July 2025.

Taylor D (2020) The Impact of Artificial Intelligence on Space Investment. https://www.geospatialworld.net/prime/the-impact-of-artificial-intelligence-on-space-investment/. Accessed 14 July 2024.

U.S. National Space Policy (2006). https://obamawhitehouse.archives.gov/sites/default/files/microsites/ostp/national-space-policy-2006.pdf. Accessed 14 July 2025.

Wedenig S-M (2023) Artificial Intelligence in Outer Space: The Responsibility of the State of the Software Developer. In: Institute of Air & Space Law. https://www.mcgill.ca/iasl/article/artificial-intelligence-outer-space-responsibility-state-software-developer. Accessed 11 July 2025/

Wedenig S-M, Nelson Wright J (2023) The Moon Agreement: Hanging by a Thread? In: Institute of Air & Space Law. https://www.mcgill.ca/iasl/article/moon-agreement-hanging-thread. Accessed 14 July 2025.

Welser WI (2016) The Democratization of Space. In: The Democratization of Space: New Actors Need New Rules. https://www.rand.org/pubs/commentary/2016/03/the-democratization-of-space.html. Accessed 16 July 2025.
What is robotics? In: WhatIs.com. https://www.techtarget.com/whatis/definition/robotics. Acccsscd 11 July 2025.
Woodruff A What is a neuron? https://qbi.uq.edu.au/brain/brain-anatomy/what-neuron. Accessed 11 July 2025.
Wright Nelson J (2018) Lost in Space? Gaps in the International Space Object Registration Regime. www.ejiltalk.org/lost-in-space-gaps-in-the-international-space-object-registration-regime/. Accessed14 July 2025.

UN Documents

LSC, Report of the Legal Sub-Committee on the Work of its Second Session (16 April – 3 May 1963) to the Committee on the Peaceful Uses of Outer Space, UNCOPUOS, 1963, UN Doc A/AC.105/12.
Report of the Committee on the Peaceful Uses of Outer Space, UNCOPUOS, 18th Sess, Annex III, Agenda Item 28, UN Doc A/5549 Add.1, (1963).
Report of the Ad Hoc Committee on the Peaceful Uses of Outer Space, 1959, UN Doc A/4141.
UNCOPUOS, Union of Soviet Socialist Republics: Draft Declaration of the Basic Principles Governing the Activities of States Pertaining to the Exploration and Use of Outer Space, UN Doc A/AC.105/L.2 (1962).
United Nations Conference on the Law of Treaties, 54th Mtg, UN Doc A/CONF.39/11 (1968).
Resolution adopted by the General Assembly on 2 March 2022, UNGA, 11th Sess, UN Doc A/Res/ES-11/1 (2022), Res ES-11/1.

Judicature

Case Concerning Application of the Convention on the Prevention and Punishment of the Crime of Genocide (Bosnia and Herzegovina v Serbia and Montenegro), [2007], ICJ Rep 40.
Case concerning the Barcelona Traction, Light and Power Company, Limited (Belgium v Spain), [1970] ICJ Rep 3.
Mavrommatis Palestine Concessions (Greece v. U.K.) (1924), PCIJ (Ser A) No 3.
North Sea Continental Shelf Cases, [1969] ICJ Rep 3.
Prosecutor v Duško Tadić, IT-94-1-A, Judgement (15 July 1999)(International Criminal Tribunal for the former Yugoslavia, Appeals Chamber).
Prosecutor v Ratko Mladić, IT-09-92-T, Judgement (22 November 2017) (International Criminal Tribunal for the former Yugoslavia).

The Steamship Lotus (Fance v Turkey) (1927), PCIJ (Seri A) No 10 at 18.

Legislation and International Treaties

51 USC § 50902; 51 USC § 20103.
Act Prohibiting Importation of Slaves, Pub L No 9-22, 2 Stat 426 (1807).
Basel Protocol on Liability and Compensation for Damage Resulting from Transboundary Movements of Hazardous Wastes and their Disposal, 10 December 1999, UNTS.
Bundesgesetz über die Genehmigung von Weltraumaktivitäten und die Einrichtung eines Weltraumregisters (Weltraumgesetz) (Austria).
Convention for the Unification of Certain Rules for International Carriage by Air, 28 May 1999, 2242 UNTS 309.
Convention for the Unification of certain Rules relating to International Carriage by Air, 12 October 1929, 137 UNTS 11.
EU, Regulation (EU) 2024/1689 of the European Parliament and of the Council of 13 June 2024 laying down harmonised rules on artificial intelligence and amending Regulations (EC) No 300/2008, (EU) No 167/2013, (EU) No 168/2013, (EU) 2018/858, (EU) 2018/1139 and (EU) 2019/2144 and Directives 2014/90/EU, (EU) 2016/797 and (EU) 2020/1828, [2024] OJ, L 2024/1689.
International Convention on Liability and Compensation for Damage in Connection with the Carriage of Hazardous and Noxious Substances by Sea, 3 May 1996.
Slave Trade Act, 1807 (UK) 47 Geo III, c 36.
Law on the Activities of Launching, Flight Operation or Guidance of Space Objects (Belgium) [Belgian Space Law]; Outer Space Act 1986 (UK).
Radio Regulations Edition of 2024, WRC-23 (Dubai, 2023).
Slave Trade Act, 1788 (UK), 28 Geo III, c 54.
Space (Launches and Returns) Act (Australia), 123/1998.
Space Development Promotion Act (Republic of South Korea).
Statute of the International Court of Justice, 18th April 1946, 33 UNTS 993, UKTS 67 (1946).
Telecommunication Union, 22 December 1992, 1825, 1826 UNTS.
Vienna Convention on Succession of States in Respect of Treaties, 23 August 1978, 1946 UNTS 3.
Vienna Convention on the Law of Treaties, 23 May 1969, 1155 UNTS 331.

References

Literature

Abass A (2012) International law: text, cases, and materials. Oxford University Press, New York
Abbott R (2018) The reasonable computer: disrupting the paradigm of tort liability. Geo Wash Law Rev 86
Abbott R (2020) The reasonable robot: artificial intelligence and the law, 1st edn. Cambridge University Press, New York
Allain JS (2013) From Jeopardy! to Jaundice: the medical liability implications of Dr. Watson and other artificial intelligence systems. LA Law Rev 73:1049
Anzilotti D (1929) Cours de droit international. Imprimerie Cadoret, Bordeaux
Aust A (2010) Handbook of international law, 2nd edn. Cambridge University Press, Cambridge
Awford I (1995) Legal liability arising from commercial space activities in outer space. In: Mosteshar S (ed) Research and invention in outer space: liability and intellectual property rights. M. Nijhoff Publishers, Dordrecht, p 95
Baiocchi D, Welser WI (2015) The democratization of space: new actors need new rules. Foreign Aff 94:98
Barboza J (2011) The environment, risk and liability in international law. Martinus Nijhoff Publishers, Leiden
Barfoot T, Burgner-Kahrs J, Diller E et al (2020) Making sense of the robotized pandemic response: a comparison of global and Canadian robot deployments and success factors. https://doi.org/10.48550/ARXIV.2009.08577
Bathaee Y (2018a) The artificial intelligence black box and the failure of intent and causation. Harv J Law Tech 31:890
Bathaee Y (2018b) Artificial intelligence opinion liability. BTLJ 35:115
Bayern S (2015) The implications of modern business-entity law for the regulation of autonomous systems. Stan Tech Law Rev 19:93
Bertolini A (2013) Robots as products: the case for a realistic analysis of robotic applications and liability rules. Law Innov Technol 5:214–247. https://doi.org/10.5235/17579961.5.2.214
Blount PJ (2011) Renovating space: the future of international space law. Den J Int Law Policy 40:515
Bourély M (1991) Quelques réflexions au sujet des législations spatiales nationales. Ann Air Space Law 16:245
Bracht G, Martinez P (2021) International challenges to the safety, security and sustainability of outer space activities. In: Robinson GS, Benkö M, Schrogl K-U (eds) Outer space: future for humankind: issues of law and policy. Eleven, The Hague, p 105
Bratu I, Lodder A, van der Linden T (2021) Autonomous space objects and international space law: navigating the liability gap. IJIL 18. https://doi.org/10.17304/ijil.vol18.3.818
Brownlie I (2008) Principles of public international law, 7th edn. Oxford University Press, New York
Brownsword R (2008) The challenge of regulatory connection. In: Rights, regulation, and the technological revolution, 1st edn. Oxford University Press, Oxford
Buckley RA (2011) The law of negligence and nuisance, 5th edn. LexisNexis, London
Burrell J (2026) How the machine ‘thinks’: understanding opacity in machine learning algorithms. Big Data Soc 3. https://doi.org/10.1177/2053951715622512
Butcher J, Beridze I (2019) What is the state of artificial intelligence governance globally? RUSI 164:88. https://doi.org/10.1080/03071847.2019.1694260
Byrd LC (2022) Soft law in space: a legal framework for extraterrestrial mining. Emory Law J 71:801
Cai H, Lin J, Han S (2022) Efficient methods for deep learning. In: Davies ER, Turk MA (eds) Advanced methods and deep learning in computer vision. Elsevier

Calo R (2015) Robotics and the lessons of cyberlaw. Cal Law Rev 103:513
Cassese A (2001) International law. Oxford University Press, New York
Castelvecchi D (2016) Can we open the black box of AI? Nat News 538:20. https://doi.org/10.1038/538020a
Čerka P, Grigienė J, Sirbikytė G (2015) Liability for damages caused by artificial intelligence. Comput Law Secur Rev 31:376–389. https://doi.org/10.1016/j.clsr.2015.03.008
Chatzipanagiotis MP (2020) Whose fault is it? Artificial intelligence and liability in international space law. In: Blount PJ et al (eds) Proceedings of the International Institute of Space Law 2020. Eleven International Publishing, The Hague
Cheng B (1965) United Nations Resolutions on Outer Space: 'instant' international customary law? Indian J Int Law 5:23
Cheng B (1997a) Space objects and their various connecting factors. In: Lafferranderie G, Crowther D (eds) Outlook on space law over the next 30 years: essays published for the 30th Anniversary of the Outer Space Treaty. Kluwer Law International, The Hague
Cheng B (1997b) Studies in international space law. Oxford University Press, New York
Cofone I (2021) AI in judicial decision-making. SCLR 102:12
Cohen J (2016) The regulatory state in the information age. Theor Inq Law 12:369
Cohen S (2021) The evolution of machine learning: past, present, and future. In: Cohen S (ed) Artificial intelligence and deep learning in pathology. Elsevier, London
Cooper JC (1968) Explorations in aerospace law: selected essays. McGill University Press, Montreal
Crepeau PA (1962) Liability for damage caused by things: from the civil law point of view. Can Bar Rev XL:222
Das HS, Roy P (2019) A deep dive into deep learning techniques for solving spoken language identification problems. In: Dey N (ed) Intelligent speech signal processing. Elsevier, London
De Frouville O (2010) Attribution of conduct to the state: private individuals. In: Crawford J, Pellet A, Olleson S, Parlett K (eds) The law of international responsibility. Oxford University Press, New York.
De Zwaart M (2017) Google in Space? How will space governance accommodate non-state actors? In: Manoli M, Habchi SB (eds) Conflicts in space and the rule of law. Centre for Research in Air and Space Law, Montreal
Dempsey PS (2017) Public international air law, 2nd edn. Centre for Research of Air and Space Law, McGill University, Montreal
Dennett DC (1998) Brainchildren: essays on designing minds. MIT Press, Cambridge
Diederiks-Verschoor IHP, Kopal V (2008) An introduction to space law, 3rd edn. Kluwer Law International, Alphen aan den Rijn
Dobbs R, Manyika J, Woetzel JR (2015) No ordinary disruption: the four global forces breaking all the trends, 1st edn. PublicAffairs, New York
Dunlop B (1962) Liability for damage caused by things: from the common law point of view. Can Bar Rev XL:240
Dworkin RM (1967) The model of rules. Univ Chic Law Rev 35:14. https://doi.org/10.2307/1598947
Easterbrook FH (1996) Cyberspace and the law of the horse. University Chicago Legal Forum
Farsaiya I, Sharma A (2014) The term 'appropriate state' and state liability for private commercial space activities. In: Jakhu RS, Kaul S, Chen K-W (eds) Emerging trends in aviation and space applications: legal, safety and policy issues. Centre for Research in Air and Space Law, Montreal
Finch ERJ (1980) Outer space liability: past, present and future. Int Lawyer 14:123
Freeland S (2011) For better or for worse? The use of 'soft law' within the international legal regulation of outer space. Ann Air Space Law 36:409
Freeland S (2012) The role of 'soft law' in public international law and its relevance to the international legal regulation of outer space. In: Marboe I (ed) Soft law in outer space: the function of non-binding norms in international space law. Böhlau Verlag, Wien

Freeland S (2017) Newspace, small satellites, and law: finding a balance between innovation, a changing space paradigm, and regulatory control. In: Ahmad MT, Su J (eds) NewSpace commercialisation and the law. Centre for Research in Air and Space Law, Montreal
Freeland S, Jakhu RS (2017) Article II. In: Hobe S, Schmidt-Tedd B, Schrogl K-U (eds) Cologne commentary on space law: outer space treaty. Berliner Wissenschafts-Verlag, Berlin
Gal GA, Santos C, Rapp L, Markovich R (2020) Artificial Intelligence in Space. https://doi.org/10.48550/arXiv.2006.12362
Gillespie T (2014) The relevance of algorithms. In: Gillespie T, Boczkowski PJ, Foot KA (eds) Media technologies. The MIT Press, Cambridge
Giuffrida I (2019) Liability for AI decision-making: some legal and ethical considerations. Fordham Law Rev 88:439
Goodfellow I, Bengio Y, Courville A (2016) Deep learning. The MIT Press, Cambridge
Goodman B, Flaxman S (2017) European Union regulations on algorithmic decision-making and a "right to explanation". AI Mag 38:50–57. https://doi.org/10.1609/aimag.v38i3.2741
Goodrich J (2013) Driving miss daisy: an autonomous Chauffeur system. Hous Law Rev 51:265
Gould H (2011) Categorical obligation in international law. Int Theory 3:254–285. https://doi.org/10.1017/S1752971911000091
Gray A (2021) The evolution from strict liability to fault in the law of torts. Hart Publishing, Oxford
Hameed H (2018) The concept of launching state in democratized NewSpace. In: Blount PJ et al (eds) Proceedings of the International Institute of Space Law 2018. Eleven International Publishing, The Hague
Heiss S (2021) Towards optimal liability for artificial intelligence lessons from the European Union's Proposals of 2020. UC Law SF Sci Tech Law J 12
Hengstler M, Enkel E, Duelli S (2016) Applied artificial intelligence and trust—the case of autonomous vehicles and medical assistance devices. Technol Forecast Soc Change 105:105–120. https://doi.org/10.1016/j.techfore.2015.12.014
Henkin L (1995) International law: politics and values. Martinus Nijhoff, Dordrecht
Henri Y, Matas A, Macedo Scavuzzi dos Santos J (2017) Regulations of telecommunications by satellites: ITU and space service. In: Jakhu RS, Dempsey PS (eds) Routledge handbook of space law. Routledge, New York
Hermida J (2004) Legal basis for a national space legislation. Kluwer Academic, Dordrecht
Hervey M, Lavy M (eds) (2021) The law of artificial intelligence, 1st edn. Sweet & Maxwell, London
Hoffman SJ, Baral P, Rogers Van Katwyk S et al (2022) International treaties have mostly failed to produce their intended effects. Proc Natl Acad Sci U S A 119:e2122854119. https://doi.org/10.1073/pnas.2122854119
Hohman F, Kahng M, Pienta R, Chau DH (2018) Visual analytics in deep learning: an interrogative survey for the next frontiers. https://doi.org/10.48550/ARXIV.1801.06889
Hurwitz BA (1992) State liability for outer space activities: in accordance with the 1972 Convention on International Liability for Damage Caused by Space Objects. Martinus Nijhoff Publishers, Dordrecht
Hutchison T, Duncan N Defining and describing what we do: doctrinal legal research. Deakin Law Rev 17:83
Jakhu RS (2006) Legal issues relating to the global public interest in outer space. J Space Law 31
Jakhu RS (ed) (2010) National regulation of space activities. Springer, Netherlands, Dordrecht
Jakhu RS (2016) Regulatory process for communications satellite frequency allocations. In: Pelton JN, Madry S, Camacho-Lara S (eds) Handbook of satellite applications. Springer New York, New York
Jakhu RS, Freeland S (2016) The relationship between the outer space treaty and customary international law. In: Blount PJ et al (eds) Proceedings of the International Institute of Space Law 2016. Eleven International Publishing, The Hague
Jakhu RS, Pelton JN (eds) (2017) Global space governance: an international study. Springer International Publishing, Cham

Jakhu RS, Jasani B, McDowell JC (2018a) Critical issues related to registration of space objects and transparency of space activities. Acta Astronautica 143:406. https://doi.org/10.1016/j.actaastro.2017.11.042
Jakhu RS, Pelton JN, Nyampong YOM (2018b) Space mining and its regulation. Springer, Cham
Jakhu RS, Dasgupta U, Freeland S (2020) Back to the future: space law in a networked world. In: Blount PJ et al (eds) Proceedings of the International Institute of Space Law 2020. Eleven International Publishing, The Hague
Jakhu RS, Freeland S, Chen DK-W (2021) The sources of international space law: revisited. German J Air Space Law 67:606. https://doi.org/10.2139/ssrn.3806175
Jankowitsch P (1998) The role of the United Nations in outer space law development: past achievements and new challenges. J Space Law 26:101
Jankowitsch P (2015) The background and history of space law. In: von der Dunk FG, Tronchetti F (eds) Handbook of space law. Edward Elgar Publishing, Cheltenham, England
Kayser V (2001) Launching space objects: issues of liability and future prospects. Springer, Netherlands, Dordrecht
Kerrest A (1997) Launching spacecraft from the sea and the outer space treaty: the sea launch project. Proc Law Outer Space 40:264
Kerrest A, Thro C (2017) Liability for damage caused by space activities. In: Jakhu RS, Dempsey PS (eds) Routledge handbook of space law. Routledge, New York
Kindred HM, Sounders PM, Currie RJ (eds) (2014) International law: chiefly as interpreted and applied in Canada, 8th edn. Emond Montgomery Publ, Toronto
Koivurova T (2003) What is the principle of due diligence. In: Petman J, Klabbers J (eds) Nordic cosmopolitanism: essays in international law for Martti Koskenniemi. Martinus Nijhoff Publishers, Leiden
Koul N, Manvi SKS (2021) Computational intelligence techniques for cancer diagnosis. In: Bhattacharyya S, Dutta P, Samanta D et al (eds) Recent trends in computational intelligence enabled research. Elsevier, London
Lachs M (2010) The law of outer space: an experience in contemporary law-making. Martinus Nijhoff Publishers, Leiden
Laude E (1910) Questions Pratiques. R Juridique Intl Locomation Aérienne 1:16
Lee R (2012) Law and regulation of commercial mining of minerals in outer space. Springer, Netherlands, Dordrecht
Lee JD, See KA (2004) Trust in automation: designing for appropriate reliance. Human Factors: J Hum Factors Ergon Soc 46:50–80. https://doi.org/10.1518/hfes.46.1.50_30392
Lemley MA, Casey B (2019) Remedies for robots. Univ Chic Law Rev 86:1311
LeValley D (2013) Autonomous vehicle liability—application of common carrier liability. 36:23
Lohmann MF (2016) Liability issues concerning self-driving vehicles. Eur J Risk Regul 2:335
Long GA (2018) Artificial intelligence and state responsibility under the outer space treaty. In: Blount PJ et al (eds) Proceedings of the International Institute of Space Law 2018. Eleven International Publishing, The Hague
Lyall' F (2000) On the privatisation of INTELSAT. J Space Law 28:101
Maes P (1995) Artificial life meets entertainment: lifelike autonomous agents. Commun ACM 38:108–114. https://doi.org/10.1145/219717.219808
Malgieri G, Pasquale F (2022) From transparency to justification: toward ex ante accountability for AI. Brooklyn Law School Legal Studies Paper
Manoli M (2017) Commercial space as a source of conflicts and the need for 'space pluralism'. In: Manoli M, Habchi SB (eds) Conflicts in space and the rule of law. Centre for Research in Air and Space Law, Montreal
Marboe I (ed) (2012) Soft law in outer space: the function of non-binding norms in international space law. Böhlau Verlag, Wien
Marboe I (2015) National space law. In: von der Dunk FG, Tronchetti F (eds) Handbook of space law. Edward Elgar Publishing, Cheltenham

Martin A-S, Freeland S (2021) The advent of artificial intelligence in space activities: new legal challenges. Space Policy 55:101408. https://doi.org/10.1016/j.spacepol.2020.101408
Martinez P (2020) The role of soft law in promoting the sustainability and security of space activities. J Space Law 44:522
Masson-Zwaan TL, Hofmann M (2019) Introduction to space law, 4th edn. Wolters Kluwer, Alphen aan den Rijn
Matte NM (1969) Aerospace law. Carswell, Toronto
Matte NM (1984) Space activities and emerging international law. Centre for Research of Air and Space Law, Montreal
Matthias A (2004) The responsibility gap: ascribing responsibility for the actions of learning automata. Ethics Inf Technol 6:175. https://doi.org/10.1007/s10676-004-3422-1
Mazzeschi R (2004) The marginal role of the individual in the ILC's articles on state responsibility. Ital Yearb Int Law XIV:39–51
Mitchell BR (2021) Overview of advanced neural network architectures. In: Cohen S (ed) Artificial intelligence and deep learning in pathology. Elsevier, London
Momtaz D (2010) Attribution of conduct to the state: state organs and entities empowered to exercise elements of governmental authority. Oxford University Press, New York
Müller VC (ed) (2018) Philosophy and theory of artificial intelligence 2017. Springer International Publishing, Cham
Munakata T (2008) Fundamentals of the new artificial intelligence: neural, evolutionary, fuzzy and more, 2nd edn. Springer, London
Muse RL (1997) The nationality of claims principle of public international law and the Helms-Burton Act. Hastings Int Comp Law Rev 20
Palkovitz N (2020) Regulating a revolution: small satellites and the law of outer space. Wolters Kluwer, Alphen aan den Rijn
Parker K, Neylon LB Jus Cogens: compelling the law of human rights. Hastings Int Comp Law Rev 12:411
Pasquale F (2017) Toward a fourth law of robotics: preserving attribution, responsibility, and explainability in an algorithmic society. University of Maryland Francis King Carey School of Law Legal Studies Research Paper No 2017-21
Pasquale F (2019) Data-informed duties in AI development. Colum Law Rev 119:1917
Paul V (1971) The legal consequences of conflict between a treaty and an imperative norm of general international law (jus cogens). Aus J Pub Int Law 21:18
Pepin E (1956) The legal status of the airspace in the light of progress in aviation and astronautics. McGill Law J 3:70
Petrovici G, Carlo A (2018) Legal challenges of Space 4.0: the framework conditions of legal certainty among states, international organisations and private actors in the changing landscape of space activities. In: Blount PJ et al (eds) Proceedings of the International Institute of Space Law 2018. Eleven International Publishing, The Hague
Pfeifer R, Scheier C (2001) Understanding intelligence, 1st edn. MIT Press, Cambridge
Phillips-Wren G (2013) Intelligent decision support systems. In: Doumpos M, Grigoroudis E (eds) Multicriteria decision aid and artificial intelligence: links, theory and applications. Wiley-Blackwell, Hoboken, New Jersey
Powell D (2020) Autonomous systems as legal agents: directly by the recognition of personhood or indirectly by the alchemy of algorithmic entities. Duke Law Tech Rev 18:306
Qizhi H (1997) The outer space treaty in perspective. J Space Law 25:93
Rapp L (2015) Building bridges on global governance issues: cyperspace shaping outer space? In: Jakhu RS, Chen K-W, Nyampong Y (eds) Global space governance. Centre for Research in Air and Space Law, Montreal
Ribeiro MT, Singh S, Guestrin C (2016) 'Why Should I Trust You?': explaining the predictions of any classifier. https://doi.org/10.48550/ARXIV.1602.04938

Rieder G, Simon J (2017) Big data: a new empiricism and its epistemic and socio-political consequences. In: Pietsch W, Wernecke J, Ott M (eds) Berechenbarkeit der Welt? Springer Fachmedien Wiesbaden, Wiesbaden
Rumelhart DE, Hinton GE, Williams RJ (1986) Learning representations by back-propagating errors. Nature 323:533
Russell SJ, Norvig P, Davis E (2010) Artificial intelligence: a modern approach, 3rd edn. Prentice Hall, Upper Saddle River
Salmeri A (2021) Collective space object as a new concept of international law. Air Space Law 46:203
Samuel AL (1959) Some studies in machine learning using the game of checkers. IBM J Res Dev 3:210–229. https://doi.org/10.1147/rd.33.0210
Schrogl K-U, Davies C (2002) A new look at the "launching state": the results of the UNCOPUOS Legal Subcommittee Working Group "Review of the Concept of the 'Launching State' 2000-2002". Proc Law Outer Space 45:286
Semenyaka V (2019) The current state of deregulation of space activities in Ukraine. ASL 3. https://doi.org/10.29202/asl/2019/3/9
Shaw MN (2008) International law, 6th edn. Cambridge University Press, New York
Siciliano B, Khatib O (2016) Robotics and the handbook. In: Siciliano B, Khatib O (eds) Springer handbook of robotics, 2nd edn. Springer, New York
Sienknecht M, Vetterlein A (2023) Conceptualizing responsibility in world politics. Int Theory 1. https://doi.org/10.1017/S1752971923000039
Smuclerova M (2018) Legal perspectives for the further development of the five United Nations Treaties on Outer Space in Light of Rising Multistakeholderism. In: Blount PJ et al (eds) Proceedings of the International Institute of Space Law 2018. Eleven International Publishing, The Hague
Soroka L, Kurkova K (2019) Artificial intelligence and space technologies: legal, ethical and technological issues. ASL 3. https://doi.org/10.29202/asl/2019/3/11.
Steels L (2018) Building agents out of autonomous behaviour systems. In: Steels L, Brooks RA (eds) The artificial life route to artificial intelligence: building embodied, situated agents. Routledge, New York
Tomaszewski JE (2021) Overview of the role of artificial intelligence in pathology: the computer as a pathology digital assistant. In: Cohen S (ed) Artificial intelligence and deep learning in pathology. Elsevier, London
Turing AM (1950) Computing machinery and intelligence. Mind 59:433
Turner J (2019) Robot rules: regulating artificial intelligence, 1st edn. Springer International Publishing, Cham
United Nations (1967) Materials on the Succession of States. United Nations, New York
van Traa-Engelman HL (ed) (1984) Problems of state responsibility in international space law. 26:139
Verney J-M, Vinçotte T (2021) Human-on-the-loop. In: Read Ahead
Vilmer J-BJ (2013) Légalité et légitimité des drones armés. Politique étrangère 2013:119. https://doi.org/10.3917/pe.133.0119
Vladeck DC (2014) Machines without principals: liability rules and artificial intelligence. Wash Law Rev 89
Von der Dunk FG (1992) Liability versus responsibility in space law: misconception or misconstruction? Space, Cyber, and Telecommunications Law Faculty Publications
Von der Dunk FG (1994) Commercial space activities: an inventory of liability - an inventory of problems. Proc Law Outer Space 37:161
Von der Dunk FG (2011a) The origins of authorisation: Article VI of the outer space treaty and international space law. In: von der Dunk FG (ed) National Space Legislation in Europe: issues of authorisation of private space activities in the light of developments in European Space Cooperation. Martinus Nijhoff Publishers, Leiden

Von der Dunk FG (ed) (2011b) National space legislation in Europe: issues of authorisation of private space activities in the light of developments in European space cooperation. Martinus Nijhoff Publishers, Leiden
Von der Dunk FG (2015) International space law. In: von der Dunk FG, Tronchetti F (eds) Handbook of space law. Edward Elgar Publishing, Cheltenham
Wachter S, Mittelstadt B, Floridi L (2017) Why a right to explanation of automated decision-making does not exist in the general data protection regulation. Int Data Priv Law 7:76–99. https://doi.org/10.1093/idpl/ipx005
Wadden JJ (2021) Defining the undefinable: the black box problem in healthcare artificial intelligence. J Med Ethics medethics-2021-107529. https://doi.org/10.1136/medethics-2021-107529
Wagner G (2018) Robot Liability. Paper presented at the Münster Colloquium on EU Law and Digital Economy Liability for Robotics and the Internet of Things, University of Münster, Münster, 12 March 2018
Watson SJ (1992) State consent and the sources of international obligations. Proc Annu Meet (Am Soc Int Law) 86:108
Wischmeyer T (2020) Artificial intelligence and transparency: opening the black box. In: Wischmeyer T, Rademacher T (eds) Regulating artificial intelligence. Springer, Cham
Zednik C (2018) Will machine learning yield machine intelligence? In: Müller VC (ed) Philosophy and Theory of Artificial Intelligence 2017. Springer International Publishing, Cham
Zednik C (2021) Solving the black box problem: a normative framework for explainable artificial intelligence. Philos Technol 34:265–288. https://doi.org/10.1007/s13347-019-00382-7

Chapter 2
Non-Contractual Liability

2.1 Introduction

Public international law, space law and AI are three incredibly broad areas. It is therefore necessary, at the outset, to carve out the boundaries of the present research and narrow down the scope to clearly limit the approach. This chapter will therefore delve deeper into non-contractual liability, also called liability *ex-delicto*.

In simple terms, non-contractual liability is the liability of a party who infringes on the legal rights of, or breaches a legal duty owed to, another party in the absence of a contract between the two parties.[1]

Generally, a person is non-contractually liable if they commit a civil wrong. For example, if A walks down the street and B throws a stone at A, then B has committed a civil wrong to A and A might be able to seek compensation for the harm under private law.[2]

[1] It is important to note that the differentiation between liability ex-delicto and cx-contractu arises from domestic law and does not exist in this form in public international law. The ILC makes this clear in the Articles on Responsibility of States for Internationally Wrongful Acts when it states in Article 12 that, "[t]here is a breach of an international obligation by a State when an act of that State is not in conformity with what is required of it by that obligation, regardless of its origin or character." See also Aust (2010) ["International Law does not draw the distinction found in domestic law between contractual and tortious responsibility (...)']; Case concerning the difference between New Zealand and France concerning the interpretation or application of two agreements, concluded on 9 July 1986 between the two States and which related to the problems arising from the Rainbow Warrior Affair (1990), RIAA 215, p. 251 ["The reason is that the general principles of International Law concerning State responsibility are equally applicable in the case of breach of treaty obligation, since in the international law field there is no distinction between contractual and tortious responsibility, so that any violation by a State of any obligation, of whatever origin, gives rise to State responsibility and consequently, to the duty of reparation."]; Verhoeven (2010).

[2] Of course, such a behaviour could also be a criminal offence.

S.-M. Wedenig, *The International Responsibility of States for AI-enabled Space Activities*, Space Regulations Library 13,
https://doi.org/10.1007/978-3-032-09506-0_2

The equivalent of this civil wrong in public international law is the breach of an international obligation (an international wrong), which is one of the requirements for State responsibility to arise (see Sect. 4.3.2.1.1). If a State A violates, for example, the sovereignty of State B, then State A has committed an international wrong and is responsible.[3]

In contrast to liability *ex-delicto* stands contractual liability, or liability *ex-contractu*. This type of liability arises when one party enters into an agreement with another party, and subsequently one party breaches the duties stipulated in that agreement. For example, if A sells their car to B and it turns out that the car has more mileage than originally guaranteed in the contract, then A is liable *ex-contractu* to right the wrong committed, which will usually take the form of a compensation payment.

The differentiation between liability *ex-contractu* and liability *ex-delicto* is not new. Indeed, it goes all the way back to Roman Law and constitutes nowadays a central building block of any municipal legal order.[4]

The tort of negligence is one of the forms in which we encounter *ex-delicto* liability nowadays in common law systems and many cases are litigated within this tort.

Therefore, this chapter will employ a bottom-up approach. First, we will discuss fault, negligence and the reasonable person test contained within. We will build upon the observations of Chap. 1 and discuss how AI challenges our current understanding of fault. This will enable us to make the necessary subsequent step towards public international law and space law. The second part of this chapter will therefore look at the fault standard contained in the Liability Convention and the Outer Space Treaty. As there is no internationally accepted definition of fault in international law, we ought to investigate the question as to how fault in international law should be understood. In part three, this chapter will therefore try to explore how other international treaties deal with fault and argue that negligence is generally seen as one way to establish fault in domestic law and is a central element in many jurisdictions. The author therefore argues that it constitutes a general principle of law recognised by nations.

This in turn will then allow us look towards public international law and space law and conclude with outlining the challenges that AI poses to our understanding of fault and how it could lead to the undesired consequences that a State might escape liability altogether under space law for damage in outer space when employing AI for their space applications.

[3] This is naturally a very superficial and simplistic example. The book discusses State responsibility in greater detail in Chap. 4.

[4] Ca. 160AD, the Roman scholar and jurist Gaius already described in his Insititutiones that "(...) obligations, quarum summa diuisio in duas species diducitur: omnis enim obligatio uel ex contractu nascitur uel ex-delictu". See Gaius Institutiones 3.88 [obligations which fall into two categories: born from contract and born from delict].

2.2 Liability and Negligence

In civil law, for a defendant to be found liable, certain conditions need to be fulfilled to the satisfaction of the court, namely (1) damage sustained by the plaintiff, (2) fault of the defendant and (3) a causal connection between the damage sustained by the plaintiff and the fault of the defendant.[5] Fault in civil law usually means the violation of a duty, objectively and subjectively, whether it results from a breach of contract (liability *ex-contractu*) or a legal duty (liability *ex-delicto*). This breach can be committed either intentionally or negligently.[6]

In common law, the inquiry is framed differently, albeit the outcome is the same. Broadly we can find three categories of torts: intentional torts, negligent torts and strict liability torts.[7] In each case the court will ascertain whether there exists a duty, a breach of the duty, harm and causation between the breach of the duty and the harm suffered.[8] Fault in this regard is framed within the question of whether the legal duty has been breached and thus refers to "what a reasonable person would not have done, or not doing what a reasonable person would have done".[9]

This section will mainly be concerned with the second element, the fault of the defendant. It will address how fault is established and how AI will challenge our current legal understanding of fault.

Before we proceed, this author would like to clarify the terminology that will subsequently be used. Reference will often be given to the term "subjective fault". But what does it mean? The author bases his understanding of fault on the notion that fault has two aspects, an objective one and a subjective one, something this book will circle back to in the chapters about State responsibility and State liability. Objective fault is concerned only with the inquiry as to what was the objective conduct required versus what was the actual conduct followed. It concerns what is called in civil law the *illicéité*, *Rechtswidrigkeit* or breach of obligation, elements that are assessed objectively. Subjective fault, on the other hand refers to the mental element of *dolus* or *culpa*.[10] It follows therefore logically that if we speak of strict

---

[5] Crepeau (1962), p. 223 It must be noted, however, that there is also a liability without fault. Strict liability will be dealt with in Sect. 2.2.3 of this Chapter.

[6] Ibid.

[7] Tort. LII / Legal Information Institute. https://www.law.cornell.edu/wex/tort. Accessed 17 July 2025.

[8] For common law Cf Green (2015); Dunlop (1962); Buckley (2011), ch. 3; Walton et al. (2018), sects 1-29;1-34; Howarth et al. (2015), ch. 6.

[9] Howarth (1995), p. 36.

[10] Or in criminal law, *mens rea*. Cf Gray (2021), p. 7ff; Barboza (2011), p. 23. To come back to the example of the stone throw above. The objective fault would be concerned with the question of what was the objective conduct required of B? Naturally, it would have been not to throw a stone at A. By throwing the stone at A, B is objectively at fault. It is important to note, that this differentiation between subjective and objective fault does not mean that the reasonable person test is a subjective test. The standard of the reasonable person is an objective standard and the test itself is objective. For the purposes of this book subjective fault is used to refer to elements that refer to the

liability, we technically speak of the irrelevance of *dolus* or *culpa* which is not required in cases of strict liability.[11]

Fault is generally based on intention or negligence.[12] This research will focus solely on negligence and will not delve further into the subject matter of intent. This is due to two reasons, (1) many cases litigated before courts concern negligence and (2) an AI absent legal personhood is unable to act intentionally. We must admit, of course, that a State can use an AI to intentionally harm another State, which could constitute a breach of an international obligation and give rise to the responsibility of that State. Intentional conduct, however, will not be an aspect this research will look at. As we are concerned with the responsibility of States under international law for AI-enabled space activities, and so far in the space domain there has not been any intentional conduct directed towards another State, it seems more appropriate to look solely at the negligence aspect.

Second, intentional conduct by a State could be considered a use of force which would mandate a different inquiry, one that would go beyond the scope of this book and the subject matter discussed herein. Therefore, when we discuss fault in general, we will focus on negligence and the challenge AI poses to that particular legal construct.

subject in general, and nothing more. We deem this necessary, as we are discussing public international law, which transcends municipal legal systems (and thus the different tests for, and the varying meaning of fault in domestic law). This was clearly described by Barboza when he describes that, "[t]he word 'fault' in English and 'faute' in French have dual meanings: one refers to the breach of an obligation—i.e., to the mere contrast between the conduct required by that obligation and the conduct which the author State has in effect followed—and the other refers to culpa lato sensu—that is, to dolus or negligence. The latter meaning points to the 'subjective' aspect of the conduct". See Barboza (2011), p. 23.

[11] The term *culpa*, like so many other things in law, finds its origins in Roman Law. Gaius mentions the element of culpa frequently, for example he stated that "*Iniuria autem occidere intellegitur, cuius dolo aut culpa id acciderit; nec ulla alia lege damnum, quod sine iniuria datur, reprenenditur; itaque inpunitus est, qui sine culpa et dolo malo casu quodam damnum committit*" [Unlawful killing means killing by intention or negligence; loss suffered by no fault of the committing person is punished by no law; therefore a person, who damages another person with no fault and malice is not being punished.]. See Gaius Institutiones 3.211.

[12] This statement should not be understood as a steadfast rule. Indeed, there are variations to it. To use the words of Professor Crépeau, "[i]t should be understood that fault, in the civil-law meaning of the term, does not necessarily mean negligence, absence of reasonable care, or conduct not up to the standard of a 'bon père de famille'. It means simply any breach of one's duty, whatever the duty may be". Crepeau (1962), p. 223.

2.2.1 *Negligence, the Duty to Take Care and the Reasonable Person Test*

Before delving deeper into the question of how negligence is established, it seems appropriate to first explain what negligence actually means. As with many things in law, there is no clear-cut definition of the term. In every-day speech negligence is often used as a synonym for carelessness.[13] Alderson called negligence "the omission to do something which a reasonable man, guided upon those considerations which ordinarily regulate the conduct of human affairs, would do, or doing something which a prudent and reasonable man would not do."[14]

In a legal context negligence can have different meanings. Charlesworth and Percy for example state that "the word [negligence] can be used in three senses: (1) in referring to the state of mind accompanying an action, when it can be contrasted, for instance, with intention; (2) in describing conduct of a careless type; and (3), (…) as the breach of a duty to take care imposed by the (…) law or arising under statute."[15] The present research will focus on the last aspect or, as Professor Dunlop denotes it, negligence as a "conduct unintentionally falling below a standard of care imposed on all members of the community".[16] To understand negligence as a breach of a duty to take care makes sense as "the idea of negligence and duty are strictly correlative, and there is no such thing as negligence in the abstract; negligence is simply neglect of some care which we are bound by law to exercise towards somebody".[17] In other words, the law must establish a duty to take care whose

---

[13] See e.g. Negligence. https://www.merriam-webster.com/dictionary/negligence. Accessed 21 July 2025; Negligence. https://www.oxfordlearnersdictionaries.com/definition/american_english/negligence. Accessed 21 July 2025.

[14] Blyth v The Company of Proprietors of The Birmingham Waterworks [1856] EWHC Exch J65 (BAILII).

[15] Walton et al. (2018), p. 3.

[16] Dunlop (1962), p. 241.

[17] Thomas v Quartermaine (1887) 18 QBD 685 at 694; LJ Bowen cited in Walton et al. (2018), p. 10. Lord McMillan similarly stated that,

> [t]he law takes no cognizance of carelessness in the abstract. It concerns itself with carelessness only where there is a duty to take care and where failure in that duty has caused damage. In such circumstances carelessness assumes the legal quality of negligence and entails the consequences in law of negligence. What, then, are the circumstances which give rise to this duty to take care? In the daily contacts of social and business life human beings are thrown into, or place themselves in, an infinite variety of relations with their fellows; and the law can refer only to the standards of the reasonable man in order to determine whether any particular relation gives rise to a duty to take care as between those who stand in that relation to each other. The grounds of action may be as various and manifold as human errancy; and the conception of legal responsibility may develop in adaptation to altering social conditions and standards. The criterion of judgment must adjust and adapt itself to the changing circumstances of life. The categories of negligence are never closed. The cardinal principle of liability is that the party complained of should owe to the party complaining a duty to take care, and that the party complaining should be able to prove that he

breach would lead to negligence and subsequently liability. It must be noted that "the duty to take care" is a formulation mainly found in common law. Civil law frames it a bit differently, but the outcome remains the same. In civil law, negligence usually forms part of the wider fault analysis and denotes a behaviour which falls below the ordinarily required due diligence and is assessed, similar to common law, by employing the reasonable person test.[18] The existence of the legal duty itself and whether that duty was objectively breached (i.e., deviation from the objectively required conduct) is ordinarily a question contained within the *illicéité*, *Rechtswidrigkeit* or breach of the legal duty assessment.

> has suffered damage in consequence of a breach of that duty. Where there is room for diversity of view, it is in determining what circumstances will establish such a relationship between the parties as to give rise, on the one side, to a duty to take care, and on the other side to a right to have care taken.

See Donoghue v Stevenson [1932] UKHL 100 (BAILII), MacMillan LJ.

[18]For example, the German Bürgerliches Gesetzbuch (BGB, German Civil Code) in § 276/2 defines negligence as "*Fahrlässig handelt, wer die im Verkehr erforderliche Sorgfalt außer Acht lässt*" [Negligence is committed by those who fail to exercise the due diligence ordinarily required]. Similarly, the Austrian Allgemeines Bürgerliches Gesetzbuch (ABGB, Austrian Civil Code) in § 1297 states that "*Es wird aber auch vermuthet, daß jeder welcher den Verstandesgebrauch besitzt, eines solchen Grades des Fleißes und der Aufmerksamkeit fähig sey, welcher bey gewöhnlichen Fähigkeiten angewendet werden kann. Wer bey Handlungen, woraus eine Verkürzung der Rechte eines Anderen entsteht, diesen Grad des Fleißes oder der Aufmerksamkeit unterläßt, macht sich eines Versehens schuldig*" [But it is also suspected that everyone who has the use of reason is capable of such a degree of diligence and attention as can be applied to ordinary capabilities. Failure to exercise this degree of diligence or attention in acts which result in the infringement of another's rights is guilty of an oversight]. The ABGB also categorises a violation of "good manners" as a breach of an obligation [Verstoß gegen die Guten Sitten § 1295/2). The Austrian Supreme Court (Oberster Gerichtshof) defined negligence as follows:

> Fahrlässigkeit ist die Außerachtlassung der gehörigen Sorgfalt. § 1297 ABGB legt den allgemeinen Sorgfaltsmaßstab fest, dessen Nichteinhaltung Fahrlässigkeit begründet. Da auf den gewöhnlichen Grad der Aufmerksamkeit und des Fleißes abzustellen ist, ist maßgeblich, wie sich ein maßgerechter Durchschnittsmensch in der konkreten Lage verhalten hätte. Bei der Beurteilung dieser Frage ist auch das Wissen einzubeziehen, das der Täter um die konkreten Umstände hatte. Das Wissenmüssen richtet sich von vornherein nach dem, was ein maßgerechter Mensch in der konkreten Situation hätte wissen müssen. Daher handelt auch fahrlässig, wer ein Verhalten für erlaubt hält, obwohl es erkennbar rechtswidrig ist; zB wer bei gehöriger Aufmerksamkeit den Eintritt des Schadens voraussehen hätte können. [Negligence is the failure to exercise due care. § 1297 ABGB defines the general standard of care, non-compliance with which justifies negligence. Since the focus is on the usual degree of attention and diligence, what is decisive is how a reasonable average person would have behaved in the specific situation. When assessing this question, the knowledge that the offender had about the specific circumstances must also be taken into account. From the outset, the need to know is based on what a reasonable person should have known in the specific situation. Therefore, anyone who considers behaviour to be permissible, even though it is clearly illegal, is also acting negligently, eg who could have foreseen the occurrence of the damage if they had paid due attention].

Oberster Gerichtshof (Supreme Court), Vienna, 22 June 2011, OGH GZ 2 Ob 112/10z.

In order for the court to determine whether such a breach of a duty to take care occurred, or to ascertain in civil law whether the behaviour fell below the required due diligence, the court will usually employ the "reasonable person test". This neutral test is removed from the individual characteristics of the defendant and allows for an objective analysis of their behaviour. To use the words of Lord Macmillan, "[t]he standard of foresight of the reasonable man is, in one sense, an impersonal test. It eliminates the personal equation and is independent of the idiosyncrasies of the particular person whose conduct is in question".[19] In essence this test tries to ascertain whether the damage was objectively foreseeable for a reasonable third person and how that person would have acted under the same circumstances.[20] This standard is a flexible one. For example, should a bus driver injure a pedestrian then the standard of care applied is the "conduct or behaviour that would be expected of the reasonably prudent bus driver in the [same] circumstances".[21] In the same manner where a child is accused of having been culpable, the standard will be that objectively be expected of a child of that age.[22]

Therefore, the reasonable person test relies on two elements, namely foreseeability and reasonableness, both of which are challenged by AI (see below). Indeed, as Charlesworth and Percy point out "[t]he word "duty" connotes a relationship by which an obligation is imposed upon one person for the benefit of another to take reasonable care in all the circumstances".[23] It is important to note that these two elements are not detached from one another. As a matter of fact, they overlap and influence each other. What is reasonable will be influenced by what is foreseeable under the given circumstances and conversely what is foreseeable will be based on the consideration of what is foreseeable for the reasonable person.[24]

---

[19] Muir v Glasgow Corporation, [1943] UKHL 2 (BAILII).

[20] Rogers and Winfield (2010), pp. 92–94; Buckley (2011), p. 51; Howarth et al. (2015), p. 292ff; Gray (2021), ch. 7; Walton et al. (2018), p. 32ff; Dunlop (1962), p. 241ff.

[21] Patoma v Clarke, 2009 BCSC 1069, para. 6 ["It is clear that bus drivers owe a duty of care to their passengers based on the reasonable foreseeability test. The standard of care is the conduct or behaviour that would be expected of the reasonably prudent bus driver in the circumstances. This is an objective test that takes into consideration both the experience of the average bus driver, and what the driver knew or should have known."].

[22] Walton et al. (2018), pp. 512–514; Arthur Guiness, Son & Co (Dublin) Ltd v Owners of the Motor vessel the Freshfield 1965).

[23] Walton et al. (2018), p. 18.

[24] McLoughlin v O'Brian, [1982] UKHL 3 (BAILII), p. 5. In the words of Lord Wilberforce, "[f]oreseeability, which involves a hypothetical person, looking with hindsight at an event which has occurred, is a formula adopted by English law, not merely for defining, but also for limiting the persons to whom duty may be owed, and the consequences for which an actor may be held responsible".

2.2.2 AI Automata: A Challenge to the Reasonable Person Test?

The question that now arises is this: Does the emergence of AI challenge our current understanding of negligence or, put differently, does AI challenge the reasonable person test? The answer to this question must be in the affirmative.

First, reasonableness and the reasonable person test naturally require a certain conduct, namely the conduct of the reasonable person and while what is reasonable might differ depending on the circumstances, it all goes back to one common fact, namely that we measure reasonableness objectively against a human standard of care. The name "reasonable person test" or, as it was called in the past, "the reasonable man test" are indicative of this already. Further, various legal interpretations in leading cases make it evident, that the reasonable person test uses a human standard of care.[25] So far, jurisprudence has not developed an AI standard of behaviour against which we could measure the actions of an AI. There are suggestions in the literature to develop a "robot common sense" standard for such cases.[26] While such a proposal is intriguing and might help courts in future to reach a decision, this book is concerned with currently available standards and norms (i.e., the *lex lata*) and we will not delve deeper into the merits of such suggestions, particularly because at present we do not know how and whether such a robot common sense will find its way into case law. Further, we do not know whether we can even find a suitable "robot common sense" standard in light of the fast-changing nature of AI.

Another proposal suggested in academic circles is to expand corporate liability for failure to maintain adequate safety standards to AI.[27] However, this approach would require a certain set of industry standards relating to the use of AI. Even if we were to create such standards, the fast-developing nature of AI could leave these standards behind very quickly.

[25] Reference is often given to 'person' or 'man'. See e.g. Hanson v City of Saint John, 1973 CanLII 145 (SCC); A.C. Billings and Sons Limited v Riden, [1957] UKHL 1 (BAILII); Carmarthenshire County Council v Lewis [1955] UKHL 2 (BAILII); Hawkins v Coulsdon and Purley Urban District Council, [1953] EWCA Civ J1217-1; Donoghue v Stevensons [1932] UKHL 100 (BAILII), MacMillan LJ; McLoughlin v O'Brian, [1982] UKHL 3 (BAILII); Blyth v The Company of Proprietors of The Birmingham Waterworks [1856] EWHC Exch J65 (BAILII); Muir v Glasgow Corporation, [1943] UKHL 2 (BAILII).

[26] Abbott (2020); Abbott (2018); Giuffrida (2019), pp. 449–450.

[27] Pasquale (2019), p. 1929; Pasquale bases his argument on the case *Thompson v Nason Hospital* in which the court established general duty to ensure safety and well-being. To that end, the court established four duties of a health care provider, (1) a duty to use reasonable care in the maintenance of safe and adequate facilities and equipment; (2) a duty to select and retain only competent physicians; (3) a duty to oversee all persons who practice medicine within its walls as to patient care; and (4) a duty to formulate, adopt and enforce adequate rules. Thompson v Nason Hospital, 591, A (2d) 703 (1991) (Pa Sup Ct).

Of course, one might raise the argument, that we could still use the human standard of behaviour against which we measure the actions of AI.[28] This is, of course, a valid argument which would not require courts to change their approach. However, the author sees some problems with such an argument for it does not take the nature of AI adequately into account. This reasoning might be suitable for currently available narrow AI, which in many ways is just an "appliance" of the human and humans are at any time either on-the-loop or in-the-loop. The driver of a Tesla, who utilises the autopilot function on a highway, will still have control over the car. Indeed, in such a case it will be reasonably expected of the driver to not divert their attention away from traffic but monitor the car carefully. The inquiry will quickly shift to the human conduct. Similarly, where a voice assistant insults a user, the liability will most likely lie with the manufacturer or programmer as they have control over the AI and can determine where things went wrong. To come back to our Roomba example—if the owner of the Roomba leaves the door of the house open and the Roomba ventures outside therefore posing an obstacle that led to a person walking on the sidewalk to stumble over the vacuum cleaner and get injured, then the liability will again most likely be anchored in the human conduct.

However, even in cases where we deal only with narrow AI, one argument must be raised: AI is ordinarily much safer than humans. For example, driverless cars cause much fewer accidents than cars operated by humans. Autonomous ridesharing company Cruise, together with General Motors and the University of Michigan Transportation Research Institute, conducted a large-scale study in San Francisco comparing crash rates of human ridehail driving with autonomous ridehail driving in relation to miles driven.[29] The study showed that there were 64.9 crashes per million miles for human ridehail driving as opposed to 23 crashes per million miles for autonomous ridehail driving.[30] We see a similar trend in aviation. While in the beginning of aviation 80% of accidents were caused by machines and 20% by humans, this has now reversed and 80% of accidents are caused by human factors.[31] Machines are generally much safer than humans. That begs the question as to whether it is adequate to still use to the human standard of behaviour which is arguably lower than that of a machine. If machines are always much safer than humans, how would a machine then be in breach of a standard of care based on human

[28] For example, Chatzipanagiotis proposes to use the human standard of behaviour as a minimum standard. See Chatzipanagiotis (2020).

[29] Zhang L (2023) A Comprehensive Study - Human Ridehail Crash Rate Benchmark | Cruise. https://web.archive.org/web/20240616184516/https://www.getcruise.com/news/blog/2023/human-ridehail-crash-rate-benchmark/?ref=warpnews.org. Accessed 21 July 2025.

[30] Ibid.

[31] Rankin W (2011) MEDA Investigation Process. Available via http://www.boeing.com/commercial/aeromagazine/articles/qtr_2_07/AERO_Q207_article3.pdf. Accessed 21 July 2025; Winingham WK (2018) Human Error in Aviation Accidents | Wilson Kehoe Winingham. https://www.wkw.com/aviation-accidents/blog/aviation-accidents-human-error/. Accessed 21 July 2025.

behaviour, which will arguably be lower?[32] Whatever the case may be, at least for narrow AI, the court could at a minimum take the use of machines into account when conducting the standard of care analysis, but it becomes problematic when AI becomes more autonomous and independent.

The challenges we encounter in the case of AI when applying the reasonable person test are in essence linked to the autonomy or independence of the AI. The more AI advances towards full autonomy, the more the reasonable person test will be challenged. As this author mentioned earlier, autonomy and control are incongruous. The more autonomy we grant AI, the more we give up control. AI, utilising a DNN for ML and operating autonomously without any human oversight, is, as mentioned, opaque. While the programmer might know where the error occurred, they will not be able to ascertain *why* it occurred. Indeed, an AI might function as intended and still cause harm. Nick Bostrom describes this problem in his "paperclip" example, in which a machine is tasked to produce paperclips and subsequently starts using up all of Earth's resources in the process.[33] An example in recent history would be Boeing's Manoeuvring Characteristics Augmentation System (MCAS) that worked as it was programmed but still caused the fatal loss of two Boeing 737-Max 8 aircraft.[34]

Ryan Abbott tries to work around this problem by proposing that if the programmer of an AI can show that the AI is safer than a reasonable person would be, then the programmer should only be liable in negligence. In this regard Abbott proposes a negligence test that focuses on the AI's "act instead of its design, and in a sense, it would treat a computer tortfeasor as a person" and proposes to use the standard of "the reasonable computer".[35] This standard should only be used when AI is safer than a human.

There are practical problems with such a suggestion, which mainly lie in the question of how we establish and imagine such a "reasonable computer" standard. The reasonable person test currently employed is based on the objective notion that all humans are similar, that is the law assumes that we have a set of traits that are more or less the same in all humans.[36] This is not the same for AI. Indeed, there are a variety of different ways to create AI and the code is ordinarily proprietary.[37] Lastly, to treat the AI (or as Abbott calls it, the computer tortfeasor) as a person

---

[32] Ryan Abbot discusses this problem and argues that once computers become safer than humans then the actions of a human should be measured against a computer standard of care. See Abbott (2018), p. 5.

[33] Bostrom (2014), pp. 123–125; See also Turner who talks about a toaster that burns down a house in the attempt to produce as many toasts as possible, Turner (2019), p. 89.

[34] For an excellent analysis see Travis G (2019) How the Boeing 737 Max Disaster Looks to a Software Developer - IEEE Spectrum. https://spectrum.ieee.org/how-the-boeing-737-max-disaster-looks-to-a-software-developer. Accessed 21 July 2025.

[35] Abbott (2018), p. 1; Abbott (2020).

[36] At least that is the starting point and subsequently the court takes other factors into account. See Turner (2019), p. 90.

[37] Ibid.

would require significant changes in the law and raise the problem of legal capacity (see Sect. 2.2.4).

Therefore, to find a suitable AI standard of behaviour would be exceedingly difficult. Even to fall back to the creator of the AI (e.g., the programmer) would cause obstacles. As mentioned earlier, negligence requires not only the existence of a duty to take care but also a breach of such duty. While the existence of a duty to take care might be easier to establish, proving a breach of said duty in the case of advanced AI will be extremely challenging. The standard of care "is a question of law, although whether or not it was achieved is a question of fact decided by reference to all the circumstances of the case".[38] The court therefore has to take multiple factors into account, such as for example the magnitude of risk involved, the likelihood of injury, predictability of harm and common practices of the industry. How would a court find a programmer liable if they programmed and tested the AI to the best standards and knowledge of the industry, after all there would be likely no negligence in these cases?

Further, as mentioned, the likelihood of injury and the risk are greatly reduced. This is already the case for narrow AI, and it applies even more so to advanced AI. In the case of DNN and ML predictability is also greatly reduced. The very essence of ML is that we cannot predict what the machine will encounter and how the machine will react to such unknown circumstances. Indeed, we specifically grant the AI the ability to learn and adjust its behaviour to deal with unpredictable situations. A programmer will, as mentioned, not even be in the position to rectify the problem as the AI is opaque and the programmer will not be able to tell why the machine reached a particular decision.

This is not to say that a programmer could not be held liable. We could, of course, make the programmer strictly liable but then we would find ourselves not in the realm of negligence anymore, and it would again require changes in the law in the form of the creation of a dedicated strict liability regime.

As mentioned, negligence relies on foreseeability. It asks the question whether the damage was objectively foreseeable for the reasonable person based on the behaviour shown. It not only defines but also limits the person "to whom duty may be owed, and the consequences for which an actor may be held responsible".[39] It thus acts as a shield against damages which would be too remote.[40]

The foreseeability requirement, on which our current understanding of negligence is based, will increasingly be challenged by autonomous highly advanced AI. As mentioned in Sect. 1.3.4, the black-box problem of AI causes some significant challenges as AI becomes increasingly opaque. This will lead to the consequence that we will have difficulty to foresee the actions of the AI. We know the

[38] Walton et al. (2018), p. 511.

[39] McLoughlin v O'Brian, [1982] UKHL 3 (BAILII).

[40] For example, in the famous Wagon Mound case, the Judicial Committee of the privy council rejected liability for carelessly ejected oil which was ignited in a manner, unforeseeable to the objective third person. Overseas Tankship (UK) Ltd v Morts Dock and Engineering Co Ltd [1961] UKPC 2 (BAILII); Buckley (2011), p. 78.

input (i.e., the instruction to the AI) and the eventual output (i.e., the end-result) but the output will only be known ex-post. The reasonable person test, however, rests on the objective foreseeability ex-ante. As the Supreme Court of Canada stated in *Rankin's Garage & Sales v J.J.*," [w]hether or not something is "reasonably foreseeable" is an objective test. The question is properly focussed on whether foreseeability was present prior to the incident occurring and not with the aid of 20/20 hindsight".[41]

The autonomy of AI and ML strike at the very heart of this issue. As has been emphasised before, the very essence of ML and autonomy is to give up control and equip the AI with the ability to programme itself in order to successfully deal with unknown situations. It thus becomes impossible for a software engineer to foresee the damage that the AI might cause. In other words, we will not be able to determine what risk the use of highly advanced AI will cause. But if this risk is unforeseeable, then there is no duty to guard against it.[42]

To account for this problem, Pasquale, for example, suggests anchoring the liability in the use of inaccurate or inappropriate data rather than looking at the decision-making process of the AI.[43] Data is usually transmitted to the AI by humans, and the use of faulty or inappropriate data might be easier to prove.

The argument could also be raised that the creator of an AI ought to have known that there is a risk, albeit minimal, that the AI could cause damage and thus should be held liable. Such an approach is problematic. First, it would go against the very issue the reasonable person test tries to address namely, to limit the liability of the defendant and not make them liable for damage that is too broad and remote. To say that a software engineer ought to have known that the AI could theoretically cause damage, is the same as to say that the driver of a car ought to have foreseen a child jumping out behind a parked car at midnight far away from a school zone or that whenever one leaves the house, one should have foreseen that one could cause damage, regardless of how remote that damage is. The theoretical possibility to cause damage is just a fact of life. Whenever we interact with one another there is the theoretical possibility that damage can occur. The reasonable person test takes account of that and makes sure that not all damage automatically leads to liability.

Further, this argument would venture more into the direction of strict liability, which will be discussed in Sect. 2.2.3 below.

Before we conclude this section, there is another issue which requires our attention. As mentioned at the beginning of this section, besides the requirement of damage sustained by the plaintiff and the fault of the defendant, we also need a third element, a causal connection between the damage sustained by the plaintiff and the fault of the defendant.[44] In addition to the foreseeability requirement contained in the reasonable person test, causality further limits the scope of liability and makes

---

[41] Rankin (Rankin's Garage & Sales) v. J.J., 2018 SCC 19, pp. 588–589.

[42] See Stanton (1994), p. 62; Roe v Minister of Health, [1954] EWCA Civ 7 (BAILII).

[43] Pasquale (2019), p. 1939.

[44] Crepeau (1962); Stanton (1994), ch. 4.

sure that only damage that resulted from the fault of the defendant is going to be compensated. In other words, the question asked is whether the loss would have occurred "but for" the fault of the defendant.[45] In the case of AI, however, the "but for" element will not always be easy to determine. As mentioned, should an autonomous AI cause damage, the software engineer might be able to determine where and when the error occurred in the code, but not why it occurred. If we are unable to determine the why, we are unable to determine causality because we fail to establish whether the negligence of the software engineer caused the error and led to the damage.[46]

In conclusion, as mentioned previously in this book, the actions of AI will become increasingly unforeseeable, "except perhaps at a very high level of abstraction and generality".[47] Further, there is no accepted "AI standard of behaviour", at least not yet, that could be employed by courts and using the human standard of behaviour is not a suitable solution as AI is proven to be much safer than humans, which would allow for an escape from liability. In other words, once we venture outside narrow AI, and thus have difficulty anchoring the liability in the human conduct, our current understanding of negligence will be challenged and may fail altogether. As Frank Pasquale succinctly puts it "there is grave danger that AI will become one more tool for deflecting liability".[48]

Of course, this is not the first time law is confronted with situations in which subjective fault might be hard to prove and over time a system has evolved that creates liability without the element of subjective fault, that is strict liability and absolute liability regimes. Let us therefore discuss these more in detail and address whether a strict liability regime might be a suitable solution for AI.

2.2.3 *Strict Liability*

The above-mentioned challenges in negligence have led many authors to advocate for a system of strict liability to adequately govern damages caused by AI. The suggestions differ in their details but can generally be divided into two camps. There are those who advocate for granting AI legal personhood, similar to corporations, to make them strictly liable either directly or via the vehicle of agency law, and those who point towards a strict products liability regime, particularly in the case of autonomous vehicles.[49] It warrants the question whether a strict liability regime is

[45] Buckley (2011), sect. 3.02.

[46] Yavar Bathaee looks at this issue in more detail and is of a similar opinion. See Bathaee (2018), p. 922ff.

[47] Turner (2019), p. 91.

[48] Pasquale (2019), p. 1918.

[49] See e.g. Allain (2013), pp. 1078–1079; Powell (2020), p. 317; Vladeck (2014), pp. 149–150 propose two ways to solve the liability issue, either by establishing a 'common enterprise' liability or establish legal personhood for the autonomous vehicle itself; Giuffrida (2019); Wagner (2018);

the appropriate way forward to address the challenges of AI. This requires us to lay some groundwork. First, we need to emphasise that liability is generally based on fault. "Fault as the basis of liability is grounded on the fundamental proposition that a person who is injured due to the fault of another person has the right to compensation from the wrongdoer".[50] However, there are certain cases in which the law makes an exception to this general rule (i.e., cases of strict or absolute liability).[51]

Second, we need to distinguish between strict liability and absolute liability. These two terms are often used interchangeably, although there is a fine but important legal distinction between them, leading to confusion and sometimes incorrect application of the terms. The common denominator of both—absolute and strict liability—is, that subjective fault (e.g., *culpa or dolus* in tort law or *mens rea* in criminal law) is irrelevant and both create a prima-facie liability.[52] The important legal difference is that in cases of strict liability, certain defences to escape liability are available to the defendant whereas in absolute liability cases, they are not.[53] For example, the Supreme Court of Canada differentiated fault-based, strict and absolute liability as follows:

> Three categories of offences are therefore now recognised (first) offences in which mens rea must be established, (second) offences of "strict liability" in which mens rea need not be established but where the defence of reasonable belief in a mistaken set of facts or the

Čerka et al. (2015); Heiss (2021) propose a strict liability regime in which losses are paid to the State. LeValley (2013) who favours product liability but also proposes to hold the vehicle manufacturer strictly liable as a common carrier; Lohmann (2016).

[50] Peixeiro v Haberman, [1997] 3 SCR 549, para. 20; Lapierre v A.G. (Que.), [1985] 1 SCR 241.

[51] In other words, a case-by-case analysis is necessary to determine whether the law provides for absolute or strict liability.

[52] It must be noted at this point that strict liability is handled a bit differently in common and civil law jurisdictions. While in common law, strict liability does not require the fault of the defendant, it does require a duty the law imposes upon the defendant. See Rylands v Fletcher [1868] UKHL 1 (BAILII) ["The question of law therefore arises, what is the obligation which the law casts on a person (…)"]. Conversely, in civil law jurisdictions neither a breach of an obligation (*Rechtswidrigkeit, illicéité*) nor the fault of the defendant is necessary. In strict liability the activity is lawful. For example, Austria imposes a strict liability on the operator of a motor vehicle for damages resulting from an accident. In this regard, the liability attaches to the damage that resulted from an accident, rather than to a breach of an obligation (*Rechtswidrigkeit*). The operation of the vehicle is perfectly legal and, should damage resulting from an accident occur, the operator will be held strictly liable. Neither an inquiry into a breach of an obligation, nor into the fault of the operator is necessary. See Riedler (2015), p. 122 ["Liability (…) is not linked (…) to culpable conduct of the liable persons, but to infliction of damage (…)".]; Barta U-PDH (2007) ziviltecht.online. https://web.archive.org/web/20230311134322/https://www.uibk.ac.at/zivilrecht/buch/kap9_0.xml?section-view=true;section=2. Accessed 21 July 2024 ["It waives the criterion of fault as a prerequisite for liability. But breach of an obligation is also no longer a prerequisite for liability, because the "hazardous activity" and any resulting damage is not caused unlawfully."]. In the course of this book we will look more towards the common law understanding of strict liability.

[53] A good example for a typical strict liability regime is products liability, which usually allows the exoneration of the manufacturer in certain cases.

> defence of reasonable care is available, and (third) offences of "absolute liability" where it is not open to the accused to exculpate himself by showing that he was free of fault.[54]

While this case concerned criminal law, similar considerations ought to apply in tort law cases.[55]

In other words, absolute liability is strict liability without any defences available.

There is again no clear-cut definition of strict liability. However, it is generally understood that the rationale for strict liability is to make sure a plaintiff is properly compensated, particularly where it is hard for the victim to prove subjective fault of the defendant,[56] to make sure people engaged in dangerous activities put adequate safety precautions in place[57] and to place the burden of liability on those that stand to benefit the most from the activity.[58]

A strict liability regime for AI would be a workable solution as it circumvents the main problem discussed above, namely, to prove subjective fault.[59] However, it does come with some challenges in case of AI. To illustrate this, let us first look a bit

---

[54] R v Sault Ste Marie, [1978] 2 SCR 1299, 1978 CANLII 11.

[55] St. Lawrence Cement Inc v Barrette, 2008 SCC 64. In *Lupu v Rabinovitch* the court interpretated Section 26 of the Animal Husbandry Act to give rise to absolute liability without any defenses available. See Lupu v. Rabinovitch, 1975 CanLII 979 (MB KB). In *Witman v Johnson* the court differentiated between absolute liability, where no defenses are available, and strict liability which allows some defenses. See Witman v. Johnson, 1990 CanLII 7975 (MB KB), paras 15–20. See also Brewer v. Saunders, 1986 CanLII 4009 (NS SC), para. 10 ["The common law also recognized that certain animals were, by their nature, so dangerous to man that the keeper of them could not be heard to say that he did not know of their character. Scienter, in such a case, was to be conclusively presumed. 'Strict liability' was imposed in such cases, with certain defences permitted."].

[56] This rationale is predominant in products liability regimes where it is generally very hard for the plaintiff to prove the fault of the manufacturer. Therefore, many products liability regimes ease the burden of proof on the plaintiff and only require the plaintiff to prove the defect, damage resulting from the defect and causation between defect and damage. See e.g. EC, Council Directive 85/374/EEC of 25 July 1985 on the approximation of the laws, regulations and administrative provisions of the Member States concerning liability for defective products, [1985] OJ, L 210/29; Consumer Protection Act 1987 (UK), c 43.

[57] See e.g. Rylands v Fletcher [1868] UKHL 1 (BAILII). Lord Cains affirming and concurring with the words of Justice Blackburn, "[w]e think that the true rule of law is, that the person who, for his own purposes, brings on his land and collects and keeps there anything likely to do mischief if it escapes, must keep it in at his peril; and if he does not do so, is primâ facie answerable for all the damage which is the natural consequence of its escape".

[58] United States v Dotterweich, 1943 US LEXIS 1100 ["Balancing relative hardships, Congress has preferred to place it upon those who have at least the opportunity of informing themselves of the existence of conditions imposed for the protection of consumers before sharing in illicit commerce."]; Stapleton (1994), p. 189 ["(…) a view that the enterprise should pay its way for this bad luck, even if unavoidable".].

[59] Indeed, the regime of State Responsibility and Liability does not require fault and, as will be argued later, provides therefore a good solution to address the responsibility of States for their AI-enabled space activities.

closer at three prominent forms in which we encounter strict liability: vicarious liability, products liability and the liability for animals.[60]

2.2.3.1 Products Liability

Charlesworth and Percy describe products liability as "civil liability for damage and loss suffered or injury sustained, or both, caused by a defect or defects in goods consumed".[61] Products liability places the emphasis on the defective state of a product, rather than the fault of the defendant and usually makes the producer liable to pay compensation for damage resulting from the defective product.[62] Let us focus briefly on two jurisdictions that use a strict liability approach in products liability, the European Union and the United States.

The EU regulates products liability in Directive 85/374/ECC and places the liability for "damage caused by a defect in his product" on the producer.[63] The Directive adopts a very wide definition for "producer" thus giving the plaintiff a range of options to choose from. Primarily, the producer is the manufacturer of the finished product, raw materials, or component parts of the product.[64] Further, any person who presents themselves as the producer is considered producer under the Directive, even though they may not have manufactured the product.[65] Secondly, also the importer of a product can be considered producer.[66] Finally, where the producer of a product cannot be identified, each supplier of the product should be considered a producer.[67] Product is defined as "all movables, with the exception of primary

---

[60] It must be noted that product liability is not the only form of strict liability. Indeed, there are various other forms in which we encounter strict liability, such as liability of owners of animals, liability of parents for their children, liability of common carriers, liability for fire. For a good comprehensive overview see, Gray (2021), ch. 1.

[61] Walton et al. (2018), p. 1167; Turner correctly summarises it as "a system of rules which establish who is liable when a given product causes harm". Turner (2019), p. 92; Cf Escola v Coca Cola Bottling Co. (1944) 24 C (2d) 453 (Cal Sup Ct), Traynor J concurring.

[62] Turner (2019), p. 92; Interestingly, this is not the case in Canada. Courts reject a strict liability for defects in products and the liability of the manufacturer is based on a negligence claim. See e.g Cassels and Jones (2005), p. 16ff; Phillips et al. v. Ford Motor Co. of Canada Ltd. et al., 1971 CanLII 389 (ON CA) ["(…) our Courts do not, in product liability cases, impose upon manufacturers, distributors or repairers, as is done in some of the States of the American union, what is virtually strict liability. The standard of care exacted of them under our law is the duty to use reasonable care in the circumstances and nothing more."].

[63] EC, Council Directive 85/374/EEC of 25 July 1985 on the approximation of the laws, regulations and administrative provisions of the Member States concerning liability for defective products, [1985] OJ, L 210/29, art. 1.

[64] Ibid, art. 3(1).

[65] Ibid.

[66] Ibid, art. 3(2).

[67] Ibid. art 3(3); EU Directive 2024/2853 replaces "producer" with "economic operator". Economic operator is "(a) the manufacturer of a defective product; (b) the manufacturer of a defective component, where that component was integrated into, or inter-connected with, a product within the

agricultural products and game, even though incorporated into another movable or into an immovable" and includes electricity.[68] This means that intangible objects, such as software, do not fall under the scope of the Directive. At the date of writing, the European Union is trying to rectify this problem, and the European Commission submitted a proposal for a new Directive on products liability to the European Parliament in September 2022. As one of the reasons for the need to update Directive 85/374 the Commission expressly lists as shortcoming that "it was legally unclear how to apply the [Product Liability Directive's] decades-old definitions and concepts to products in the modern digital economy and circular economy (e.g. software and products that need software or digital services to function, such as smart devices and autonomous vehicles)."[69] The draft Directive came into force on 4th December 2024 as Directive 2024/2853. However, it will only apply to products placed on the market or put into service after 9th December 2026.[70] This chapter will therefore discuss primarily Directive 85/374.

The Directive Directive 2024/2853 affirms that AI systems and AI-enabled goods are considered to be products and that not only the hardware manufacturer but also software providers as well as providers for digital services can be held strictly liable.[71]

The European Union adopts a wider approach as to when a product is considered to be defective. A product can be considered defective "when it does not provide the safety which a person is entitled to expect, taking all circumstances into account"

---

manufacturer's control and caused that product to be defective, and without prejudice to the liability of the manufacturer referred to in point (a); and (c) in the case of a manufacturer of a product or a component established outside the Union, and without prejudice to the liability of that manufacturer: (i) the importer of the defective product or component; (ii) the authorised representative of the manufacturer; and (iii) where there is no importer established within the Union or authorised representative, the fulfilment service provider." It further clarifies that "[a]ny natural or legal person that substantially modifies a product outside the manufacturer's control and thereafter makes it available on the market or puts it into service shall be considered to be a manufacturer of that product" See EU, Directive (EU) 2024/2853 of the European Parliament and the Council of 23 October 2024 on liability for defective products and repealing Council Directive 85/374/EEC, [2024] OJ, L 2024/2853.

[68] EC, Council Directive 85/374/EEC of 25 July 1985 on the approximation of the laws, regulations and administrative provisions of the Member States concerning liability for defective products, [1985] OJ, L 210/29, art. 2.

[69] EU, Commission, Proposal for a Directive of the European Parliament and of the Council on liability for defective products, [2022] COM(2022) 495 final, p. 1.

[70] EU, Directive (EU) 2024/2853 of the European Parliament and the Council of 23 October 2024 on liability for defective products and repealing Council Directive 85/374/EEC, [2024] OJ, L 2024/2853, art. 2.

[71] Interestingly the European Union also attempted to tackle the question of fault-based liability for AI and originally adopted a draft Directive on adapting non-contractual fault-based civil liability rules to artificial intelligence. This draft Directive sought to alleviate the burden of proof for a plaintiff in cases where damage was caused by AI. See EU, Commission, Proposal for a Directive of the European Parliament and of the Council on adapting non-contractual civil liability rules to artificial intelligence, [2022] COM(2022) 496 final [Commission AI Liability Draft Directive]. In the end, the Directive did not go ahead as no foreseeable agreement could be reached.

this includes the presentation of the product, the reasonable use of the product and the time when the product was put into circulation.[72]

On the other hand, the US Restatement (Third) of Products Liability adopts a narrower approach and requires that defects fall into one of three categories, (1) manufacturing defect, (2) design defect and (3) instruction or warning defect.[73] It links the liability to the manufacturing or non-manufacturing commercial seller ("[o]ne engaged in the business of selling") or the Distributor.

The suggestion to bring AI under a product liability regime is attractive as it presents some advantages. The first, and probably most obvious one, is that a product liability regime brings clarity and removes all doubt as to who will be liable for a defect. It provides a viable avenue for the consumer to seek compensation for a defective product from the producer (or alternatively the supplier). It further removes a significant obstacle for the consumer, insofar as it creates a prima-facie liability for the producer. A negligence-based liability regime would put the burden of proof for fault on the consumer rather than the producer, which is a standard very difficult to meet. How would a consumer prove that a producer breached a standard of care during the manufacturing process? These processes are typically proprietary and not public knowledge.[74]

---

[72] EC, Council Directive 85/374/EEC of 25 July 1985 on the approximation of the laws, regulations and administrative provisions of the Member States concerning liability for defective products, [1985] OJ, L 210/29, art. 6. In comparison Directive 2024/2853 considers a product defect "where it does not provide the safety that a person is entitled to expect or that is required under Union or national law. In assessing the defectiveness of a product, all circumstances shall be taken into account, including: (a) the presentation and the characteristics of the product, including its labelling, design, technical features, composition and packaging and the instructions for its assembly, installation, use and maintenance; (b) reasonably foreseeable use of the product; (c) the effect on the product of any ability to continue to learn or acquire new features after it is placed on the market or put into service; (d) the reasonably foreseeable effect on the product of other products that can be expected to be used together with the product, including by means of inter-connection; (e) the moment in time when the product was placed on the market or put into service or, where the manufacturer retains control over the product after that moment, the moment in time when the product left the control of the manufacturer; (f) relevant product safety requirements, including safety-relevant cybersecurity requirements; (g) any recall of the product or any other relevant intervention relating to product safety by a competent authority or by an economic operator as referred to in Article 8; (h) the specific needs of the group of users for whose use the product is intended; (i) in the case of a product whose very purpose is to prevent damage, any failure of the product to fulfil that purpose".

[73] American Law Institute (1998), § 2. It must be noted that in the US there are no federal laws that address product liability. Instead, US states regulate these matters. The Restatement on Product Liability is the result of the efforts of the American Law Institute to compile existing jurisprudence and laws on that subject and bring clarity to it. It is a commentary often relied on by courts and States.

[74] This is made clear in the preamble to EU Directive 85/371 when it states that "[w]hereas liability without fault on the part of the producer is the sole means of adequately solving the problem, peculiar to our age of increasing technicality, of a fair apportionment of the risks inherent in modern technological production".

A products liability regime requires the plaintiff to only prove the existence of the defect, the damage and the causal connection between the defect and the damage, which will ordinarily be much easier than proving fault of the producer.

To strike a balance between consumer protection and facilitating product development, products liability regimes typically allow for exoneration of the producer if certain conditions are met. Therefore, the producer is prima-facie liable but can escape liability under certain circumstances.[75]

Such a strict products liability regime also encourages caution and safety in product development. It encourages producers to manufacture products safely and put adequate control mechanism into place.[76]

On the producer's side, clarity in liability brings the advantage that the business can put appropriate safety measures in place, obtain adequate insurance coverage for any damages and ultimately be able to calculate potential costs better. The risk of possible damages can be priced into the product already and allows for better projections.[77]

In the case of a faulty AI, it would allow the victim to seek compensation not only from the immediate supplier but also the original manufacturer or any other supplier involved in the supply chain. For example, let us assume a faulty AI in an autonomous car causes an accident which kills the driver. The family could not only sue the car manufacturer but also anybody in the supply chain who contributed to the harm.

Albeit there are advantages of a product liability regime, there are also some shortcomings when applied to AI.

First, current products liability regimes only apply to tangible objects and exclude software. While a robot causing damage would be covered by the scope of products liability, AI itself would not.[78] This is one of the shortcomings the European Union

---

[75] EC, Council Directive 85/374/EEC of 25 July 1985 on the approximation of the laws, regulations and administrative provisions of the Member States concerning liability for defective products, [1985] OJ, L 210/29, art. 7; American Law Institute (1998), § 2.

[76] See e.g. American Law Institute (1998), p. 15; EC, Commission, Report from the Commission on the Application of Directive 85/374 on Liability for Defective Products, [2001] COMM (2000) 893 final; Turner (2019), p. 95.

[77] See e.g. Stapleton (1994), p. 205ff; Escola v Coca Cola Bottling Co. (1944) 24 C (2d) 453 (Cal Sup Ct), Traynor J concurring:

> The cost of an injury and the loss of time or health may be an overwhelming misfortune to the person injured, and a needless one, for the risk of injury can be insured by the manufacturer and distributed among the public as a cost of doing business. It is to the public interest to discourage the marketing of products having defects that are a menace to the public. If such products nevertheless find their way into the market it is to the public interest to place the responsibility for whatever injury they may cause upon the manufacturer, who, even if he is not negligent in the manufacture of the product, is responsible for its reaching the market. However intermittently such injuries may occur and however haphazardly they may strike, the risk of their occurrence is a constant risk and a general one. Against such a risk there should be general and constant protection and the manufacturer is best situated to afford such protection.

[78] However, AI forms an integral part of the object itself without which it could not function. We will discuss this a little further in Sect. 3.3.1.3.

tries to address in EU Directive 2024/2853. In the Directive product is defined as "all movables, even if integrated into, or inter-connected with, another movable or an immovable; it includes electricity, digital manufacturing files, raw materials and software."[79] The Directive further clarifies that a related service shall be treated as a component of a product and explains that related service means "a digital service that is integrated into, or inter-connected with, a product in such a way that its absence would prevent the product from performing one or more of its functions."[80]

However, as mentioned the Directive only applies to products placed on the market or put into service after 9 December 2026 and therefore does not apply to any products at the date of writing. We will therefore not delve into it deeper.

Another challenge when applied to AI is, that products liability regimes usually assume that a product remains static once it has been released.[81] This is not the case for AI, especially when equipped with machine learning.[82] As mentioned in Sect. 1.3.3 machine learning essentially means that we give the AI the ability to programme itself and give up control to gain independence.

Further, the premise products liability is usually based on, is that the producer is in a position to rectify the problem.[83] The producer is in the best position to ascertain what went wrong in the manufacturing process, put adequate safety measure in place to correct the problem, or is able to recall and pull the product from the market if necessary. While for narrow AI this would not change, more advanced autonomous AI will create some obstacles. We come back to our example of autonomous AI equipped with ML utilising a DNN. As previously mentioned, it is opaque (a black box) and while the software engineer might be able to pinpoint where and when the problem in the code occurred, they will not be able to pinpoint why it

[79] While this Directive of the EU is a first step in trying to capture AI and attempt to lay down rules on how to regulate liability claims arising from defective AI, it does come with its own set of issues. First, to strike a balance between the need to protect consumers and to encourage development in the area of AI, the Directive states in Article 2 that it "should not apply to free and open-source software developed or supplied outside the course of a commercial activity". This is an odd provision in the Directive as it fundamentally disregards the developments in the AI sector. Albeit there are some companies open source their code, the vast majority of AI development happens behind closed doors and is treated strictly confidentially. No company voluntarily parts with their valuable software to not loose revenue. Thus, this provision seems to miss the target, as it does not really help to counterbalance the strict liability regime created by it. Ordinarily, mostly educational institutions open source their code.

[80] EU, Directive (EU) 2024/2853 of the European Parliament and the Council of 23 October 2024 on liability for defective products and repealing Council Directive 85/374/EEC, [2024] OJ, L 2024/2853.

[81] Turner (2019), p. 95.

[82] EU Directive 2024/2853 considers this in Article 7 and clarifies that in assessing the defectiveness of a product, "the effect on the product of any ability to continue to learn or acquire new features after it is placed on the market or put into service" shall be taken into account. It makes the economic operator liable for any harm caused by ML. The author remains critical of this due to the same arguments illustrated in the main text.

[83] Cf Bathaee (2018), p. 932.

occurred. This makes it impossible, or at least very difficult, for the manufacturer to put adequate safety measures in place or correct the problem.

In the same sense, it would allow manufacturers to escape liability. Under Directive 85/374 the producer is not liable if they, *inter alia*, prove that "having regard to the circumstances, it is probable that the defect which caused the damage did not exist at the time when the product was put into circulation by him or that this defect came into being afterwards" or "that the state of scientific and technical knowledge at the time when he put the product into circulation was not such as to enable the existence of the defect to be discovered".[84] The fact that the AI is equipped with ML will mean that there is a real possibility that the problem was not present when the AI was released to the market. Further, AI development is rapidly increasing and moves along quickly. Indeed, what is considered state-of-the-art today, can very well be outdated tomorrow.

The case is similar in the US. Albeit the Restatement (Third) of Products Liability does not contain a dedicated provision with express defences for the manufacturer, apart from affirmative defences in §17, it does allow for exoneration when certain conditions are met. These conditions are contained within the definition of defect in §2. First, a requirement for products liability is that the defect must be present at the time of sale or distribution.[85] The same considerations from above, are applicable here. ML would mean that the problem could not be present at all during the sale or distribution of the software but rather appeared only later through the ML of the AI. Another challenge that is posed is the definition for manufacturing defect, design defect and instruction/warning defect.

A product contains a manufacturing defect, "when the product departs from its intended design even though all possible care was exercised in the preparation and marketing of the product".[86] A manufacturing defect is therefore a "departure from a product unit's design specifications" and common examples ordinarily include physically flawed, incorrectly assembled or damaged products.[87] This touches upon

[84] EC, Council Directive 85/374/EEC of 25 July 1985 on the approximation of the laws, regulations and administrative provisions of the Member States concerning liability for defective products, [1985] OJ, L 210/29, art. 7. Interestingly, Directive 2024/2853 deviates from this. While it maintains the exemption of the non-existence of the defect at the time the product was put into circulations as well as the exemption of scientific knowledge, it deviates from the former by declaring that "[b]y way of derogation from paragraph 1, point (c)[non-existence of defect at product distribution], an economic operator shall not be exempted from liability, where the defectiveness of the product is due to any of the following, provided that it is within the manufacturer's control: (a) a related service; (b) software, including software updates or upgrades; (c) the lack of software updates or upgrades necessary to maintain safety; (d) substantial modification of the product". However, the question remains how much of the subsequent ML for the AI would be under the manufacturers control. As mentioned, we give up control for the sake of gaining independence and automation. Art. 11, EU Directive 2024/2853.

[85] American Law Institute (1998), §2 ["A product is defective when, at the time of sale or distribution, it contains a manufacturing defect, is defective in design, or is defective because of inadequate instructions or warnings"].

[86] Ibid, § 2(a).

[87] Ibid, p. 18.

a fundamental question, namely whether the undesired outcome was actually caused by an error in the code? What if the AI worked as intended and solely within the parameters given to it? This touches upon a myriad of moral and philosophical questions, which will not be the focus of the present research. Great minds like Stephen Hawking, Geoffrey Hinton and Steven Wozniak have warned of this effect, that is that AI could work exactly as intended but interpret parameters differently and surpass the human race.[88] In a recently published statement over 400 signatories, among them the biggest names in tech, asked that "[m]itigating the risk of extinction from AI should be a global priority alongside other societal-scale risks such as pandemics and nuclear war".[89]

A product is defective in its design when "the foreseeable risks of harm posed by the product could have been reduced or avoided by the adoption of a reasonable alternative design".[90]

Finally, a product is defective when "because of inadequate instructions or warnings when the foreseeable risks of harm posed by the product could have been reduced or avoided by the provision of reasonable instructions or warnings".[91]

Both, design and instruction/warning defect, are therefore only defects when the risks are reasonably foreseeable. The author directs the reader to Sects. 2.2.1 and 2.2.2 in which this book discusses at length the problem of reasonableness and foreseeability.

It follows therefore, that currently available product liability regimes are difficult to apply to AI without modification, even when the damage is cause by a robot (and therefore by a tangible object). Although the European Union has initiated steps in the right direction by proposing to update the products liability regime, the proposal was only recently adopted, does not yet apply to currently available products, and contains some ambiguities which still need to be addressed.

Another option, brought forward in literature, is that of governing AI applications under the rules of the liability for animals.

[88] (2023)AI risks leading humanity to 'extinction,' experts warn. In: NBC News. https://www.nbcnews.com/tech/tech-news/ai-risks-leading-humanity-extinction-experts-warn-rcna86791. Accessed 17 July 2025; Cellan-Jones R (2014) Stephen Hawking warns artificial intelligence could end mankind. https://www.bbc.com/news/technology-30290540. Accessed 22 July 2025.

[89] Statement on AI Risk | CAIS. In: Center for AI Safety. https://www.safe.ai/statement-on-ai-risk. Accessed 14 June 2023; Collier K (2023) Artificial intelligence may lead humanity to 'extinction,' experts warn. https://www.nbcnews.com/tech/tech-news/ai-risks-leading-humanity-extinction-experts-warn-rcna86791. Accessed 22 July 2025; Cellan-Jones R (2014) Stephen Hawking warns artificial intelligence could end mankind. https://www.bbc.com/news/technology-30290540. Accessed 22 July 2025.

[90] American Law Institute (1998), § 2(b).

[91] Ibid, § 2(c).

2.2.3.2 Liability for Animals

The doctrine of strict liability for animals imposes legal responsibility on the keeper of an animal regardless of the keeper's intent, negligence or the measures taken to prevent the harm.[92]

Under common law, strict liability is imposed on the owner or possessor for animals *ferae naturae* (i.e., the animal belongs to a dangerous species) or for animals *mansuetae naturae* (i.e., animals not belonging to a dangerous species) on the condition that the keeper knew of the vicious characteristics of the animal.[93] The US Restatement (Third) on Liability for Physical Harm classifies animals *ferae naturae* as wild animals or animals that are abnormally dangerous and imposes a strict liability on the owner or possessor of such kind of animals.[94] For an animal to be considered wild, it must fulfil two requirements: (1) it must belong to a category of animal that is not generally domesticated and (2) that is likely to cause personal injuries if not restrained.[95] Therefore, the owner of a cheetah will be strictly liable for any physical harm it causes, but the owner of an iguana will not be subjected to the same standard as these animals are not likely to cause injury, even though they are not domesticated.[96]

The rationale behind imposing strict liability on owners and keepers of wild animals is based on the notion that wild animals are inherently dangerous, and that ownership of such animals is an unusual activity enjoyed by few yet poses significant risk to others.[97] Additionally, more often than not, the danger of keeping such animals is known to the owner.[98]

The second category subject to strict liability is that of abnormally dangerous animals. For this category of animal, the owner or possessor is strictly liable if they know or have reason to know that the animal has dangerous tendencies which are abnormal for the animal's category.[99] This type covers domesticated animals (e.g., dogs, cats etc.) and is also commonly referred to as the "first bite rule".[100] The premise behind this rule is that animals which are not considered to be "wild" are generally assumed to be safe and a strict liability regime in these cases would not be just, unless the animal displays an abnormal tendency and the owner has a reason to

[92] This section discusses the liability for animals under common law, primarily US common law. Some common law jurisdictions enacted specific legislation to govern these issues differently or impose certain additional requirements. For example, California imposes a general strict liability for all dog bites. See https://leginfo.legislature.ca.gov/faces/codes_displaySection.xhtml?sectionNum=3342.&lawCode=CIV. Accessed 22 July 2025.

[93] Rogers and Winfield (2010), sect. 16.3.

[94] American Law Institute (2010), p. § 22.

[95] Ibid.

[96] Ibid, p. 294; see also Nichols (2023).

[97] American Law Institute (2010), p. 295.

[98] Ibid, p. 296.

[99] Ibid, § 23.

[100] Nichols (2023), p. 196.

know or knows of this abnormal tendency.[101] Further, such animals generally provide a benefit for society.

It has been suggested in the literature to apply the "first bite rule" to AI. Nichols for example argues that AI fits the same criteria and rational behind the liability for domesticated animals.[102] Such application would allow businesses to properly anticipate legal challenges, help courts to rely on an existing standard and facilitate AI development.[103]

The author submits that the application of the "first bite rule" seems attractive on its face. There seems to be a certain resemblance between AI and animals seeing both can show erratic or unpredictable behaviour while living side-by-side with humankind.[104] It would incentivise innovation while striking a balance of holding developers only strictly liable if they knew or had reason to know that the AI would show behaviour that could cause harm to others. It further would allow us to categorise different AI applications and view them either as "wild" or "domesticated". However, the analogy of animals in an AI context is, in this author's view, problematic.

First, the differentiation between "wild" and "domesticated" is difficult in the context of AI. An AI with a relatively innocent purpose could still be able to cause significant harm. A domesticated animal has gone through a process of domestication and is generally obedient from birth.[105] This is applicable to the whole category of animal. For example, generally all cats, regardless of their specific race, are domesticated. This is not so for AI. While AI can be domesticated in the technological sense of the word, each AI application is different.[106] If equipped with ML and autonomy, the ensuing black-box makes this differentiation extremely challenging, and a court might not to be able to ascertain a classification. As previously mentioned, the rationale behind imposing strict liability for wild animals is that these animals are assumed to be inherently dangerous and pose a significant risk to others. This is not the case for AI. How would we accurately determine that an AI is inherently dangerous and pose a significant risk to others, particularly in light of the rapid technological development of AI?

Second, AI applications are specifically created by humans to fulfil a certain purpose. This does not apply to animals. Animals evolved without human interference to become what they are today. "Their unpredictability stems from the fact

---

[101] American Law Institute (2010), p. 303. For example, if a guide dog, who has performed admirably for many years and never shown any aggression, suddenly bites a pedestrian, then the owner would not be held strictly liable for this "first-bite", unless the owner failed to adhere to safety standards that are commonly required (e.g. to have the dog on a leash or in an harness). However, if the dog would subsequently bite another pedestrian two months later, then the owner would be held strictly liable because in that case the owner knew of the dangerous behaviour of the guide dog.

[102] Nichols (2023), p. 210.

[103] Ibid, pp. 214–215.

[104] Lior (2020), p. 1061.

[105] Ibid, p. 1062.

[106] Ibid, p. 1062.

they are non-human animals with needs and desires separate from our needs and desires of them".[107]

Third, animals are known. Humankind has devoted centuries of exploration to nature. We generally know the typical characteristics of animals, may they be domesticated or wild, and this allows us to properly classify them and assign the appropriate type of liability. This is not the case for AI. Each application is different, the source codes are often not public knowledge and the aforementioned BBP will prevent us from properly classifying them.[108] The addition of ML could enable the AI to develop into something humans did not foresee or anticipate. The developer will not be able to know or have reason to know about any potential harmful side-effects of the AI application. It could be argued that, should the AI cause harm, then the developer at a minimum will know ex-post of the "dangerous tendency" of the specific AI application. However, as illustrated already, the black-box that modern AI creates, makes it impossible for the developer to ascertain what exactly led to the specific outcome. The only known variable is the outcome itself (ex-post). In other words, a developer will not necessarily be in a position to rectify the problem apart from perhaps withdrawing the application from the market entirely. Even in a scenario where the programmer can ascertain the cause of the problem (e.g., in narrow AI applications), and thus make appropriate corrections in the code to avoid a similar problem, an analogy to liability for animals is challenging. If an AI is reprogrammed, can we still consider it the same AI or do we need to treat it as a new AI?[109] Many software engineers would argue that the nature of the AI changes in the reprogramming process. This would mean that the "first bite rule" could be applied again. Further, the application of the "first bite rule" would essentially provide the software developer with a free "get out of jail" pass as long as they adhered to safety and industry standards. In the author's view this would disproportionally affect the end-consumer. As mentioned, even AI that can be considered "domesticated" is capable of causing great harm and it would be difficult to hold the developer accountable when harm first occurs.

Fourth, the liability for animals is generally linked to physical harm (e.g., a dog bite). While embodied AI (i.e., a robot) may be capable of causing physical harm, other AI has no physical form and are not capable of causing physical but can cause types of non-physical harm.[110] An AI-enabled booking engine could create fraudulent bookings.[111] An AI-powered hiring software could discriminate based on sexual

[107] Ibid, p. 1062.

[108] Even two AI applications dealing with the same issue are different and have a different coding structure. For example, the AI used by Uber to answer chat questions will be different from the AI used by Amazon to handle the same type of application.

[109] Nichols (2023), p. 213.

[110] Ibid, p. 212.

[111] Ibid.

orientation.[112] How do we categorise this type of damage? Is it less than, greater than, or equivalent to a dog bite?[113]

In light of the foregoing challenges, we are of the view, that an analogy to the liability for animals is interesting and has merit but there are still too many issues that would arise from such an approach. The regime will, at a minimum, need to be adjusted to reflect the nature of AI adequately. In its current form, comparing AI to animals poses more problems than it provides solutions.

Perhaps another suggestion, which seems to be recurring in literature, namely to make a legal person vicariously liable for the actions of the AI, could be the better solution? It seems therefore warranted to discuss this option briefly.

2.2.3.3 Vicarious Liability

The paradigm underpinning liability is that generally one is responsible only for one's own acts. Vicarious liability can be seen as an exception to this principle.[114]

"Vicarious liability arises where one person is held to be liable for torts committed by a second person, even though without fault himself and herself".[115] In other words, "one person takes the place of another so far as liability is concerned".[116] Therefore, A could be vicariously liable for the damage done to C by the negligence of B. Vicarious liability imposes strict liability on A for the actions done by B. A neither needs to have committed a tort or participated in any way nor is there a duty owed from A to C necessary.[117] The focus of vicarious liability is on the special relationship between A and B. However, vicarious liability does not shield B from liability.[118] Indeed, B can potentially remain liable and in certain circumstances A could claim indemnities from B.

Three elements are generally required, namely (1) tort or civil wrong committed by the agent, (2) a relationship between the principal and the agent and (3) a connection between the relationship and the wrong committed.[119] Most cases nowadays focus on the special relationship between employer and employee (sometimes called a master-servant relationship), but vicarious liability is not limited to this

[112] Ibid.

[113] Ibid. Nichols, although in favour of applying the "first bite rule", admits similar arguments against.

[114] See e.g. Rogers and Winfield (2010), pp. 943–944; Turner (2019), p. 99; McCarthy (2004); Walton et al. (2018), ch. 7.

[115] Walton et al. (2018), p. 465.

[116] Launchbury v Morgans, [1971] EWCA Civ J0120-2, MR.

[117] Cf Rogers and Winfield (2010), p. 944; Howarth et al. (2015), p. 1065ff.

[118] Rogers and Winfield (2010), p. 94; Walton et al. (2018), p. 465.

[119] See e.g. Atiyah (1967), p. 3; Walton et al. (2018), p. 466; Howarth et al. (2015), p. 1065; Rogers and Winfield (2010), p. 944.

category alone.[120] For example, there is the liability of parents for the actions of their child, or, more generally, the liability of the principal for the agent. They may slightly differ in their details, but they are based centrally on the same idea, namely that one is liable for the acts of another.[121]

Vicarious liability has been proposed in the literature to address the challenges arising from AI. On its face, this seems to be an attractive suggestion because it recognises the independence of AI and strikes a balance between acknowledging this independence and holding currently recognised legal persons liable for the actions of an AI.[122] As becomes evident from the previous discussion, negligence and product liability regimes tend to see AI as an object whereas vicarious liability, since it forms part of the broader field of agency law, recognises the AI as an independent agent. Nevertheless, vicarious liability is not an entirely satisfactory solution either.

First, this proposal is only really viable for currently available narrow AI and not for highly advanced autonomous AI. Vicarious liability is tightly linked to the special relationship between the principal and the agent and where the agent deviates too far from that special relationship, vicarious liability fails. If employer A sends his employee B to the bank to withdraw money from the company bank account and B shoots the bank clerk, then A will not be held vicariously liable for the murder of the clerk.[123] The same applies to AI. When AI advances and becomes more autonomous, it could significantly deviate from the ascribed path. This would then in turn lead to a liability gap and we would need to be able to determine when the AI is cut loose from the principal-agent relationship.[124]

Second, and perhaps most importantly, vicarious liability would recognise AI as an agent and thus would need to recognise it, at least to a certain degree, as an independent legal subject. This means that the law would need to recognise the legal capacity of AI. However, as we will discuss in the next section, AI lacks legal capacity and subjectivity.

---

[120] Interestingly this seems to stem from ancient times. Under Roman Law the master was held liable for the actions of their slaves. With the abolishment of slavery and the rise of the industrial age, the master-slave relationship became the master-servant relationship. For a more detailed discussion see Johnston (1995).

[121] Vicarious liability is a very broad and frequently discussed area of law. While it is beyond the scope of the present research to delve deeper into this fascinating area of the law, I encourage the reader to frequent more details sources, such as Atiyah (1967); Gray (2018).

[122] Turner (2019), p. 101.

[123] This relates to the 'close connection' test developed by the Supreme Court of Canada in *Bazley v Curry*, which is nowadays more frequently used. In essence the fundamental question is whether the act was sufficiently related to the conduct authorised by the principal and whether the principal created or enhanced the risk which resulted in the wrongful act.

[124] This is similar to the parent-child relationship. Generally, the more children age, the more they are cut loose from the parent-child relationship. Once the child reaches legal adulthood, they become responsible for their own acts.

2.2.4 AI Lacks Legal Subjectivity

Generally, a system of law—be it national or international, secular or religious—tells subjects what they should and should not do.[125] In order to accomplish this, each system of laws generally determines the subjects to which it is applicable. These legal subjects can be different, depending on the legal system in question. For example, in public international law, States are one of the legal subjects to which the regime of public international law applies.[126]

The system itself needs to confer such legal subjectivity.[127] In national legal systems, we usually find human and non-human legal subjects.[128] This makes it necessary to differentiate legal subjectivity from legal capacity.

All that hold legal capacity are legal subjects, but not all legal subjects hold legal capacity. In very simple terms, the term legal capacity describes what a legal subject can and cannot do within a legal framework: the ability to be the bearer of legal rights and obligations.[129] The pre-requisite to hold legal capacity is that the system of norms recognises one as legal subject. However, a legal subject can have varying degrees of legal capacity. In humans, full legal capacity usually encompasses full

[125] Turner (2019), p. 42.

[126] The Steamship Lotus (Fance v Turkey) (1927), PCIJ (Seri A) No 10, p. 18 ["International law governs relations between independent States"]; See also Kindred et al. (2014), ch. 2. States are only one category of international law subjects and there is substantive literature dedicated to the discussion as to what is a State and what other international law subjects exist. For the purposes of this book we will solely focus on States as those are the subjects that are responsible and liable under international space law. It must further be noted that there are other international law areas, such as international human rights law, where international norms can be applicable to private individuals.

[127] Dartmouth College v Woodward, 17 US 580 (1819), p. 17 ["A corporation is an artificial being, invisible, intangible, and existing only in contemplation of law. Being the mere creature of law, it possesses only those properties which the charter of its creation confers upon it either expressly or as incidental to its very existence."].

[128] A typical example of a non-human legal subject is a corporation.

[129] See Law Commission of Ontario (2017) Legal Capacity, Decision-making and Guardianship: Final Report. Available via https://www.lco-cdo.org/wp-content/uploads/2017/03/CG-Final-Report-EN-online.pdf. Accessed 22 July 2025.

The legal concept of 'capacity' is central to the law related to decision-making, serving as both its rationale and the threshold for its application. Generally, persons who are considered to have legal capacity are entitled to make decisions for themselves and are held responsible for those decisions, including decisions that others may consider reckless or unwise. On the other hand, persons who have been determined to lack legal capacity in a particular domain or for a particular decision may lose the right to make decisions for themselves independently in that area: others will be responsible for making decisions on their behalf, and can in law be held accountable for how those decisions are made (p. 57).

Kindred et al. (2006), p. 13 ["a capacity similar to that of an individual person in domestic law, to enter into legal relations, and to create the consequent rights and duties attached to that capacity. Without this capacity an entity will be unable to maintain any claims."].

age of majority and full mental capacity.[130] Children are a good example of that: the moment they are born, indeed in certain jurisdictions from the moment of conception, they are legal subjects, but they largely lack legal capacity. The older they get and the more their mental capacity develops, the more rights and obligations they can bear.[131]

Another example is a person of full age suffering from a mental illness. Ordinarily, the law will create a protective supervision for a person that is unable to care for themselves. The person remains a legal subject, but their legal capacity may be limited depending on the degree of the person's incapacity.[132]

Now that we have discussed this basic differentiation, let us turn back towards AI.

At the time of writing AI does not possess legal capacity as no legal system has recognised AI as an independent legal subject. As previously pointed out, there are voices in the literature that advocate exactly for that, to recognise AI as a legal subject and thus make our laws, even if they might not be entirely suitable due to the nature of AI, applicable. Indeed, the European Union has started to look into the idea of an "electronic personhood" and is actively discussing the idea of creating such a category of legal subjects and equip them with legal capacity.[133] So far this

---

[130] See e.g. Public Guardian and Trustee of British Columbia (2021) Definitions and Tests of Mental Capacity. Available via https://www.trustee.bc.ca/sites/default/files/2025-02/definitions-tests-mental-capacity.pdf. Accessed 22 July 2025; Arts 153-154 Civil Code of Quebec.

[131] For example, the Civil Code of Austria (Allgemeines Bürgeliches Gesetzbuch – ABGB) in §170 talks about the legal capacity of minors. It states,

[e]in minderjähriges Kind kann ohne ausdrückliche oder stillschweigende Einwilligung seines gesetzlichen Vertreters rechtsgeschäftlich weder verfügen noch sich verpflichten. (2) Nach erreichter Mündigkeit kann es jedoch über Sachen, die ihm zur freien Verfügung überlassen worden sind, und über sein Einkommen aus eigenem Erwerb so weit verfügen und sich verpflichten, als dadurch nicht die Befriedigung seiner Lebensbedürfnisse gefährdet wird. (3) Schließt ein minderjähriges Kind ein Rechtsgeschäft, das von Minderjährigen seines Alters üblicherweise geschlossen wird und eine geringfügige Angelegenheit des täglichen Lebens betrifft, so wird dieses Rechtsgeschäft, auch wenn die Voraussetzungen des Abs. 2 nicht vorliegen, mit der Erfüllung der das Kind treffenden Pflichten rückwirkend rechtswirksam.

[A minor child can neither dispose of nor undertake a legal transaction without the express or tacit consent of his legal representative. (2) After reaching the age of majority, however, he can dispose of things that have been left to him to freely dispose of and his income from his own acquisition and commit himself to the extent that this does not jeopardize the satisfaction of his vital needs. (3) If a minor child enters into a legal transaction which is usually concluded by minors of his age and which concerns a minor matter of everyday life, this legal transaction, even if the requirements of para 2 are not met, is retroactively valid]. This is a very good example how a legal subject can have different legal capacities depending on age and mental capacity.

[132] Articles 256ff of the Quebec Civil Code deal with protective supervision of person with incapacity.

[133] In the European Parliament Resolution on Civil Law on Robotics the EU stated in point 59(f) that "creating a specific legal status for robots in the long run, so that at least the most sophisticated autonomous robots could be established as having the status of electronic persons responsible for making good any damage they may cause, and possibly applying electronic personality to cases where robots make autonomous decisions or otherwise interact with third parties independently". See EU, European Parliament resolution of 16 February 2017 with recommendations to the Commission on Civil Law Rules on Robotics (2015/2103(INL)). It must be borne in mind, how-

has not resulted in any meaningful legislation however and the *lex lata* does not recognise AI as a separate legal subject at the moment. This does not seem too surprising. Other than the fact that legislation is generally re-active rather than pro-active,[134] our currently existing legal systems are built around humans. As Yavar Bathaee accurately puts it,

> [m]any have forcefully called for regulation before [the risks of AI] manifest, but there is a more pressing problem looming on the horizon: the law is built on legal doctrines that are focused on human conduct, which when applied to AI, may not function.[135]

If our laws were built around advanced machines, we would not necessarily be confronted with our current dilemma and ambiguities.

Jacob Turner touches upon this issue from the different angle of agency.[136] He describes agency in its wider philosophical meaning as requiring the knowledge of, and engagement with, relevant legal norms and concludes that it is an interactive process which is at present reserved only to humans.[137] This points towards a wider theoretical and philosophical problematique that the legal community will have to face in due course. For the present research, it will be sufficient to have mentioned it briefly to illustrate that AI will not just challenge solely the application of our current legal principles but also the theoretical framework upon which our understanding is placed.

In conclusion, we can therefore say that, within the *lex lata,* AI lacks legal subjectivity and consequently also possesses no legal capacity. This means that any legal notion that would accept AI as an independent agent or entity would fail.[138]

2.2.5 *Summary and Recapitulation*

Before we make the step into the realm of public international law, it seems beneficial to quickly recapitulate and summarise the main conclusions drawn from the previous discussion. The foregoing discussion served mainly two purposes, (1) to illustrate and provide a general overview of fault-based liability in civil and common law jurisdictions and (2) to highlight the problems that arise. This inquiry was necessary to evaluate whether we can find suitable solutions in domestic law that are

---

ever, that this is just a resolution of the European Parliament and no legislation, apart from draft proposals, have been introduced so far.

[134] As Oliver Wendell Holmes famously claimed, "[t]he life of the law has not been logic: it has been an experience". Holmes (2020), p. 5.

[135] Bathaee (2018), pp. 890–891.

[136] Agency in this sense should not be understood within the concept of principal-agent relationship but rather in a wider philosophical sense. See Turner (2019), p. 42.

[137] Ibid, pp. 43–44.

[138] As illustrated below, this problem does not occur in international space law as States are the legal subjects of this regime and accept direct responsibility.

practised by the majority of States and can be transformed into the international legal arena or seen as general principles of law recognised by nations.[139]

We discussed that fault-based liability will increasingly be challenged the more AI develops and will eventually fail in the case of highly advanced autonomous AI. We explored whether products liability, the liability for animals or vicarious liability could be seen as a viable solution to solve our current dilemma. The preceding section pointed out, that albeit strict liability is an attractive solution to govern liability arising from the use of AI, products liability, liability for animals and vicarious liability are not entirely adequate. The reader of the present research may now rightfully raise the question as to why this author attempts to discuss the beforementioned issues at such length when the present research is concerned with the responsibility of States for their AI-enabled space activities and thus squarely contained within the scope of public international law.

The answer to this question lies in the simple fact that fault plays an important role in space law to assign the liability of the launching State for damage in outer space.

However, fault is neither defined in the Liability Convention and the Outer Space Treaty nor in any of the other space treaties. We therefore need to address the fundamental question as to how fault is established in the Liability Convention and the Outer Space Treaty. To do this we had to look towards the national legal regimes to ascertain how fault is established in common and civil law jurisdictions more generally. This allows us to apply the gained knowledge to the international legal instruments that will be discussed in the next section. Therefore, let us now turn our attention towards the Liability Convention as well as the Outer Space Treaty and the fault standard contained within.

2.3 Fault in the Liability Convention and the Outer Space Treaty for Damage Caused by a Space Object in Outer Space

The Liability Convention is an interesting legal instrument, insofar as it makes a fundamental distinction in public international law between absolute liability and fault-based liability. In essence, the Liability Convention establishes a two-tiered liability regime. "A launching State shall be absolutely liable (…) for damage caused by its space object on the surface of the earth or to aircraft in flight" whereas in "the event that of damage caused elsewhere than on the surface of the earth [the

[139] Statute of the International Court of Justice, 18th April 1946, 33 UNTS 993, UKTS 67 (1946), Art. 38(c).

launching State] shall be liable only if the damage is due to its fault or the fault of persons for whom it is responsible."[140]

The Liability Convention was conceived as dedicated regime to the more general norms of the Outer Space Treaty.[141] Accordingly, the Outer Space Treaty, in Article VII, contains a provision that addresses liability for the launching State. However, contrary to the Liability Convention, the text of the Outer Space Treaty does not mention fault, or establish a two-tiered regime as the Liability Convention does. This has led some authors to suggest that Article VII does not require fault of the launching State to be liable and the liability in the Outer Space Treaty is absolute.[142] This author disagrees with this argument as it does not take the *travaux préparatoires* of the Outer Space Treaty into account. When interpreting the Liability Convention or the Outer Space Treaty, one ought to be aware of the fact that they were negotiated at the same time in the 1960s, albeit the Liability Convention took a bit longer to be concluded. During the negotiation of the Outer Space Treaty the United States of America favoured absolute liability but ultimately had to make concessions as the Soviet Union was not ready to accept such absolute liability.[143] An early draft of what later became Article VII of the Outer Space Treaty, submitted by the Soviet Union proposed that

> (e)ach State Party to the Treaty which launches or organizes the launching of an object into outer space and on to celestial bodies, and each State from whose territory or facility an object is launched, is internationally liable for damage to another State Party to the Treaty or to its natural or juridical persons by such object or its component parts on the earth, in air space, in outer space or on the celestial body.[144]

India, sharing the view of the United States, subsequently proposed an amendment to the Soviet draft and suggested to substitute the word "absolutely" for the word

---

[140] Arts. II-III, Convention on the international liability for damage caused by space objects (29 March 1972) 961 UNTS 187. [Liability Convention].

[141] Ibid, Preamble.

[142] See e.g. Kerrest and Smith (2017); Ziemblicki and Oralova (2021); Albert (2014); Pfeifer (1981).

[143] Christol (1980); United States of America: revised proposal, UNCOPUOS, 1965, UN Doc A/AC.105/C.2/L.8/Rev; LSC, Report of the Legal Sub-Committee on the work of its fifth session (12 July–4 August and 12–16 September 1966) to the Committee on the Peaceful Uses of Outer Space, UNCOPUOS, 1966, UN Doc A/AC.104/3; Malanczuk (1991), pp. 776–778; LSC, Summary Records of the 29th to 37th meetings held at the Palais des Nations, Geneva from 9 to 26 March 1964, UNCOPUOS 1964, Un Doc A/AC.105/C.2/SR.29-37, p. 28 ["Article III, paragraph 1 [of the Principles declaration] stated the fundamental principle that liability should be absolute; that was that an injured party would not have to prove negligence on the part of the launching authorities."]; ibid, p. 86 ["The Hungarian draft also advanced a satisfactory solution to the extra-ordinarily complex theoretical question of the principle underlying liability. (…) In the present case, therefore, it was necessary to rely on experience, logic and common sense. In the Hungarian draft, liability for damage on the ground or in the atmosphere was regarded as absolute, whereas liability for damage in outer space was considered to arise only when the party inflicting the damage was at fault. This was a clear and logical concept and a good basis on which to draft the agreement."].

[144] LSC, Report of the Legal Sub-Committee on the Work of Its Fifth Session (12 July–4 August and 12–16 September 1966) to the Committee on the Peaceful Uses of Outer Space, UNCOPUOS, 1966, UN Doc A/AC.105/35 at 14 [UN Doc A/AC.105/35].

"internationally".[145] This proposal did not find broad support, was expressly criticized by the Australian delegate and was ultimately not adopted in the final draft of the Outer Space Treaty.[146] Additionally, many delegates pointed toward the need to elaborate and clarify the principles laid down in Article VII, in a dedicated legal regime.[147] The rejection of the Indian proposal together with the fact that State parties subsequently expressly included a fault standard in the Liability Convention lends support to the argument that the drafters did not attempt to create a stricter regime in the Outer Space Treaty than in the more specialised Liability Convention.[148] This author therefore submits that we need to "read" the two-tiered fault standard *mutatis mutandis* into the Outer Space Treaty and the liability in Article VII is thus not absolute.[149] This section will proceed to discuss the fault standard contained in the Liability Convention but it should be understood that the same considerations are given to Article VII of the Outer Space Treaty.

Although the Liability Convention sets out fault-based liability for damage in outer space, it neglects to define the term "fault" and how fault ought to be established. This lacuna led to some academic discussion and was subsequently brought into the focus of the academic community again after the Iridium-Cosmos collision

---

145 Ibid, Annex III, Working Paper No 21.

146 LSC, Summary Record of the Seventy-First Meeting, UNCOPUOS, 1966, UN Doc A/AC.105/C.2/SR.71 and Add.1 at 14 ["Work was already in progress on those subjects, however, and for that reason his [Australian] delegation had some doubts regarding the feasability of the Indian proposal (Working Paper No. 21, para.1) that the concept of absolut liability should be embodied in the text. At earlier sessions the Sub-Committee had found that absolute liability was necessarily subject to limitations and qualifications if justice was to be achieved."]; Austria similarly expressed that, where the meaning of liability in the draft of the Outer Space Treaty would differ from the drafts of the Return and Rescue Agreement and the Liability Convention, the draft of the Outer Space Treaty should be amended. See ibid, p. 10 ["Where the present text of the articles on assistance and liability departed from the principles stated in the two draft conventions, it should be amended"].

147 So done for example by Italy, Austria, Belgium, Canada, the Soviet Union, Argentina. See LSC, Summary Records of the 29th to 37th meetings held at the Palais des Nations, Geneva from 9 to 26 March 1964, UNCOPUOS 1964, Un Doc A/AC.105/C.2/SR.29-37.

148 In other words: If we were to accept the argument that the Outer Space Treaty does not require fault, then the liability in the Outer Space Treaty would be strict in all cases, even for damage in outer space, whereas in the Liability Convention only certain damage gives rise to absolute liability.

149 Prof. Smith supports this view. See Smith (2009), pp. 256–257. Interestingly Prof. Bin Cheng contradicts himself and is not clear in this regard. In one part he argues that the liability contained in Article VII is absolute, only to cast doubt on his words later. As mentioned in the main text, we do not agree with the notion that the liability is absolute in Article VII Outer Space Treaty and if Prof. Cheng indeed argued for such a view, then he did not look at both treaties together and failed to reach an, in our view, logical conclusion. It simply would not make sense that the same States that negotiated and concluded the Outer Space Treaty would agree to bind themselves to a stricter regime in the more general treaty than in the more specialised subsequent treaty, especially in the light that a dedicated convention on liability was on the mind of UNCOPUOS almost as long as it existed, even though the Soviet Union was originally against it. Cheng (1997), pp. 291, 326. See also Summary Record of the Fourteenth Meeting, UNCOPUOS, 14th Sess, UN Doc A/AC.105/C.2/SR.14 (1962), p. 3 ["In the case of damage caused by a space vehicle, even under existing law, compensation would undoubtedly be payable."}.

in 2009.[150] Authors correctly point to this problem, but they do not go further to ask the question as to how we should understand fault in international law. The only indication as to how fault can be established could be seen in Article VI of the Liability Convention which allows for exoneration of the launching State if "damage has resulted either wholly or partially from gross negligence or from an act or omission done with intent to cause damage on the part of a claimant State or of natural or juridical persons it represents".[151] Perhaps this can be seen as indication that contracting States saw negligence as an element to establish fault?

A quick survey of the other U.N. space treaties is not enlightening as they neglect to mention fault altogether. We therefore need to expand the inquiry and look towards other instruments in general international law outside of the specialised regime of space law to determine what can be understood under the term fault in international law. To do this, we need look towards what is widely considered the sources of international law stipulated in Article 38 of the Statute of the International Court of Justice (ICJ Statute).[152]

To the best knowledge of the author there exists to date no international agreement or treaty that expressly defines "fault". However, negligence is occasionally mentioned in exoneration clauses of private and public international law treaties.[153]

---

150 Hurwitz (1992), pp. 33–34; Lyall and Larsen (2018), p. 109; Von der Dunk (2009), pp. 202–205; Smith (2009); Mejía-Kaiser (2009).

151 Art. VI, Liability Convention.

152 Article 38 of the ICJ Statute states:

The Court, whose function is to decide in accordance with international law such disputes as are submitted to it, shall apply: international conventions, whether general or particular, establishing rules expressly recognized by the contesting states; international custom, as evidence of a general practice accepted as law; the general principles of law recognized by civilized nations; subject to the provisions of Article 59, judicial decisions and the teachings of the most highly qualified publicists of the various nations, as subsidiary means for the determination of rules of law. See also Kindred et al. (2014), p. 3; Castel (1976), p. 10ff; Oppenheim (1955), p. 23ff; Brownlie (2008), p. 3ff. Prof. Jakhu supports this view and likewise argues that an answer ought to be sought in the realm of general international law. See Jakhu (2010), pp. 255–256.

153 Arts. 20, 22(5), Convention for the Unification of certain Rules relating to Carriage by Air, 12 October 1929, 137 UNTS 11; Arts. 20, 22(5), Convention for the Unification of Certain Rules for International Carriage by Air, 28 May 1999, 2242 UNTS 309 ["If the carrier proves that the damage was caused or contributed to by the negligence or other wrongful act or omission of the person claiming compensation (…)"; "[t]he foregoing provisions of paragraphs 1 and 2 of this Article shall not apply if it is proved that the damage resulted from an act or omission of the carrier, its servants or agents, done with intent to cause damage or recklessly and with knowledge that damage would probably result."]; Art. III (2c) International Convention on Civil Liability for Oil Pollution Damage, 29 November 1969, 973 UNTS 3 ["No liability for pollution damage shall attach to the owner if he proves that the damage: was wholly caused by the negligence or other wrongful act of any Government or other authority responsible for the maintenance of lights or other navigational aids in the exercise of that function."]; Art. VIII (3), General Agreement on Tariffs and Trade, 30 October 1947, 55 UNTS 187. ["In particular, no penalty in respect of any omission or mistake in customs documentation which is easily rectifiable and obviously made without fraudulent intent or gross negligence shall be greater than necessary to serve merely as a warning."]; Art. 29, Agreement on Trade-Related Aspects of Intellectual Property Rights (as amended on 23 January 2017). Available via online https://www.wto.org/english/docs_e/

This seems to be an indication, that contracting parties lean towards the same understanding across different jurisdictions, namely negligence is needed to establish subjective fault of the subject of public international law, when it is required. This view might be further supported by the fact that subjective fault is never concretely defined but rather it seems that there exists a pre-determined understanding of subjective fault and negligence.

Likewise, this applies to various judgement and proceedings of international tribunals that seem to lean towards the understanding that subjective fault in public international law is established via negligence without discussing in detail how it is established.[154] Interestingly, the *Neer* Case references the reasonable person test

legal_e/31bis_trips_01_e.htm. Accessed 22 July 2025 ["For the purpose of this provision, "a manner contrary to honest commercial practices" shall mean at least practices such as breach of contract, breach of confidence and inducement to breach, and includes the acquisition of undisclosed information by third parties who knew, or were grossly negligent in failing to know, that such practices were involved in the acquisition"]; Art 7(3), International Convention on Liability and Compensation for Damage in Connection with the Carriage of Hazardous and Noxious Substances by Sea, 3 May 1996 ["If the owner proves that the damage resulted wholly or partly either from an act or omission done with intent to cause damage by the person who suffered the damage or from the negligence of that person, the owner may be exonerated wholly or partially from liability to such person."]; Art. 1, Convention for the Suppression of Unlawful Acts Against the Safety of Civil Aviation, 23 September 1971, 974 UNTS 177 ["Any person commits an offence if he unlawfully and intentionally (...)"]; Arts. 4, 6(1) Convention on Damage Caused by Foreign Aircraft to Third Parties on the Surface, 7 October 1952, 310 UNTS 181 ["(...) unless he proves that he has exercised due care shall not be liable (...); Any person who would otherwise be liable under the provisions of this Convention shall not be liable for damage if he proves that the damage was caused solely through the negligence or other wrongful act or omission of the person who suffers the damage (...)"]; Art. 1, Convention on the Suppression of Unlawful Acts Relating to International Civil Aviation, 10 September 2010, 337 UNTS ["Any person commits an offence if that person unlawfully and intentionally (...)"]; Art. II, Convention on the Prevention and Punishment of the Crime of Genocide, 9 December 1948, 78 UNTS 277 ["In the present Convention, genocide means any of the following acts committed with intent to destroy, in whole or in part, a national, ethnical, racial or religious group (...)"].

[154] Case Concerning Application of the Convention on the Prevention and Punishment of the Crime of Genocide (Bosnia and Herzegovina v Serbia and Montenegro), [2007] ICJ Rep 43, para. 186 ["Killing" must be intentional, as must "causing serious bodily or mental harm". Mental elements are made explicit in paragraphs (c) and (d) of Article II by the words "deliberately" and "intended", quite apart from the implications of the words "inflicting" and "imposing"; and forcible transfer too requires deliberate intentional acts. The acts, in the words of the ILC, are by their very nature conscious, intentional or volitional acts (...)"]; Prosecutor v Vidoje Blagojevi, IT-02-60-T, Judgement (17 January 2005) at para 656 (International Criminal Tribunal for the former Yugoslavia, Trial Chamber) ["The Appeals Chamber has held that "the specific intent requires that the perpetrator seeks to achieve the destruction, in whole or in part, of a national, ethnical, racial or religious group, as such," although it found that the existence of a plan or policy is not a legal requirement of the crime. It is not sufficient that the perpetrator simply knew that the underlying crime would inevitably or likely result in the destruction of the group. The destruction, in whole or in part, must be the aim of the underlying crime(s)"]; Prosecutor v Ratko Mladić, IT-09-92-T, Judgement (22 November 2017) (International Criminal Tribunal for the former Yugoslavia), para. 3558; Corfu Channel Case (United Kingdom v Albania) [1949] ICJ Rep 4, p. 22. The *Corfu Channel Case* frequently touches upon the element of knowledge culminating in the often-cited sentence 'and every State's obligation not to allow knowingly its terriotry to be used for acts con-

directly providing further evidence that negligence is seen as a way to establish fault.[155]

Finally, the element of fault has also been discussed in academic writings and commentaries. One example is the academic discussion whether subjective fault of the State is necessary to give rise to its responsibility.[156] The traditional view, which originated from the writings of Hugo Grotius and is now widely rejected, saw subjective fault of the State as a necessary element of State responsibility.[157] Also, more generally, when authors in international law refer to the element of fault, they do so by referring to, *inter alia*, negligence.[158] All seems to point towards the same.

It seems therefore appropriate to conclude that to establish fault in the Liability Convention and Outer Space Treaty, indeed in public international law more generally when specific norms require subjective fault, negligence of the injuring State is needed. This is not surprising if we consider how treaties come into being and how judgements are handed down. Treaties are negotiated by States via delegations and these delegations consist of people, occasionally even lawyers or delegates with a legal education, and they all enter negotiations with a pre-conceived understanding of fault, ordinarily the same way their respective legal system understands the term fault. This applies equally to arbitrators and justices who all come from various legal backgrounds and base their judgements on their own legal understanding and reasoning. Therefore, it might not even occur to them to actually define what they understand under the term fault.[159]

---

trary to the rights of other States'. Home Frontier and Foreign Missionary Society of the United Brethren in Christ (United States) v Great Britain (1920), 6 RIAA 42, p. 43 ["the British Government wholly failed to take proper steps for the maintenance of order and the protection of life and property; that the loss of life and damage to property was the result of this neglect and failure of duty, and therefore that it is liable to pay compensation."].

155 L. F. H. Neer and Pauline Neer (U.S.A.) v. United Mexican States (1926), 4 RIAA 60 at 61–62 [Neer Case]. The claims commission states that

> [w]ithout attempting to announce a precise formula, it is in the opinion of the Commission possible to go a little further than the authors quoted, and to hold (first) that the propriecy of governmental acts should be put to the test of international standards, and (second) that the treatment of an alien, in order to constitute an international delinquency, should amount to an outrage, to bad faith, to wilful neglect of duty, or to an insufficiency of governmental action so far short of international standards that every reasonable and impartial man would readily recognize its insufficiency.

156 It must be noted, however, that a State itself cannot possess a mental element and therefore subjective fault attaches to the organ or public official.

157 See e.g. Grotius (2005), p. 1187; Oppenheim (1955), p. 343. Oppenheim and Lauterpracht state that "[a]n act of a State injurious to another State is nevertheless not an international delinquency if committed neither willfully and maliciously [i.e., intentionally] nor with culpable negligence."].

158 Cassese (2001), p. 191; Castel (1976), p. 1091; Abass (2012), pp. 266–267; O'Connell (1965), pp. 1020–1023; Shaw (2008), p. 783; Stern (2010), p. 210; Brownlie (2008), pp. 437–441; Kindred et al. (2014), p. 381; Brownlie (1983), p. 40ff; Kiss and Shelton (2007), p. 1131ff.

159 There is no point in pointing out the obvious and usually what is obvious to one, one hardly every defines or talks in detail about.

Even if we were to reject the arguments brought forward thus far, there is yet another argument that clearly supports this view: The general principles of law recognised by nations. The ICJ Statute lists the general principle of law recognised by nations as one of the primary sources of international law.[160] As should be evident by now, domestic law, regardless of whether it is of common or civil law nature, always differentiates between liability *ex-delicto* and liability *ex-contractu*. While negligence might have different thresholds to be established or excluded depending on different circumstances, it all rests upon the same principle: Fault requires a mental element of either *dolus* or *culpa*.

This is a principle taught in every law school, inherent to any legal system and familiar to anyone with a legal background. It is the backbone of our legal systems and a cornerstone of any liability, may it be criminal or private. It is enshrined in our respective domestic legal orders. It can therefore be seen as a principle of law recognised by nations and can thus be viewed as source of international law.

Turning back to the Liability Convention and the Outer Space Treaty, the author therefore submits that 'fault' in both treaties requires at a minimum negligence on the part of the launching State.[161]

2.4 Conclusion

Building on the observations of Chap. 1, the aim of this chapter was to further narrow down the scope and continue to lay the legal foundation for the subsequent chapters. The chapter, at length, discussed the element of fault and built a bridge between the domestic understanding of fault, and what fault means in public international law, and thereby what it means in the Liability Convention and the Outer Space Treaty.

We looked at negligence in greater detail, highlighted the problems and concluded that the further AI advances, the more it will challenge our understanding of negligence until a point where foreseeability and reasonableness will fail, and negligence cannot be established anymore.

While strict liability regimes might alleviate the problems arising from our dilemma, it is not a one-stop solution either. Especially, vicarious liability and products liability in their current form are not entirely suitable to govern AI.

---

[160] Art. 38(c), Statute of the International Court of Justice, 18th April 1946, 33 UNTS 993, UKTS 67 (1946).

[161] As already mentioned, intent is another element that can establish fault. However, since this research focuses on the negligence aspect, the author decided to not mention intent in the main text. This should not be misunderstood as to mean that only negligence can establish fault. Negligence is only one of the mental elements needed. In this regard it can be seen as the minimum threshold that has to be met for a defendant to be at fault. Intent is generally harder to prove than negligence and requires more than just unreasonable behaviour.

Additionally, AI lacks legal capacity entirely which makes it increasingly hard to integrate it into our currently available legal systems.

To conclude, let us therefore recapitulate the observations made:

(1) The more AI advances, the more it will challenge our understanding of fault. The reasonable person test will fail, negligence cannot be established anymore, and no fault-based liability will be available.
(2) Strict liability seems on its face a viable solution. However, product liability, in its current form, is not entirely applicable to AI. While it could work for a robot, it will not work for AI software. While vicarious liability might be a workable solution for currently available narrow AI, it will fail once AI advances more. Further, the liability for animals also does not provide a satisfying solution.
(3) AI lacks legal capacity, and thus legal subjectivity, which makes it difficult to recognise it as a separate entity.
(4) Fault in public international law requires negligence on the part of the international legal subject (i.e., the State) and thus rests on the same understanding as domestic law.

With these observations in mind, let us now move on towards the norms of public international law and address the challenges that AI causes, and will cause, in the space law legal regime for determining liability.

Websites and Online Sources

AI risks leading humanity to 'extinction,' experts warn. In: NBC News. https://www.nbcnews.com/tech/tech-news/ai-risks-leading-humanity-extinction-experts-warn-rcna86791. Accessed 17 July 2025.

Barta U-PDH (2007) ziviltecht.online. https://web.archive.org/web/20230311134322/https://www.uibk.ac.at/zivilrecht/buch/kap9_0.xml?section-view=true;section=2. Accessed 21 July 2024.

Cellan-Jones R (2014) Stephen Hawking warns artificial intelligence could end mankind. https://www.bbc.com/news/technology-30290540. Accessed 22 July 2025.

Collier K (2023) Artificial intelligence may lead humanity to 'extinction,' experts warn. https://www.nbcnews.com/tech/tech-news/ai-risks-leading-humanity-extinction-experts-warn-rcna86791. Accessed 22 July 2025.

https://leginfo.legislature.ca.gov/faces/codes_displaySection.xhtml?sectionNum=3342.&lawCode=CIV. Accessed 22 July 2025.

Law Commission of Ontario (2017) Legal Capacity, Decision-making and Guardianship: Final Report. Available via https://www.lco-cdo.org/wp-content/uploads/2017/03/CG-Final-Report-EN-online.pdf. Accessed 22 July 2025

Negligence. https://www.merriam-webster.com/dictionary/negligence. Accessed 21 July 2025.

Negligence.https://www.oxfordlearnersdictionaries.com/definition/american_english/negligence. Accessed 21 July 2025.
Public Guardian and Trustee of British Columbia (2021) Definitions and Tests of Mental Capacity. Available via https://www.trustee.bc.ca/sites/default/files/2025-02/definitions-tests-mental-capacity.pdf. Accessed 22 July 2025.
Rankin W (2011) MEDA Investigation Process. Available via http://www.boeing.com/commercial/aeromagazine/articles/qtr_2_07/AERO_Q207_article3.pdf. Accessed 21 July 2025.
Statement on AI Risk | CAIS. In: Center for AI Safety. https://www.safe.ai/statement on ai-risk. Accessed 17 July 2025
tort. In: LII / Legal Information Institute. https://www.law.cornell.edu/wex/tort. Accessed 17 July 2025.
Travis G (2019) How the Boeing 737 Max Disaster Looks to a Software Developer - IEEE Spectrum. https://spectrum.ieee.org/how-the-boeing-737-max-disaster-looks-to-a-software-developer. Accessed 21 July 2025.
Winingham WK (2018) Human Error in Aviation Accidents | Wilson Kehoe Winingham. https://www.wkw.com/aviation-accidents/blog/aviation-accidents-human-error/. Accessed 21 July 2025.
Zhang L (2023) A Comprehensive Study - Human Ridehail Crash Rate Benchmark | Cruise. https://web.archive.org/web/20240616184516/https://www.getcruise.com/news/blog/2023/human-ridehail-crash-rate-benchmark/?ref=warpnews.org. Accessed 21 July 2025.

UN Documents

LSC, Report of the Legal Sub-Committee on the work of its fifth session (12 July - 4 August and 12-16 September 1966) to the Committee on the Peaceful Uses of Outer Space, UNCOPUOS, 1966, UN Doc A/AC.104/3.
LSC, Report of the Legal Sub-Committee on the Work of Its Fifth Session (12 July - 4 August and 12 - 16 September 1966) to the Committee on the Peaceful Uses of Outer Space, UNCOPUOS, 1966, UN Doc A/AC.105/35.
LSC, Summary Record of the Seventy-First Meeting, UNCOPUOS, 1966, UN Doc A/AC.105/C.2/SR.71 and Add.1.
LSC, Summary Records of the 29th to 37th meetings held at the Palais des Nations, Geneva from 9 to 26 March 1964, UNCOPUOS 1964, Un Doc A/AC.105/C.2/SR.29-37.
Summary Record of the Fourteenth Meeting, UNCOPUOS, 14th Sess, UN Doc A/AC.105/C.2/SR.14 (1962).
United States of America: revised proposal, UNCOPUOS, 1965, UN Doc A/AC.105/C.2/L.8/Rev.

Judicature

A.C. Billings and Sons Limited v Riden, [1957] UKHL 1 (BAILII).
Blyth v The Company of Proprietors of The Birmingham Waterworks [1856] EWHC Exch J65 (BAILII).
Brewer v. Saunders, 1986 CanLII 4009 (NS SC).
Carmarthenshire County Council v Lewis [1955] UKHL 2 (BAILII).
Case Concerning Application of the Convention on the Prevention and Punishment of the Crime of Genocide (Bosnia and Herzegovina v Serbia and Montenegro), [2007] ICJ Rep 43.
Corfu Channel Case (United Kingdom v Albania) [1949] ICJ Rep 4.
Dartmouth College v Woodward, 17 US 580 (1819).
Donoghue v Stevenson [1932] UKHL 100 (BAILII).
Escola v Coca Cola Bottling Co. (1944) 24 C (2d) 453 (Cal Sup Ct).
Hanson v City of Saint John, 1973 CanLII 145 (SCC).
Hawkins v Coulsdon and Purley Urban District Council, [1953] EWCA Civ J1217-1.
L. F. H. Neer and Pauline Neer (U.S.A.) v. United Mexican States (1926), 4 RIAA 60.
Lapierre v A.G. (Que.), [1985] 1 SCR 241.
Launchbury v Morgans, [1971] EWCA Civ J0120-2, MR.
Lupu v. Rabinovitch, 1975 CanLII 979 (MB KB).
McLoughlin v O'Brian, [1982] UKHL 3 (BAILII).
Muir v Glasgow Corporation, [1943] UKHL 2 (BAILII).
New Zealand and France concerning the interpretation or application of two agreements, concluded on 9 July 1986 between the two States and which related to the problems arising from the Rainbow Warrior Affair (1990), RIAA 215.
Oberster Gerichtshof (Supreme Court), Vienna, 22 June 2011, OGH GZ 2 Ob 112/10z.
Overseas Tankship (UK) Ltd v Morts Dock and Engineering Co Ltd [1961] UKPC 2 (BAILII).
Patoma v Clarke, 2009 BCSC 1069.
Peixeiro v Haberman, [1997] 3 SCR 549.
Phillips et al. v. Ford Motor Co. of Canada Ltd. et al., 1971 CanLII 389 (ON CA).
Prosecutor v Ratko Mladić, IT-09-92-T, Judgement (22 November 2017) (International Criminal Tribunal for the former Yugoslavia).
Prosecutor v Vidoje Blagojevi, IT-02-60-T, Judgement (17 January 2005) (International Criminal Tribunal for the former Yugoslavia, Trial Chamber).
R v Sault Ste Marie, [1978] 2 SCR 1299, 1978 CANLII 11.
Rankin (Rankin's Garage & Sales) v. J.J., 2018 SCC 19.
Roe v Minister of Health, [1954] EWCA Civ 7 (BAILII).
Rylands v Fletcher [1868] UKHL 1 (BAILII).
St. Lawrence Cement Inc v Barrette, 2008 SCC 64.
The Steamship Lotus (Fance v Turkey) (1927), PCIJ (Seri A) No 10.

Thomas v Quartermaine (1887) 18 QBD 685 at 694.
Thompson v Nason Hospital, 591, A (2d) 703 (1991) (Pa Sup Ct).
United States v Dotterweich, 1943 US LEXIS 1100.
Witman v. Johnson, 1990 CanLII 7975 (MB KB).

Legislation and International Treaties

Agreement on Trade-Related Aspects of Intellectual Property Rights (as amended on 23 January 2017). Available via online https://www.wto.org/english/docs_e/legal_e/31bis_trips_01_e.htm. Accessed 22 July 2025.
Allgemeines Bürgerliches Gesetzbuch (ABGB, Austrian Civil Code).
Bürgerliches Gesetzbuch (BGB, German Civil Code).
Civil Code of Quebec.
Consumer Protection Act 1987 (UK), c 43.
Convention for the Suppression of Unlawful Acts Against the Safety of Civil Aviation, 23 September 1971, 974 UNTS 177.
Convention for the Unification of Certain Rules for International Carriage by Air, 28 May 1999, 2242 UNTS 309.
Convention for the Unification of certain Rules relating to Carriage by Air, 12 October 1929, 137 UNTS 11.
Convention on Damage Caused by Foreign Aircraft to Third Parties on the Surface, 7 October 1952, 310 UNTS 181.
Convention on the international liability for damage caused by space objects (29 March 1972) 961 UNTS 187.
Convention on the Prevention and Punishment of the Crime of Genocide, 9 December 1948, 78 UNTS 277.
Convention on the Suppression of Unlawful Acts Relating to International Civil Aviation, 10 September 2010, 337 UNTS.
EC, Council Directive 85/374/EEC of 25 July 1985 on the approximation of the laws, regulations and administrative provisions of the Member States concerning liability for defective products, [1985] OJ, L 210/29.
EC, Council Directive 85/374/EEC of 25 July 1985 on the approximation of the laws, regulations and administrative provisions of the Member States concerning liability for defective products, [1985] OJ, L 210/29.
EU, Directive (EU) 2024/2853 of the European Parliament and the Council of 23 October 2024 on liability for defective products and repealing Council Directive 85/374/EEC, [2024] OJ, L 2024/2853.
General Agreement on Tariffs and Trade, 30 October 1947, 55 UNTS 187/
International Convention on Civil Liability for Oil Pollution Damage, 29 November 1969, 973 UNTS 3.
International Convention on Liability and Compensation for Damage in Connection with the Carriage of Hazardous and Noxious Substances by Sea, 3 May 1996.
Statute of the International Court of Justice, 18th April 1946, 33 UNTS 993, UKTS 67 (1946).

Other

EC, Commission, Report from the Commission on the Application of Directive 85/374 on Liability for Defective Products, [2001] COMM (2000) 893 final.
EU, Commission, Proposal for a Directive of the European Parliament and of the Council on liability for defective products, [2022] COM(2022) 495 final.
EU, European Parliament resolution of 16 February 2017 with recommendations to the Commission on Civil Law Rules on Robotics (2015/2103(INL)).
Gaius Institutiones 3.88.
Gaius Institutiones 3.211.

References

Literature

Abass A (2012) International law: text, cases, and materials. Oxford University Press, New York
Abbott R (2018) The reasonable computer: disrupting the paradigm of tort liability. Geo Wash Law Rev 86
Abbott R (2020) The reasonable robot: artificial intelligence and the law, 1st edn. Cambridge University Press, New York
Albert C (2014) Liability in international law and the ramifications on commercial space launches and space tourism. Loy LA Int Comp Law J 36:30
Allain JS (2013) From Jeopardy! to Jaundice: the medical liability implications of Dr. Watson and other artificial intelligence systems. LA Law Rev 73:1049
American Law Institute (ed) (1998) Restatement of the law third, torts: products liability. American Law Institute Publishers, St. Paul
American Law Institute (ed) (2010) Restatement of the law third, torts: liability for physical and emotional harm. American Law Institute Publishers, St. Paul
Atiyah PS (1967) Vicarious liability in the law of torts. Butterworths, London
Aust A (2010) Handbook of international law, 2nd edn. Cambridge University Press, Cambridge
Barboza J (2011) The environment, risk and liability in international law. Martinus Nijhoff Publishers, Leiden
Bathaee Y (2018) The artificial intelligence black box and the failure of intent and causation. Harv J Law Tech 31:890
Bostrom N (2014) Superintelligence: paths, dangers, strategies, 1st edn. Oxford University Press, Oxford
Brownlie I (1983) State responsibility. Oxford University Press, New York
Brownlie I (2008) Principles of public international law, 7th edn. Oxford University Press, Oxford
Buckley RA (2011) The law of negligence and nuisance, 5th edn. LexisNexis, London
Cassels J, Jones CE (2005) The law of large-scale claims: product liability, mass torts, and complex litigation in Canada. Irwin Law, Toronto
Cassese A (2001) International law. Oxford University Press, Oxford
Castel JG (1976) International law, chiefly as interpreted and applied in Canada, 3d edn. Butterworths, Toronto
Čerka P, Grigienė J, Sirbikytė G (2015) Liability for damages caused by artificial intelligence. Comput Law Secur Rev 31:376–389. https://doi.org/10.1016/j.clsr.2015.03.008

Chatzipanagiotis MP (2020) Whose fault is it? Artificial intelligence and liability in international space law. In: Blount PJ et al (eds) Proceedings of the International Institute of Space Law 2020. Eleven International Publishing, The Hague
Cheng B (1997) Studies in international space law. Oxford University Press
Christol CQ (1980) International liability for damage caused by space objects. Am J Int Law 74:346–371. https://doi.org/10.2307/2201505
Crepeau PA (1962) Liability for damage caused by things: from the civil law point of view. Can Bar Rev XL:222
Dunlop B (1962) Liability for damage caused by things: from the common law point of view. Can Bar Rev XL:240
Giuffrida I (2019) Liability for AI decision-making: some legal and ethical considerations. Fordham Law Rev 88:439
Gray A (2018) Vicarious liability: critique and reform. Hart Publishing, Oxford, UK; Portland, Oregon
Gray A (2021) The evolution from strict liability to fault in the law of torts. Hart Publishing, Oxford
Green S (2015) Causation in negligence. Hart Publishing, Oxford
Grotius H (2005) The rights of war and peace. Liberty Fund, Indianapolis
Heiss S (2021) Towards optimal liability for artificial intelligence lessons from the European Union's Proposals of 2020
Holmes OW (2020) The common law, 1st edn. Routledge, New York
Howarth D (1995) Textbook on tort. Butterworths, London
Howarth D, Matthews MH, Morgan J et al (2015) Hepple and Matthews' tort law: cases and materials, 7th edn. Oxford University Press, Oxford
Hurwitz BA (1992) State liability for outer space activities: in accordance with the 1972 Convention on International Liability for Damage Caused by Space Objects. Martinus Nijhoff Publishers, Dordrecht
Jakhu RS (2010) Iridium-Cosmos collision and its implications for space operations. In: Schrogl K-U, Rathgeber W, Baranes B, Venet C (eds) Yearbook on Space Policy 2008/2009. Springer, Vienna
Johnston D (1995) Limiting liability: Roman law and the civil law tradition. Chic-Kent Law Rev 70:1515
Kerrest A, Smith LJ (2017) Article VII. In: Hobe S, Schmidt-Tedd B, Schrogl K-U (eds) Cologne Commentary on Space Law. 1: Outer Space Treaty
Kindred HM, Saunders PM, Brunnée J (eds) (2006) International law, chiefly as interpreted and applied in Canada, 7th edn. Emond Montgomery Publications, Toronto
Kindred HM, Saunders PM, Currie RJ (eds) (2014) International law: chiefly as interpreted and applied in Canada, 8th edn. Emond Montgomery Publ, Toronto
Kiss A, Shelton D (2007) Strict liability in international environmental law. In: Mensah TA, Ndiaye TM, Wolfrum R, Kojima C (eds) Law of the sea, environmental law, and settlement of disputes: Liber Amicorum Judge Thomas A. Mensah. Martinus Nijhoff, Leiden
LeValley D (2013) Autonomous vehicle liability—application of common carrier liability. Seattle Univ School Law Digital Commons 36:5
Lior A (2020) AI entities as AI agents: artificial intelligence liability and the AI Respondeat Superior Analogy. Mitchell Hamline Law Rev 46:1043
Lohmann MF (2016) Liability issues concerning self-driving vehicles. Eur J Risk Regul 2:335
Lyall F, Larsen PB (2018) Space law: a treatise, 2nd edn. Routledge, New York
Malanczuk P (1991) Haftung. In: Böckstiegel K-H, Benkö M (eds) Handbuch des Weltraumrechts. Heymann, Köln
McCarthy L (2004) Vicarious liability in the agency context. QUT Law Rev 4. https://doi.org/10.5204/qutlr.v4i2.204
Mejía-Kaiser M (2009) Collision Course: 2009 Iridium-Cosmos Crash. In: Jorgenson C (ed) Proceedings of the International Institute of Space Law 2009. American Institute of Aeronautics and Astronautics, Washington D.C.

Nichols H (2023) The first byte rule: a proposal for liability of artificial intelligences. Wm Mary Law Rev 14:189
O'Connell DP (1965) International law. Oceana Publications, New York
Oppenheim L (1955) International law, 8th edn. Longmans, London
Pasquale F (2019) Data-informed duties in AI development. Colum Law Rev 119:1917
Pfeifer J (1981) International liability for damage caused by space objects. German J Air Space Law 30:44
Powell D (2020) Autonomous systems as legal agents: directly by the recognition of personhood or indirectly by the alchemy of algorithmic entities. Duke Law Tech Rev 18:306
Riedler A (2015) Schuldrecht BT - Gesetzliche Schuldverhältnisse, 4th edn. Johannes Kepler Universität Linz Multimediale Studienmaterialien GmbH, Linz
Rogers WVH, Winfield PH (2010) Winfield and Jolowicz on tort, 18th edn. Sweet & Maxwell, London
Shaw MN (2008) International law, 6th edn. Cambridge University Press
Smith LJ (2009) Facing up to third party liability for space activities: some reflections. In: Jorgenson C (ed) Proceedings of the International Institute of Space Law 2009. American Institute of Aeronautics and Astronautics, Washington D.C.
Stanton KM (1994) The modern law of tort. Sweet & Maxwell, London/
Stapleton J (1994) Product liability. Butterworths, London/
Stern B (2010) The elements of an internationally wrongful act. In: Crawford J, Pellet A, Olleson S, Parlett K (eds) The law of international responsibility. Oxford University Press, New York
Turner J (2019) Robot rules: regulating artificial intelligence, 1st edn. Springer International Publishing, Cham
Verhoeven J (2010) The law of responsibility and the law of treaties. In: Crawford J, Pellet A, Olleson S, Parlett K (eds) The law of international responsibility. Oxford University Press, New York
Vladeck DC (2014) Machines without principals: liability rules and artificial intelligence. Wash Law Rev 89
Von der Dunk F (2009) Too-close encounters of the third-party kind: will the liability convention stand the Test of the Cosmos 2251-Iridium 33 Collision? In: Jorgenson C (ed) Proceedings of the International Institute of Space Law 2009. American Institute of Aeronautics and Astronautics, Washington D.C.
Wagner G (2018) Robot liability. In: Münster Colloquium on EU law and digital economy, liability for robotics and the internet of things
Walton CT, Armitage M, Cooper R et al (eds) (2018) Charlesworth & Percy on negligence, 14th edn. Sweet & Maxwell, London
Ziemblicki B, Oralova Y (2021) Private entities in outer space activities: liability regime reconsidered. Space Policy 56:101427. https://doi.org/10.1016/j.spacepol.2021.101427

Chapter 3
The Liability of the Launching State Under the Outer Space Treaty and the Liability Convention

3.1 Introduction

The previous two chapters laid the groundwork for our subsequent academic discourse. Building on this, this chapter will look at the liability of the launching State under the Outer Space Treaty and the Liability Convention in more detail. This chapter will first provide the reader with a comprehensive overview of the liability regime that governs space law before critically examining whether Article VII of the Outer Space Treaty and the Liability Convention are adequate to govern advanced and emerging AI. It will conclude by arguing that Article VII of the Outer Space Treaty and the Liability Convention are not entirely suitable to address liability issues arising from the use of AI in all cases and highlight the problems that this can cause.

3.2 Liability of the Launching State Under Article VII of the Outer Space Treaty

The liability of the launching State is not only addressed in the Liability Convention but also in the Outer Space Treaty. Article VII of the Outer Space Treaty provides that,

> [e]ach State Party to the Treaty that launches or procures the launching of an object into outer space, including the Moon and other celestial bodies, and each State Party from whose territory or facility an object is launched, is internationally liable for damage to another State Party to the Treaty or to its natural or juridical persons by such object or its

S.-M. Wedenig, *The International Responsibility of States for AI-enabled Space Activities*, Space Regulations Library 13,
https://doi.org/10.1007/978-3-032-09506-0_3

> component parts on the Earth, in air space or in outer space, including the Moon and other celestial bodies.[1]

By doing so the Outer Space Treaty accomplishes two things, namely (1) it separates the liability from the responsibility aspect and (2) it links international liability for damage caused by a space object to the launching State. The separation of responsibility and liability is particularly interesting as it is a frequently debated issue in the realm of general international law, something this book will address in more detail in Chap. 4.

Article VII was subsequently expanded upon in a dedicated treaty, the Liability Convention.[2] This research will therefore discuss the issues pertaining to the liability of the launching State under the Liability Convention in the next section with the understanding that the same considerations are applicable in most part also to Article VII of the Outer Space Treaty. As highlighted in Sect. 2.3 above, although Article VII of the Outer Space Treaty does not mention fault or any fault standard, we nevertheless need to read the two-tiered liability regime of the Liability Convention into the Outer Space Treaty. Therefore, any and all problems relating to the fault standard in the Liability Convention discussed below, are equally applicable to Article VII of the Outer Space Treaty. At this point, we need to address a few differences in the liability provisions of the Outer Space Treaty and the Liability Convention.

First, the Liability Convention speaks of damage caused by a "space object on the surface of the earth or to an aircraft in flight" while the Outer Space Treaty avoids such a formulation and only speaks of damage to another State Party on the Earth or in airspace. This would mean that the Outer Space Treaty would cover damages to things, which are not considered aircraft, in the airspace of a State. However, at present, it is hard to imagine anything traversing the airspace of a State that does not fall under the definition of aircraft as set out in Annex 7 to the Chicago Convention.[3] Aircraft means "any machine that can derive support from the reactions of the air other than the reaction of the air against Earth's surface".[4] This definition covers all currently used devices in airspace, such as conventional aircraft, helicopters, UAVs and balloons. It would further also extend, for example, to high-altitude platform stations.

Second, the Outer Space Treaty speaks of damage caused by a space object "to another State Party to the Treaty or to its natural or juridical persons" on Earth, in

[1] Art. VII, Treaty on Principles Governing the Activities of States in the Exploration and Use of Outer Space, including the Moon and Other Celestial Bodies, 27 January 1967, 610 UNTS 205 [Outer Space Treaty].

[2] Indeed, during the negotiation of the Outer Space Treaty, the delegations frequently pointed towards the need of a dedicated treaty expanding on Article VII and address liability claims. So argued for example by Italy, Austria, Belgium, Canada, the Soviet Union. Argentina. LSC, Summary Records of the 29th to 37th meetings hela at the Palais des Nations, Geneva from 9 to 26 March 1964, UNCOPUOS 1964, Un Doc A/AC.105/C.2/SR.29-37, pp. 31, 35, 36, 38, 42, 44.

[3] Convention on International Civil Aviation, 7 December 1944, 15 UNTS 295.

[4] Ibid, Annex 7, art 1.

airspace or in outer space, including the Moon and other celestial bodies. The Liability Convention in contrast speaks of damage to "a space object of one launching State or to persons or property on board such a space object". This formulation makes the Outer Space Treaty broader, and Article VII would also cover damage caused to persons and property not onboard of a space object, such as astronauts on a spacewalk or persons and property traversing the surface of a celestial body.

Third, there is a slight but important difference as to whom compensation is owed. International organisations can declare their acceptance of the Liability Convention. Thus, while Article VII of the Outer Space Treaty only applies to damage to another State party or its natural or juridical persons, the Liability Convention also includes damage to property of an international organisation.[5]

3.3 The Liability of the Launching State Under the Liability Convention

The Liability Convention was concluded in 1972 as a result of the work undertaken by the United Nations Committee on the Peaceful Uses of Outer Space (UNCOPUOS). It elaborated and built upon Article VII of the Outer Space Treaty and established a framework for liability claims arising from damage caused by a space object that ensures full and equitable compensation and has been widely regarded as a victim-oriented convention.[6] On its face, the Liability Convention seems to be straightforward: it makes the launching State liable for damage caused by a space object. However, as is the case with many instruments of international law, the wording is far from unambiguous and has caused a large academic debate, even though the Liability Convention was conceived as an attempt to elaborate and clarify Article VII of the Outer Space Treaty.[7]

[5] Arts. I (a), XXII Convention on the International Liability for Damage caused by Space Objects, 29 March 1972, 961 UNTS 18 [Liability Convention]. Article XXII further states that

> [i]n this Convention, with the exception of articles XXIV to XXVII, references to States shall be deemed to apply to any international intergovernmental organization which conducts space activities the organization declares its acceptance of the rights and obligations provided for in this Convention and if a majority of the States members of the organization are States Parties to this Convention and to the [Outer Space Treaty].

[6] Hurwitz (1992), p. 9; Matte (1984), p. 305; Kayser (2001), p. 35. States also regarded the Liability Convention as 'victim oriented'. See e.g. Canada in LSC, Summary Record of the 117th Meeting held on Tuesday, 17 June 1969, at 11 a.m., UNCOPUOS 1969, Un Doc A/AC.105/C.2/SR.117, p. 70; USA, Czechoslovakia and Austria in LSC, Summary Record of the 121st Meeting held on Friday, 20 June 1969, at 10.50 a.m., UNCOPUOS 1969, Un Doc A/AC.105/C.2/SR.121, pp. 103, 104, 106; Bulgaria in LSC, Summary Record of the 122nd Meeting held on Tuesday, 24 June 1969, at 11:00 a.m., UNCOPUOS 1969, Un Doc A/AC.105/C.2/SR.122, p. 113.

[7] As mentioned in footnote 2, the need for a specialised legal regime for liability claims had been discussed by delegates already during the negotiation of the Outer Space Treaty.

Therefore, it seems appropriate to briefly review the academic debate relating to certain provisions of the Liability Convention, and by extension the Outer Space Treaty, and determine how AI factors into this debate.

3.3.1 *Some Preliminary Considerations*

3.3.1.1 Launching State

The first ambiguity relates to the notion of what State exactly is the "launching State" and the interpretational problems are vast. The Liability Convention itself adopts the wording of the Outer Space Treaty and defines launching State as the "State which launches or procures the launching of a space object" and "from whose territory or facility a space object is launched".[8] As mentioned, many authors point out that the definition of "launching State" leaves room for interpretation and there could be more than one launching State at any given time, a problem which is significant in the context of the multinational space industry of the 21st Century.[9] Contrary to the responsible State in Article VI of the Outer Space Treaty, which can change depending on the circumstances, the launching State does not, and ownership of the space object is irrelevant for the classification as launching State. In other words, once a launching State always a launching State, and thus always liable.[10] This can lead to significant challenges, especially in the case of an in-orbit transfer of ownership of a space object, as there could be a case where a State is liable by virtue of being a launching State while another State has *de facto* control over the space object and is responsible under Article VI of the Outer Space Treaty since the space object would be part of that State's national space activity.[11]

Some authors, when discussing the question of the interpretation of the term "launching State", further express the view that a narrow interpretation of the term could allow for a case of "no launching State" if a launch is conducted purely privately and not on the territory of any State.[12] However, such a narrow interpretation would fail to take into account the Outer Space Treaty, particularly Article VI, which makes States responsible for the activities of non-governmental entities. Further, even if the launch would be done purely privately and not on the territory of any State, the company or person involved will ordinarily have a nationality which would link it to a State and as such could be seen as procuring the launch making

[8] Art. I, Liability Convention.

[9] See Sect. 1.4.1.

[10] Von der Dunk (2017), p. 36; Hertzfeld and Von der Dunk (2005), p. 89; Trepczynski (2007), p. 224; Dasgupta (2016), p. 648; Cheng (1997), p. 239.

[11] Dasgupta (2013a); Von der Dunk (2017), p. 33.

[12] Von der Dunk frequently discusses this problem and mentions the national space legislation of specific countries. Von der Dunk (2015), pp. 83–84; Von der Dunk (1998); Kerrest and Smith (2017), p. 137.

their State liable and thus ensure to have a launching State as addressee of the liability claims.[13]

The discussion is also vivid regarding the correct interpretation of the term "to procure a launch" insofar as it is not clear from the treaty text what this term entails and what elements must be present to regard a State as a launching State which procured the launch. This ambiguity was also raised during the negotiation of the Liability Convention and it was pointed out early that "there was a possibility that the words 'procures the launching' might be subject to different interpretations".[14] It seems however, that States leaned towards the understanding that "procure" means a more substantive involvement in the launch that would allow the State to influence decisions regarding the launch.[15] However, States decided to continue using the term "procure" to avoid discrepancies with the wording of the Outer Space Treaty.[16] In the literature various interpretations have been provided, reaching from the State which finances the launch, requests the launch or benefits from the launch to the State whose nationals have financed or ordered the launch.[17]

AI is already being used in launch and landing procedures, and, as the technology evolves, AI will be capable of conducting all launch and landing procedures without any human involvement.[18] Should a State use its own AI software to conduct a launch in another State, it could be seen to "procure" the launch or to "launch",

[13] Hurwitz (1992), p. 22.

[14] LSC, Report of the Legal Sub-Committee on the work of the second part of Its Third Session (5–23 October 1964) to the Committee on the Peaceful Uses of Outer Space, UNCOPUOS 1964, UN Doc A/AC.105/21, Annex IV, p. 20.

[15] For example, at one point the United States proposed to define launching State as "the State that launches or actively and substantially participates in the launching of an object into outer space". LSC, Report of the Legal Sub-Committee on the Work of Its Sixth Session (19 June–14 July 1967) to the Committee on the Peaceful Uses of Outer Space, UNCOPUOS 1967, UN Doc A/AC.105/37, Annex II. The US originally used the term "procure" but changed their proposal to "actively and substantially participates in the launching" because various delegations objected to the term "procure". See LSC, Summary Records of the seventy-seventh meeting held at the Palais des Nations, Geneva on Friday, 23 June 1967, UNCOPUOS 1967, Un Doc A/AC.105/C.2/SR.77, p. 4; The UK also favoured the term "actively and substantively participates". See LSC, Summary Records of the 90th to 101st meetings held at the Palais des Nations, Geneva from 4 to 18 June 1968, UNCOPUOS 1968, Un Doc A/AC.105/C.2/SR.90-101, p. 99.

[16] Indeed, as the US delegate expressly stated "he himself would prefer to translate expression 'fait preceder' by the English word 'arranges' but the word used in the 1967 Treaty was 'procures' and both words could not correspond to the same French word". LSC, Summary Records of the 90th to 101st meetings held at the Palais des Nations, Geneva from 4 to 18 June 1968, UNCOPUOS 1968, Un Doc A/AC.105/C.2/SR.90-101, p. 74.

[17] Martin (1980); Böckstiegel (1994a); Nesgos (1984); Wirin (1994); Hurwitz (1992); Matte (1984); Hobe (2019), p. 80.

[18] Marr B (2023) Artificial Intelligence In Space: The Amazing Ways Machine Learning Is Helping To Unravel The Mysteries Of The Universe. https://www.forbes.com/sites/bernardmarr/2023/04/10/artificial-intelligence-in-space-the-amazing-ways-machine-learning-is-helping-to-unravel-the-mysteries-of-the-universe/. Accessed 26 July 2025; Chatterjee P (2022) How SpaceX is using AI to advance its ambitions. https://analyticsindiamag.com/how-spacex-is-using-ai-to-advance-its-ambitions/. Accessed 26 July 2025.

even when the launch takes place on the territory of another State, and there is no human involvement.

3.3.1.2 Damage

The term damage is a central element as it constitutes a core requirement for liability to arise. Without damage, there is no liability under the Liability Convention, or under Article VII of the Outer Space Treaty.[19]

The Liability Convention defines the term damage as "loss of life, personal injury or other impairment of health; or loss or damage to property of States or of persons, natural or juridical, or property of international intergovernmental organizations". The damage must be caused by a space object.[20]

Thus, discussion within UNCOPUOS quickly arose as to whether indirect damage (i.e., damage that does not directly flow from the act but from the consequences or result of such an act) falls within the meaning of the term damage and thus within the scope of the Liability Convention.[21] The opinion amongst literature is divided. While some reject the view to include indirect damage, others accept that such damage lies within the scope of the Liability Convention.[22]

We can resolve a dispute in literature by looking towards the *travaux préparatoires*. However, States in this case were equally divided on the issue with varying proposals being brought forward and no express agreement being reached.[23] On the contrary, proposals that were aimed to include indirect damage in the definition of "damage" were not adopted. In an early draft, Hungary for example expressed the opinion that a State "shall assume full liability for damage caused directly or indirectly on the ground, in the atmosphere or in outer space".[24] India, similarly

---

[19] The Liability Convention is clear in this regard when it provides, in Articles II and III, that a State is liable if a space object causes damage. So is the Outer Space Treaty which uses a similar formulation in Article VII. See also Hurwitz (1992), p. 12.

[20] Art. I, Liability Convention.

[21] The Canadian delegation considered the term "damage" broad enough to include direct, indirect and nuclear damage. The US, on the other hand, did not accept any suggestion that the definition covered indirect damage. See e.g. LSC, Summary Records of the eighty-fourth meeting held at the Palais des Nations, Geneva on Friday, 14. July 1967, UNCOPUOS, 1967, Un Doc A/AC.105/C.2/SR.84, p. 8.

[22] For rejection see Finch (1980); Beresford (1964). For inclusion see Van Bogaert (1986), p. 172; Wiewiorowska (1979), p. 33; Christol (1980), p. 363; Hurwitz (1992), p. 12ff.

[23] LSC, Report of the Legal Sub-Committee on the work of its Seventh Session 94-28 June 1968) to the Committee on the Peaceful Uses of Outer Space, UNCOPUOS, 1968, UN Doc. A/AC.105/45, p. 76 ["No agreement was reached on the inclusion of indirect damage and delayed damage in the definition."].

[24] LSC, Report of the Legal Sub-Committee on the Work of Its Third Session (9–26 March 1964) to the Committee on the Peaceful Uses of Outer Space, UNCOPUOS 1964, Annex II, UN Doc A/AC.105/19, p. 8.

proposed to expressly include "indirect damage" in the convention.[25] The discussions in the Legal Subcommittee indicate that many States were leaning towards the understanding that any proximate damage should be covered by the Liability Convention.[26] Therefore this author supports the opinion of other authors that express the view that this matter is better handled in the realm of proximate or adequate causality.[27]

Proximate cause is a legal doctrine that is closely related to the cause-in-fact doctrine, or as it is frequently called: the "but for" test. As mentioned earlier, the "but for" test asks the question whether the damage would have occurred "but for" the actions of the defendant. This is a factual test that creates a causal link between the fault of the defendant and the damage that occurred. However, while the "but for" test addressed the question of whether the damage would have occurred but for the fault of the defendant, the proximate cause doctrine addresses the foreseeability of the damage itself. In this sense it is more nuanced and limited than the "but for" test. As one author puts it,

> [the] factual causation analysis asks whether the accident would have happened even if the breach identified by the plaintiff had not occurred. In this sense, factual causation analysis works backward from the accident to the moment of the breach. In contrast, proximate causation analysis starts with identification of a specific breach and looks forward to determine whether the accident that occurred was foreseeable given the breach.[28]

For example, let us assume the satellite of State A malfunctions and forces State B to redirect its satellite to avoid a collision. A few hours later, Satellite B is hit by an unexpected solar flare and suffers a complete system failure. If State B did not have

---

[25] LSC, Report of the Legal Sub-Committee on the Work of Its Sixth Session (19 June–14 July 1967) to the Committee on the Peaceful Uses of Outer Space, UNCOPUOS 1967, UN Doc A/AC.105/37, p. 20.

[26] See for example, Sweden, Hungary, Italy, France and Austria. LSC, Summary Records of the 90th to 101st meetings held at the Palais des Nations, Geneva from 4 to 18 June 1968, UNCOPUOS 1968, Un Doc A/AC.105/C.2/SR.90-101, pp. 37, 38, 40–43; The discussion was perhaps most clearly summarised by the Japanese delegation in a working paper submitted to the LSC, stating that

> [t] The question whether so called 'indirect damage' or 'delayed damage' should be covered by the convention was discussed in the previous sessions within the framework of the definition of damage. It is well-known that the content or extent of these two terms is differently interpreted in the general international law and case law of international arbitration (…). In order to avoid endless discussion on whether to include those terms of 'indirect damage' or 'delayed damage' in the definition of damage, we should discuss the problem of these two terms not in the context of definition of damage but in the context of the manner in which the damage occurred, by introduction the notion of adequate relationship of cause and effect or so called 'the existence of proximity' (…).

See LSC, Report of the Legal Sub-Committee on the Work of its Eight Session (9 June–4 July 1969) to the Committee on the Peaceful Uses of Outer Space, UNCOPUOS 1969, Un Doc A/AC.105/58, p. 31.

[27] Cheng (1997), p. 323; Gorove (1991), p. 225; Malanczuk (1991), p. 792; Kayser (2001), pp. 48–49; Hobe (2019), pp. 80–82.

[28] Hylton (2016), p. 227.

to correct course, then its satellite would have avoided the solar flare. It is evident that the "but for" test is fulfilled. Satellite B would not have had to correct course, and thus being hit by the solar flare, but for the malfunction of satellite A. However, damage claims against State A would fail on proximate cause grounds as damage caused by the solar flare was not foreseeable given the breach that occurred (the malfunction of the satellite of State A). In other words, the fault of State A did not increase the rationally estimated probability of the events leading to injury.[29]

This rationale seems to inform the argument of many authors in space legal literature to suggest assessing indirect damage within the doctrine of proximate causation. This is a convincing argument as it allows to adequately address indirect damage without having to assess whether the treaty text includes indirect damage within its scope.

Another issue relates to the question as to whether non-physical damage, or damage caused by non-physical means, can be considered as damage under the Outer Space Treaty and the Liability Convention. During the negotiation of the Liability Convention States were divided on the issue.[30]

3.3.1.3 Space Object

Only damage that is caused by a space object is compensable under the Liability Convention and Article VII of the Outer Space Treaty. However, space object is a term which is not clearly defined in either treaty text. The term "space object" is the foundation, a necessary requirement, upon which the space law regime attaches liability. In addition to the Liability Convention and the Outer Space Treaty, a number of other norms of space law give reference to the term "space object", such as the Registration Convention, the Return and Rescue Agreement, and national space legislation.[31] It seems therefore necessary, to more closely examine the term "space object" in relation to AI.

---

[29] Ibid, p. 229.

[30] LSC, Report of the Legal Sub-Committee on the Work of its Eight Session (9 June–4 July 1969) to the Committee on the Peaceful Uses of Outer Space, UNCOPUOS 1969, Un Doc A/AC.105/58, p. 32 ["The Japanese delegation interprets that the damage in the text agreed during the last session with regard to the damage to a space object by another space object means a physical damage of a space object, and that it does not include harmful interference itself with radio communications"]; ibid, p. 18 ["This definition refers to damage in general, without any exception. Consequently, nuclear damage should be considered as being included."]; Summary Records of the One Hundred and Thirty-Second to the One Hundred and Fifty-First Meetings, UNCOPUOS, 1970, Un Doc A/AC.105/C.2/SR.132-151, p. 28 ["Damage to a space object or to persons or property on board it might well be due to other causes, such as jamming of or interference with transmission frequencies."].

[31] See e.g. Art. 5, Agreement on the Rescue of Astronauts, the Return of Astronauts and the Return of Objects Launched into Outer Space, 22 April 1968, 672 UNTS 119 [Return and Rescue Agreement]; Arts. I-II, IV-VI, Convention on Registration of Objects Launched into Outer Space, 12 November 1974, 1023 UNTS 15 [Registration Convention]; Art. 3, Law on the Activities of Launching, Flight Operation or Guidance of Space Objects (Belgium); Outer Space Act (Denmark)

The problem one is inevitably confronted with, is the fact that the Outer Space Treaty, the Registration Convention and the Liability Convention do not fully define the term "space object" and no legally binding definition has been agreed upon by States so far. The Liability Convention and the Registration Convention only clarify that the term space object also encompasses "component parts of space objects as well as its launch vehicles and parts thereof".[32] Judge Manfred Lachs, for example, pointed to this definitional lacuna as early as 1972 and expressed his support for a definition that is broad enough to include any object that is designed to be placed in orbit or on celestial bodies and is capable to traverse to, in or through outer space.[33] This led to vivid academic discussion in the literature, which can essentially be divided into two schools of thought.

The first school of thought includes authors that argue that intangible objects are not strictly excluded from the definition of the term "space object". This problem is usually raised within the discussion of liability for damage caused by signals of Global Navigation Satellite Systems (GNSS). Lyall and Larson, for example, base their support for this school on the fact that "[n]either Article VII, nor its origin para 5 of the UNGA 'Declaration of Legal Principles Governing Activities in Outer Space', UNGA Res. 1962 (XVIII) 13 December 1963, specify a narrow view of liability".[34] Henaku, similarly argues that a signal (i.e., intangible object) could be considered an independent space object.[35] If one were to follow this view and additionally see AI as a separate independent part of the space object, then AI itself would fall under the scope of the definition of space object, even though AI is not tangible. This author does not agree with this view (see below).

The second, and predominant, school of thought sees "space object" as a tangible object with physical properties and would thus exclude anything intangible. Stephen Gorove, attributes to object the notion that it is a material thing that can be seen or touched and is stable in form.[36] Bin Cheng, in a similar fashion, supports the view that a space object must be tangible and defines it as any "object, including components, launch vehicles, and parts thereof, which humans launch, attempt to launch, or have launched into space".[37] This school of thought finds broad support by a

2016, part 2; Sec 1c, Rules Concerning Space Activities and the Establishment of a Registry of Space Objects (Space Activities Act) 2006 (Netherlands); Outer Space and High-altitude Activities Act 2017 (NZ), 2017/29, part 1, s 4; Outer Space Act 1986 (UK), c 38, s 1; National Aeronautics and Space Act, Pub L No 111-314, § 3, 124 Stat 3330; Space (Launches and Returns) Act (Austl), 123/1998, s 8; Loi n° 2008-518 du 3 juin 2008 relative aux opérations spatiales JO, 4 June 2008 (France), art 1.

[32] Art. I, Registration Convention.

[33] Lachs (2010), p. 65.

[34] Lyall and Larsen (2018), p. 352.

[35] However, Henaku points out that it is "ridiculous to seek an answer in the esoteric realm when a particular object orbiting in space is obviously present and emitting signals (erroneous signals causing damage)". Henaku (1996), p. 165. See also Smith (2015).

[36] Gorove (1993), p. 25.

[37] Cheng (1997), p. 615.

majority of publicists.[38] If we were to apply this view to AI, then the software itself, if seen as separate from the rest of the object, could not be considered a space object in itself.

Whenever there is a conflict in literature, or the meaning of a treaty provision is ambiguous, we ought to look towards the "traditional" modes of treaty interpretation as set out in Article 31 of the Vienna Convention on the Law of Treaties (VCLT),[39] which has been widely considered to be a codification of customary international law.[40] Thus, treaty provision have to be interpreted "in good faith in accordance with the ordinary meaning to be given to the terms of the treaty in their context and in the light of its object and purpose".[41]

The ordinary meaning of the word "object" suggests that it has physical properties and can be touched or seen.[42] This understanding of the word space object seems to have informed the five UN Space Treaties.

First, the UN Space Treaties use various terms for objects. The Outer Space Treaty prohibits the establishment of any "military bases", "installations" as well as "fortifications" and requires that all "stations", "installations", "equipment" and "space vehicles" are open to representatives of other State parties.[43] The Return and Rescue Agreement employs the term "spacecraft" alongside the term "space object".[44] The Moon Agreement refers to "space vehicles", "equipment", "facilities", "stations" and "installations".[45]

Second, as mentioned above, the Liability Convention and Registration Convention both clarify that space object includes "component parts of space objects as well as its launch vehicles and parts thereof". The ordinary meaning of component part is a part that combines with other parts, which points towards a tangible nature.[46]

---

[38] Kopal (1994); Böckstiegel (1994b); Kerrest and Smith (2017); Kerrest and Thro (2017); Jakhu et al. (2021); De Lucia (2021), p. 221 ff; Ogunbanwo (1975), p. 60.

[39] Vienna Convention on the Law of Treaties, 23 May 1969, 1155 UNTS 331 [VCLT].

[40] Golder v United Kingdom, (1975) 18 ECHR (Ser A), 16 YB Eur Conv HR 482; Sinclair (1984), p. 20.

[41] Art. 31, VCLT.

[42] The Cambridge Dictionary defines object as "a thing that you can see or touch but that is not usually a living animal, plant, or person". The Collins dictionary suggests that "An object is anything that has a fixed shape or form, that you can touch or see, and that is not alive". Similarly, the Oxford Learner's Dictionary sees object as "a thing that can be seen and touched but is not alive". See Cambridge Dictionary. https://dictionary.cambridge.org/dictionary/english/object. Accessed 25 July 2025; Collins. https://www.collinsdictionary.com/dictionary/english/object. Accessed 25 July 2025; Oxford Learner's Dictionary. https://www.oxfordlearnersdictionaries.com/definition/english/object_1. Accessed 25 July 2025.

[43] Arts. IV, XII, Outer Space Treaty.

[44] Arts. 1–4, Return & Rescue Agreement.

[45] Art. 8, Agreement Governing the Activities of States on the Moon and Other Celestial Bodies, 05 December 1979, 1363 UNTS 3.

[46] The Cambridge dictionary defines component as "a part that combines with other parts to form something bigger". The Oxford Learners Dictionary classifies it as "one of several parts of which

Third, the ITU Radio Regulations likewise employ terms that seem to indicate that a space object should be understood of having tangible properties. For example, space radiocommunication is defined as "any radiocommunication involving the use of one or more *space stations* or the use of one or more *reflecting satellites* or other objects in space [emphasis added]".[47]

Fourth, the Space Protocol to the Cape Town Convention[48] speaks of "space asset" and defines it as

> any man-made uniquely identifiable asset in space or designed to be launched into space, and comprising of a spacecraft, such as a satellite, space station, space module, space capsule, space vehicle or reusable launch vehicle (…), a payload (whether telecommunications, navigation, observation, scientific or otherwise) in respect of which a separate registration may be effected in accordance with the regulations; or a part of a spacecraft or payload such as a transponder, in respect of which a separate registration may be effected in accordance with the regulations, together with all installed, incorporated or attached accessories, parts and equipment and all data, manuals and records relating thereto.[49]

Further, no evidence for the inclusion of intangible objects can be found in the negotiation history of the Outer Space Treaty and the Liability Convention.[50] States were uniformly leaning towards the understanding that space object needs to be a physical object.[51]

---

something is made. The Collins Dictionary says that "the components of something are the parts that it is made of". See Cambridge Dictionary. https://dictionary.cambridge.org/dictionary/english/component. Accessed 25 July 2025; Oxford Learner's Dictionary. https://www.oxfordlearnersdictionaries.com/definition/english/component_1. Accessed 25 July 2025; Collins. https://www.collinsdictionary.com/dictionary/english/component. Accessed 25 July 2025.

[47] Radio Regulations Edition of 2024, WRC-23 (Dubai, 2023) (entered into force 1 January 2025, s I at 1.8.

[48] Convention on International Interests in Mobile Equipment, 16 November 2001, 2307 UNTS 285.

[49] Art. 1(k), Protocol to the Convention on International Interests in Mobile Equipment on Matters Specific to Space Assets, 9 March 2012.

[50] See e.g. Report of the Ad Hoc Committee on the Peaceful Use of Outer Space, 14th Sess, UN Doc A/4141 (1959), Agenda Item 25, Annexes, at 21–23, 64ff; LSC, Report of Legal Sub-Committee on the Work of its First Session (28 May–20 June 1962), UNCOPUOS, 1962, UN Doc A/AC.105/6, p. 6; LSC, Report of the Legal Sub-Committee on the Work of Its Third Session (9–26 March 1964) to the Committee on the Peaceful Uses of Outer Space, UNCOPUOS, 1964, UN Doc A/AC.105/19, Annex II, p. 2 [US Proposal]; Ibid, Annex II, p. 7 [Hungary Proposal]; Ibid., Annex II, p. 11 [Belgian Proposal]; International co-operation in the peaceful uses of outer space, UNGA, 17th Sess, UN Doc A/5181, GA Res 1802 (XVII), Article I, para 3; LSC, Report of the Legal Sub-Committee on the Work of Its Fifth Session (12 July–4 August and 12–16 September 1966) to the Committee on the Peaceful Uses of Outer Space, UNCOPUOS, 1966, UN Doc A/AC.105/35, p. 2.

[51] The United States of America spoke of "space vehicle" while Belgium defined "space device" as "any device which is intended to move in space, remaining there by means other than the reaction of the air. See LSC, Report of the Legal Sub-Committee on the work of its second session (16 April–3 May 1963) to the Committee on the Peaceful Uses of Outer Space, UNCOPUOS, 1963, UN Doc A/AC.105/12, Annex I, pp. 10–11; LSC, Summary Records of the 90th to 101st meetings held at the Palais des Nations, Geneva from 4 to 18 June 1968, UNCOPUOS, 1968, Un Doc A/AC.105/C.2/SR.90-101, p. 30 ["With regard to the text itself, his [Canadian] delegation would

This seems to suggest that the drafters of the UN Space Treaties saw space object as a tangible object. This view is also supported by national space legislation of various States which generally lean towards the same understanding.[52]

Finally, the Liability Convention aims to establish "elaborate effective international rules and procedures concerning liability caused by a space object and to ensure, in particular, the prompt payment (...) of a full and equitable measure of compensation to victims of such a damage".[53] The main objective and the purpose of the Liability Convention seems therefore to ensure the adequate compensation for victims in case damage is caused by a space object. This is the reason why the Liability Convention has widely been considered a victim-oriented international agreement.[54] States put great emphasis on creating a dedicated liability regime that enables quick and adequate access to compensation of paramount importance.[55] In other words, States wanted to make sure that damage caused by a space object is compensated. In this light, Bratu for example argues that "a broader interpretation of the term "space object" cannot be deemed inappropriate".[56]

---

recommend the use of the term "space object" rather than "space device" or "space vehicle", because the word "object" was more general and also covered risks arising from falling fragments."]; India clarified that space object "means spaceship, satellite, or any other vehicle, device or object howscever [sic] designated, designed for movement in outer space and intended to sustain there otherwise than by the reaction of air and includes its component parts and apparatus or equipment used in the launching". See also LSC, Report of the Legal Sub-Committee on the work of the second part of Its Third Session (5–23 October 1964) to the Committee on the Peaceful Uses of Outer Space, UNCOPUOS, 1964, UN Doc A/AC.105/21, Annex II, p. 28.

[52] See e.g. Space (Launches and Returns) Act (Australia), 123/1998, s 8 ["space object means a thing consisting of: (a) a launch vehicle; and (b) a payload (if any) that the launch vehicle is to carry into or back from outer space"]; Bundesgesetz über die Genehmigung von Weltraumaktivitäten und die Einrichtung eines Weltraumregisters (Weltraumgesetz) (Austria), § 2/2 ["*Weltraumgegenstand": Gegenstand, der in den Weltraum gestartet wurde oder gestartet werden soll, einschließlich seiner Bestandteile*]; Law on the Activities of Launching, Flight Operation or Guidance of Space Objects (Belgium), Art. III(1) ["space object" means, (a) any object launched or intended to be launched, on an orbital trajectory around the Earth or to a destination beyond the earth orbit; (b) any device whose purpose is to launch an object on a trajectory as mentioned under (a), even when such a device is operated without payload for the sole purpose of its development and validation phase; (c) any constitutive element of an object as mentioned under (a) of (b)"]; Outer Space Act 1986 (UK), s 13 ["space object includes the component parts of a space object, its launch vehicle and the component parts of that"]; Space Development Promotion Act (Republic of South Korea), Art. 2(3) ["objects designed and manufactured for use in outer space including space launch vehicles, artificial satellites, and spaceships and their components"]; US, 51 USC § 50902 [defining a payload as "an object that a person undertakes to place in outer space by means of a launch vehicle or reentry vehicle, including components of the vehicle specifically designed or adapted for that object"]; US, 51 USC § 20103 [defining "aeronautical and space vehicles" as "aircraft, missiles, satellites, and other space vehicles, manned and unmanned, together with related equipment, devices, components, and parts"].

[53] Preamble, Liability Convention.

[54] See footnote 6.

[55] See footnote 2.

[56] Bratu (2024), p. 145.

After an extensive review of the negotiation history and the discussion pertaining to the term "space object", as well as the overwhelming use of references indicating the tangible nature of a space object, this author firmly counts himself amongst the second school of thought and argues that only tangible objects can be considered space objects.

The author mentioned earlier that this view would not allow AI to be considered a space object as the software itself is intangible. But this only applies if the AI can be seen as separate, independent from the rest of the space object. However, AI utilised on a space object needs to be assessed differently, especially highly advanced next generation AI. While currently used narrow AI, and computer software, might allow humans to interact with the space object remotely (human-in-the-loop, human-on-the-loop), this will not necessarily be the case for highly advanced AI. Indeed, the AI will be the sole decision maker, without which the space object will not function and become mere space debris. The AI is the space object, and the space object is the AI. One cannot separate one from the other.[57] For practical purposes this means that when the AI malfunctions, it is still the space object that causes damage and we do not necessarily need a new or clarified definition for the term "space object" to account for AI or other software.[58] Therefore, when the present research speaks of "damage caused by AI" it should be understood as to mean "damage caused by a space object", and *vice versa.*

Another aspect that needs to be explored is the question as to when an object becomes and, conversely, when it ceases to be a "space object" as this can have implications on the liability of States under the norms of the Liability Convention and the Outer Space Treaty.

The Liability Convention clarifies that launching also includes an attempt to launch.[59] Consequently, even when a launch is unsuccessful, for example the rocket explodes during the launch phase, the rocket would still be considered a space object. Professor Cheng bases his definition of space object on the very same understanding and accordingly states that "the term space object designates any object which humans launch, attempt to launch or have launched in outer space".[60] Various

---

[57] Bratu, for example, seems to lean towards the same understanding as her definition concerns "any object launched or attempted to be launched physically into outer space. It includes all its components, software and hardware, equipment, installations, launch vehicles and other parts thereof without which the full operation of the space object would not be construed as possible". See ibid, p. 147; Mishra seems to share this view by using the term 'intelligent space object'. See Mishra (2022); Cf Navas (2020), p. 167.

[58] This would not necessarily change when an AI on the ground remotely pilots a space object. If the satellite causes damage, even when it was due to a fault in the AI on the ground, we can determine that it was damage caused by a space object. In this regard, it is not legally different from a human pilot error.

[59] Art. I (b), Liability Convention.

[60] Cheng (1997), p. 464. Interestingly, Prof. Cheng includes humans in his definition indicating that humans need to launch. However, neither the UN Space Treaties, nor national legislation (see below) make it a requirement that humans need the one to launch. Consequently, the *lex lata* does not make a distinction as to whether an actual human launches the space object or an AI.

national legislations adopt the understanding that a space object is an object, which is either launched, intended to be launched or attempted to be launched.[61] However, States neglect to define what "intended to be launched" actually means. The ordinary meaning of the term "intend" is to have a plan or purpose when undertaking something.[62]

Therefore, it seems that a space object that is ready at the launch facility, would likely fall under the definition while an object that is still being transported to the launch facility, or is in the manufacturing process, would likely not be considered a space object. The same has to apply in reverse, that is when a reusable launch vehicle has successfully returned to the surface of the Earth and the controlled landing process has been completed, it ceases to be a space object within the meaning of the UN Space Treaties.

Consequently, an object becomes a space object the moment it is at the launch facility and ready to be launched until the moment the landing process has been successfully completed after the return to the designated landing facility.[63]

There has also been a discussion in the literature as to whether a space object must be *launched* into outer space to be considered a space object. The problem arises because Article VII of the Outer Space Treaty speaks of objects that have been launched into outer space while the Liability Convention avoids such a formulation. Two views emerge in the literature. Some authors argue that some form of launch is necessary, while others reject this and express the view that even objects constructed in outer space can fall under the liability provisions set out in the Liability Convention and the Outer Space Treaty.

Stephen Gorove, for example, maintains that a space object needs to originate from Earth because the other space treaties "speak of the "return" to earth of space objects, thereby implying that the objects had to originate from earth".[64] Bruce Hurwitz on the other hand points out that the Liability Convention "contains no such provision, except within the (...) definition of launching state" and elaborates that "the title of the [Liability] Convention has some bearing on the issue: it is the "Convention on International Liability for Damage Caused by Space Objects", *not* the Convention on International Liability for Damage Caused by *Objects Launched into Outer Space* (...) [and] therefore the definition of "space object" must include objects constructed or assembled in outer space".[65]

---

[61] See footnote 52.

[62] The Oxford Learner's Dictionary defines "intend" as "to have a plan, result or purpose in your mind when you do something". The Cambridge Dictionary similarly sees "intend" as "to have as a plan or purpose". See Cambridge Dictionary. https://dictionary.cambridge.org/dictionary/english/intend. Accessed 25 July 2025; Oxford Learner's Dictionary. https://www.oxfordlearnersdictionaries.com/definition/english/intend. Accessed 25 July 2025.

[63] This definition only includes controlled landings where the space object successfully returns to the designated landing facility. It does not encompass situations in which the space object returns uncontrollably or causes damage.

[64] Gorove (1983), p. 375.

[65] Hurwitz (1992), pp. 23–24.

However, caution must be exercised with the latter interpretation because the Liability Convention links the liability to the launching State thereby indicating that there needs to be some sort of "launch".[66] Further, in addition to adopting the definition of launching State of the Liability Convention and the Outer Space Treaty, the Registration Convention speaks of the registration of objects that are "launched into earth orbit or beyond".[67] Also, the Outer Space Treaty makes the launching State liable for any damage caused by a space object.[68] Additionally, various national space law regimes speak of launch.[69] Finally, delegates also frequently spoke of launch. The Argentinian delegate, for example, pointed out that "the term [object] was supposed to refer to anything launched into outer space" and added that the various different terms used to refer to space object "all shared the particular attribute of being launched into outer space".[70] The US and India similarly spoke of "damage caused by the launching of space vehicles"[71] and States were broadly discussing the damage caused by a space object in connection with a launching State. All of this seems to indicate that the current space law regime makes a launch (or attempted launch) a necessary element in order for an object to be considered a space object.

This puts the discussion of whether *in-situ* created objects (i.e., objects not launched into outer space but rather constructed from materials found in outer space) can be considered "space object" in an interesting light.

While it could be argued that excluding *in-situ* created objects from the scope of "space object" would run contrary to the object and purpose of the Liability Convention, that is to enable quick and equitable access to compensation and to make sure damage is compensated properly, the negotiation history is clear evidence that States made launch a necessary element. Placing the Liability Convention and Article VII of the Outer Space Treaty in the larger context of the other treaties would also lend further support to this view.

In other words, for *in-situ* created space objects, there is no launch and thus no launching State to which liability could attach. Since the Liability Convention, and Article VII of the Outer Space Treaty, link the liability to the launching State, claims would be unsuccessful for *in situ* created space objects. Even so, this problem is alleviated as, for *in situ* created objects in outer space, the State will have to bear

---

[66] Art. I, Liability Convention.

[67] Art. II, Registration Convention.

[68] Art. VII, Outer Space Treaty.

[69] See e.g. Law of the Russian Federation "About Space Activity", Decree No. 5663-1; Space Development Promotion Act (Republic of South Korea Loi n° 2008-518 du 3 juin 2008 relative aux opérations spatiales JO, 4 June 2008, art 1; Outer Space Act 1986 (UK), s 1; *Danish Outer Space Act*, *supra* note 465, part 2; Outer Space Act (Denmark) 2016, s 1; Space (Launches and Returns) Act (Australia), 123/1998, s 8, Outer Space and High-altitude Activities Act 2017 (NZ), 2017/29, s4.

[70] LSC, Summary Records of the seventy-seventh meeting held at the Palais des Nations, Geneva on Friday, 23 June 1967, UNCOPUOS 1967, Un Doc A/AC.105/C.2/SR.77, pp. 13–14.

[71] Ibid, pp. 3, 13.

responsibility pursuant to Article VI of the Outer Space Treaty as the construction and use of such objects would likely be considered a "national activity in outer space".[72]

In light of the above discussion, and to stay in line with the meaning of the term found in the negotiation history, this book interprets space object as follows:

> A space object is a tangible object, that is launched, intended to be launched or has been attempted to be launched into outer space from the moment the object is ready for launch at the launch facility until after all and any necessary landing procedures are completed.[73]

As this author has pointed out earlier, the AI forms part of the overall space object, and this book will therefore not include AI or the computer software as a separate element in its interpretation of the term "space object". Indeed, the author thinks that the AI component of a space object falls squarely withing the same meaning the States ascribed to the term in the 1960s and 1970s.

3.3.1.4 The Delimitation Issue

Lastly, brief attention must be paid to the issue that there is no internationally agreed definition of the term "outer space", particularly relating to the question as to where airspace ends, and outer space begins. Form a legal point of view, this is a fundamental question to determine what fault standard needs to be applied to a given case.

Generally, there is support that the demarcation line between airspace and outer space is located somewhere between 80 and 100 km above the Earth's surface, because the air becomes too thin to support flight, unless the object travels at orbital velocity.[74] The exact location of this boundary is, however, still very much debated. In 2020 UNCOPUOS disseminated a summary of the considerations brought forward by States concerning the delimitation issue.[75] On the one hand, some States that support a precise demarcation line argue that it can reduce disputes between States, facilitate the principle of freedom of use of outer space for peaceful purposes and clearly define the sphere of influence of private and State actors in outer space.[76] On the other hand, States are against a definition of a demarcation line because, in their opinion, it has not caused any practical problems so far and a delimitation, given the current state of development of space technologies, is not necessary.[77]

---

[72] For a detailed discussion regarding Article VI of the Outer Space Treaty, see Chap. 4.

[73] The author points out that the above-mentioned definition is purely a working definition for the present book and should not been seen as an attempt to definitively define the term "space object" in the realm of space law.

[74] See e.g. Dasgupta (2013b), p. 245; Tronchetti, p. 178; Wedenig (2020), p. 16.

[75] Historical summary on the consideration of the question on the definition and delimitation of outer space, UNCOPUOS, 2020, UN Doc A/AC.105/769/Add.1.

[76] Ibid.

[77] Ibid.

Nationally, Australia has enacted legislation which considers a space object an object which goes into or comes back from an area beyond the distance of 100 km above mean sea level.[78] The Russian Federation suggested an "altitude not exceeding 110 kilometres above sea level."[79] The Draft Treaty on the Prevention of Placement of Weapons in Outer Space (PPWT), submitted by the Russian Federation and China, defined outer space as "the space above Earth in excess of 100 km above sea level".[80] Interestingly, this definition was not retained in the second draft of the PPWT.[81] Serbia proposed 2 million kilometres above the Earth as the boundary line between airspace and outer space.[82]

Although no agreement on a definitive demarcation line had been reached during the negotiation history of the Outer Space Treaty and the Liability Convention, early proposed definitions of the term "space object" indicate that the air needs to be too thin to support ordinary flight. In this regard, States placed their definitions of space object vis-à-vis the definition of aircraft found in Annex 7 to the Chicago Convention. Belgium for example defined "space device" as "any device which is intended to move in space, remaining there by means other than the reaction of the air".[83] Hungary, in a similar fashion proposed that "space object" is an object that is "designed for movement in outer space and sustained there otherwise than by the reaction of the air".[84]

---

[78] Thus, outer space begins 100km above the Earth's Surface. Australian Space Launch and Returns Act 2018, s.8.

[79] LSC, Matters relating to the Definition and, or Delimitation of Outer Space and Outer Space Activities, Bearing in Mind inter alia, Questions Relating to the Geostationary Orbit, UNCOPUOS, 1983, UN Doc A/AC.105/C.2/L.139. See also Draft Basic Provisions of the General Assembly Resolution on the Delimitation of Air Space and Outer Space and on the Legal Status of the Geostationary Satellites' Orbital Space: USSR Working Paper, UNCOPUOS, 22nd Sess, UN Doc A/AC.105/L.122 (1979) Agenda Item 4 (c).

[80] Conference on Disarmament, Letter dated 12 February 2008 from the Permanent Representative of the Russian Federation and the Permanent Representative of Chine to the Conference on Disarmament addressed to the Secretary-General of the Conference transmitting the Russian and Chinese Texts of the Draft "Treaty on the Prevention on Placement of Weapons in Outer Space and of the Threat or Use of Force against Outer Space Objects (PPWT)" introduced by the Russian Federation and China, UNODA, 2008, UN Doc CD/1839 at 2.

[81] See Conference on Disarmament, Letter dated 10 June 2014 from the Permanent Representative of the Russian Federation and the Permanent Representative of China to the Conference on Disarmament addressed to the Acting Secretary-General of the Conference transmitting the updated Russian and Chinese texts of the draft treaty on prevention of the placement of weapons in outer space and of the threat or use of force against outer space objects (PPWT) introduced by the Russian Federation and China, UNODA, 2014, UN Doc CD/1985.

[82] See LSC, National legislation and practice relating to the definition and delimitation of outer space, UNCOPUOS, 49th Sess, UN Doc A/AC.105/865/Add.6 (2010).

[83] LSC, Report of the Legal Sub-Committee on the work of its second session (16 April–3 May 1963) to the Committee on the Peaceful Uses of Outer Space, UNCOPUOS 1963, UN Doc A/AC.105/12, Annex I, p. 11.

[84] LSC, Report of the Legal Sub-Committee on the Work of Its Third Session (9–26 March 1964) to the Committee on the Peaceful Uses of Outer Space, UNCOPUOS 1964, UN Doc A/AC.105/19, Annex II p. 8.

In light of this, the present book will accept the Von Kármán Line as the boundary between airspace and outer space. The physicist Von Kármán calculated that 100 km is the height at which a vehicle would have to start travelling at orbital velocity in order to generate enough support from the atmosphere.[85] Accordingly, when this book speaks of outer space, it means the area above 100 km from the Earth's surface.

3.3.1.5 Conclusion

The purpose of the preceding sections was to make the reader aware that the legal regime governing space activities is far from unambiguous, even when we exclude AI from the equation. Many important terms, such as space object, launching State and outer space, are still very much debated by academia and the international community. The introduction of AI will only add another layer of complexity onto an already ambiguous legal regime, and we shall be content in the present research to examine the impact AI has on the norms that relate to the responsibility and liability of States for their space activities. Therefore, let us now turn towards the fault standard contained within the Liability Convention and show how AI will bring the Outer Space Treaty and the Liability Convention, at least in certain cases, to their breaking point.

3.3.2 Fault in the Liability Convention and the Outer Space Treaty

In the course of this book, it has already been pointed out that the Liability Convention establishes a two-tiered liability regime. For damage on the surface of the Earth or to an aircraft in flight the launching State incurs absolute liability, while the liability for damage anywhere else than on the surface of the Earth (i.e., in outer space) is tied to the fault of the launching State.[86]

It must be noted that the Liability Convention was the first, and to date the only, public international law treaty that adopts the term "absolute liability". Caution must therefore be employed when using this term for other public international legal norms as there is to date not sufficient State practice or case law that would allow us to freely use this term in the realm of international law outside the Liability Convention. This book will therefore adopt the term "liability without subjective fault" to indicate the absence of the mental element of *culpa* or *dolus*. We will refer

[85] Fernández de Cordoba S (2017) 100km Altitude Boundary for Astronautics | World Air Sports Federation. https://www.fai.org/page/icare-boundary. Accessed 25 July 2025.

[86] Arts. II-III, Liability Convention.

to the term "absolute liability" only in relation to the Liability Convention as the treaty text itself adopts this wording.

The differentiation between absolute and fault-based liability in the Liability Convention makes it necessary that we address these issues separately when we discuss the liability of States for their AI-enabled space activities.

3.3.2.1 Damage on the Surface of the Earth or to an Aircraft In-Flight

The perhaps less problematic scenario for AI-enabled space activities is the case of surface damage or damage to an aircraft in flight as the liability in these cases is not dependent on fault. Subjective fault is not a necessary element to give rise to the liability of the launching State. The claimant State only needs to prove the existence of the damage, that the damage was caused by a space object, and that the defendant State can be considered a launching State.[87] In this regard, it is irrelevant how the damage was caused and whether the actions that led to the damage were foreseeable. This means that the issues this research discussed regarding subjective fault, are not applicable. The launching State will be liable regardless of how advanced the AI was. The reasonable person test, along with foreseeability and a standard of care, are simply not relevant in such cases and the whole problematique discussed in detail above will be circumvented.

It is therefore submitted that in cases of surface damage or damage to an aircraft in flight caused by an AI, the Liability Convention is applicable and adequate to govern these instances. Accordingly, for damage on Earth or in airspace, Article VII of the Outer Space Treaty is equally sufficient to govern claims arising from this kind of damage.[88] This does not only ensure adequate safeguards for civil aviation and third parties (i.e., third countries) not involved in the space activities, but is also in line with the intent of the drafters to shift the burden to the State that conducts the space activities.[89]

3.3.2.2 Damage Elsewhere Than on the Surface of the Earth

The situation changes for damage anywhere else than on the surface of the Earth (i.e., damage in outer space). For this kind of damage, the Liability Convention requires the fault of the launching State. This is already a very difficult threshold to

[87] Ibid, art. II; Hurwitz (1992), p. 31; Lachs (2010), p. 116; Kerrest and Smith (2017), pp. 141–142.

[88] The author reminds the reader that the two-tiered liability standard established in the Liability Convention has to be equally applied to Article VII of the Outer Space Treaty. For the detailed discussion in this regard see Sect. 2.3.

[89] See footnotes 2 and 6. See especially the statement of the French delegate in LSC, Summary Records of the 90th to 101st meetings held at the Palais des Nations, Geneva from 4 to 18 June 1968, UNCOPUOS 1968, Un Doc A/AC.105/C.2/SR.90-101, p. 9 [verbatim quote can be found in footnote 150].

meet under ordinary circumstances. In fact, many authors point towards the difficulty of the claimant State to establish the fault of the launching State for accidents that occur in outer space as data is limited and sometimes it is not clear what led to a specific damage.[90] Interestingly, this was seemingly also on the minds of certain States while drafting the Liability Convention. Italy, for example, proposed a liability regime with a reversed burden of proof in which the liability for surface damage should be absolute, the liability for damage occurring in the air based on fault but with a rebuttable presumption of fault against the space object, and the liability for damage in outer space with a rebuttable presumption of fault on both sides.[91] States were therefore aware of the challenges fault can pose in cases of liability for damage caused by a space object but chose to adopt a fault standard regardless. However, while in non-AI related cases, the subjective fault might be difficult to prove, it becomes impossible to do so in cases involving autonomous AI based on ML.

This research argued in Sect. 2.3 that subjective fault in public international law, just like subjective fault in domestic law, requires negligence. This means that to establish subjective fault in the Liability Convention, the claimant State would need to prove, at a minimum, negligence on the launching State's part. Therefore, our argument rests on the understanding that foreseeability and reasonableness are required. However, as we concluded above, both these elements will fail in the case of highly advanced next generation autonomous AI, which in turn means that subjective fault cannot be determined anymore.

But if subjective fault is impossible to determine, then liability for damage in outer space under the Liability Convention and the Outer Space Treaty cannot arise and launching States that utilised highly advanced autonomous AI for their respective space activities would *de facto* be entirely shielded from any liability claims, apart from claims arising from surface damage, under the Liability Convention and the Outer Space Treaty. This would run contrary to the very purpose of the Liability Convention, namely, to embody "the principles of a full measure of compensation to victims and effective procedures which would lead to prompt and equitable settlement of claims".[92]

For cases involving narrow AI, the author admits that that this impossibility threshold is not yet met, and it seems appropriate to assess the damage resulting from the use of narrow AI under the currently available fault-based regime, even though it might be difficult. As highlighted in Sects. 1.3.4 and 1.5, as long as we are able to reverse engineer what led to the undesired outcome, we can apply our

[90] Palkovitz (2020), p. 104; Jakhu (2010), sect. 8.3.1.

[91] LSC, Report of the Legal Sub-Committee on the Work of Its Sixth Session (19 June–14 July 1967) to the Committee on the Peaceful Uses of Outer Space, UNCOPUOS 1967, UN Doc A/AC.105/37, p. 25; LSC, Working Paper submitted by the Italian Delegation draft convention concerning liability for damage caused by the launching of objects into outer space, UNCOPUOS, 1968, UN Doc A/AC.105/C.2/L.40. A reversal of the burden of proof is an interesting and attractive suggestion as it would alleviate the very problems we are facing right now, namely that fault for damage caused by a space object in outer space is difficult to prove.

[92] Preamble, Liability Convention.

available liability standards. Further in the case of narrow AI, humans are generally either in-the-loop or at the very least on-the-loop, so the liability can be anchored in their conduct (see Sect. 1.5).

The question that now arises is, how do we solve this problem and move forward? Although space law literature addressing this question is at present very limited, a few suggestions have been brought forward.

First, there is Chatzipanagiotis who argues that due to the victim-oriented character of the Liability Convention the human standard of behaviour should be used as a minimum standard in AI-enabled space applications.[93] This author argued that AI is much safer than humans and already addressed the shortcomings of such proposal in Sect. 2.2.2 and will therefore not repeat it here.

Second, there are authors that support the establishment of new rules. Martin and Freeland advocate for non-binding transparency and confidence-building measures (TCBMs) to address the challenges brought by AI in space law.[94] Chatzipanagiotis agrees with this view and supports the creation of non-binding rules of conduct that utilise "international performance-based safety standards [to] contribute to legal certainty"[95] in cases where fault is still problematic, even when we adopt the human standard of behaviour as minimum standard.

In a GNSS-enabled AI context, Bratu advocates for a broad definition of the terms "space objects" and "damage", a case-by-case analysis of the causal link between damage and the space object and a new definition for "space object" to deal with issues in the upstream level.[96]

Finally, there are those that prefer a new international legal system consisting of strict laws specifically designed to deal with AI in outer space.[97]

To avoid the creation of an entirely new international legal regime dealing with AI, which can be lengthy, a possible solution could be an amendment to the Liability Convention. State Parties could either extend the scope of absolute liability to also include damage anywhere else than on the surface of the Earth, or they could adopt the proposal originally brought forward by Italy and use a system which presumes the fault but where the fault can be rebutted.

Work in this regard is already underway. The European Union originally proposed a draft directive on adapting non-contractual liability rules to artificial intelligence but abandoned the endeavour in 2025 citing "no foreseeable agreement".[98] In the explanatory memorandum to the draft directive, the Commission explained that,

[93] Chatzipanagiotis (2020), p. 5.

[94] Martin and Freeland (2020); Martin and Freeland (2021).

[95] Chatzipanagiotis (2020), p. 7.

[96] Bratu (2024), p. 194.

[97] Soroka and Kurkova (2019).

[98] EU, Annexes to the Communication from the European Commission to the European Parliament, the Council, the European Economic and Social Committee of the Regions: Commission Work Programme 2025, [2025] COM(2025) 45 final; EU, Commission, Proposal for a Directive of the European Parliament and of the Council on adapting non-contractual civil liability rules to artificial intelligence, [2022] COM(2022) 496 final.

> [c]urrent national liability rules, in particular based on fault, are not suited to handling liability claims for damage caused by AI-enabled products and services. Under such rules, victims need to prove a wrongful action or omission by a person who caused the damage. The specific characteristics of AI, including complexity, autonomy and opacity (the so-called "black box" effect), may make it difficult or prohibitively expensive for victims to identify the liable person and prove the requirements for a successful liability claim.[99]

Therefore, the draft directive would have introduced a presumption of causality where it is difficult to prove that "a specific input for which the potentially liable person is responsible had caused a specific AI system output that led to the damage at stake".[100] It must be noted that the draft directive would have only created a rebuttable presumption of causality and not of the fault of the defendant. The question of how fault is established would have been left to the national courts to decide.[101]

Remarkably, the draft directive stated that "while this Directive does not apply with respect to criminal liability, it may be applicable with respect to [S]tate liability".[102] This statement needs to be underlined as it could have had an impact on how we assess liability claims in public international law. If the draft directive had been adopted and come into force, it would have left the door open for the 27 Member States of the European Union to assess State liability claims for AI under the rules established in the draft directive which directly impact the problematique addressed in this book.

In any case, the problem that all these suggestions have in common is that they advocate for either the amendment of the existing or the creation of an entirely new legal system. As we argued above, States are increasingly unwilling to subject themselves to binding legal regimes, and in the light of the current political climate it is hard to envision a new binding global legal regime without the support of the Russian Federation and China. We must therefore discard all proposals for a new binding legal regime on those grounds. A dedicated binding regime is certainly desirable but in our current environment of Realpolitik simply unattainable.

The argument of non-binding confidence building measures, or generally more soft law, is more realistic. However, what makes it more realistic is also its biggest drawback. Non-binding measures are just that, non-binding. How can we hold States and other actors in outer space accountable if we follow a non-binding framework? Such a framework is without teeth and based on the notion that States see themselves honour bound to follow these non-binding rules. However, honour is arguably in short supply at the moment. Therefore, we submit that non-binding measures ought to be equally discarded for the regulation of the responsibility of States for their AI-enabled space activities.

---

[99] Ibid, p. 1.

[100] Ibid, p. 20.

[101] Ibid.

[102] Ibid, p. 11.

Lastly, one could address damage caused by AI under Article VI of the Outer Space treaty, or the responsibility aspect.[103] However, this is legally and doctrinally a different area and will be addressed further below in Chap. 4.

Therefore, none of the above discussed solutions are viable in our case, which leaves us with the undesired consequence that for damage in outer space, from a public international law perspective, the Liability Convention and Article VII of the Outer Space Treaty abandon their rationale entirely and become what they try to avoid, a shield for the launching State to escape liability.[104]

They create a legal framework with a fault standard and burden of proof which is impossible to meet thus ruling out any possibility, theoretically and practically, for the claimant State to seek compensation from the launching State for damage caused by a space object in outer space using AI.

In the light of these arguments, the questions that arise are: How can States be held liable for their space activities, and how can we ensure recourse for States that have been harmed by space activities of other States that employ highly advanced next generation AI?

This book explores the question of whether a solution can be found in the realm of existing public international law and how these general norms can be successfully applied to liability arising from AI-enabled space activities. However, we are confronted with the fact that we have two validly concluded and in-force treaties, namely the Outer Space Treaty and the Liability Convention, which are not, as this author has concluded, entirely adequate to govern the liability of States for their AI-enabled space activities.[105]

Although it has been pointed out above that space law is embedded in general international law and the rules of public international law are equally applicable and must be taken into account, one cannot simply seek a solution solely within the regime of public international law without discussing the specialised treaty regime of space law first. A principle of any treaty, just as for any contract in private law, is not only to regulate a specific matter, but more importantly, by doing so to create specialised norms applicable to the parties that can deviate from general norms.[106]

---

[103] Gal et al. (2020) who address it very superficially.

[104] In cases of highly advanced AI built on machine learning. As mentioned earlier, in cases of narrow AI this threshold is not met. This book's argument does not preclude solutions found in domestic law or European law. For example, the European Union is charging ahead with drafting ambitious AI legislation. This, however, would only apply to the Member States and would not affect third States. The present research is concerned with responsibility and liability under public international law only, and therefore does not assess any viable avenues that could be found in domestic or European Law.

[105] The sole exception, as pointed out, might be cases of currently available narrow AI.

[106] To use the words of the ILC, '[v]ery often new rules or regimes develop precisely in order to deviate from what was earlier provided by general law'. See Koskenniemi M Fragmentation of International Law: Difficulties arising from the Diversification and Expansion of International Law, ILC, 58th Sess, UN Doc A/CN.4/L.702, p. 6. This book will look more closely at a possible hierarchy of the sources of law in Chap. 4.

The US and the Russian Federation are both parties to the Liability Convention, so they agree that for claims arising from damage caused by a space object between them, the norms of the Liability Convention are primarily applicable. This means that, should a space object for which the US is the launching State fall onto Russian territory and cause damage, the US's responsibility may primarily be assessed under the norms of the Liability Convention.

In case of two international treaties regulating the same or a similar matter, we may look towards the more specialised norm first, and should a conflict arise solve that conflict via established principles, such as *lex specialis derogat legi generali.*[107]

For example, the Liability Convention was adopted specifically to create specialised rules regarding liability for damage caused by a space object, and to elaborate Article VII of the Outer Space Treaty.[108] Coming back to our example of the US and the Russian Federation, liability will still primarily be assessed under the Liability Convention, and not the Outer Space Treaty, albeit both States are parties to both treaties.[109]

As long as rules of international law do not have the character of *ius cogens*, States can contract out of them and even though the treaty might stand in conflict with certain rules in general international law, it would not make the treaty necessarily void.[110]

Treaties are binding and the bedrock of international treaty law, indeed even domestic contract law, is the principle "*pacta sunt servanda*". Consequently, international law only allows the termination or suspension of a treaty under special limited circumstances.

This research will therefore investigate the question of whether the Outer Space Treaty or the Liability Convention cease to apply in cases of responsibility of States for their AI-enabled space activities. In particular, these subsequent paragraphs will assess the possibility that the adoption of highly advanced next generation AI in space activities could lead to a case of supervening impossibility (Article 61 VCLT) or a fundamental change of circumstances (Article 62 VCLT).

---

[107] The ICJ views the *lex specialis* principle both, as a method of solving normative conflicts and a rule of interpretation to avoid normative conflicts. For example, in its Advisory Opinion on the Legality of the Threat or Use of Nuclear Weapons the ICJ used the law of armed conflict (*lex specialis)* to interpret the meaning of "arbitrary deprivation of life" in Article 6 of the International Covenant on Civil and Political Rights. See Legality of the Threat or Use of Nuclear Weapons, Advisory Opinion, [1996] ICJ Rep 226, p. 240; The court used the lex specialis principle to avoid a normative conflict between international humanitarian law and human rights law: see Legal Consequences of the Construction of a Wall in the Occupied Palestinian Territory, Advisory Opinion, [2004], ICJ Rep 136, p. 178.

[108] As made clear by the Preamble of the Liability Convention.

[109] However, this does not prevent a State from additionally arguing that liability also arises under the Outer Space Treaty and general international law. It simply means that the Liability Convention will be primarily used to assess a claim.

[110] Aust (2013), p. 279. This argument goes back to the element of hierarchy of the sources of law discussed in more detail in Chap. 4.

The reason behind this inquiry is two-fold. First, should the introduction of AI lead to a supervening impossibility or a fundamental change in circumstances, the Outer Space Treaty and the Liability Convention could be suspended in such instances. This means that a conflict of norms, and a corresponding application of the *lex specialis* principle to resolve a conflict, will not arise as the treaty provision that could stand in conflict with general international law is suspended. Second, the introduction of highly advanced next generation AI is not only purely a matter for space law. Indeed, an eventual widespread adoption of this technology will penetrate other areas of international law, such as international humanitarian law, international environmental law, the law of armed conflict to name a few, and the question of whether it could lead to a suspension of a public international law treaty is an important question to investigate in general. We will therefore look at a possible application of Articles 61 and 62 VCLT before addressing other avenues to go beyond the Outer Space Treaty and the Liability Convention.

3.4 The Termination and Suspension of the Outer Space Treaty and the Liability Convention

To talk about treaties, or contracts in domestic law, goes hand in hand with the principle of *pacta sunt servanda* which constitutes the foundation of any agreement and is a principle dating back to at least Roman times.[111] It is a basic rule of the law of treaties and is universally recognised by all nations.[112] For this reason, international law allows the termination and suspension of treaties only in certain circumstances, which are laid down in Articles 54 to 64 VCLT. These circumstances are, termination of or withdrawal from a treaty under its provisions or by consent of the parties (Article 54); reduction of the parties to a multilateral treaty below the number necessary for its entry into force (Article 55); denunciation of or withdrawal from a treaty containing no provision regarding termination, denunciation or withdrawal (Article 56); suspension of the operation of a treaty under its provisions or by consent of the parties (Article 57); suspension of the operation of a multilateral treaty by agreement between certain of the parties only (Article 58); termination or suspension of the operation of a treaty implied by conclusion of a later treaty (Article 59); termination or suspension of the operation of a treaty as a consequence of its breach (Article 60); supervening impossibility of performance (Article 61);

[111] Digesta 2.14.7.7. (Ulpian) ["pacta conventa, quae neque dolo malo, neque adversus leges plebis scita senatus consulta decreta edicta principum, neque quo fraus cui eorum fiat facta erunt, servabo" (I will keep the pacts agreed upon, which have not been made by malice, nor against the laws of the people)].

[112] The ILC calls it 'a fundamental principle of the law of treaties'. See Report of the International Law Commission on the work of the second part of its seventeenth session" (UN Doc A/6309/Rev.1) in Yearbook of the International Law Commission 1966, vol 2 (New York: UN, 1967) at 258 (Un Doc A/CN.4/SER.A/1966/Add. 1), p. 211; see also Villiger (2009), p. 363; Schmalenbach (2018).

Fundamental change of circumstances (Article 62); severance of diplomatic or consular relations (Article 63); emergence of a new peremptory norm of general international law ("[i]us cogens") (Article 64).

Of the above-mentioned situations, two are of special interest in the present research, namely supervening impossibility and fundamental change of circumstances. In the next section, we will therefore look more closely at these two doctrines and discuss whether the emergence of highly advanced next generation AI could fulfill Articles 61 and 62 of the VCLT and therefore allow us to temporarily suspend, withdraw or terminate, both the Liability Convention and the Outer Space Treaty when AI is being used.

Before we can engage in a detailed inquiry into this issue, we ought to lay some groundwork and address a few things pre-emptively at the beginning of this section. It seems therefore appropriate, though unconventional, to point out what the following inquiry is not concerned with.

First, this author argued that only highly advanced next generation AI built on machine learning will challenge the fault standard in a way that brings it to its limits. In other words, currently available narrow AI, albeit it might raise challenges in the realm of subjective fault, does not bring our fault standard to its absolute limits. Indeed, as discussed earlier, in cases of narrow AI a human is either in-the-loop, or at the very least on-the-loop, and liability can therefore be anchored in human conduct.

Second, this book concluded that in cases of surface damage, both the Outer Space Treaty and the Liability Convention can deal with cases of narrow AI and highly advanced next generation AI as the liability is absolute. This means that the present inquiry concerns itself only with damage that occurs in outer space, and as such falls under Article VII of the Outer Space Treaty and Article III of the Liability Convention.

Thirdly, we are not concerned at this stage with State responsibility. The responsibility aspect is doctrinally different and will be address in Chap. 4 later on.

Therefore, the following discussion and all conclusions drawn are based on the notion that the damage in outer space was caused by highly advanced next generation AI built on ML.

Further, the VCLT came into force in 1980 and as such is not applicable to the Outer Space Treaty and the Liability Convention which came into force in 1967 and 1972 respectively. However, the ICJ considers Article 61 and Article 62 in many respects a codification of existing customary law and can therefore be applied to both conventions on those grounds.[113]

---

[113] Case concerning the Gabčíkovo-Nagymaros Project (Hungary v Slovakia), [1997] ICJ Rep 7, para. 46; Fisheries Jurisdiction Case (United Kingdom of Great Britain and Northern Ireland v Iceland), [1973] ICJ Rep 3, para. 36; ECJ, A Racke GmbH&Co v Hauptzollamt Mainz, C-162/96, [1998] ECR I-3688, para. 46. As regards the *clausula rebus sic stantibus*, some authors argue that it forms part of *ius cogens* and can therefore not be excluded by the parties. Haraszti for example states that, "[i]n our opinion the enforcement of the clause cannot be excluded even by the will of the parties for changes entailing consequences which cannot be assessed beforehand." Haraszti

Both Article 61 and 62, should their conditions be fulfilled, allow for a suspension of, withdrawal from or termination of the whole treaty.[114]

With this in mind, let us now turn our attention towards the doctrines of supervening impossibility and fundamental change of circumstances, stipulated in Article 61 and 62 respectively.

3.4.1 Article 61 of the VCLT: Supervening Impossibility of Performance

Supervening impossibility is set out in Article 61, according to which a party to a treaty "may invoke the impossibility of performing a treaty as a ground for terminating or withdrawing from it if the impossibility results from the permanent disappearance or destruction of an object indispensable for the execution of the treaty".[115] As such, supervening impossibility of performance can be seen as a special variation of the doctrine of *rebus sic stantibus* as both are based on the same idea of a fundamental change in conditions that constitute a basis for the obligation contained in the treaty.[116] However, the International Law Commission (ILC) rightly determined that juridically impossibility of performance and fundamental change of circumstances are two distinct grounds and ought to be kept separate, even though there may be borderline cases in which these two doctrines could overlap.[117]

The crucial difference between the two is that a case of supervening impossibility does not permit the continued performance of the treaty and it is therefore "not so much one of a change in, as of a total disappearance of the only circumstances to

---

bases his argument mainly on the fact that, according to international practice, States generally do not preclude the existence of the clause. While State practice and literature suggest the acceptance of the clause, and the ICL rightly included it in the VCLT as an objective rule of international law, this author does not agree with the argument that such an acceptance is indication that the *clausula rebus sic stantibus* forms part of *ius cogens*. This should only be seen as an indication and proof of the customary nature of the rule. See Haraszti (1973), pp. 389–390.

[114] Indeed, the VCLT establishes this as the norm and states in Article 44 that "[a] ground for invalidating, terminating, withdrawing from or suspending the operation of a treaty recognized in the present Convention may be invoked only with respect to the whole treaty expect as provided in the following paragraphs". One of these exceptions is the separability of a treaty provision.

[115] Art. 61, VCLT.

[116] Bodeau-Livinec and Morgan-Foster (2011), p. 1385; Haraszti (1973), p. 421; "Second Report on the Law of Treaties, by Sir Humphrey Waldock, Special Rapporteur" (UN Doc A/CN.4/156) in Yearbook of the International Law Commission 1963, vol 2 (New York: UN, 1964) (U Doc A/CN.4/Ser A/1963/Add.1), p. 78.

[117] "Fifth Report on the Law of Treaties, by Sir Humphrey Waldock, Special Rapporteur" (Un Doc A/CN.4/183) in Yearbook of the International Law Commission 1966, vol 2 (New York: UN, 1967) (A/CN.4/SER.A/1966/Add.1), p. 38.

which the treaty could have any application".[118] Therefore, while in cases of supervening impossibility the treaty arrives at insurmountable obstacles which will eventually culminate in the termination of the treaty, in the cases of fundamental change of circumstances no such insurmountable obstacles need to be produced.[119] The "performance [of the treaty] would, even if possible, be absurd, inappropriate and meaningless and (...) is really no longer a question of performance, because there is no longer any field of action to which the treaty relates, or in which performance can take place".[120]

The impossibility can be the result of the extinction of a physical object to which the treaty relates, or the disappearance of an object of legal nature.[121] Whether of legal or physical nature, the object must have been indispensable for the execution of the treaty.[122]

In the light of the above discussion, we now need to ask ourselves the question whether the introduction of highly advanced next generation AI could lead to such a supervening impossibility of performance and thus allow for a termination or suspension of the Liability Convention and the Outer Space Treaty. In this author's opinion, the answer to this question is "no".

As this research has argued earlier, highly advanced AI will challenge our current understanding of fault and the fault standard contained in the Liability Convention and the Outer Space Treaty for damage caused by a space object in outer space. While this arguably poses a significant obstacle, indeed an obstacle making it impossible for the claimant State to prove subjective fault, it does not constitute a total disappearance of the only circumstances to which the treaty could be applied. Indeed, the circumstances are still there, albeit changed, as we still have the element of damage, that damage is caused by as space object and the damage occurred in outer space. The treaty provision may shield States that employ highly advanced next generation AI and run contrary to the object and purpose of the Liability Convention and the Outer Space Treaty, but it nevertheless could still be applicable

[118] "Second report by G.G. Fitzmaurice, Special Rapporteur" (UN Doc A/CN.4/107) in Yearbook of the International Law Commission 1957, vol 2 (New York: UN, 1958), para. 102. See also Bodeau-Livinec and Morgan-Foster (2011), p. 1385.

[119] Haraszti (1973), pp. 380–381.

[120] "Second report by G.G. Fitzmaurice, Special Rapporteur" (UN Doc A/CN.4/107) in Yearbook of the International Law Commission 1957, vol 2 (New York: UN, 1958), para. 101.

[121] Ibid, para. 97 ["Extinction of the physical object to which the treaty relates for instance, the disappearance of an island owing to a subsidence in the seabed; the drying up of the bed of a river permanently, the destruction of a railway by an earthquake; the destruction of plant, installations, a canal, a lighthouse, etc."]; "Second Report on the Law of Treaties, by Sir Humphrey Waldock, Special Rapporteur" (UN Doc A/CN.4/156) in Yearbook of the International Law Commission 1963, vol 2 (New York: UN, 1964) (U Doc A/CN.4/Ser A/1963/Add.1) ["Paragraph 2 covers cases where the treaty is literally impossible to perform by reason of the disappearance of its subject-matter. This may happen in two ways, either through the disappearance of the physical subject of the rights and obligations of the treaty or through the disappearance of a legal state of affairs which was the raison d'etre of those rights and obligations."].

[122] Art. 61, VCLT.

to these cases. A case of supervening impossibility could be argued in instances in which, for example, outer space becomes totally inaccessible to humans. On these grounds the doctrine of supervening impossibility of performance, especially in light of the restrictive nature of the application of the norm, must be rejected.[123]

3.4.2 *Article 62 of the VCLT: Fundamental Change in Circumstances*

Similar to Article 61, Article 62 of the VCLT deals with cases of unforeseen developments, events and circumstances occurring outside of the treaty after conclusion and have an effect on the subsequent execution of the treaty.

Article 62 is a safety valve and stands as an exception to the *pacta sunt servanda* principle, "the lifeblood of the international legal order" by allowing for an escape from a treaty for which the circumstances have fundamentally changed since its inception.[124] In its entirety, Article 62 states,

1. A fundamental change of circumstances which has occurred with regard to those existing at the time of the conclusion of a treaty, and which was not foreseen by the parties, may not be invoked as a ground for terminating or withdrawing from the treaty unless:
   (a) the existence of those circumstances constituted an essential basis of the consent of the parties to be bound by the treaty; and
   (b) the effect of the change is radically to transform the extent of obligations still to be performed under the treaty.
2. A fundamental change of circumstances may not be invoked as a ground for terminating or withdrawing from a treaty:
   (a) if the treaty establishes a boundary; or
   (b) if the fundamental change is the result of a breach by the party invoking it either of an obligation under the treaty or of any other international obligation owed to any other party to the treaty.
3. If, under the foregoing paragraphs, a party may invoke a fundamental change of circumstances as a ground for terminating or withdrawing from a treaty it may also invoke the change as a ground for suspending the operation of the treaty.

It is important to point out that the ILC opted to formulate the article in the negative, thus emphasizing its exceptional nature and highlighting the tension between Article

[123] Case concerning the Gabčíkovo-Nagymaros Project (Hungary v Slovakia), [1997] ICJ Rep 7, para. 46; Fisheries Jurisdiction Case (United Kingdom of Great Britain and Northern Ireland v Iceland), [1973] ICJ Rep 3.

[124] Giegerich (2018), p. 1145.

62 and the *pacta sunt servanda* principle.[125] Article 62 thus presents us with five cumulative conditions that need to be fulfilled in order for the provision to be applicable: (1) a subsequent (or supervening) change of circumstances, (2) the change needs to be fundamental, (3) the change must not have been foreseen by the parties, (4) the circumstances must have been an essential basis of consent of the contracting parties and (5) radical transformation of the obligations still to be performed under the treaty.

In order to explore whether the use of highly advanced next generation AI could cause such a fundamental change of circumstances, we will address each of these conditions separately. The following sections will therefore deal with each of the requirements of Article 62 individually and discuss if and how AI fits into them. This will allow us to determine whether AI could trigger an Article 62 application.

3.4.2.1 Subsequent Fundamental Change of Circumstances

The first requirement, which needs to be fulfilled, is that of a fundamental change of circumstances "which has occurred with regard to those existing at the time of the conclusion of a treaty" unforeseen by the contracting parties.[126]

The change in circumstances need to have occurred subsequently (i.e, at a later date) after the conclusion of a treaty. This means that the conclusion of the treaty serves as both, the time limit when the circumstances must have existed (*terminus ante quem*) and the starting point for any change, which must have occurred after the conclusion (*terminus post quem*).[127] Therefore, Article 62 evolves around the point in time of the conclusion of the treaty and as such does not consider any circumstances that come into being after the treaty was concluded. This point in time can vary and needs to be assessed on a case-by-case basis. The term "conclusion" in the sense of Article 62 is not directly defined in the VCLT, neither has a definition

---

[125] Indeed, this was constantly on the mind of the ILC when drafting the article as they were mindful of the fact to formulate the article in a way that would not allow a subjective, at will, use of the clause by States to escape unfavorable treaties. Special Rapporteur Fitzmaurice was correct when he called it an attractive but dangerous doctrine and stated that,

> [t]here are few [doctrines] which could so easily reduce the main principle of treaty law, pacta sunt servanda, to a mere form of words (...) [and] [i]t is all too easy to find grounds for alleging a change of circumstances, since in fact, in international life, circumstances are constantly changing. But these changes are not, generally speaking, of a kind that can or should affect the continued operation of treaties. As a rule, they do not render the execution of the treaty either impossible or materially very difficult, or its objects impossible of further realization, or destroy its value or raison d'etre. What they may tend to influence is the willingness of one or other of the parties, on ideological or political grounds—often of an internal character—to continue to carry it out.

"Second report by G.G. Fitzmaurice, Special Rapporteur" (UN Doc A/CN.4/107) in Yearbook of the International Law Commission 1957, vol 2 (New York: UN, 1958), para. 142.

[126] Art. 61(1), VCLT.

[127] "Second report by G.G. Fitzmaurice, Special Rapporteur" (UN Doc A/CN.4/107) in Yearbook of the International Law Commission 1957, vol 2 (New York: UN, 1958), para. 171; Giegerich (2018), p. 1159; Villiger (2009), p. 773.

been provided in the reports of the ILC. Very early on, Special Rapporteur Fitzmaurice used the wording "entered into" instead of "conclusion". A terminology which was retained by Special Rapporteur Waldock and subsequently worked into what was then Article 22 which stated that "[a] change in the circumstances which existed at the time when the treaty was entered into (...)".[128] Waldock used the same wording until 1966 but it was ultimately changed to "conclusion" in the final version of the draft without any explanation.[129] However, this difference in wording could have a significant impact on the application of the principle. The term "entered into" could be seen as the point in time when a party expresses its consent to be bound to the treaty (e.g., signature) while the term "conclusion" is arguably more restrictive and would indicate the point in time when the negotiations are concluded, and the final treaty text is adopted. For bilateral treaties, this would be less of a problem as we only have two States that negotiate, and if agreement is reached, sign. However, it would give rise to more difficulties in multilateral treaties open to subsequent signature of States.

For the purposes of the Outer Space Treaty and the Liability Convention this theoretical problem is less problematic as most States became parties to the two treaties largely between the 1960s and 1980s, when AI did not yet exist beyond mere imagination.

The time of conclusion is also the point in time against which we ought to assess whether the change was unforeseen by the parties. This means a State, which subsequently expressed its consent to be bound to the treaty, cannot invoke any change that occurred before that point in time.[130]

---

[128] "Second Report on the Law of Treaties, by Sir Humphrey Waldock, Special Raporteur" (UN Doc A/CN.4/156) in Yearbook of the International Law Commission 1963, vol 2 (New York: UN, 1964) (U Doc A/CN.4/Ser A/1963/Add.1), p. 79.

[129] "Fifth Report on the Law of Treaties, by Sir Humphrey Waldock, Special Rapporteur" (Un Doc A/CN.4/183) in Yearbook of the International Law Commission 1966, vol 2 (New York: UN, 1967) (A/CN.4/SER.A/1966/Add.1), p. 44; "Reports of the International Law Commission on the second part of its seventeenth session and on its eighteenth session" (UN Doc A/6309/Rev.1) in Yearbook of the International Law Commission 1966, vol 2 (New York: UN, 1967) (Un Doc A/CN.4/SER.A/1966/Add.1), pp. 256–257.

[130] For example, Croatia only ascended to the Outer Space Treaty in March 2023. It is doubtful that Croatia could avail herself of Article 62 VCLT as autonomous AI is under development at the moment, and thus the use of highly advanced autonomous AI is not unforeseen by Croatia. See also Giegerich (2018), p. 1160 In this regard it is logical to interpret the term 'conclusion' as to mean 'entered into' (i.e., the point in time when a State Party expresses its consent to be bound to the treaty) otherwise it would undermine the rationale of this article. To go back to our example of Croatia. If we were to interpret the term 'conclusion' as to mean the point in time when the treaty is concluded (i.e., the negotiations are concluded and the final treaty text is adopted), then we also need to measure the element of 'unforeseen' against this point in time. In other words, Croatia could then argue that in the 1960s AI was unforeseen and therefore it would allow her to suspend the treaty.

This change in circumstances can either be of factual or legal nature.[131] When Article 62 speaks of "circumstances" it talks about objective circumstances that are external and outside of the treaty and come about by operation of the law independent from the subjective will of the parties to the treaty.[132] As such, subjective motives of a contracting party cannot be used as a ground to invoke the fundamental change in circumstances contained in Article 62. This does not mean, however, that we can entirely divorce the subjective element from the rule as it would otherwise be impossible to ascertain what the parties deemed as essential basis for consent to be bound to the treaty (see below).[133] Thus, there will always be a certain degree of subjectivity found in the application of the rule. However, this subjectivity is strictly limited because what the parties considered to be an essential basis to be bound to the treaty "must appear from an objective interpretation of the treaty and the circumstances surrounding its conclusion that the parties contracted on the assumption that the fact or situation in question was a necessary basis for the operation of the treaty".[134] Thus, "the intentions, expectations and objectives of the parties to a treaty are "subjective," the ascertainment of their existence (...) requires reliance on objective elements".[135]

Can the use of highly advanced AI constitute a subsequent change in circumstances? The author submits that it can.

First, highly advanced next generation AI has not yet emerged and AI was neither a concern at the time the treaties were drafted, nor when States signed and became parties to them in the years that followed. Albeit the drafters were aware of outer space as a technological advanced area, and the potential for private actors to become involved in the space industry, they cannot have anticipated circumstances in which the human is taken out of the equation entirely. Both, the Outer Space Treaty and the Liability Convention, were conceived around human interaction, maybe even human-machine interaction, but certainly not independent machine interaction outside of human interaction. Once highly advanced AI emerges, and is being used in outer space, it will cause the law to operate differently and independently from the will of the parties, insofar as it transforms Article VII of the Outer Space Treaty and the Liability Convention, from a means to obtain compensation for damage in outer space, to a legal shield against any claims. As subjective fault will be impossible to prove, it will effectively provide an avenue for States to escape

[131] Fisheries Jurisdiction Case (United Kingdom of Great Britain and Northern Ireland v Iceland), [1973] ICJ Rep 3, para. 32.

[132] Cf "Second report by G.G. Fitzmaurice, Special Rapporteur" (UN Doc A/CN.4/107) in Yearbook of the International Law Commission 1957, vol 2 (New York: UN, 1958), pp. 32–33.

[133] "Second Report on the Law of Treaties, by Sir Humphrey Waldock, Special Rapporteur" (UN Doc A/CN.4/156) in Yearbook of the International Law Commission 1963, vol 2 (New York: UN, 1964) (U Doc A/CN.4/Ser A/1963/Add.1), p. 84.

[134] Ibid, p. 84.

[135] Lissitzyn (1967), p. 915.

their liability under both treaties.[136] Therefore, the introduction of general AI can be seen as a subsequent change in circumstances.

A change alone is not enough, the change also needs to be fundamental. It relates to the circumstances rather than the treaty itself and must be of considerable and substantial importance, insofar as circumstances will no longer be what they were before.[137] The VCLT does not directly define the term "fundamental". However, the ILC explained that a change is fundamental in the sense that the existence of the fact or situation constituted an essential basis of consent, and the effect of the change is to transform the character of the obligations undertaken in the treaty in an essential respect.[138] Looking at the text of Article 62 VCLT itself, it seems that the term "fundamental" is closely linked to "essential" and "radically".[139] This can arguably be seen as an indication that a change is fundamental when it was essential for the consent of the parties and has the ability to radically transform the obligations to be performed under the treaty. It is very difficult to imagine a change that was essential to the consent of the parties and radically transforms the treaty obligations without it being fundamental.[140]

Consequently, to determine whether a change was fundamental, we first need to ascertain whether the circumstances that were changed were essential for the consent of the parties and the subsequent change in those very circumstances radically transforms the treaty obligations.

---

[136] The author believes that States might use this to their advantage, insofar as they could purposefully use highly advanced AI to escape their obligations under the Outer Space Treaty and the Liability Convention.

[137] Villiger (2009), p. 771.

[138] "Report of the International Law Commission covering the work of its fifteenth session" (UN Doc A/5509) in Yearbook of the International Law Commission 1963, vol 2 (New York: UN, 1964) (UN Doc A/CN.4/SER.A/1987/ADD.1), p. 210; It is interesting to note that the ILC used the term essential instead of fundamental in early drafts. Special Rapporteur Waldock considered a change essential when it is linked to the "change in circumstances forming the basis of the treaty". See "Second Report on the Law of Treaties, by Sir Humphrey Waldock, Special Rapporteur" (UN Doc A/CN.4/156) in Yearbook of the International Law Commission 1963, vol 2 (New York: UN, 1964) (U Doc A/CN.4/Ser A/1963/Add.1), p. 79; Capotorti (1971), p. 543 ["(...) et enfin qu'il soit «fondamental», c'est-à-dire qu'il ait eu pour effet «de transformer radicalement la portée des obligations qui restent à exécuter en vertu du traité»."].

[139] The ILC seems to lean towards the same conclusion. They explained that change must be a fundamental one "in the sense that: (a) "the existence of the fact or situation constituted an essential basis of the consent of the parties to the treaty", and (b) "the effect of the change is to transform in an essential respect the character of the obligations undertaken in the treaty". See "Report of the International Law Commission covering the work of its fifteenth session" (UN Doc A/5509) in Yearbook of the International Law Commission 1963, vol 2 (New York: UN, 1964) (UN Doc A/CN.4/SER.A/1987/ADD.1), p. 210.

[140] See especially Giegerich (2018), p. 1161.

3.4.2.2 Essential Basis for Consent of the Parties

Article 62 (1) (a) further narrows the scope of application by adding yet another requirement that needs to be fulfilled to invoke a fundamental change of circumstances successfully, namely that of the "essential basis of the consent". Not only must the change be fundamental, it must also change the very circumstances that the parties regarded as an essential basis for their consent. Thus para (a) compares the circumstances that were present at the time of the conclusion of the treaty with those arising after.[141] Subsequent changes in circumstances are nothing out of the ordinary. Indeed, they happen quite regularly and are just a fact of life, particularly in the realm of international law where treaties remain in force for a long time. Activities in outer space can be seen as an example of such change in circumstances. At the conclusion of the Outer Space Treaty and the Liability Convention, States were the main actors in outer space, and it was only a few nations that were operating in this domain. That changed in the years following the conclusion of the treaties, and nowadays, as mentioned above, private actors are the main players in outer space and devote significant resources towards the commercial exploitation and exploration of space. The change in space actors is undoubtedly a change in circumstances compared to those that existed at conclusion, but it did not constitute an essential basis for the consent of the parties, neither does it, from a purely legal point of view, make a difference whether States or private actors are the main actors in outer space.[142]

The question whether the circumstances constituted an essential basis for the consent of the parties is a hypothetical one, and just like the rest of Article 62, needs to be interpreted objectively based on evidence which can be drawn from the negotiation history of the treaty.[143] In essence, we are trying to ascertain whether, had the parties foreseen the subsequent fundamental change, they would not have committed themselves to the treaty, or, at the very least, would have drafted it differently.[144]

---

[141] See also Villiger (2009), p. 774.

[142] This change in space actors was foreseen by the drafters, and they made States directly internationally responsible and liable for the activities of non-governmental entities.

[143] "Second Report on the Law of Treaties, by Sir Humphrey Waldock, Special Rapporteur" (UN Doc A/CN.4/156) in Yearbook of the International Law Commission 1963, vol 2 (New York: UN, 1964) (U Doc A/CN.4/Ser A/1963/Add.1), p. 84; "Record of the 695th Meeting" (UN Doc A/CN.4/156) in Yearbook of the International Law Commission 1963, vol 1 (Un Doc A/CN.4/SER.A/1963), p. 149 ["Establishing the essential basis of consent requires an objective examination of the historical background and the circumstances surrounding the conclusion of the treaty. An objective approach is all the more called for since, on the one hand, it is likely that ex post the parties will draw different conclusions from the original facts, and, on the other, the requirement of the essential basis remains fundamental to the security of the treaty"].

[144] Villiger (2009), p. 774; "Second report by G.G. Fitzmaurice, Special Rapporteur" (UN Doc A/CN.4/107) in Yearbook of the International Law Commission 1957, vol 2 (New York: UN, 1958), p. 63 [what is necessary (...) is not so much to show that the parties intended the treaty to terminate if there was a change in certain then existing circumstances, but that in the absence of those circumstances they would not (that is, neither of them would) have entered into the treaty at all, or that they would have drafted it differently. It is only on that basis that the circumstances can be

This is again an objective test. Indeed, as Villiger put it, "in most cases the parties will most likely not have given much thought to the circumstances which subsequently changed".[145]

Finally, the circumstances must have been essential for the basis of the consent of the "parties". Therefore, it is not enough that "just" one party regarded the circumstance as essential. By using the plural "parties" the VCLT seems to be rather clear in this regard. In bilateral treaties this would mean that the circumstances must have constituted an essential basis for both parties. For multilateral treaties, it becomes more challenging. Does the term "parties" imply that all parties must have seen it as an essential basis for their consent, or only the "majority" of the parties? In his commentary on Article 62 of the VCLT, Giegerich, for example, argues that ""[b]asis of the consent of the parties" means that the existence of the circumstances must have been the determining factor for all the parties to enter the treaty"[146] In this author's opinion, this conclusion is a bit too far reaching. While the author agrees that in multilateral treaties the circumstances must have been essential for more than a few parties, he disagrees that it needs to be the case for all parties. This would too narrowly limit the application of the *rebus sic stantibus* principle and render it in almost all cases inapplicable, which would go against the very reason why the rule was accepted in the first place.[147] Further, as was stated above, the element of "time of conclusion" means the point in time when a party entered into the treaty and this can vary case-by-case. If one were to take Giegerich's argument at face value, it would mean one needs to re-assess anew essentially whenever a new party joins.[148] Therefore the author proposes for multilateral treaties that a majority of States is enough to satisfy the requirement, especially as it would still ensure that the rule is firmly placed on an objective foundation and removed from the arbitrary and

regarded as being such that a fundamental change in them should give a faculty of termination or suspension of the treaty obligation."]; "Second Report on the Law of Treaties, by Sir Humphrey Waldock, Special Rapporteur" (UN Doc A/CN.4/156) in Yearbook of the International Law Commission 1963, vol 2 (New York: UN, 1964) (U Doc A/CN.4/Ser A/1963/Add.1), p. 84 ['Secondly, it must appear from the object and purpose of the treaty and the circumstances surrounding its conclusion that the parties assumed the existence and continued existence of that fact or situation to be a necessary foundation of the obligations accepted by them. In other words, it must appear from an objective interpretation of the treaty and the circumstances surrounding its conclusion that the parties contracted on the assumption that the fact or situation in question was a necessary basis for the operation of the treaty."].

[145] Villiger, *supra* note 545.

[146] Giegerich (2018), p. 1163.

[147] Namely to be a safety valve to escape a treaty.

[148] For example, Croatia joined the Outer Space Treaty in March 2023. Were we to follow Giegerich's view, it would mean that we cannot invoke a change of circumstances anymore for the use of AI as Croatia seemingly has accepted that highly advanced AI can shield a launching State from liability. This would then effectively remove the safety valve for all other States that joined the treaty when AI was a mere figment of imagination. For States that subsequently join a multilateral treaty, the change in circumstances would not have been unforeseen anymore and a successful application would fail on those grounds.

unilateral.[149] This also makes sense if we consider that the States that did not regard the change in circumstances as fundamental or for which the change was not unforeseen, cannot invoke the rule in the first place.

For the purposes of the present inquiry, the question that needs to be asked is whether the parties, had they known that highly advanced next generation AI could be introduced into the space domain and subsequently challenge the fault standard in such a way that it becomes impossible to prove and a such transforms the Liability Convention and Article VII of the Outer Space Treaty effectively into a shield against any liability claims, the States would have either not agreed to the treaty or drafted it differently. As mentioned above, this assessment needs to be based on objective elements drawn from the negotiation history of the treaty in question.

The question of liability had been before the UNCOPUOS almost as long as it existed. Particularly pressing was the matter of surface damage, especially in the light of the fact that at the time of drafting there were only a handful of space powers and the majority of States were excluded from the space domain, and therefore States favoured rules that would deal with damage caused by the space object to something or someone within their territory.[150] During the drafting of the Liability Convention, the negotiations came to a standstill as States were arguing about the extent of the restoration the Liability Convention needs to grant.[151] While this discussion on its face is concerned with the extent of restoration, it is placed upon the

---

[149] "Second report by G.G. Fitzmaurice, Special Rapporteur" (UN Doc A/CN.4/107) in Yearbook of the International Law Commission 1957, vol 2 (New York: UN, 1958), p. 63.

[150] Cheng (1997), p. 288. The possibility of damage caused by a space object was a real danger. In 1962 the US presented a metal weighing around 20 pounds which was believed to be from Sputnik IV. In 1970 the US brought to the attention of the United Nations that it had been showered by fragments, one weighing more than 650 pounds, that were supposedly debris from soviet launches; See Verbatim Record of the Fifteenth Meeting, UNCOPUOS, 1962, UN Doc A/AC.105/PV/15 (1963), p. 33; Cheng (1997), p. 287; The French delegate summarised it aptly when he said,

> Liability had to be regarded as having been incurred without fault whenever an inequality in the form of unequal possibilities of causing or sustaining damage was established between the respondent State and the victim. In other words, whenever damage was caused as a result of the launching of a space vehicle in the territory of third States which had neither participated in nor had any influence on the space activities of the launching State or States, the system of liability without fault had to be adopted, under which only the party which derived advantage from the space vehicle was required to make good the damage. That decision originated in the idea that it was necessary for the international community to protect victims of damage caused by a space vehicle because it was considered equitable to favour the victim over the party causing the damage, even if the latter was not at fault, or to give the general interest, that of the third parties which had suffered damage, precedence over the particular interest, that of the State which caused the damage. Equity demanded compensation for any damage; justice, however required that the State whose role had been purely passive should be favoured over the State whose role had been active, particularly as the latter derived benefit from its activities. The principle of liability based on risk must therefore be applied in all cases where damage was sustained by States, or by persons in their territory, that had played no part in the space activities which caused the damage.

See LSC, Summary Records of the 90th to 101st meetings held at the Palais des Nations, Geneva from 4 to 18 June 1968, UNCOPUOS 1968, Un Doc A/AC.105/C.2/SR.90-101, p. 9.

[151] Cheng (1997), p. 296 LSC, Report of the Legal Sub-Committee on the work of its Ninth Session (8 June–3 July 1970 to the Committee on the Peaceful Uses of Outer Space, UNCOPUOS, 1970, UN Doc A/AC.105/85; LSC, Letter Dated 27 April 1970 from the Chairman of the Committee on

notion that compensation is payable due to damage caused by a space object. For damage in outer space this also requires subjective fault. Since the Soviet Union insisted on full compensation, it could be argued that had they known that there could be instances in which the Liability Convention ceases to provide such access to compensation, they would not have consented to it in the current form. The possibility to access compensation is further closely linked to the object and purpose of the treaty.[152] This can arguably be seen as an essential basis for the consent of the parties. This is different for the Outer Space Treaty.

As opposed to the Liability Convention, which is a dedicated treaty dealing with liability for damage caused by a space object, the Outer Space Treaty is much broader and deals with a wide variety of different issues. Liability is but one of the principles enumerated in the treaty. Albeit liability being an issue mentioned as early as 1962, Article VII does not seem to have been a central element of the negotiations. Rather, as Professor Cheng correctly points out "[i]t is merely the logical consequence of Article VI"[153] and it would thus be very likely that States would not have withdrawn their consent, or changed Article VII in any meaningful way, even if they considered highly advanced general AI. This is due to multiple reasons.

First, the Outer Space Treaty deals with numerous important principles, such as the prohibition to place nuclear weapons in Earth's orbit, non-appropriation and freedom of exploration and use (and as a consequence access to outer space). These principles can arguably be seen as more pressing, especially in light of Article VI.

Second, Article VI makes States responsible for their national activities in Outer Space and directly attributes actions of non-governmental entities to the appropriate State party. As will be discussed in more detail in Chap. 4, State responsibility also entails the obligation to make reparation.[154] Therefore, State responsibility and liability are "two facets of one same fact: a State will have to compensate the victim of a damage which that State has caused".[155] In other words, liability could arise as a result of State responsibility and compensation can be ensured that way.

Third, the Outer Space Treaty and the Liability Convention were negotiated at the same time with many delegates being involved in both negotiations. Therefore, States were aware that there would eventually be a separate treaty dealing with

the Peaceful Uses of Outer Space Addressed to the Chairman of the Legal Sub-Committee, UNCOPUOS, 1970, UN Doc A/AC.105/C.2/8.

[152] Case concerning the Gabčíkovo-Nagymaros Project (Hungary v Slovakia), [1997] ICJ Rep 7, para. 104. The court linked the element of 'essential consent' to the object and purpose of the treaty ["In the Court's view, the prevalent political conditions were thus not so closely linked to the object and purpose of the Treaty that they constituted an essential basis of the consent of the parties and, in changing, radically altered the extent of the obligations still to be performed"].

[153] Cheng (1997), p. 238.

[154] See Case Concerning the Factory at Chorzów (Germany v Poland), (1928) PCIJ (Ser A) No 17; See also Lee (2006).

[155] Kayser (2001), p. 32.

liability for damage caused by space objects and many delegates pointed to the need to negotiate separately a treaty specifically addressing the issue of liability.[156]

It follows therefore that, as far as Article VII Outer Space Treaty is concerned, it cannot be seen as an essential basis of consent of the parties, and the author doubts that States would have drafted it differently had they known about the potential emergence of highly advanced general AI. This is supported by the fact, that States chose to not textually include a fault standard in Article VII Outer Space Treaty.[157]

Thus, it seems highly unlikely that a State could successfully invoke the fundamental change in circumstances regarding the Outer Space Treaty. This section will therefore not look at the Outer Space Treaty anymore but focus its inquiry on the Liability Convention.

3.4.2.3 Radical Transformation of Obligations

Finally, the fundamental change of circumstances must have the effect of radically transforming "the extent of obligations still to be performed under the treaty."[158] This means that the change in circumstances will substantially hinder the continued realisation of the object and purpose of the treaty and render the performance of the treaty something essentially different from what was originally undertaken.[159] It is interesting to note that the ICJ in the *Fisheries Jurisdiction* held that the "change must have increased the burden of the obligations to be executed" under the treaty.[160] It is equally interesting that authors dealing with Article 62 VCLT seemingly brush this statement of the Court aside and do not regard it any further. This seems overly dismissive in this author's opinion, as this statement could indicate that the Court interprets Article 62 in a way that sees the formulation "radically to transform the extent of obligations still to be performed" as to mean an *increase* in the burden

[156] *Supra*, note 2.

[157] As we pointed out above, we need to read the two-tiered liability standard into Article VII of the Outer Space Treaty, especially when we take the Liability Convention into account. However, when we assess whether a circumstance constituted an essential basis for the consent of the parties, we ought to assess this objectively based on the negotiation history of the respective treaty. Therefore, we ought to solely look at the Outer Space Treaty and not the negotiation of the Liability Convention. Interestingly, Bin Cheng toyed with the idea that the liability in Article VII is absolute. However, we believe that this is because he wrote his assessment of the Outer Space Treaty in 1968, before the Liability Convention came into being. At that time, taking the norms of general international law into account, it seemed logical to arrive at such a conclusion. Despite this, his language remained quite cautious ["(…) it would appear that (…)]. See Cheng (1997), p. 238.

[158] Art. 62 (1)(b), VCLT.

[159] Villiger (2009), p. 774; "Second report by G.G. Fitzmaurice, Special Rapporteur" (UN Doc A/CN.4/107) in Yearbook of the International Law Commission 1957, vol 2 (New York: UN, 1958), p. 60; Fisheries Jurisdiction Case (United Kingdom of Great Britain and Northern Ireland v Iceland), [1973] ICJ Rep 3, para. 43.

[160] Fisheries Jurisdiction Case (United Kingdom of Great Britain and Northern Ireland v Iceland), [1973] ICJ Rep 3, para. 43.

of obligations to be performed. In other words, it would mean that Article 62 VCLT only would find application in cases in which a fundamental change in circumstances changes the obligations to be performed under the treaty in a way that increases the burden of one party. Consequently, a change, even though it would hinder the continued realisation of the object and purpose of the treaty, would not allow a party to invoke a fundamental change in circumstances if it did not increase the burden on the party. It is wholly unclear to this author, how and why the Court arrived at such a formulation, and he disagrees with such an interpretation of Article 62 (1)(b) VLCT.

First, there is no indication, neither in the negotiation history, nor in the commentary of the ILC that Article 62 (1)(b) ought to be interpreted in such a way. The ILC never used such a formulation, and usually links the term "obligations" to the object and purpose of the treaty.

Second, the treaty text itself avoids such a formulation but rather only speaks of "obligations" and not the "burden of obligations". This becomes even more evident when we look at the development of Article 62. Special Rapporteur Fitzmaurice, in what was then Article 22, proposed that,

> [t]he change must have the effect either (a) of rendering impossible the realization, or further realization, of the objects and purposes of the treaty itself, or of those to which the particular obligation concerned relates; or (b) of destroying or completely altering the foundation of the obligation based on the situation of fact or state of affairs referred to in subparagraph (ii) above.[161]

This formulation was largely retained by Special Rapporteur Waldock who argued that "in determining the relation which the change of circumstances must have to the original treaty, the relevant consideration is rather the nature and extent of the effect upon the performance of the treaty obligations".[162] He likewise did not speak of "burden". In his fifth report, Waldock continued to adhere to this formulation but inserted the formulation "obligations to be performed" in the treaty text, only after Australia suggested to include "continued performance" to make clear that it does not apply to treaties whose provisions have already been fully executed on both sides, and as such this formulation is only of temporal character.[163] Once again, the States and the Special Rapporteur did not speak of the burden of obligations.

---

[161] "Second report by G.G. Fitzmaurice, Special Rapporteur" (UN Doc A/CN.4/107) in Yearbook of the International Law Commission 1957, vol 2 (New York: UN, 1958), p. 33. This makes the fact that Special Rapporteur Fitzmaurice, who was also one of the ICJ judges in this case, did not engage with this formulation in his separate opinion.

[162] "Second Report on the Law of Treaties, by Sir Humphrey Waldock, Special Rapporteur" (UN Doc A/CN.4/156) in Yearbook of the International Law Commission 1963, vol 2 (New York: UN, 1964) (U Doc A/CN.4/Ser A/1963/Add.1), p. 84.

[163] "Fifth Report on the Law of Treaties, by Sir Humphrey Waldock, Special Rapporteur" (Un Doc A/CN.4/183) in Yearbook of the International Law Commission 1966, vol 2 (New York: UN, 1967) (A/CN.4/SER.A/1966/Add.1), p. 43.

Third, the ICJ itself seems to abandon this wording in the *Gabčikovo-Nagymaros* case, and only speaks of "obligations to be performed" and that the changes must be closely linked to the object and purpose of the treaty.[164]

Fourth, if we were to accept such an interpretation, then Article 62 would miss its purpose as a safety valve, as it could only be applied in very narrow cases and it would realise the fear that the drafters shared, namely that States, without an option to otherwise get out of the treaty, would need to seek a solution which might be contrary to public international law (e.g., to breach treaty obligations).[165]

Certainly, a change in circumstances can increase the burden of the obligation(s) of one party. However, it is not limited to it but must also include other instances in which the burden of the obligations does not increase per se but, for example, diminishes the value to be gained by further performance of the treaty.[166]

Thus, in this author's view, as stated above, the wording "obligations to still be performed under the treaty" ought to be interpreted to mean that the change in circumstances will substantially hinder the continued realisations of the object and purpose of the treaty and render the performance of the treaty something essentially different from what was originally undertaken and is not confined to an increase in the burden of obligations alone.

In the circumstances discussed in the present research, namely the use of highly advanced next generation AI in outer space which subsequently causes damage, this problem is less pronounced because in cases in which the Liability Convention shields the launching State from any liability claims, the other States are forced to tolerate it and, should they suffer damage, bear all the costs themselves without any possibility of recourse under the Liability Convention. As such, their burden arguably increases as they are obligated to bear their own costs without the possibility of obtaining compensation. Seeing that the object and purpose of the Liability Convention is to ensure access to just and equitable compensation and allow a

[164] Case concerning the Gabčíkovo-Nagymaros Project (Hungary v Slovakia), [1997] ICJ Rep 7, para. 104.

[165] "Reports of the International Law Commission on the second part of its seventeenth session and on its eighteenth session" (UN Doc A/6309/Rev.1) in Yearbook of the International Law Commission 1966, vol 2 (New York: UN, 1967) (Un Doc A/CN.4/SER.A/1966/Add.1), p. 258; Giegerich (2018), pp. 1145–1146.

[166] "Second report by G.G. Fitzmaurice, Special Rapporteur" (UN Doc A/CN.4/107) in Yearbook of the International Law Commission 1957, vol 2 (New York: UN, 1958), p. 60

Frequently, the suggestion is not that the change of circumstances has rendered realization by performance impossible, but that it has so altered the conditions of performance. for the party concerned (either by increasing their onerousness or diminishing the value to be gained by further performance) that such party can no longer carry out, or can no longer be expected to continue performing, the treaty. That this is liable to be the plea is readily seen from the fact that the great majority of treaties involve continuing obligations. (…) The objects of the treaty are therefore, or have been, in principle realizable, and are being realized, so that, short of some event creating an actual and literal impossibility of further performance, or rendering further performance pointless for both or all parties, there is actually nothing to prevent the continued execution of the treaty. The plea put forward in such cases usually is that performance has become vexatious or unduly burdensome for one of the parties, or that events have occurred such that, for one of the parties, the treaty has lost a large part of its value, or is no longer worthwhile.

wronged State to obtain such adequate compensation, the author submits that the further performance of the treaty not only greatly diminishes the value to be gained, but also substantially hinders the realisation of the object and purpose of the treaty and make the performance something essentially different from what was originally undertaken. Adequate access to compensation is not possible anymore.

3.4.2.4 Unforeseen by the Parties

Lastly, the fundamental change of circumstances must have been unforeseen by the parties.[167] This means that the change, which subsequently occurred, must not have been reasonably foreseeable by the parties. In other words, we ought to ask the question whether that fundamental change of circumstances was reasonably and objectively foreseeable for the parties at the time of the conclusion of the treaty. If it was, then it could be considered a case of *venire contra factum proprium* and would not allow for a suspension or termination based on a fundamental change of circumstances.[168]

For the purposes of this research, we need to assess the question of whether the parties to the Liability Convention foresaw the introduction of highly advanced AI and the possibility that the Liability Convention would be transformed into a shield for liability claims. In the author's view, it is acceptable to argue both sides. As mentioned earlier, the Liability Convention, just like the other space law treaties, were conceived at a time when AI was but a figment of imagination. As pointed out above, the treaties were all drafted around human interaction, with a human standard of care and based on the belief that there will always be a human in whom we can anchor the liability. Highly advanced next generation AI will change this dynamic, take the human out of the equation and make it impossible to prove fault. The human standard of behaviour cannot be successfully applied which will lead to the unfortunate consequence that a State employing general AI will be effectively shielded from any liability claims under the Liability Convention. It goes against its very object and purpose, and it would be quite difficult to argue that States had foreseen this development and consented to the treaty in this form regardless.

States did foresee that private actors might become a major driving force in space applications and accounted for this by making States directly responsible (and liable) for the activities of non-governmental entities.[169] However, this assumption was based on the same belief, namely that the liability will be anchored in human conduct. It is difficult to imagine that States could objectively foresee such a development even when they thought about private companies.

---

[167] Art. 61(1), VCLT.

[168] Villiger (2009), p. 773. *Venire contra factum proprium* [to go against one's own fact] is a principle that does not allow to go against and contradict one's previous conduct. In a way, it is a principle close to *pacta sunt servanda*.

[169] Art. VI, Outer Space Treaty.

If we were to follow this argument, we are able to conclude that the introduction of highly advanced next generation AI constitutes a fundamental change of circumstances, which was an essential basis for the consent of the parties and thus allows the successful application of the clause. A State can thus suspend or terminate the Liability Convention in cases of damage caused by general AI.[170]

On the other hand, it would also be permissible to argue that a State cannot invoke a fundamental change in circumstances. Indeed, there might even be more arguments against than for the application of a fundamental change in circumstances.

The first issue would arise in the realm of foreseeability. One could argue that highly advanced next generation AI is merely a result of a logical technological development. The space sector has always been amongst the most technological advanced industries. Devices that were originally designed for the harsh and unforgiving environment of outer space, have been adapted for use on Earth.[171] Space objects in the 1970s and 1980s used, what was then considered, state-of-the-art technology and the development of technology had always been one of the prime drivers of the space industry.[172] It could be argued that, although the emergence of highly advanced AI was not objectively foreseeable for the contracting parties, modern technology was always meant to be included in the scope of the treaties. After all, works of science-fiction like Kubrick's Space Odyssey and its HAL-9000 are evidence that humankind was already discussing such technology.

---

[170] The present analysis does not list withdrawal as an option because the Liability Convention itself provides for a withdrawal procedure in Article XXVII. As highlighted, Article 62 VCLT serves as a safety valve in cases in which the treaty itself does not provide adequate means of escaping the treaty obligations. The Liability Convention provides for withdrawal, but not for termination or suspension. In this author's view, a termination should only be considered if a suspension would not suffice. The principle of *pacta sunt servanda* requires that treaties stay valid as much as possible and therefore a temporary suspension of a treaty seems preferable to a termination, even though Article 62 does not list a hierarchy but rather grants the parties the choice. See Giegerich (2018), p. 1173 ["[w]here the legitimate interests of parties affected by a fundamental change can be sufficiently protected by suspension, terminating the treaty is not justified and should not be allowed under Article 62"].

Further, as discussed at the very beginning of this section, a fundamental change in circumstance can only be argued in cases of highly advanced AI. It would not be possible to do so in other instances or where narrow AI is used. If a State were to withdraw from or terminate the treaty on the basis of a fundamental change of circumstances, the treaty would also cease to apply to all other cases, such as damage caused by a space object not utilising AI. In order to adhere to the principle of *pacta sunt servanda* in our case, a State can invoke a fundamental change in circumstances only in cases in which the highly advanced AI causes damage.

[171] NASA: 60 Years & Counting - Technology. https://www.nasa.gov/specials/60counting/tech.html. Accessed 19 July 2025.

[172] Ben-Itzhak S (2022) The Future of Space Technology and How It May Benefit Humanity. https://web.archive.org/web/20240527154714/global.upenn.edu/sites/default/files/perry-world-house/space-ben-itzhakthoughtpiece.pdf. Accessed 30 July 2025.

Second, a change cannot be considered to be entirely unforeseen if the parties made arrangements in the treaty itself to deal with changes.[173] It was on this reasoning, amongst others, the ICJ rejected the view of Hungary that developments in new environmental knowledge and environmental law can be considered to be unforeseen in the *Gabčikovo-Nagymaros* case.[174] As Giegerich in his commentary correctly points out, "a common device to provide for future changes of circumstances in treaties is the use of revision clauses"[175] and should such a provision clause exist, then a party will not be able to invoke a fundamental change of circumstances. Article XXVI of the Liability Convention contains such a revision clause.[176] This means that the Liability Convention itself gives the parties the option to revise it afterwards. This can be seen as strong support for the fact that States did foresee changes that might make the Liability Convention not adequate anymore, especially when we consider the language used in Article XXVI. It gives the States the ability to revise the Convention if they feel that practical application does not adequately safeguard the object and purpose of the treaty. This would also be in line with Article 62 VCLT which was conceived as an *ultima ratio* solution and safety valve to provide a legal avenue to escape a treaty when all other attempts fail.

Third, the development in AI has been progressing in recent history and as highlighted earlier, AI is already being used in space applications to assist astronauts, conduct docking maneuvers and utilise accurate navigation. States seem to have accepted this development and to the best knowledge of the author have not opposed the use of AI in space applications. According to Article 45 of the VCLT a State loses the right to invoke a fundamental change in circumstances when it either expressly agreed to it or by reason of its conduct indicates that it has acquiesced to the validity of the treaty or it remaining in force.[177] This means that should a State not react *bona fide* within a reasonable period of time to the change, then it could be

---

[173] Giegerich (2018), p. 1162; "Fifth Report on the Law of Treaties, by Sir Humphrey Waldock, Special Rapporteur" (Un Doc A/CN.4/183) in Yearbook of the International Law Commission 1966, vol 2 (New York: UN, 1967) (A/CN.4/SER.A/1966/Add.1), p. 43 ["f a treaty makes provision for the consequences of a change of circumstances, the will of the parties must prevail; and this would appear to form part of the general conditions for the operation of the article rather than to be an 'exception'."].

[174] Case concerning the Gabčíkovo-Nagymaros Project (Hungary v Slovakia), [1997] ICJ Rep 7, p. 65 ["What is more, the formulation of Articles 15, 19 and 20, designed to accommodate change made it possible for the parties to take account of such developments and to apply them when implementing those treaty provisions."].

[175] Giegerich (2018), p. 1162.

[176] Article XXVI states that

[t]en years after the entry into force of this Convention, the question of the review of this Convention shall be included in the provisional agenda of the United Nations General Assembly in order to consider, in the light of past application of the Convention, whether it requires revision. However, at any time after the Convention has been in force for five years, and at the request of one third of the States Parties to the Convention, and with the concurrence of the majority of the States Parties, a conference of the States Parties shall be convened to review this Convention.

[177] Art. 45, VCLT.

considered as having acquiesced to the change.[178] Article 45 is based on the principle of preclusion (estoppel) which is an aspect of *bona fide* and may arise from both an act or an omission. This principle was recognised by the ICJ in the *Temple* case.[179] Article 45 could therefore be seen as a declaration of a rule of customary law and as such applicable to the Liability Convention.

Coming back to the issue discussed in the present research, States are aware that narrow AI is currently being used, while development in the area of highly advanced next generation AI is underway. Although it can be argued that the reasonable timeframe for States to object has not yet passed – narrow AI has only recently started to enjoy more widespread use – it must be noted that only academia and legal literature have so far raised some concerns. In the space domain, States do not seem to be particularly concerned with the problem, even though private companies, such as SpaceX are utilising AI in their day-to-day space operations already. Further, as mentioned previously, the development towards highly advanced autonomous AI is progressing and experts in the industry warn of potential repercussions. Nevertheless, States seem to accept this development, at least so far.

It could therefore be argued that States have acquiesced to AI being used in space applications and the application of the Liability Convention to these circumstances.

Based on the observations of the preceding paragraphs one could therefore deny an application of a fundamental change of circumstances, which means that it would not be possible for a State to opt-out of the treaty on these grounds. In this author's view, under the present circumstances and in light of the above discussion, there are more convincing arguments against the application of a fundamental change of circumstances and it might be better to perhaps look for other possibilities to avoid the Liability Convention and the Outer Space Treaty.

[178] Villiger (2009), p. 777; "Second Report on the Law of Treaties, by Sir Humphrey Waldock, Special Rapporteur" (UN Doc A/CN.4/156) in Yearbook of the International Law Commission 1963, vol 2 (New York: UN, 1964) (U Doc A/CN.4/Ser A/1963/Add.1), pp. 39–40.

[179] Case Concerning the Temple of Preah Vihear (Cambodia v Thailand), [1962] ICJ Rep 6, p. 32

Even if there were any doubt as to Siam's acceptance of the map in 1908, and hence of the frontier indicated thereon, the Court would consider, in the light of the subsequent course of events, that Thailand is now precluded by her conduct from asserting that she did not accept it. She has, for fifty years, enjoyed such benefits as the Treaty of 1904 conferred on her, if only the benefit of a stable frontier. France, and through her Cambodia, relied on Thailand's acceptance of the map. Since neither side can plead error, it is immaterial whether or not this reliance was based on a belief that the map was correct. It is not now open to Thailand, while continuing to claim and enjoy the benefits of the settlement, to deny that she was ever a consenting party to it.

3.5 A Question of Consent

Finally, the question arises whether Article VII Outer Space Treaty and the Liability Convention are applicable to harm caused by highly advanced next generation AI. This issue arises due to the nature of such AI and how it will challenge our fault standard. As argued throughout this book, highly advanced next generation AI will challenge our currently applied fault standards. Case analysis parameters that courts utilise to assess a claim, and determine whether subjective fault was present, were built on human behaviour and conceived to be applied to human interaction.[180] The same applies to the fault-based liability set out in the Liability Convention and the Outer Space Treaty for damage in outer space. However, next generation AI will make it impossible to prove the subjective fault of the launching State.

As discussed above, this will lead to the consequence that Article VII of the Outer Space Treaty and the Liability Convention will essentially shield a launching States from liability claims. This would run contrary to the object and purpose of the international instruments, a problem particularly pronounced in the Liability Convention.[181] We are thus confronted with the question of how to assess a treaty that, through changes outside of the treaty context (i.e., the emergence of AI), prevents itself from fulfilling its own objective and purpose. In essence, we are dealing with a problem of execution. The Liability Convention would make it impossible to prove subjective fault and execute the remedy provisions set out in the treaty text. In municipal law such cases may be addressed within the doctrine of supervening impossibility or frustration. However, as we have determined in the preceding sections, the doctrine of supervening impossibility in international law is much more limited and would not apply to the issues presently discussed. Similarly, while there can be arguments found on both sides, a fundamental change of circumstance would likely also fail.

However, there is yet another aspect, which should not be neglected in this regard. International law is a legal system of cooperation that governs relations between subjects of international law.[182] International law, and its binding effect on States, flows from their own free will. This free will manifests in the consent of States.[183] Consent therefore underlies all public international law.[184] Consent as the necessary foundation of international law is particularly visible in treaty law.[185]

[180] See Chaps. 1 and 2.

[181] The Outer Space Treaty provides in Article VI for the responsibility of States for their space activities. This essentially establishes a separate avenue to obtain compensation from another State.

[182] Rousseau (1932); Oppenheim (1955), p. 4; The Steamship Lotus (Fance v Turkey) (1927), PCIJ (Seri A) No 10; Kindred et al. (2006), pp. 13, 107; Brownlie (1983), p. 2ff; Buergenthal and Murphy (2002), p. 1ff; Damrosch (2001), p. 1.

[183] The Steamship Lotus (Fance v Turkey) (1927), PCIJ (Seri A) No 10, p. 18; Damrosch (2001), p. 1; Gould (2011), p. 262; Contra Ago, who calls it a myth. See Ago (1957), p. 699.

[184] Oppenheim (1955), p. 17; The Steamship Lotus (Fance v Turkey) (1927), PCIJ (Seri A) No 10, p. 18; Henkin (1989).

[185] Henkin (1989), p. 47.

Without consent, there can be no treaty. A treaty can thus only become a source of international law if States consent to it. If consent is not present, a treaty relationship, and all rights and obligations flowing from it, cannot arise.[186] Consent needs to be given freely (without duress) and must be free of any error.[187] The Liability Convention, and Article VII of the Outer Space Treaty, were created to ensure damage caused by a space object is compensable and to guarantee a system to give equitable and quick access to compensation. The question was never whether there should be access to compensation but rather how this access can be facilitated for space activities. This becomes evident when we consider that States in the Liability Convention only allow an escape from liability in very narrow circumstances while the Outer Space Treaty is completely silent on this question. It seems therefore highly unlikely that States have consented to a situation in which the Liability Convention itself would be transformed from a facilitator of to a shield against all liability claims for damage in outer space involving AI.

As mentioned earlier, States have worked the human standard of behaviour for fault into the treaty. The Liability Convention and the Outer Space Treaty are predicated on the human interaction and do not account for singular machine interaction. Accordingly, it could be argued that States have not consented to this. They gave consent to the legal doctrines that involve human interaction, even human-machine interaction, but not to a system where the human is taken out of the equation entirely as regards the fault analysis for damage caused by a space object in outer space.

One could raise the argument, as this research has done above, that States accounted for technological development, made the treaty "future-proof", and the emergence of AI is merely a logical consequence of the technological advancement. On its face, this argument makes sense. States indeed accounted for future development, emphasised by the fact that they made States directly responsible and liable for the activities of non-governmental entities. However, this was still based on the understanding that human conduct will be present in the chain of causation.[188]

While an absolute liability regime, due to its nature of not requiring subjective fault, can be applied to cases of AI causing the damage, a fault-based regime cannot.

It could therefore be argued that consent to make the treaty applicable to liability claims arising from damage in outer space caused by highly advanced next generation AI, was not given.

It could be argued that Article 48 VCLT would be the more appropriate avenue to handle problems arising in the consent of the States. However, an error can only be invoked if consent is given in the first place. The error depends on the existence

[186] Ibid.

[187] Ibid.

[188] This research discussed this argument when it looked at whether the fundamental change of circumstances was unforeseen by the parties. This is an entirely different inquiry than the one we are concerned with here. A fundamental change in circumstances requires a treaty to arise, while the question of consent arises before, or at the minimum the moment, a treaty comes into being and is a determining factor whether a treaty relationship itself arises or not.

of consent. Article 48 VCLT is reflective of this by giving a State the option to invoke an error to invalidate its consent to be bound by the treaty.[189]

Further, it is also doubtful whether Article 48 has customary character, so it cannot be applied to the Liability Convention and the Outer Space Treaty.

While the issue of consent poses an interesting inquiry, the present research will not delve deeper into it as it would go beyond its cope. However, the author thinks its important to, albeit briefly, mention it to provide better context.

3.6 Conclusion

In conclusion, can the introduction of highly advanced next generation AI be seen as a fundamental change in circumstances which would justify the application of Article 62 VCLT? While an application of a fundamental change of circumstances must be denied for the Outer Space Treaty on grounds that Article VII was not an essential basis for the consent of the parties, the answer is more blurred for the Liability Convention. In this author's view arguments for both sides can be found, although it seems there are more arguments against the successful application of the clausula than for it.

Seeing that Article 62 of the VCLT was conceived as a very narrow exception to the principle of *pacta sunt servanda*, the ILC employed great caution in the drafting of the Article and the ICJ has thus far not permitted a successful application of a fundamental change of circumstances, we think that an application will likely fail even in cases in which the Liability Convention would abandon its object and purpose. Not only does the principle of *pacta sunt servanda* demand adherence to, and the continuity of, validly concluded treaties, but the Liability Convention also contains a revision clause which would provide the States with a viable way to amend the convention.

Given the political landscape at the time of writing, an amendment of the Liability Convention is highly unlikely. However, this circumstance does not influence the assessment of whether a fundamental change of circumstances can be invoked or not. This is a question purely of legal nature, and an objective legal analysis therefore must be employed. Realpolitik cannot influence this analysis.

As the preceding section has underlined, highly advanced next generation AI will bring with it significant challenges and we ought to think about ways to set the treaties aside. In this author's view, the nature of highly advanced next generation

[189] Article 48(1) VCLT states:

A State may invoke an error in a treaty *as invalidating its consent* to be bound by the treaty if the error relates to a fact or situation which was assumed by that State to exist at the time when the treaty was concluded and formed an essential basis of its consent to be bound by the treaty [emphasis added].

AI made it necessary to look towards the principle of supervening impossibility and fundamental change of circumstances.

Regardless of the view taken, whether one allows or denies the application of a fundamental change of circumstances or whether one invokes missing consent, the treaties themselves allow to look towards norms of general international law. This underlines the intent of the drafters: to create a dedicated regime for space activities that is firmly embedded in general international law. This book therefore looks towards this solution in the next chapter.

Websites and Online Sources

Ben-Itzhak S (2022) The Future of Space Technology and How It May Benefit Humanity. https://web.archive.org/web/20240527154714/global.upenn.edu/sites/default/files/perry-world-house/space-ben-itzhakthoughtpiece.pdf. Accessed 30 July 2025.

Cambridge Dictionary. https://dictionary.cambridge.org/dictionary/english/object. Accessed 25 July 2025.

Cambridge Dictionary. https://dictionary.cambridge.org/dictionary/english/component. Accessed 25 July 2025.

Cambridge Dictionary. https://dictionary.cambridge.org/dictionary/english/intend. Accessed 25 July 2025.

Chatterjee P (2022) How SpaceX is using AI to advance its ambitions. https://analyticsindiamag.com/how-spacex-is-using-ai-to-advance-its-ambitions/. Accessed 26 July 2025.

Collins. https://www.collinsdictionary.com/dictionary/english/component. Accessed 25 July 2025.

Collins. https://www.collinsdictionary.com/dictionary/english/object. Accessed 25 July 2025.

Fernández de Cordoba S (2017) 100km Altitude Boundary for Astronautics | World Air Sports Federation. https://www.fai.org/page/icare-boundary. Accessed 25 July 2025.

https://www.oxfordlearnersdictionaries.com/definition/english/intend. Accessed 25 July 2025.

Marr B (2023) Artificial Intelligence In Space: The Amazing Ways Machine Learning Is Helping To Unravel The Mysteries Of The Universe. https://www.forbes.com/sites/bernardmarr/2023/04/10/artificial-intelligence-in-space-the-amazing-ways-machine-learning-is-helping-to-unravel-the-mysteries-of-the-universe/. Accessed 26 July 2025.

NASA: 60 Years & Counting - Technology. https://www.nasa.gov/specials/60counting/tech.html. Accessed 19 July 2025.

Oxford Learner's Dictionary.

Oxford Learner's Dictionary. https://www.oxfordlearnersdictionaries.com/definition/english/object_1. Accessed 25 July 2025.

Oxford Learner's Dictionary. https://www.oxfordlearnersdictionaries.com/definition/english/component_1. Accessed 25 July 2025.

UN Documents

Conference on Disarmament, Letter dated 10 June 2014 from the Permanent Representative of the Russian Federation and the Permanent Representative of China to the Conference on Disarmament addressed to the Acting Secretary-General of the Conference transmitting the updated Russian and Chinese texts of the draft treaty on prevention of the placement of weapons in outer space and of the threat or use of force against outer space objects (PPWT) introduced by the Russian Federation and China, UNODA, 2014, UN Doc CD/1985.

Conference on Disarmament, Letter dated 12 February 2008 from the Permanent Representative of the Russian Federation and the Permanent Representative of Chine to the Conference on Disarmament addressed to the Secretary-General of the Conference transmitting the Russian and Chinese Texts of the Draft "Treaty on the Prevention on Placement of Weapons in Outer Space and of the Threat or Use of Force against Outer Space Objects (PPWT)" introduced by the Russian Federation and China, UNODA, 2008, UN Doc CD/1839.

Draft Basic Provisions of the General Assembly Resolution on the Delimitation of Air Space and Outer Space and on the Legal Status of the Geostationary Satellites' Orbital Space: USSR Working Paper, UNCOPUOS, 22nd Sess, UN Doc A/AC.105/L.122 (1979) Agenda Item 4 (c).

"Fifth Report on the Law of Treaties, by Sir Humphrey Waldock, Special Rapporteur" (Un Doc A/CN.4/183) in Yearbook of the International Law Commission 1966, vol 2 (New York: UN, 1967) (A/CN.4/SER.A/1966/Add.1).

International co-operation in the peaceful uses of outer space, UNGA, 17th Sess, UN Doc A/5181, GA Res 1802 (XVII).

Koskenniemi M (2006) Fragmentation of International Law: Difficulties arising from the Diversification and Expansion of International Law, ILC, 58th Sess, UN Doc A/CN.4/L.702.

LSC, Letter Dated 27 April 1970 from the Chairman of the Committee on the Peaceful Uses of Outer Space Addressed to the Chairman of the Legal Sub-Committee, UNCOPUOS, 1970, UN Doc A/AC.105/C.2/8.

LSC, Matters relating to the Definition and, or Delimitation of Outer Space and Outer Space Activities, Bearing in Mind inter alia, Questions Relating to the Geostationary Orbit, UNCOPUOS, 1983, UN Doc A/AC.105/C.2/L.139.

LSC, National legislation and practice relating to the definition and delimitation of outer space, UNCOPUOS, 49th Sess, UN Doc A/AC.105/865/Add.6 (2010).

LSC, Report of Legal Sub-Committee on the Work of its First Session (28 May-20 June 1962), UNCOPUOS, 1962, UN Doc A/AC.105/6.

LSC, Report of the Legal Sub-Committee on the Work of its Eight Session (9 June - 4 July 1969) to the Committee on the Peaceful Uses of Outer Space, UNCOPUOS 1969, Un Doc A/AC.105/58.
LSC, Report of the Legal Sub-Committee on the Work of its Eight Session (9 June - 4 July 1969) to the Committee on the Peaceful Uses of Outer Space, UNCOPUOS 1969, Un Doc A/AC.105/58.
LSC, Report of the Legal Sub-Committee on the Work of Its Fifth Session (12 July - 4 August and 12 – 16 September 1966) to the Committee on the Peaceful Uses of Outer Space, UNCOPUOS, 1966, UN Doc A/AC.105/35.
LSC, Report of the Legal Sub-Committee on the work of its Ninth Session (8 June - 3 July 1970 to the Committee on the Peaceful Uses of Outer Space, UNCOPUOS, 1970, UN Doc A/AC.105/85.
LSC, Report of the Legal Sub-Committee on the work of its second session (16 April - 3 May 1963) to the Committee on the Peaceful Uses of Outer Space, UNCOPUOS, 1963, UN Doc A/AC.105/12.
LSC, Report of the Legal Sub-Committee on the work of its Seventh Session 94-28 June 1968) to the Committee on the Peaceful Uses of Outer Space, UNCOPUOS, 1968, UN Doc. A/AC.105/45.
LSC, Report of the Legal Sub-Committee on the Work of Its Sixth Session (19 June - 14 July 1967) to the Committee on the Peaceful Uses of Outer Space, UNCOPUOS 1967, UN Doc A/AC.105/37.
LSC, Report of the Legal Sub-Committee on the Work of Its Third Session (9 - 26 March 1964) to the Committee on the Peaceful Uses of Outer Space, UNCOPUOS 1964, UN Doc A/AC.105/19.
LSC, Report of the Legal Sub-Committee on the work of the second part of Its Third Session (5-23 October 1964) to the Committee on the Peaceful Uses of Outer Space, UNCOPUOS 1964, UN Doc A/AC.105/21.
LSC, Summary Record of the 117th Meeting held on Tuesday, 17 June 1969, at 11 a.m., UNCOPUOS 1969, Un Doc A/AC.105/C.2/SR.117.
LSC, Summary Record of the 121st Meeting held on Friday, 20 June 1969, at 10.50 a.m., UNCOPUOS 1969, Un Doc A/AC.105/C.2/SR.121.
LSC, Summary Record of the 122nd Meeting held on Tuesday, 24 June 1969, at 11:00 a.m., UNCOPUOS 1969, Un Doc A/AC.105/C.2/SR.122.
LSC, Summary Records of the 29th to 37th meetings hela at the Palais des Nations, Geneva from 9 to 26 March 1964, UNCOPUOS 1964, Un Doc A/AC.105/C.2/SR.29-37
LSC, Summary Records of the 90th to 101st meetings held at the Palais des Nations, Geneva from 4 to 18 June 1968, UNCOPUOS 1968, Un Doc A/AC.105/C.2/SR.90-101.
LSC, Summary Records of the eighty-fourth meeting held at the Palais des Nations, GenevaonFriday,14.July1967,UNCOPUOS,1967,UnDocA/AC.105/C.2/SR.84.
LSC, Summary Records of the seventy-seventh meeting held at the Palais des Nations, Geneva on Friday, 23 June 1967, UNCOPUOS 1967, Un Doc A/AC.105/C.2/SR.77.

LSC, Working Paper submitted by the Italian Delegation draft convention concerning liability for damage caused by the launching of objects into outer space, UNCOPUOS, 1968, UN Doc A/AC.105/C.2/L.40.
"Record of the 695th Meeting" (UN Doc A/CN.4/156) in Yearbook of the International Law Commission 1963, vol 1 (Un Doc A/CN.4/SER.A/1963).
Report of the Ad Hoc Committee on the Peaceful Use of Outer Space, 14th Sess, UN Doc A/4141 (1959), Agenda Item 25, Annexes, at 21–23.
"Report of the International Law Commission covering the work of its fifteenth session" (UN Doc A/5509) in Yearbook of the International Law Commission 1963, vol 2 (New York: UN, 1964) (UN Doc A/CN.4/SER.A/1987/ADD.1).
"Report of the International Law Commission covering the work of its fifteenth session" (UN Doc A/5509) in Yearbook of the International Law Commission 1963, vol 2 (New York: UN, 1964) (UN Doc A/CN.4/SER.A/1987/ADD.1).
"Report of the International Law Commission on the work of the second part of its seventeenth session" (UN Doc A/6309/Rev.1) in Yearbook of the International Law Commission 1966, vol 2 (New York: UN, 1967) (Un Doc A/CN.4/SER.A/1966/Add. 1).
"Second report by G.G. Fitzmaurice, Special Rapporteur" (UN Doc A/CN.4/107) in Yearbook of the International Law Commission 1957, vol 2 (New York: UN, 1958).
"Second Report on the Law of Treaties, by Sir Humphrey Waldock, Special Rapporteur" (UN Doc A/CN.4/156) in Yearbook of the International Law Commission 1963, vol 2 (New York: UN, 1964) (U Doc A/CN.4/Ser A/1963/Add.1).
Summary Records of the One Hundred and Thirty-Second to the One Hundred and Fifty-First Meetings, UNCOPUOS, 1970, Un Doc A/AC.105/C.2/SR.132-151.
UNCOPUOS, 2020, UN Doc A/AC.105/769/Add.1.
Verbatim Record of the Fifteenth Meeting, UNCOPUOS, 1962, UN Doc A/AC.105/PV/15 (1963).

Judicature

Case concerning the Gabčíkovo-Nagymaros Project (Hungary v Slovakia), [1997] ICJ Rep 7.
Case Concerning the Temple of Preah Vihear (Cambodia v Thailand), [1962] ICJ Rep 6.
ECJ, A Racke GmbH&Co v Hauptzollamt Mainz, C-162/96, [1998] ECR I-3688.
Fisheries Jurisdiction Case (United Kingdom of Great Britain and Northern Ireland v Iceland), [1973] ICJ Rep 3.
Golder v United Kingdom, (1975) 18 ECHR (Ser A), 16 YB Eur Conv HR 482; Sinclair (1984).
Legal Consequences of the Construction of a Wall in the Occupied Palestinian Territory, Advisory Opinion, [2004], ICJ Rep 136.

Legality of the Threat or Use of Nuclear Weapons, Advisory Opinion, [1996] ICJ Rep 226.
The Steamship Lotus (Fance v Turkey) (1927), PCIJ (Seri A) No 10.

Legislation and International Treaties

Agreement Governing the Activities of States on the Moon and Other Celestial Bodies, 05 December 1979, 1363 UNTS 3.
Agreement on the Rescue of Astronauts, the Return of Astronauts and the Return of Objects Launched into Outer Space, 22 April 1968, 672 UNTS 119.
Bundesgesetz über die Genehmigung von Weltraumaktivitäten und die Einrichtung eines Weltraumregisters (Weltraumgesetz) (Austria).
Convention on International Interests in Mobile Equipment,16 November 2001, 2307 UNTS 285.
Convention on Registration of Objects Launched into Outer Space, 12 November 1974, 1023 UNTS 15.
Convention on the International Liability for Damage caused by Space Objects, 29 March 1972, 961 UNTS 18
Law of the Russian Federation "About Space Activity", Decree No. 5663-1.
Law on the Activities of Launching, Flight Operation or Guidance of Space Objects (Belgium); Outer Space Act (Denmark) 2016.
Loi n° 2008-518 du 3 juin 2008 relative aux opérations spatiales JO, 4 June 2008 (France).
National Aeronautics and Space Act, Pub L No 111-314, § 3, 124 Stat 3330
Outer Space Act 1986 (UK)
Outer Space and High-altitude Activities Act 2017 (NZ), 2017/29.
Protocol to the Convention on International Interests in Mobile Equipment on Matters Specific to Space Assets, 9 March 2012.
Radio Regulations Edition of 2024, WRC-23 (Dubai, 2023) (entered into force 1 January 2025.
Rules Concerning Space Activities and the Establishment of a Registry of Space Objects (Space Activities Act) 2006 (Netherlands).
Space (Launches and Returns) Act (Australia), 123/1998.
Space Development Promotion Act (Republic of South Korea).
Treaty on Principles Governing the Activities of States in the Exploration and Use of Outer Space, including the Moon and Other Celestial Bodies, 27 January 1967, 610 UNTS 205.
US, 51 USC § 20103.
Vienna Convention on the Law of Treaties, 23 May 1969, 1155 UNTS 33.

Others

Digesta 2.14.7.7. (Ulpian).
EU, Annexes to the Communication from the European Commission to the European Parliament, the Council, the European Economic and Social Committee of the Regions: Commission Work Programme 2025, [2025] COM(2025) 45 final.
EU, Commission, Proposal for a Directive of the European Parliament and of the Council on adapting non-contractual civil liability rules to artificial intelligence, [2022] COM(2022) 496 final.

References

Literature

Ago R (1957) Positive law and international law. Am J Int Law 51:691–733. https://doi.org/10.2307/2195350
Aust A (2013) Modern treaty law and practice, 3rd edn. Cambridge University Press, Cambridge
Beresford SM (1964) Requirements for an International Convention on Spacecraft Liability. In: Haley A (ed) Proceedings of the International Institute of Space Law 1964. American Institute of Aeronautics and Astronautics, Washington D.C.
Böckstiegel K-H (1994a) The term 'launching state' in international space law. In: Proceedings of the International Institute of Space Law 1994. American Institute of Aeronautics and Astronautics, Washington D.C.
Böckstiegel K-H (1994b) Term appropriate state in international space law. In: Proceedings of the International Institute of Space Law 1994. American Institute of Aeronautics and Astronautics, Washington D.C.
Bodeau-Livinec P, Morgan-Foster J (2011) Article 61 - Supervening impossibility of performance. In: Corten O, Klein P (eds) The Vienna Conventions on the Law of Treaties: a commentary. Oxford University Press, Oxford
Bratu I (2024) Chartering the unchartered waters: non contractual liabilities for damage caused by GNSS-enabled artificial intelligence. PhD Thesis, University of Amsterdam
Brownlie I (1983) State responsibility. Oxford University Press, New York
Buergenthal T, Murphy SD (2002) Public international law in a nutshell, 3rd edn. West Group, St. Paul
Capotorti F (1971) L'extinction et las suspension des traités. Rec des Cours 134:423
Chatzipanagiotis MP (2020) Whose fault is it? Artificial intelligence and liability in international space law. In: Blount PJ et al (eds) Proceedings of the International Institute of Space Law 2020. Eleven International Publishing, The Hague
Cheng B (1997) Studies in international space law. Oxford University Press
Christol CQ (1980) International liability for damage caused by space objects. Am J Int Law 74:346–371. https://doi.org/10.2307/2201505
Damrosch LF (ed) (2001) International law: cases and materials, 4th edn. West Group, St. Paul
Dasgupta U (2013a) On-orbit transfer of satellites between states legal issues – with special emphasis on liability and registration. Master's Thesis, McGill University
Dasgupta U (2013b) Legal issues on sub-orbital space tourism: international and national law perspectives. Ann Air Space Law 38:237

Dasgupta U (2016) On-orbit transfer of satellites between states legal issues – with special emphasis on liability and registration. In: Blount PJ et al (eds) Proceedings of the International Institute of Space Law 2016. Eleven International Publishing, The Hague
De Lucia V (2021) Oceanic dumping of space objects and the conservation of marine biodiversity in areas beyond national jurisdiction. In: Robinson GS, Benkö M, Schrogl K-U (eds) Outer space: future for humankind: issues of law and policy. Eleven, The Hague
Finch ERJ (1980) Outer space liability: past, present and future. Int Lawyer 14:123
Gal GA, Santos C, Rapp L et al (2020) Artificial intelligence in space. arXiv:200612362
Giegerich T (2018) Article 62 - fundamental change of circumstances. In: Dörr O, Schmalenbach K (eds) Vienna Convention on the Law of Treaties: a commentary, 2nd edn. Springer, Berlin
Gorove S (1983) Liability in space law: an overview. Ann Air Space Law 8:373
Gorove S (1991) Developments in space law: issues and policies. Martinus Nijhoff, Dordrecht
Gorove S (1993) Toward a clarification of the term space object - an international legal and policy imperative. J Space Law 21:11
Gould H (2011) Categorical obligation in international law. Int Theory 3:254–285. https://doi.org/10.1017/S1752971911000091
Haraszti G (1973) Some fundamental problems of the law of treaties. Akadémiai Kiadó, Budapest
Henaku BDK (1996) The International Liability of the GNSS Space Segment Provider. Ann Air Space Law 21:143
Henkin L (1989) International law: politics, values and functions general course on public international law. Brill, The Hague
Hertzfeld HR, Von der Dunk F (2005) Bringing space law into the commercial world: property rights without sovereignty. Chic J Int Law 6:1
Hobe S (2019) Space law, First edition. Nomos Verlagsgesellschaft, Baden-Baden
Hurwitz BA (1992) State liability for outer space activities: in accordance with the 1972 Convention on International Liability for Damage Caused by Space Objects. Martinus Nijhoff Publishers, Dordrecht
Hylton KN (2016) Tort law: a modern perspective, 1st edn. Cambridge University Press, Cambridge
Jakhu RS (2010) Iridium-Cosmos collision and its implications for space operations. In: Schrogl K-U, Rathgeber W, Baranes B, Venet C (eds) Yearbook on Space Policy 2008/2009. Springer, Vienna
Jakhu RS, Pelton JN, Mishra N (2021) Satellite constellations and orbital pollution. In: Robinson GS, Benkö M, Schrogl K-U (eds) Outer space: future for humankind: issues of law and policy. Eleven, The Hague
Kayser V (2001) Launching space objects: issues of liability and future prospects. Springer, Netherlands, Dordrecht
Kerrest A, Smith LJ (2017) Space object. In: Hobe S, Schmidt-Tedd B, Schrogl K-U (eds) Cologne Commentary on Space Law. 1: Outer Space Treaty. Berliner Wissenschafts-Verlag, Berlin
Kerrest A, Thro C (2017) Liability for damage caused by space activities. In: Jakhu RS, Dempsey PS (eds) Routledge handbook of space law. Routledge, New York
Kindred HM, Saunders PM, Brunnée J (eds) (2006) International law, chiefly as interpreted and applied in Canada, 7th edn. Emond Montgomery Publications, Toronto
Kopal V (1994) Some remarks on issues relating to legal definitions of "space object", "space debris" and "Astronaut". In: Proceedings of the International Institute of Space Law 1994. American Institute of Aeronautics and Astronautics, Washington D.C.
Lachs M (2010) The law of outer space: an experience in contemporary law-making. Martinus Nijhoff Publishers
Lee RJ (2006) The Liability Convention and Private Space Launch Services. Ann Air Space Law 31
Lissitzyn OJ (1967) Treaties and changed circumstances (Rebus Sic Stantibus). Am J Int Law 61:895
Lyall F, Larsen PB (2018) Space law: a treatise, 2nd edn. Routledge, New York
Malanczuk P (1991) Haftung. In: Böckstiegel K-H, Benkö M (eds) Handbuch des Weltraumrechts. Heymann, Köln

Martin RJ (1980) Legal ramifications of the uncontrolled return of space objects to earth. J Air Law Com 45:457

Martin A-S, Freeland S (2020) Artificial intelligence - a challenging realm for regulating space activities. Ann Air Space Law 45:275

Martin A-S, Freeland S (2021) The advent of artificial intelligence in space activities: new legal challenges. Space Policy 55:101408. https://doi.org/10.1016/j.spacepol.2020.101408

Matte NM (1984) Space activities and emerging international law. Centre for Research of Air and Space Law, McGill University, Montreal

Mishra N (2022) The need for an international rules-based framework for artificial intelligence technologies & systems in space activities. Master's Thesis, McGill University

Navas S (2020) Robot machines and civil liability. In: Ebers M, Navas S (eds) Algorithms and law, 1st edn. Cambridge University Press, Cambridge

Nesgos PD (1984) International and domestic law applicable to commercial launch vehicle transportation. 27:98

Ogunbanwo OO (1975) International law and outer space activities. Nijhoff, The Hague/

Oppenheim L (1955) In: Lauterpacht H (ed) International law, 8th edn. Longmans, London

Palkovitz N (2020) Regulating a revolution: small satellites and the law of outer space. Wolters Kluwer, Alphen aan den Rijn

Rousseau C (1932) De La Compatibilité des Normes Juridiques Contradictoires dans L'Ordre International. RGDIP 133

Schmalenbach K (2018) Article 26. In: Dörr O, Schmalenbach K (eds) Vienna Convention on the Law of Treaties: a commentary, 2nd edn. Springer, Berlin, p 476

Sinclair I (1984) The Vienna Convention on the Law of Treaties, 2nd edn. Manchester University Press, Manchester

Smith LJ (2015) Legal aspects of satellite navigation. In: von der Dunk FG, Tronchetti F (eds) Handbook of space law. Edward Elgar Publishing, Cheltenham

Soroka L, Kurkova K (2019) Artificial intelligence and space technologies: legal, ethical and technological issues. ASL 3. https://doi.org/10.29202/asl/2019/3/11

Trepczynski S (2007) The effect of the liability convention on national space legislation. J Space Law 33:221

Tronchetti F Regulating sub-orbital flights traffic: using air traffic control as a mode. Proc Int Inst Space Law 56:176

Van Bogaert ERC (1986) Aspects of space law. Kluwer Law and Taxation Publishers, Deventer

Villiger ME (2009) Commentary on the 1969 Vienna Convention on the Law of Treaties. Martinus Nijhoff Publishers, Leiden

Von der Dunk F (1998) The 1972 Liability Convention, The Addenda. In: Proceedings of the International Institute of Space Law 1998. American Institute of Aeronautics and Astronautics, Washington D.C.

Von der Dunk F (2015) International space law. In: Von der Dunk F, Tronchetti F (eds) Handbook of space law. Edward Elgar Publishing, Cheltenham

Von der Dunk F (2017) Transfer of ownership in orbit: from fiction to problem. In: Hofmann M, Loukakis A (eds) Ownership of satellites: 4th Luxembourg workshop on space and satellite communication law, 1st edn. Hart Publishing, Baden-Baden

Wedenig S-M (2020) Suborbital point-to-point flights —applicability of air navigation law and aviation criminal law. Master's Thesis, McGill University

Wiewiorowska K (1979) Some problems of state responsibility in outer space law. J Space Law 7

Wirin WB (1994) Practical implications of launching state - appropriate state definitions. In: Proceedings of the International Institute of Space Law 1994. American Institute of Aeronautics and Astronautics, Washington D.C.

Chapter 4
State Responsibility for AI-enabled Space Activities

4.1 Introduction

The present research so far has looked solely at the treaty regime that governs the space activities of States and it has not yet devoted much attention to other ways outside international treaty law to make States responsible and liable for their AI-enabled space activities. This was done because treaties constitute an avenue in public international law that allows States to regulate a specific subject matter if they deem it prudent.[1]

It is also a question of practicality. In an international dispute, a court will usually give preference to a validly concluded treaty rather than to fall back to the more general, and sometimes ambiguous, norms of public international law (i.e., custom and general principles of law).

However, as described above, Article VII of the Outer Space Treaty and the Liability Convention are largely inadequate to govern liability questions that arise from the use of highly advanced-next generation AI. While narrow AI, such as the AI currently being used in space activities, can fall under the scope of the current treaty regime—liability issues arising in this regard can be anchored in human conduct—highly advanced next generation AI will bring the treaties to their limits.

To this author, it seems therefore better to look towards the norms of general international law to address the responsibility and liability of States for their AI-enabled space activities. Indeed, the author believes that the norms of general international law are adequate to govern both narrow AI and general AI.

However, before we can look towards these rules we ought to make some preliminary considerations because the Liability Convention and the Outer Space

[1] The five UN Space Treaties are evidence of this: States felt the urgency to regulate outer space after the launch of Sputnik I in 1957. Indeed, the need was so strong that all the treaties were concluded, as mentioned, in rather remarkably quick fashion.

S.-M. Wedenig, *The International Responsibility of States for AI-enabled Space Activities*, Space Regulations Library 13,
https://doi.org/10.1007/978-3-032-09506-0_4

Treaty demand subjective fault for damage in outer space, while such fault is generally not required for responsibility and liability claims assessed under the norms of general international law.[2] We therefore need to explore how we should handle two norms in public international law which deviate from one another (i.e., subjective fault under Liability Convention and Outer Space Treaty versus no subjective fault under norms of general international law), especially in light of the difficulty of a successful application of supervening impossibility or a fundamental change of circumstances.

This raises the question of a hierarchy of the sources of international law and how to deal with provisions that seemingly differ from one another. It makes it therefore necessary to devote a bit of time to this discussion before moving on to assess whether the norms of general international law, as they exist and are accepted at the date of writing, constitute a viable way to address the responsibility and liability of States for their AI-enabled space activities.

First, this chapter, in Sect. 4.2, will look at the question of whether there exists a hierarchy in the sources of international law and argue that there is none.

Afterwards, we will turn our focus towards whether our issue is in fact a question of a conflict of laws.

Lastly, the chapter will then assess the viability of utilising the norms of general international law to address damages arising from the use of AI in space activities. In this regard, the author will look at the responsibility of States, as well as the liability of States for injurious consequences not prohibited by law to find and propose a suitable solution within the norms of public international law.

4.2 The Sources of International Law: A Hierarchy?

The present research discussed treaty law as it pertains to the responsibility and liability of States for their AI-enabled space activities. Therefore, the focus has mostly been on the Outer Space Treaty and the Liability Convention. It has been concluded that the fault standard contained in the Liability Convention will lead to the unfortunate consequence that should States employ highly advanced next generation AI, subjective fault could not be proven anymore and the Liability Convention, as well as Article VII of the Outer Space Treaty, will act as a shield preventing a claimant State to successfully obtain compensation. This issue leads us to consider other avenues, outside of international treaty law, that can be applied in these circumstances.

International treaties as such are only one of the sources of public international law. Article 38 of the ICJ Statutes enumerates international conventions, international custom and the general principles of law recognised by nations as primary sources of international law, and it has been widely accepted in literature that this

[2] This will be addressed in more detail in Sect. 4.3.

enumeration presents the traditional sources of international law.[3] Since the ICJ Statutes is only an international agreement, it is subject to amendment by States. It does therefore not define international law but is rather part of it.[4] As outlined in Article 38 itself, the Court shall decide disputes in accordance with international law and therefore Article 38 is not being viewed as an exhaustive enumeration of all the sources of international law valid at all times.[5] For example, the ICJ has started to address whether unilateral acts of States and acts of international organisations can be seen as a new source of international law.[6]

The question that now arises is, does Article 38 establish a normative hierarchy between the different sources of public international law? The answer to this question must be "no".

First, international law "governs relations between independent [S]tates".[7] International law as rules binding upon States flows from their own free will "as expressed in conventions or by usages generally accepted as expressing principles of law and established in order to regulate the relations between these coexisting independent communities" or to achieve common aims.[8] States are both creators and subjects of international law and unlike in municipal legal systems there is no higher law making authority. The creation of international law depends on the consent of States, which can either be given expressly (such as in treaties) or tacitly by conduct "which [States] would not follow in case [they] did not consent"[9] (such as custom).[10] As Charles Rousseau aptly put it, "*[l]e droit de gens est un droit de cooperation et non de subordination*".[11] In other words, and as pointed out at the very beginning of this book, all norms of public international law flow from the same source (i.e., State consent) and therefore they possess the same binding value and can logically not be subject to any normative hierarchy.[12] This means, with some exceptions (see below), that international conventions neither prevail over custom, nor does custom prevail over the general principles of law. Generally, all validly

---

[3] Pauwelyn (2003), p. 89; Castel (1976), p. 10ff; Brownlie (2008), p. 3ff; Kindred et al. (2006), p. 103ff, Oppenheim (1955), p. 25ff.

[4] Pauwelyn (2003), p. 90.

[5] Ibid, p. 90; Brownlie (2008), p. 5.

[6] Pauwelyn (2003), p. 90; Armed Activities on the Territory of the Congo (Democratic Republic of Congo v Rwanda) [2006] ICJ Rep 6, para. 43; Case Concerning the Frontier Dispute (Burkina Faso v Republic of Mali), [1986] ICJ Rep 554, para. 39; Armed Activities on the Territory of the Congo (Democratic Republic of Congo v Rwanda) [2006] ICJ Rep 6, paras. 46ff; Obligation to Negotiate Access to the Pacific Ocean (Bolivia v Chile), Advisory Opinion, [2018], ICJ Rep 507, paras. 146ff. However, whether unilateral acts can be seen as a source of law is still debated and not settled albeit the ICJ is indicating some consideration on this point.

[7] The Steamship Lotus (Fance v Turkey) (1927), PCIJ (Seri A) No 10, p. 18.

[8] Ibid, p. 18.

[9] Oppenheim (1955), p. 25.

[10] Pauwelyn (2003), p. 95; Brownlie (2008), pp. 3ff.

[11] Rousseau (1932) [Public International Law is a law of cooperation not subordination].

[12] Pauwelyn (2003), p. 95; Oppenheim (1955), pp. 15–18..

concluded international norms have the same binding effect.[13] The only exception to this principle would be that of *ius cogens* which prevails over international agreements. It is an accepted principle of international law that should a treaty provision violate *ius cogens*, then that provision becomes void.[14] Thus, two States could not validly conclude a treaty that legalises slavery and regulates slave trade. Additionally, UN Charter obligations typically prevail over other treaty provisions.[15]

Second, Article 38 is silent on this question and the sources "are not stated to give an order and in one draft the word "successively" appeared".[16] Rather, Article 38 seems to represent an informal preference the Court would assign to the rules in a given case.[17] For example, a court would first logically assess a validly concluded agreement between two States, which are parties to the court proceedings, first before looking towards rules of customary law or the general principles of law.[18] However, this would only, if at all, be an informal hierarchy of application and it does not allow us to determine a normative hierarchy between the different sources of law. Consequently, the principle of *lex superior derogat legi inferiori* does not apply in international law and we cannot say that the Liability Convention and the Outer Space Treaty, as international conventions, would prevail over the customary norms of State responsibility and liability.

Third, this author argues that there is in fact no conflict between the liability provisions of both, the Outer Space Treaty and the Liability Convention on the one hand, and the norms of general international law, on the other. According to Professor Pauwelyn, a conflict of norms occurs when following one norm would lead to the breach of another norm or when the existence of one norm in itself breaches another norm (norm conflict in the narrow sense), in which case we would need to solve the conflict via principles, such as *lex specialis derogat legi generali* or assess the question whether States have "contracted-out" of norms of general international law thus making the treaty norm to prevail over the norms of general international law.[19]

---

[13] Pauwelyn (2003), p. 95.

[14] Art. 53, Vienna Convention on the Law of Treaties, 23 May 1969, 1155 UNTS 331 [VCLT].

[15] Art. 103, UN Charter, 26 June 1945, Can TS 1945 No 7.

[16] Brownlie (2008), p. 5.

[17] Pauwelyn (2003), p. 95.

[18] In this author's view this is a natural consequence of the fact that treaties are usually much clearer defined and easier for the court to interpret and assess than custom or general principles of law. For example, should the space object of one State cause damage to another State and both are parties to the Outer Space Treaty and the Liability Convention, then the court will first look towards these specialised treaties to assess the validity of any liability claims. The ILC is of a similar opinion and calls it an "informal hierarchy". See Koskenniemi M (2006) Fragmentation of International Law: Difficulties arising from the Diversification and Expansion of International Law UN Doc A/CN.4/L.682, para 85.

[19] Pauwelyn (2003), pp. 212ff, 275–276; De Wet and Vidmar (2012), p. 1; Koskenniemi M (2006) Fragmentation of International Law: Difficulties arising from the Diversification and Expansion of International Law UN Doc A/CN.4/L.682, para 25.

Neither do the liability provisions of the Outer Space Treaty and the Liability Convention breach other norms of general international law, nor do they stand in conflict with them. Rather they lead to the same outcome, namely that a State (e.g., the launching State) is liable (and responsible) for damage caused by a space object. Both treaties confirm obligations that already exist under general international law.[20] Indeed, the customary norms of international State liability and responsibility underlying Articles VI and VII of the Outer Space Treaty and the Liability Convention continue to exist in parallel and thus provide a separate avenue States can choose to obtain compensation.[21] As the ICJ in *Nicaragua* correctly stated, "customary international law continues to exist and to apply, separately from international treaty law, even where the two categories of law have an identical content" and we cannot hold that "when customary international law is comprised of rules identical to those of treaty law, the latter "supervenes" the former, so that customary international law has no further existence of its own".[22]

In other words, a State can choose to base its claims on the norms of customary law rather than the provisions of the Outer Space Treaty and the Liability Convention. This is also important because not all sovereign States are party to either treaty.[23]

Fourth, even if one were to argue that there is a conflict of norms between the Outer Space Treaty and the Liability Convention on the one hand, and general international law on the other, it would be different in the light of the problematique discussed in the present research. This is so because in our case the specialised regime (i.e., Liability Convention and Article VII of the Outer Space Treaty) largely fails to achieve the purpose for which it was created, namely, to ensure equitable and quick access to compensation for damage caused by a space object. In cases where the dedicated treaty regime cannot be sufficiently applied anymore, we ought to fall back towards the norms of general international law which continue to exist.[24]

---

[20] Pauwelyn (2003), p. 155 ["However, particular international law can also confirm or add to rights and obligations set out in general international law. To that extent, particular international law simply confirms or complements general international law. Both can apply simultaneously and no situation of conflict arises."].

[21] Case Concerning Military And Paramilitary Activities in and Against Nicaragua (Nicaragua v United States) [1986], ICJ Rep 14, para. 178 ["There are a number of reasons for considering that, even if two norms belonging to two sources of international law appear identical in content, and even if the States in question are bound by these rules both on the level of treaty-law and on that of customary international law, these norms retain a separate existence."]; See also Pauwelyn (2003), p. 155; Kindred et al. (2006), pp. 109–110.

[22] Case Concerning Military And Paramilitary Activities in and Against Nicaragua (Nicaragua v United States) [1986], ICJ Rep 14, para. 177.

[23] As of 1st January 2025 the Outer Space Treaty has 116 ratifications and 23 signatures while the Liability Convention has 100 ratifications and 18 signatures. UNCOPUOS, "Status of International Agreements relating to activities in outer space as at 1 January 2025" (2025) UN Doc A/AC.105/C.2/2025/CRP.9.

[24] Koskenniemi M (2006) Fragmentation of International Law: Difficulties arising from the Diversification and Expansion of International Law, ILC, UN Doc A/CN.4/L.682, para. 190.

Fifth, the treaty text of both instruments supports this argument. The Outer Space Treaty and the Liability Convention do not prohibit other legal avenues to obtain compensation. Both conventions are remarkably clear in this regard. The Outer Space Treaty in Article II provides that, State Parties to the treaty "shall carry on activities in the exploration and use of outer space, including the moon and other celestial bodies, *in accordance with international law, including the Charter of the United Nations*" [emphasis added]. This important provision, placed at the very beginning of the treaty, makes it clear that the drafters did not intend to take away any existing rights and obligations under general international law but rather provide guidance and more clarity to States in their space activities. This sentiment is also echoed in the title of the Outer Space Treaty as a Treaty on *Principles* Governing the Activities of States in the Exploration and Use of Outer Space, including the Moon and Other Celestial Bodies [emphasis added]. Indeed, in this author's view, the name simultaneously underlines the important aspect general international law plays in the conduct of space activities. The Outer Space Treaty is just that, an instrument to provide international principles for the exploration of space and not a separate legal instrument detached from general international law.

The Liability Convention goes in a similar direction and "ordinary international law [i.e., general international law] might, and could still, be invoked, as, in an appropriate instance, might national law".[25] Article XI of the Liability Convention considers the option of damage being pursued using different means outside of the convention and Article XII stipulates that compensation shall be determined in accordance with international law and the principles of justice and equity.

In conclusion, it is possible to look toward the norms of general international law to find a solution to appropriately govern the responsibility and liability of States for their AI-enabled space activities. Indeed, the norms of general international law, as will be shown, provide an attractive and cohesive legal framework on which to base responsibility and liability claims. Instead of adhering, in our case, to inadequate treaties and elevating them to a non-existing privileged position in public international law as many authors in space law legal literature tend to do, this author suggests, in cases where they cannot sufficiently govern AI applications, to set the treaties largely aside and go to the norms of general international law to govern cases involving AI. The present research aims to show the reader that a solution in general international law can be found to govern cases of narrow AI and highly advanced next generation AI.

[25] Lyall and Larsen (2018), p. 95.

4.3 The Responsibility of States for Their Internationally Wrongful Acts

4.3.1 Introduction

The present research thus far was mainly concerned with the liability of States for their AI-enabled space activities and the respective liability provisions found in Article VII of the Outer Space Treaty and the Liability Convention. It is now time to go beyond the treaty regime and look towards the rules of general international law. To this end, this section will use as a starting point the responsibility of States for their international wrongful acts as expressed in the ILC Articles on State Responsibility.[26] The section will conclude by pointing out that States can be held responsible for their AI-enabled space activities under the existing norms of public international law.

As has been done before, the book will lay some groundwork before delving deeper into the responsibility aspect to clearly outline how the chapter will progress from here.

This research will separate the responsibility from the liability aspect and address the latter in the next section. This is done for several reasons.

First, as pointed out, the Outer Space Treaty and the Liability Convention address responsibility and liability separately. It seems therefore appropriate to follow a similar distinction in a book that is concerned with the responsibility of States for their AI-enabled space activities.

Second, the author supports to a certain degree the view that State responsibility and State liability are two different concepts. They overlap and influence each other but each has a proper role. The ILC found in 1962 that the topic of international liability should be addressed separately in order to avoid confusion with international responsibility as, in the ILC's view, it entails a different concept than State responsibility does.[27] International liability simply means to bear the consequences for activities that are lawful but fall under a norm establishing a duty to compensate.[28] Let us emphasise here again what has already been pointed out above: The breach of an international obligation giving rise to responsibility also entails the obligation to make reparation (i.e., to be liable).[29] It follows therefore that State responsibility and liability are two sides of the same coin: a State will be under the

[26] Resolution adopted by the General Assembly: Responsibility of States for Internationally Wrongful Acts, UNGA, 56th Sess, UN Doc A/Res/56/83.

[27] "Report on the International Law Commission on the work of its twenty-first session" (UN Doc A/7610/Rev.1) in Yearbook of the International Law Commission 1969, vol 2 (New York: UN, 1970) (A/CN.4/SER. A/1969/Add. 1), para. 83; Stubbe (2018), pp. 108–109.

[28] Cheng (1998), p. 9; Stubbe (2018), p. 62.

[29] Case Concerning the Factory at Chorzów (Germany v Poland), (1928) PCIJ (Ser A) No 17; Lee (2006), p. 359. In other words, liability is part of responsibility. While liability is only concerned with the duty to compensate, responsibility is much wider.

obligation to compensate for damage which that State has caused.[30] This led to the somewhat misleading practice of using these two terms (State responsibility and liability) interchangeably.[31] Nevertheless, some authors and the ILC support a distinction between these two terms because in their view State responsibility arises from an internationally wrongful act or omission (see below) while international liability could crucially arise even in the absence of such a wrongful act or omission.[32] The present research will circle back to this issue in more detail in Sect. 4.4.

Third, the present research has not yet discussed Article VI of the Outer Space Treaty, which deals with the responsibility of States for their national activities in outer space. Although this section will, as mentioned, go beyond treaty law and as such will not look too much towards the Outer Space Treaty, it seems appropriate to discuss Article VI in this section, especially when we consider that a few elements of this Article have crystallised into customary law, and as such must be assessed outside international treaty law. The author wants to remind the reader, here again, that there is *a priori* no hierarchy between the sources of international law and these sources co-exist in parallel. This will become more evident when we consider Article VI of the Outer Space Treaty, which can, in certain cases, be successfully applied to AI, and in many regards just reemphasises existing rules of responsibility in general international law, albeit Article VI was, as mentioned, remarkably innovative. This interaction will be present in the subsequent inquiry.[33]

4.3.2 State Responsibility for Internationally Wrongful Acts

State responsibility in its most basic sense means answerability of a State "for [its] acts and omissions, for being in conformity with whichever system of norms, whether moral, legal, religious political or any other, which may be applicable, as well as answerability for their consequences whether beneficial or injurious".[34] The source of this answerability, as emphasised in Sect. 1.2.2 above, is the consent of States, namely their consent to be answerable for their acts and omissions.[35]

---

[30] Kayser (2001), p. 32.

[31] "Second report on international liability for injurious consequences arising out of acts not prohibited by international law, by Mr. Julio Barboza, Special Rapporteur" (UN Doc A/CN.4/402) in Yearbook of the International Law Commission 1986, vol 2, part 1 (New York: UN, 1988) (UN Doc A/CN.4/SER.A/1986/Add.1), p. 146; Goldie (1985), p. 180.

[32] See e.g. Montjoie (2010), p. 503; Barboza (2011), p. 23ff.

[33] This should not be understood as to mean that customary rules and treaty law are the same. They exist, and can sometimes be applied, in parallel but in itself they are different vehicles with varying normative value.

[34] Cheng (1998), p. 9.

[35] It is important to note, however, that international responsibility is concerned with the responsibility of all subjects of international law, and this includes more than just States. Indeed, the ILC Articles on State responsibility expressly state in Article 57 that, "[t]hese articles are without prejudice to any question of the responsibility under international law of an international organization,

State responsibility describes the legal relations which arise under public international law for an internationally wrongful act or omission, and "[e]very internationally wrongful act of a State entails the international responsibility of that State"[36] As Judge Huber pointed out "*[l]a responsabilité est le corollaire nécessaire du droit. Tous droits d'ordre international ont pour conséquence une responsabilité internationale*".[37] In a practical sense the question of responsibility is a matter of "insistence on performance or restoration of normal standards of international conduct".[38]

State responsibility constitutes such an important building block of the international legal order that the General Assembly of the United Nations charged the ILC in 1953 to undertake the codification of the principles on international law governing State responsibility.[39] The ILC adopted its final draft in 2001 and presented it to the General Assembly, which adopted the Articles.

---

or of any State for the conduct of an international organization." The ICJ itself recognised that, "[the UN] is a subject of international law and capable of possessing international rights and duties, and that it has capacity to maintain its rights by bringing international claims". See Reparation for injuries suffered in the service of the United Nations, Advisory Opinion, [1949] ICJ Rep 174, p. 179. The necessary and logical result of the ability to possess international rights and duties is also to bear responsibility for the breach of such duties. It is because of this that the ILC has taken up the task of codifying the rules pertaining the responsibility of international organisations. See "Eight Report on responsibility on international organizations by Mr. Giorgio Gaja, Special Rapporteur" (UN Doc A/CN.4/640) in Yearbook of the International Law Commission 2018, vol 2, part 1 (New York: UN, 2010) (UN Doc A/CN.4/SER.A/2011/Add.1); However, the ILC seemingly uses the Articles on State responsibility as a departure point, which is problematic as States and international organisations are not the same and, in many respects, fundamentally different. This is something the ICJ itself pointed out when recognising the legal personality of the UN. The court clearly stated that, "it is not the same thing as saying that [the UN] is a State, which it certainly is not, or its legal personality and rights and duties are the same as those of a State. It does not even imply that all its rights and obligations must be upon the international plane." See Reparation for injuries suffered in the service of the United Nations, Advisory Opinion, [1949] ICJ Rep 174, p. 179. There is further no consensus so far on the content of the rules. Naturally, international organisations will also adopt the use of AI applications, and it will be interesting to see the development of the responsibility of international organisations in this regard. However, we will not further pursue this train of thought in the present research. First, as mentioned, the issue is far from settled and it would add a layer to the present research which does not serve a purpose. Second, this topic would certainly warrant its own dedicated research which would extend the scope of the present research too far. We will therefore not delve deeper into it. For a more detailed discussion see e.g. Ahlborn (2011), pp. 397–482.

[36] Resolution adopted by the General Assembly: Responsibility of States for Internationally Wrongful Acts, UNGA, 56th Sess, UN Doc A/Res/56/83, art. 1.

[37] Affaire des biens brittaniques au Maroc espagnol (Espagne contre Royaume-Uni) (1925), RIAA 615, p. 641 ["Responsibility is the necessary corollary of a right. All rights of an international character result in international responsibility"]. Case concerning the Barcelona Traction, Light and Power Company, Limited (Belgium v Spain), [1970] ICJ Rep 3, para 36 ["Responsibility is the necessary corollary of a right"].

[38] Brownlie (1983), p. 22.

[39] Request for the codification of the principles of international law governing State responsibility, UNGA, 8th Sess, UN Doc A/Res/798(VIII) (1953) GA Res 799(VIII).

For a State to be internationally responsible, it is accepted that two elements are required: (1) there has to be a breach of an international obligation and (2) the breach must be attributable to the State.[40] Whether a third element of damage, be material or immaterial, is required was debated in the past. The traditional conception, originating from Hugo Grotius, made damage a necessary element to give rise to State responsibility.[41] The now predominant view of the literature and jurisprudence rejects this understanding and rightly sees damage only as an optional element.[42] Further, the ILC Articles do not list damage as a requirement for responsibility to arise.[43]

However, this should not be misunderstood as to mean that damage can never be a prerequisite for State responsibility. The question of "whether damage is a prerequisite for a breach becomes a matter to be determined by the relevant primary rule"[44] and some primary rules may well contain such a requirement.[45]

4.3.2.1 Internationally Wrongful Act

State Responsibility is grounded in an internationally wrongful act. Article 2 of the ILC Articles sets out the two cumulative conditions that need to be fulfilled in order for a State to have committed an internationally wrongful act: there needs to be (1)

[40] Resolution adopted by the General Assembly: Responsibility of States for Internationally Wrongful Acts, UNGA, 56th Sess, UN Doc A/Res/56/83, art. 2; See also Condorelli and Kress (2010); Stern (2010); Bedjaoui (1987), p. 359; Palkovitz (2020), p. 72; Legal Consequences of the Separation of the Chagos Archipelago from Mauritius in 1965, [2019] ICJ Rep 95; Venezuela US, S.R.L. (Barbados) v The Bolivarian Republic of Venezuela (2021), Case-No 2013-34 (Permanent Court of Arbitration), paras 154–55; Consutel Group S.P.A. in liquidazione (Italy) v La République algérienne démocratique et populaire (2020), Case-No 2017-33 (Permanent Court of Arbitration), para. 317.

[41] Grotius (2005); De Visscher (1935); Stern (2010), p. 194; Bedjaoui (1987), p. 359; Oppenheim and Lauterpacht seem to lean towards the same understanding. See Oppenheim (1955), p. 352.

[42] Correctly this author might add. It makes sense if we consider that State Responsibility is grounded in the breach of an international obligation that is attributable to a State. See Corfu Channel Case (United Kingdom v Albania) [1949] ICJ Rep 4, p. 35; Cheng (1997), p. 602; Stern (2010), p. 194; Kindred et al. (2006), p. 380; "Fourth report on State Responsibility by Mr. James Crawford, Special Rapporteur" (UN Doc A/CN.4/517) in Yearbook of the International Law Commission 2001, vol 2, part 1 (New York: UN, 2010) (UN Doc A/CN.4/SER.A/2001/Add.1), p. 8.

[43] Resolution adopted by the General Assembly: Responsibility of States for Internationally Wrongful Acts, UNGA, 56th Sess, UN Doc A/Res/56/83, art. 2.

[44] Crawford (2013), p. 57.

[45] For example, the Liability Convention in Article 2 provides that a "launching State shall be absolutely liable to pay compensation for damage caused by its space object (…)" and as we have pointed out in Sect. 3.3.1.2 "no damage, no liability under the Liability Convention and Article VII Outer Space Treaty".

certain behaviour which is attributable to the State and (2) a breach of an international obligation as a result of such behaviour.[46]

If one of these elements is not present, then there is no internationally wrongful act. Therefore, the discussion in the following paragraphs relates to the necessary elements for an internationally wrongful act to arise and should be read as such. These elements are not to be read separately from the notion of internationally wrongful act, but rather are the very essence that allow for such an internationally wrongful act to arise.

It is important to note, as mentioned above, that although the ILC Articles speak of an internationally wrongful *act*, it can also be an internationally wrongful *omission*.[47] An internationally wrongful act is driven by conduct, which can consist of action or omission contrary to an international obligation.[48] Therefore, an international obligation may impose a duty to act or a duty to abstain.[49] For example, the prohibition of the use of force constitutes and obligation to abstain from such conduct, and should a State not do so, the State would act in contravention to public international law. Conversely, there exist obligations that require certain actions. If these actions are not taken, then a State would omit its obligations under international law.[50]

The use of AI does not change this assessment. For example, a State that fails to put adequate safety protocols in place to prevent the AI from malfunctioning, thus causing damage to another State, could be seen as having committed an internationally wrongful omission, provided the elements of breach and attribution are

---

[46] Stern (2010), p. 201; Resolution adopted by the General Assembly: Responsibility of States for Internationally Wrongful Acts, UNGA, 56th Sess, UN Doc A/Res/56/83, art. 2; Case Concerning United States Diplomatic and Consular Staff in Tehran (United States v Iran [1980] ICJ Rep 3, p. 29 ["First, it must determine how far, legally, the acts in question may be regarded as imputable to the Iranian State. Secondly, it must consider their compatibility or incompatibility with the obligations of Iran under treaties in force or under any other rules of international law that may be applicable."]; Phosphates in Morocco Case (Italy v France) (1938), PCIJ (Ser A/B) No 74 ["This act being attributable to the State and described as contrary to the treaty right of another State, international responsibility would be established immediately as between the two States"].

[47] Resolution adopted by the General Assembly: Responsibility of States for Internationally Wrongful Acts, UNGA, 56th Sess, UN Doc A/Res/56/83; Corfu Channel Case (United Kingdom v Albania) [1949] ICJ Rep 4. In this case the court clearly distinguished between the actions of the UK and the omissions of Albania; see also Latty (2010); Case concerning the difference between New Zealand and France concerning the interpretation or application of two agreements, concluded on 9 July 1986 between the two States and which related to the problems arising from the Rainbow Warrior Affair (1990), RIAA 215; B3 Croatian Courier Coöperatief U.A. v. Republic of Croatia (2019) ICSID Case No ARB/15/5 (International Centre for Settlement of Investment Disputes), para. 1050.

[48] Kolb (2017), p. 38.

[49] Ibid.

[50] A typical example of an obligation to act would be the protection of diplomatic personnel. For example, Iran's failure to protect US diplomatic staff and the embassy was considered an internationally wrongful omission. See Case Concerning United States Diplomatic and Consular Staff in Tehran (United States v Iran [1980] ICJ Rep 3.

fulfilled. Conversely, where a State employs AI to attack and spoof vital communication systems of another State, the State could be seen of having acted in contravention of its international obligations.

4.3.2.1.1 Breach of an International Obligation

In general terms, an international obligation means "an obligation owed under international law by one State to another State".[51] This obligation can either be owed to a single or to several States.[52] In this regard, State responsibility is often divided into two categories, namely State responsibility for breaches of international obligations that protect reciprocal interests of States (e.g., treaties) and State responsibility for violations of fundamental obligations owed to the international community as a whole, so-called *obligationes erga omnes*.[53]

The difference between these two categories is who can invoke responsibility. For breaches of obligations that protect reciprocal interests, responsibility only arises between the delinquent and the wronged State, while a breach of an obligation *erga omnes*, which is an obligation that protects fundamental values, such as human-rights, peace, self-determination etc., entitles all States to invoke responsibility as the obligation is owed to the international community as a whole.[54]

Professor Antonio Cassese categorises them, rather unfortunately in this author's view, as responsibility for "ordinary" breaches of international law and "aggravated responsibility".[55] In this author's view such a distinction could lead to confusion and make it appear that there is a hierarchy. The international legal regime does not prescribe categories to breaches of international obligations, or any degree of responsibility. A breach of *obligationes erga omnes* gives rise to responsibility of the delinquent State in the same way any other breach of an international obligation does. In this author's view, this differentiation is a procedural, rather than a material one. It concerns the question of who has the right to invoke the responsibility. As Article 12 of the ILC Articles makes clear, "[t]here is a breach of an international obligation by a State when an act of that State is not in conformity with what is

[51] Aust (2010), p. 377.

[52] Cassese (2001), p. 185.

[53] Ibid, p. 185; Crawford (2013), p. 66; Case concerning the Barcelona Traction, Light and Power Company, Limited (Belgium v Spain), [1964] ICJ Rep 6, paras 33–34; These *erga omnes* obligations also exist in treaty law. The ICJ calls them *obligationes erga partes* and are owed to all State Parties to the treaty. See e.g. Application of the Convention on the Prevention and Punishment of the Crime of Genocide in the Gaza Strip, Order of 26 January 2024 [2024], p. 12; Application of the Convention on the Prevention and Punishment of the Crime of Genocide (The Gambia v Myanmar), [2022] ICJ Rep 477, pp. 516–517.

[54] Case concerning the Barcelona Traction, Light and Power Company, Limited (Belgium v Spain), [1964] ICJ Rep 6, para. 35.

[55] Cassese (2001), sect. 9.4-9.5.

required of it by obligation, *regardless of its origin or character* [emphasis added]". In the *Rainbow Warrior Case*, the Court further underlined that,

> the general principles of International Law concerning State Responsibility are equally applicable in the case of breach of treaty obligation, since in the international law field there is no distinction between contractual and tortious responsibility, so that the violation by a State of any obligation, of whatever origin gives rise to State responsibility (…).[56]

This view was further confirmed by the ICJ in *Gabčikovo-Nagymaros*.[57]

These obligations are substantive rules of international law which determine the rights and obligations of States, and the ILC calls them primary rules of international law, whose breach would give rise to State responsibility. State responsibility itself deals with the consequences of such a breach of a primary rule and is a such a secondary rule of international law.[58] What exactly amounts to a breach of an international obligation and when a State is internationally responsible depends on the exact content of each State's international obligation and this can differ from one State to the next, which makes a case-by-case analysis necessary by applying the primary rules (e.g., customs, treaties etc.) to each case.

Since a breach of an international obligation can either be an internationally wrongful act or omission, the basis of international responsibility is not grounded in risk or damage but rather in the breach of an international obligation.[59] Once a State acts in a manner inconsistent with its international obligation, a breach has occurred. In this regard, it does not matter what the nature of the obligation is (breach of treaty, customary law, general principles of law, *ius cogens* etc.). It only needs to be an international obligation, and the responsibility is anchored in the breach of that obligation.[60] This is an important aspect to highlight as it allows us to bring AI under the umbrella of this regime (see below).

Since State responsibility is grounded in the breach of the international obligation, negligence should not be a required element to give rise to responsibility. Accordingly, the ILC did not mention fault in the ILC Articles. The author differentiated early on in this research between objective fault on the one hand, and subjective fault on the other hand (Sect. 2.2). In this author's view this differentiation is also necessary when discussing State responsibility. When authors in international law speak of the absence of fault in the ILC Articles, and within the doctrine of State

---

[56] Case concerning the difference between New Zealand and France concerning the interpretation or application of two agreements, concluded on 9 July 1986 between the two States and which related to the problems arising from the Rainbow Warrior Affair (1990), RIAA 215, para. 75.

[57] Case concerning the Gabčíkovo-Nagymaros Project (Hungary v Slovakia), [1997] ICJ Rep 7, para. 47 ["It is moreover well established that, when a State has committed an internationally wrongful act, its international responsibility is likely be involved whatever the nature of the obligation it has failed to respect"].

[58] Gourgourinis (2011), p. 1016; Stubbe (2018), p. 62; Combacau and Alland (1985), pp. 107–108; Pellet (2010), p. 28.

[59] State liability, on the other hand, is grounded in damage.

[60] Resolution adopted by the General Assembly: Responsibility of States for Internationally Wrongful Acts, UNGA, 56th Sess, UN Doc A/Res/56/83, art. 12.

responsibility more generally, they are in fact talking about the absence of subjective fault, rather than objective fault.

Indeed, objective fault is necessary to give rise to State responsibility, and this author argues that it has been included in the ILC Articles. As has been pointed out above, objective fault concerns the inquiry of what was the conduct objectively required versus what was the actual conduct followed. It thus looks purely at objective elements. For example, when Iran allowed a violent mob to break into the US embassy and abduct diplomatic personnel, the objective fault element was fulfilled. What was objectively required of Iran under international law was to protect the US embassy from any intrusion and prevent any attack on the person and freedom of the diplomatic staff.[61] However, the actual conduct shown was Iran's failure to initiate any such steps to protect the US embassy and its staff, which constituted an internationally wrongful omission.

The reader might realise that objective fault is quite like what international law denotes as international obligation, and they would be correct in this assessment. Indeed, objective fault is contained within the breach of an international obligation. Whether or not a breach of an international obligation occurred is an objective test and exactly concerned with the question of required conduct (i.e., the international obligation) versus actually shown conduct (i.e., the breach). Therefore, in this author's view, objective fault is a necessary element to give rise to State responsibility.

The other side of the coin, namely subjective fault and whether it is required to successfully hold a State responsible, was debated in the past. Proponents of subjective State responsibility, a view originating again from the writings of Hugo Grotius, saw subjective fault as a mandatory element without which State responsibility cannot arise. Oppenheim and Lauterpracht, two supporters of subjective responsibility, base their view on the *Corfu Channel Case* and argue that the case is "an instructive example of the affirmation of the principle that there is no liability without fault".[62] They base their view mainly on the fact that the Court stated that "knowledge of the minelaying cannot be imputed to the Albanian Government by reason merely of the fact that a minefield discovered in Albanian territorial waters caused the explosions of which the British warships were the victims" and "[the] fact, by itself and apart from other circumstances, neither involves prima facie responsibility nor shifts the burden of proof".[63] This view was rightly criticized by Brownlie who correctly reminded us that the Court "was concerned with the particular question of *responsibility* for the creation of danger in the North Corfu Channel by laying of mines, warning of which was not given" and the "[l]iability thus rested upon a violation of a particular legal duty".[64] In this case the obligation in itself required knowledge and

[61] Case Concerning United States Diplomatic and Consular Staff in Tehran (United States v Iran [1980] ICJ Rep 3, para. 62.

[62] Oppenheim (1955), p. 343.

[63] Corfu Channel Case (United Kingdom v Albania) [1949] ICJ Rep 4, p. 18.

[64] Brownlie (1983), p. 43.

the court was not concerned with the question of subjective fault.[65] It must also be mentioned that while the Court speaks of "every State's obligation not to allow *knowingly* its territory to be used for acts contrary to the rights of other States" [emphasis added], the word knowingly does not appear in the equally authentic French text of the judgement, possibly lending support to an objective view.[66] It is even more interesting when we consider that the case was argued in French.

In any case, this understanding of State responsibility has largely been rejected, and the now predominant view of literature and judicature holds that subjective fault is not a necessary element to give rise to State responsibility.[67]

However, this does not mean that subjective fault plays no role in the modern understanding of State responsibility. Indeed, there is a "proper role of [subjective] fault" contained in the conceptual foundations of international State responsibility.[68] For example, the ICJ in the *Corfu Channel Case* developed a general duty of due diligence and, in this regard, subjective fault can play an important part.[69] Such obligations are, *inter alia*, encountered in cases of acts of private actors, in which the State is under the due diligence obligation to prevent a certain conduct. For example, in the *Youmans Case*, the claim submitted by the US rested upon "the failure of the Mexican Government to exercise due diligence to protect the father of the claimant from the fury of the mob".[70] This led Professor Brownlie to conclude that there is "consistent [S]tate practice supporting the duty to exercise due diligence".[71]

Nonetheless, this should not be understood as an argument to see subjective fault as a separate mandatory element required to give rise to State responsibility. Indeed, this due diligence obligation is not related to attributability but rather contained in the State's primary obligation.[72]

The same applies to the notion of *dolus* or *culpa*. Although not a required element it can be helpful in several ways. First, if *dolus* or *culpa* are proven on the part

---

[65] Ibid., pp. 43–44.

[66] The French version speaks of "*l'obligation', pour tout Etat, de ne pas laisser utiliser son territoire aux fins d'actes contraires aux droits d'autres États*".

[67] See e.g. Cassese (2001), pp. 191–192; Latty (2010), p. 355; Brownlie (2008), pp. 437–439; Abass (2012), pp. 267–269; L. F. H. Neer and Pauline Neer (U.S.A.) v. United Mexican States (1926), 4 RIAA 60; Jesse Lewis (United States) v. Great Britain (David J. Adams case) (1921), 6 RIAA 85; Gustave Caire (France) v United Mexican States, (1929), 5 RIAA 590.

[68] Brownlie (1983), p. 44.

[69] Corfu Channel Case (United Kingdom v Albania) [1949] ICJ Rep 4, p. 22.

[70] Thomas H Youmans (USA) v United Mexican States (1926), 4 RIAA 110, p. 114. Similarly in the Janes and Massey claims the tribunal considered the notion of negligence; Laura M. B. Janes et al (USA) v United Mexican States (1925), 4 RIAA 82, p. 87; Massey, Getrude Parker Massey (U.S.A) v United Mexican States (1927), 4 RIAA 155, p. 155.

[71] Brownlie (1983), p. 162.

[72] Kindred et al. (2014), p. 399; Oppenheim and Lauterpracht argue that the "Corfu Channel case between Great Britain and Albania provided an instructive example of the affirmation of the principle that there is no liability without fault". See Oppenheim (1955), p. 343.

of, for example, State organs, it will help to solve the problem of attributability.[73] Second, it can assist in establishing a breach of an international obligation and be important in the determination of the appropriate damages.[74]

Further, subjective fault can be made a mandatory element in international agreements.[75] A prominent example of this is the herein discussed Liability Convention, which makes subjective fault a mandatory element to make the launching State liable for damage caused by a space object anywhere else than on the surface of the Earth.[76]

Fault is, therefore, generally not required to give rise to State responsibility. This view would also be supported by the fact that the ILC did not include fault in its final draft of the Articles on State Responsibility. Indeed, in the commentary to the final version of the ILC Articles, the ILC clarified that, "[i]n the absence of any specific requirement of a mental element in terms of primary obligation, it is only the act of a State that matters, independently of any intention".[77] Only in two cases the ILC referred to the notion of fault, namely (1) when a State directs and controls another State in the commission of an internationally wrongful act and does so with the knowledge of the circumstances of the wrongful act and (2) when one State coerces another State to commit a wrongful act.[78]

In both cases, however, the notion of subjective fault is in fact contained in the primary obligation itself, rather than being a separate requirement. On the other hand, the ILC Articles also do not expressly exclude the notion of subjective fault either.[79] In this author's opinion this makes sense in light of the discussion above, namely that subjective fault can play an important part when assessing the responsibility of States, but it is not grounded in it.

Since State responsibility is grounded in the breach of an international obligation, it can cover a breach caused by an AI. This is possible because the breach is objectively assessed. When a State acts in contravention to its obligations, regardless of the nature of the obligation in question, a breach will occur.[80] A breach of an

---

[73] Brownlie (1983), p. 46.

[74] Ibid, p. 46.

[75] Ibid, p. 46.

[76] Art. III, Convention on the International Liability for Damage caused by Space Objects, 29 March 1972, 961 UNTS 187.

[77] "Report of the International Law Commission on the work of its fifty-third session" (Un Doc A/56/10) in Yearbook of the International Law Commission 2001, vol 2, part 2 (UN Doc A/CN.4/SER.A/2001/Add.1), p. 36.

[78] Resolution adopted by the General Assembly: Responsibility of States for Internationally Wrongful Acts, UNGA, 56th Sess, UN Doc A/Res/56/83, arts 17–18.

[79] Kindred et al. (2006), p. 637.

[80] Resolution adopted by the General Assembly: Responsibility of States for Internationally Wrongful Acts, UNGA, 56th Sess, UN Doc A/Res/56/83, art. 12; Case concerning the difference between New Zealand and France concerning the interpretation or application of two agreements, concluded on 9 July 1986 between the two States and which related to the problems arising from the Rainbow Warrior Affair (1990), RIAA 215.

international obligation simply means conduct contrary to the rights of others.[81] This means that the problems discussed at length above, such as autonomy of AI, machine learning and foreseeability, do not arise in this inquiry. Whether a breach of an international obligation occurred is a matter of "if" and not "how", the latter being assessed within the question of attribution.[82] Therefore, we only need to assess whether an international obligation in the abstract has been breached, and this analysis is detached from the question of the nature of the AI involved.

When the substantive threshold of that breach is reached, that is what the content of the obligation in question is and whether it was breached, would go beyond the scope of the present research. Indeed, in the author's opinion it would not be appropriate to make general assertions and determine it in the abstract as it depends on the content and interpretation of the primary obligation which is done on a case-by-case basis.[83] The purpose of the present research is to show that AI can be addressed within the *lex lata*, albeit a practical application (i.e., to determine when a primary obligation is breached) has to be done case-by-case.

Even Article VI of the Outer Space Treaty, which addresses the responsibility of State parties for their national activities in outer space, also requires a case-by-case analysis and interpretation. It is true that Article VI mandates States to assure that "national activities are carried out in conformity with the provisions set forth in the present Treaty" but it does not tell us when exactly such a provision is substantively breached.[84]

4.3.2.1.2 Attribution

The State as an imagined political construct cannot act without some kind of agency.[85] It is a well-established principle in international law that a State can only be responsible for its own behaviour and therefore international responsibility only arises when the breach of an international obligation is also attributable to the

---

[81] "Report of the International Law Commission on the work of its fifty-third session" (Un Doc A/56/10) in Yearbook of the International Law Commission 2001, vol 2, part 2 (UN Doc A/CN.4/SER.A/2001/Add.1), p. 35.

[82] For example, the failure of a State to put adequate safety protocols in place to prevent AI to cause damage to another State, could be seen as a breach of a due diligence obligation which could invoke the responsibility of the State.

[83] "Report of the International Law Commission on the work of its fifty-third session'" (Un Doc A/56/10) in Yearbook of the International Law Commission 2001, vol 2, part 2 (UN Doc A/CN.4/SER.A/2001/Add.1), p. 36.

[84] While Article VI speaks of "conformity with the provisions set forth in the present Treaty", it must be noted that Article III requires States to act in accordance with international law. This would essentially mean that if a State breached an obligation under general international law, it would also breach Article III of the Outer Space Treaty.

[85] Kindred et al. (2006), p. 646.

State.[86] The topic of attribution "or whether an act may be imputed to a [S]tate, is a key element in international responsibility".[87] Since a State cannot act on its own but only through other persons or entities (i.e., its agents), it will generally only be held responsible for acts of its organs, for actions of person or entities empowered to exercise governmental authority or for private actors acting under the instruction or control of the State.[88] Provided that none of these circumstances are present, a State is generally not internationally responsible for the conduct of foreign nationals or private individuals, unless the State fails to act upon an international obligation to prevent a certain conduct of private individuals.[89]

4.3.2.1.2.1 State Organ

The conduct of a State organ "shall be considered an act of that State under international law, whether the organ exercises legislative, executive, judicial or any other function, whatever position it holds in the organization of the State, and whatever its character as an organ of central Government or of territorial unit of the State".[90]

This principle has long been applied in the realm of State responsibility, is widely accepted by courts and literature and has rightly been seen as a customary norm of international law.[91] The question arising now is, what can be considered a State organ? Article 4 of the ILC Articles states that "an organ includes any person or entity which has that status in accordance with internal law of the State". However, this formulation must be taken with a degree of caution and should only be seen as

[86] Momtaz (2010); Shaw (2008), p. 781ff; Abass (2012), p. 245ff; Cassese (2001), p. 187ff; Aust (2010), p. 378ff; Tulip Real Estate and Development Netherlands BV v Republic of Turkey (2015) Case-No ARB/11/28 (International Centre for Settlement of Investment Disputes), para. 183; Phosphates in Morocco Case (Italy v France) (1938), PCIJ (Ser A/B) No 74, para. 48; Dickson Car Wheel Company (USA v United Mexican States) (1931), RIAA 669, p. 678 ["Under international law, apart from any convention, in order that a State may incur responsibility it is necessary that an unlawful international act be imputed to it, that is, that there exist a violation of a duty imposed by an international juridical standard"].

[87] Kindred et al. (2014).

[88] Resolution adopted by the General Assembly: Responsibility of States for Internationally Wrongful Acts, UNGA, 56th Sess, UN Doc A/Res/56/83, arts. 4, 5, 8.

[89] Kindred et al. (2014), p. 389. However, in this case it is not the actions of the private actors themselves that impute the State but rather its own failure to prevent the conduct. It is not the private actors who breach an obligation but the State, which acts in contravention of a primary obligation that established a duty to prevent a certain conduct of private individuals. For example, if a State would allow a private actor to commit genocide, then the State would breach an obligation to prevent genocide on its territory.

[90] Resolution adopted by the General Assembly: Responsibility of States for Internationally Wrongful Acts, UNGA, 56th Sess, UN Doc A/Res/56/83, art. 4(1).

[91] Question relating to Settles of German Origin in Poland (1931), Advisory Opinion, PCIJ (Ser B) No 6, p. 22; Anzilotti (1929), p. 469; Cassese (2001), p. 188; Momtaz (2010), p. 2378; Staur Eiedom AS, Ebo Invest AS & Rox Holding AS v Republic of Latvia (2020), ARB/16/38, ICSID, para. 312 ["It is common ground that under Article 4, the conduct of a State organ acting as such is attributable to the State"].

a floor rather than a ceiling. If the internal laws of a State designate a certain entity or person as a State organ, then it shall definitively be considered as such, but it is not a requirement. In the words of the United Kingdom (UK):

> [I]f that [internal] law itself designates the organ as an organ of the State, it may be appropriate for international law to adopt a similar position. If, however, the municipal law of a State does not treat an organ as part of the State, it does not necessarily follow that the organ's acts are not attributable to the State. The municipal law cannot have determinative effect in this context: attribution is a matter for international law.[92]

Internal law ordinarily varies across States and therefore the definition of a State organ is a question of fact which is not related to any formal or regular tests provided by a State's constitution or internal law.[93] In other words, an entity or person can be considered a State organ either *de iure* (i.e., pursuant to municipal law) or *de facto*.[94] Further, any internal hierarchical structures, separation of powers or whether the act is of judicial, legislative or administrative character is irrelevant for the question of attribution under international law.[95]

4.3.2.1.2.1.1 State Organ de facto, Persons or Entities Acting Under the Instruction or Control of a State

There might be cases in which a person or entity cannot be considered a State organ *de iure* but there exists a certain factual relationship between the person or entity which would make their conduct attributable to the State. In other words, a person or entity would be seen as acting as a *de facto* State organ.

Although Article 8 of the ILC Articles only speaks of a person or group of persons, this term also encompasses both natural and legal persons (i.e., entities).[96]

---

[92] UN ILC, State Responsibility: Comments and observations received by Governments, UN Doc A/CN.4/488, March 1998, p. 106.

[93] See especially Brownlie (1983), p. 136. An example frequently given is that of the police force in the UK which is not directly under the authority of the Secretary of Home Affairs but their acts would still be attributable to the UK.

[94] Kindred et al. (2006), p. 647; Staur Eiedom AS, Ebo Invest AS & Rox Holding AS v Republic of Latvia (2020), ARB/16/38, ICSID, p. 313 ["It has nevertheless been recognized in the Commentary to the ILC Articles, other doctrinal writings and in the jurisprudence of international tribunals that a person or entity may be characterized as an organ of the State as a matter of international law even if it does not possess that character under the State's internal law"].

[95] Kindred et al. (2006), p. 647.

[96] "Report of the International Law Commission on the work of its fifty-third session" (Un Doc A/56/10) in Yearbook of the International Law Commission 2001, vol 2, part 2 (UN Doc A/CN.4/SER.A/2001/Add.1), pp. 47, 49

> ["as a general principle, the conduct of private persons or entities is not attributable to the State under international law. Circumstances may arise, however, where such conduct is nevertheless attributable to the State because there exists a specific factual relationship between the person or entity engaging in the conduct and the State. Article 8 deals with two such circumstances." (...) "Article 8 uses the words 'person or group of persons', reflecting the fact that conduct covered by the article may be that of a group lacking separate legal

To be considered a *de facto* State organ, the person or entity must be "in fact act under such strict control by the State that they must be treated as its organs for purposes of the necessary attribution leading to the State's responsibility for an internationally wrongful act".[97] Differently put,

> persons, group of persons or entities may, for purposes of international responsibility, be equated with State organs even if that status does not follow from internal law, provided that in fact the persons, groups or entities act in "complete dependence" on the State, of which they are ultimately merely the instrument.[98]

Therefore, to treat a person or entity as a *de facto* State organ, must be exceptional and requires proof of a particularly great degree of State control over them (i.e., complete dependence).[99]

Even *ultra vires* acts, that is conduct of a State organ exceeding its authority or in contradiction to its instructions, are attributable to the State and a State cannot use it as an excuse to escape responsibility.[100] However, the *ultra vires* actions must have at a minimum been taken at least under the cover of their official character.[101]

---

personality but acting on a de facto basis. Thus, while a State may authorize conduct by a legal entity such as a corporation, it may also deal with aggregates of individuals or groups that do not have legal personality but are nonetheless acting as a collective."].

[97] Case Concerning Application of the Convention on the Prevention and Punishment of the Crime of Genocide (Bosnia and Herzegovina v Serbia and Montenegro), [2007] ICJ Rep 43, para. 391; Case Concerning Military And Paramilitary Activities in and Against Nicaragua (Nicaragua v United States) [1986], ICJ Rep 14, para. 109.

[98] Case Concerning Application of the Convention on the Prevention and Punishment of the Crime of Genocide (Bosnia and Herzegovina v Serbia and Montenegro), [2007] ICJ Rep 43, para. 392.

[99] Ibid, para 393.

[100] Resolution adopted by the General Assembly: Responsibility of States for Internationally Wrongful Acts, UNGA, 56th Sess, UN Doc A/Res/56/83, art. 7; "Report of the International Law Commission on the work of its fifty-third session" (Un Doc A/56/10) in Yearbook of the International Law Commission 2001, vol 2, part 2 (UN Doc A/CN.4/SER.A/2001/Add.1), p. 45 ["The State cannot take refuge behind the notion that, according to the provisions of its internal law or to instructions which may have been given to its organs or agents, their actions or omissions ought not to have occurred or ought to have taken a different form. This is so even where the organ or entity in question has overtly committed unlawful acts under the cover of its official status or has manifestly exceeded its competence. It is so even if other organs of the State have disowned the conduct in question."].

[101] Kindred et al. (2014), p. 394; Brownlie (2008), pp. 147–150; Aust (2010), p. 380; Petrolane, Inc Eastman Whipstock Manufacturing, Inc., And Seahorse Fleet, Inc. v The Government of The Islamic Republic of Iran, Iranian Pan American Oil Company, National Iranian Oil Company, And Oil Services Company of Iran (1991) (Iran-United States Claims Tribunal), Case- No 131, para. 83; *Caire Case* cited in "Report of the International Law Commission on the work of its fifty-third session" (Un Doc A/56/10) in Yearbook of the International Law Commission 2001, vol 2, part 2 (UN Doc A/CN.4/SER.A/2001/Add.1), p. 46 ["that the two officers, even if they are deemed to have acted outside their competence … and even if their superiors countermanded an order, have involved the responsibility of the State, since they acted under cover of their status as officers and used means placed at their disposal on account of that status"].

From this, we must separate cases in which the person or entity cannot be considered a State organ (neither *de iure* nor, absent the "complete dependence" element, *de facto)* but is acting under the instruction and control of the State.

Article 8 of the ILC Articles clarifies that, "conduct of a person or group of persons shall be considered an act of a State under international law if the person or group of persons is in fact acting on the instructions of, or under the direction or control of, that State in carrying out the conduct"

According to the ICJ, effective control of the State is needed and simple participation "even if preponderant or decisive in the (…) organizing (…) and the planning of the whole operation" would not be enough to attach international responsibility to the State.[102] The European Court of Human Rights deviates from the ICJ's view a little and uses the wider criterion of "effective overall control" to attach responsibility, while the Appeals Chamber of the International Criminal Tribunal for the former Yugoslavia, applies an "overall control" test.[103]

We must at this point devote some attention to the question of whether AI can, under certain circumstances be considered an organ of the State and give rise to State responsibility when it commits an internationally wrongful act. The ILC Articles do not confine the status of State organ to humans alone but rather they define it as "any person or *entity* which has the status in accordance with the internal law of the State [emphasis added]".[104] The term "person and entity" ought to be understood in a broad sense and includes any natural or legal person that can either *de iure* or *de facto* be considered a State organ.[105] Indeed, according to the ILC it would even include a group "lacking separate legal personality but acting on a *de*

---

[102] Case Concerning Military And Paramilitary Activities in and Against Nicaragua (Nicaragua v United States) [1986], ICJ Rep 14, para. 115; Case Concerning Application of the Convention on the Prevention and Punishment of the Crime of Genocide (Bosnia and Herzegovina v Serbia and Montenegro), [2007] ICJ Rep 43, paras 396–397

> ["[T]he Court must now determine whether the massacres at Srebrenica were committed by persons who, though not having the status of organs of the Respondent, nevertheless acted on its instructions or under its direction or control (…).The Court must emphasize, at this stage in its reasoning, that the question just stated is not the same as those dealt with thus far. It is obvious that it is different from the question whether the persons who committed the acts of genocide had the status of organs of the Respondent under its internal law; nor however, and despite some appearance to the contrary, is it the same as the question whether those persons should be equated with State organs de facto, even though not enjoying that status under internal law"].

[103] Loizidou v Turkey, No 15318/89, [1996] ECHR, p. 16; Prosecutor v Dusko Tadic, IT-94-1-A, Judgement (15 July 1999) (International Criminal Tribunal for the former Yugoslavia, Appeals Chamber), pp. 51ff.

[104] Resolution adopted by the General Assembly: Responsibility of States for Internationally Wrongful Acts, UNGA, 56th Sess, UN Doc A/Res/56/83, art. 4.

[105] Ibid, p. 42 ["The term "person or entity" is used in article 4, paragraph 2, as well as in articles 5 and 7. It is used in a broad sense to include any natural or legal person, including an individual office holder, a department, commission or other body exercising public authority, etc."].

facto basis [and] deal with aggregates of individuals or groups that do not have legal personality but are nonetheless acting as a collective".[106]

There is nothing in the law that would *a priori* prevent AI from being considered a State organ. However, AI must be considered an entity, that is it must be recognised as legal person under the law. As discussed earlier, AI neither possesses legal capacity nor legal personhood, at least not yet. No State has enacted legislation, and no legal system thus far exists that would recognise the legal personhood of an AI. Although there are, as mentioned, suggestions in this direction, they have not been put into practice yet and remain suggestions.[107]

Whatever the case may be, should our legal systems begin to recognise the legal personhood of AI, then there is nothing to prevent AI from being considered an entity under Article 4 of the ILC Articles. Indeed, it may even be appropriate to do so because international law would apply to these circumstance and States would be responsible provided all other elements for State responsibility are fulfilled.

As mentioned, whether a person or entity is a State organ is a question of fact and assessed under international law. If legal systems recognise AI as a legal person, and thus give it legal capacity, then an AI is capable of being either a State organ *de iure* (i.e., the laws of the State expressly recognise it as organ) or *de facto* (i.e., when it acts like a State organ).[108] Once AI is granted legal personhood, it will also possess legal capacity, can be the bearer of rights and obligations, and thus be integrated into the legal system. Nothing would prevent municipal law or international law to treat it as a State organ *de iure.*

The case of AI being a *de facto* State organ will be more difficult. Due to the uncontrollable nature of advanced next generation AI, the current standard applied to the category—control, direction and instruction—would likely fail. Effective control, as required by the ICJ in Nicaragua, will be quite difficult to achieve, given the autonomous nature of such highly advanced AI. This problem would be even more pronounced in outer space where a command signal would need to travel long distances which increases the further away the space object travels. The standard of "effective overall control" developed by the European Court of Human Rights, might perhaps be a better standard in this regard. However, it leaves open the question of how to assess "effective overall control" in the case of autonomous advanced

[106] Ibid, p. 49.

[107] Interestingly, if we were to follow the ILC's view that groups or entities lacking separate legal personality but acting as a collective could involve the responsibility of the State, then this could be applicable to AI applications. Although AI lacks legal personality, it is not too far-fetched to consider what would happen if different separate AI applications start interacting, working together and appear as a collective. Since the ILC ties their view to the element of "acting as a collective", AI could fulfil this requirement. And while an AI application would not have legal personality separately, their collective could be seen as possessing such under international law.

[108] Although it will be extremely difficult to argue that highly advanced AI should be considered a de-facto State organ, as it will be problematic to prove the "great degree of State control". As we have seen, the very nature of autonomous AI is that we do not have control over it. Therefore, once deployed, for example, in outer space, a State would have very limited control over it. In these cases, it might be better to establish attribution via different avenues.

AI and what would be needed to fulfill this requirement. In either case, both standards would need to be re-assessed.

4.3.2.1.2.2 Persons or Entities Empowered to Exercise Elements of Governmental Authority

The next category encompasses cases in which a person or entity, which can neither *de iure* nor *de facto* be considered a State organ, commits an internationally wrongful act that can impute the State.[109] This category is to be understood broadly and can include, *inter alia*, public corporations, semi-public entities, public agencies of various kinds and even private companies.[110] However, in all these cases the municipal law must authorise the exercise of the governmental authority and grant them the power to carry out governmental functions.[111]

Whether AI can be granted the power to exercise governmental authority is subject to the same considerations that were highlighted in Sect. 4.3.2.1.2. Should our legal systems start to recognise AI as a legal person, then it can be considered an entity. As such it can have legal capacity to bear rights and obligations.[112] Consequently, behaviour of AI leading to an internationally wrongful act could then impute the State under international law. The existing legal system would be able to handle these issues provided that AI is granted legal personhood.

---

[109] Resolution adopted by the General Assembly: Responsibility of States for Internationally Wrongful Acts, UNGA, 56th Sess, UN Doc A/Res/56/83, art. 5.

[110] "Report of the International Law Commission on the work of its fifty-third session" (Un Doc A/56/10) in Yearbook of the International Law Commission 2001, vol 2, part 2 (UN Doc A/CN.4/SER.A/2001/Add.1), p. 43.

[111] Aust (2010), p. 380; An example for this is private prisons. For instance, the US increasingly authorises private prisons, which accounted for approximately 8 percent of the total state and federal prison population in 2020. Another example for such an entity empowered to exercise elements of governmental authority would be NAV Canada. It coordinates roughly 3.3 million flights a year and has been granted the authority by Canada to handle air traffic control. NAV Canada is a fully private capital cooperation and thus NAV Canada cannot be considered an organ of Canada, neither de-facto nor de-jure. Indeed, the Civil Air Navigation Services Commercialization Act, in which Canada transfers her rights to NAV Canada, explicitly states that "[f]or all purposes the Corporation [i.e., NAV Canada] is not an agent of Her Majesty in right of Canada and, when providing civil air navigation services, is not doing so on behalf of Her Majesty in right of Canada". Therefore, NAV Canada's behaviour is attributable to Canada and could give rise to international responsibility for an internationally wrongful act. See Civil Air Navigation Services Commercialization Act, SC 1996, c 20, s 7; NAV CANADA: About Us - Who We Are. https://www.navcanada.ca/en/about-us/pages/who-we-are.aspx. Accessed 5 August 2025.

[112] States are already utilizing AI for governmental activities. For example, Immigration Canada uses an AI in the decision making process of visa applications. See CIMM – Question Period Note - Use of AI in Decision-Making at IRCC – November 29, 2022. https://www.canada.ca/en/immigration-refugees-citizenship/corporate/transparency/committees/cimm-nov-29-2022/question-period-note-use-ai-decision-making-ircc.html. Accessed 5 August 2025.

4.3.2.1.2.3 Acts of Private Actors

The third category, which can give rise to State responsibility, is that of the acts of private actors. It is generally understood, as mentioned above, that a State is not internationally responsible for these acts unless specific requirements are fulfilled.

In this regard we ought to differentiate between, on the one hand, actions under the State's instruction, under its direction or under its control, and, on the other hand, the actions of private actors for which the State was under the obligation to prevent that conduct. For the latter, as we have already discussed above, it is not the actions of the private actors as such that give rise to State responsibility but rather the omission of the State, which was under a primary obligation to prevent that conduct. In this regard it is not actually the private actors that impute the State but its own omission to prevent a certain conduct.[113] For the former, in current case law, these actions would lead the private individuals and entities to be considered a State organ *de facto*, if the element of complete dependence is fulfilled, or impute the State because of instructions or control exercised by its organs as already discussed in Sect. 4.3.2.1.2.1.1. In any case, States are generally not responsible for the acts of private actors.

Article VI of the Outer Space Treaty can be seen as an exception to these requirements. This is quite remarkable because Article VI does something to which the norms of general international law attach additional requirements. It does away with the requirement of effective control and declares that the acts of private entities are applicable to the State, the only requirement being that they are national space activities. The State will be imputed regardless of the degree of its involvement in the space activities, and this provision adds a layer of clarity to the whole issue.

The same argument that AI could be covered under the previous categories provided that legal systems recognise its legal personality, can be made here.

The first category—the obligation of a State to prevent certain conduct—would be easier to determine. Should the legal system recognise the legal personhood of AI, then such an AI could be seen as an entity whose conduct a State could be under the obligation to prevent. Of course, it would require a case-by-case analysis to determine the exact extent of the obligation, and what behaviour exactly must be prevented. It must be noted, however, that this would raise the issue of the ability of the State to prevent the conduct of the AI. As this research has pointed out, highly advanced next generation AI built on ML will make it impossible to foresee the actions of the AI, investigate them *ex-post* or re-programme the AI. If we grant autonomy to AI, we must give up control. It will therefore be difficult to put the State under the obligation to prevent a certain conduct, when the State has no means of preventing it in the first place, apart from perhaps not using AI at all.

[113] Similar considerations ought to be given to actions taken by private actors under the instruction, direction, or control of the State. It is not the private actors themselves that impute the State, it is the fact that they committed actions under the instruction, control or direction of the State. Without the element of instruction, direction or control, the actions of private actors would be just that, private actions not imputable to the State.

In the case of space activities, this assessment may change as the State is directly responsible for the activities of non-governmental entities. In other words, should the AI be considered as a legal person, then its behaviour would be directly attributable to the State if that AI is engaged in what can be considered a national activity in outer space.

4.3.3 State Responsibility Applied to Artificial Intelligence

Even though this book is not primarily concerned with the *lex ferenda*, a short discussion in this regard was necessary. This was done to underline that the norms of public international law concerning attribution, will be able to handle cases even when legal systems change and start recognising AI as a separate legal person. However, since this is reliant on a proposal *de lege ferenda* based on the assumption that AI is seen as a separate entity, and AI has thus far not been granted legal personhood, we need to also discuss a scenario in which the law remains unchanged, that is AI is not recognised as a legal person. In essence, this comes back to the question of how to treat the AI. While this author argued earlier that in cases of narrow AI a human will still be in-the-loop, or at the very least, on-the-loop, thus the AI can be seen in many regards as an appliance of the human, and the liability could be anchored in the human conduct, these issues were considered in the light of the fault standard found in the Liability Convention. State responsibility is different, that is it has a different scope and AI, regardless of how technologically advanced it is, does not need to be seen as a separate element but rather falls under the umbrella of existing actors in international law.

In theory, any conduct of human beings, corporations or other actors might be linked to the State via habitual residence, nationality, or any other national link whether they have any connection to the government or not.[114] This would inevitably lead to a much too broad application of attribution, and international law avoids such a problem. This is done to limit State responsibility on the one hand, and to recognise the autonomy of persons or entities and their actions on the other hand.[115] This is why the ILC re-stated the attribution principles in its Articles. The inquiry above was done under the fiction that AI is granted legal personhood. While this could lead to an AI being considered an organ, and entity equipped with governmental authority or even a private actor, and the attribution be accomplished that way, it is, in this author's view, not actually necessary to ensure State responsibility. This is so because the AI, whether it is narrow or general, can always be linked back to either one of the categories stipulated above. This link is an objective one, and therefore its assessment is objective. In this regard we do not ask the question of

[114] "Report of the International Law Commission on the work of its fifty-third session" (Un Doc A/56/10) in Yearbook of the International Law Commission 2001, vol 2, part 2 (UN Doc A/CN.4/SER.A/2001/Add.1), p. 38.

[115] Ibid.

whether the AI itself is attributed to the State, which under the *lex lata*, lacking legal personhood, it likely cannot, but rather whether the AI can be objectively linked to the categories set out in the ILC Articles. In other words, we bring the AI objectively under the umbrella of a State organ, a person or entity equipped with governmental authority or a private actor.

Let us illustrate this with an example: Assume that State A's military employs a fully autonomous surveillance drone to gather intel on State B. This drone suddenly deviates from its prescribed instructions and self-destructs into a government building of State B. Leaving aside the responsibility of State A for the breach of sovereignty of State B by employing the drone in the airspace of State B, State A will also be responsible for the damage and loss of life the AI caused even though there was objectively no indication that the drone would do such a thing. It is not the AI itself that is attributed to State A but rather the entity equipped with governmental authority (e.g. the military of State A) that employed the drone. The drone is objectively linked to the military and the military is subsequently attributed to State A.

In the author's view, such an approach is possible under public international law since the only elements required to give rise to State responsibility are the breach of an international obligation and attribution. This is purely an objective analysis free from the shackles of subjective fault.[116] The nexus of the inquiry is different and all the problems highly autonomous AI causes within the fault analysis are not relevant when we assess State responsibility. In other words, we only need to assess whether the AI can objectively be linked to an organ, or a person or entity equipped with governmental authority. Once the link is established, the actions of the AI become the actions of the organ or the person or entity equipped with governmental authority and, should those actions breach an international obligation, impute the State and give rise to responsibility in international law. It is the act of the State that counts, and not necessarily the question of whether an AI was used or not.

This view makes sense when we consider international law more generally. As mentioned above, international law is a legal system of cooperation that governs relations between subjects of international law. Responsibility is but one aspect of it. Therefore, the nature of international law casts a much broader net and we are primarily concerned with the actions of the subjects of international law. Technological advancement, no matter how sophisticated, is not able to change this fundamental tenet. Indeed, we have seen this with the technological advancements over the past century: while public international law can and has evolved—in certain instances accounting for new technologies such as nuclear weapons—the fundamentals have remained the same. This is the reason why the ILC Articles, "seek to formulate, by way of codification and progressive development, the basic rules of international law concerning the responsibility of States for their internationally

[116] As mentioned earlier, the historic view was that fault is required to give rise to State responsibility. Since a State is just a political construct and cannot act without agents, it also does not make sense to prescribe fault as a necessary element, and this view has rightfully been rejected nowadays.

wrongful acts",[117] it is the reason why many authors refer to the ILC Articles as a codification of customary law, it is the reason why we often refer to authors like Hugo Grotius. The system of public international law has grown over centuries largely unaffected by technological developments but bringing them into its scope. As Judge Manfred Lachs put it, "as the activities of States expanded, law began to cover new areas".[118] Space activities were undoubtedly a new technology in the 1950s and 1960s but they were never lawless. International law "has followed [humankind] throughout [its] journey in time and space, for this is its function and destiny reflected by history".[119] Thus public international law was applicable to new technologies in the past, and it will continue to be applied to technologies yet to come.

The same argument of the "objective link" can be applied to space activities. Indeed, Article VI, as mentioned, alleviates the attribution problem significantly by declaring that "State Parties to the Treaty shall bear international responsibility for national activities in outer space (…) whether such activities are carried on by governmental agencies or by non-governmental entities". Article VI of the Outer Space Treaty therefore makes States directly responsible for governmental and non-governmental entities, the only requirement being that the activity in question can be considered a national activity in outer space, and thus takes away problems relating to imputability as a necessary requirement.[120]

How advanced the AI is, what degree of autonomy it possesses and whether or not it is equipped with ML—in short all elements that cause problems in the subjective fault analysis—are also not relevant for the question of responsibility under Article VI.[121]

One could object here and raise the argument that Article VI is a treaty provision, and the author often voiced that a better approach would be to go outside of the space treaties to adequately govern responsibility arising from AI. The author still stands by this point, but it warrants some clarification.

First, there is an underlying customary rule that exists in parallel to Article VI. Jakhu and Freeland, for example, argue that Article VI of the Outer Space treaty has crystallised into customary international law.[122] While this author does not believe that the entirety of Article VI has the character of customary law, he does think that

[117] "Report of the International Law Commission on the work of its fifty-third session" (Un Doc A/56/10) in Yearbook of the International Law Commission 2001, vol 2, part 2 (UN Doc A/CN.4/SER.A/2001/Add.1), p. 31.

[118] Lachs (2010), p. 11.

[119] Ibid, p. 11.

[120] This argument becomes especially attractive if we consider that the Outer Space Treaty (Article VIII) makes clear that the State, on whose register the space object appears, retains jurisdiction and control. This can be seen as one way to help establish a link to a State. Since a State, on whose registry the space object is carried, retains jurisdiction and control, it creates a link to that State.

[121] Indeed, it some cases it might even be easier establishing an objective link since space objects are often registered in a national space register.

[122] Jakhu and Freeland (2016), p. 9.

the direct responsibility aspect of Article VI has transformed into customary law.[123] To date, no State has objected to the fact that States are directly responsible for their national activities in outer space, whether they are conducted by governmental or non-governmental entities.

If we accept this view, then States will be responsible under general international law for all space-related activities conducted by their public and private entities without the necessary element of imputability.[124] Even if one rejects this view, and thus imputability is necessary, it can still be established, as mentioned above by establishing the "objective link" and bringing AI under the umbrella of existing attribution rules.

Second, Article VI Outer Space Treaty can be applied in some cases, while in others we need to look beyond the treaty regime.

The above discussion only relates to the attribution of the conduct of private actors in space activities, and nothing more. It is important to note that the direct responsibility of States for national space activities of non-governmental entities is only one of the obligations set out in Article VI of the Outer Space Treaty. Article VI established three other obligations, namely (1) States need to ensure that national activities are carried out in conformity with the Outer Space Treaty, (2) States need to authorize and provide continuing supervision of the activities of non-governmental entities and (3) that States are jointly responsible with an international organisation of which they are part. These are separate distinct obligations, something that is often overlooked in space law literature. Accordingly, we need to also assess them individually. Particularly in the context of AI, we need to investigate these obligations separately. Due to the varying degree of autonomy of AI and the fast-paced nature of its development, it gives rise to separate issues.

While the attribution provision of Article VI will be perfectly capable of addressing both currently available AI and highly advanced next generation AI, this is not the case for the obligation to authorise and provide continuing supervision. A State will be able to authorise and supervise currently available narrow AI. It will also be able to authorise the use of highly advanced next generation AI. However, it will be extremely challenging, if not impossible, to provide adequate continuing supervision of highly advanced next generation AI. This is due to the autonomy and independence of such AI, an element this book has already discussed and will not repeat here.

---

[123] In this author's view there is not enough evidence to consider the whole Article VI as having crystallised into customary law. For example, States frequently fail to register their space objects, thus not adhering to Article VIII of the Outer Space Treaty, which in turn would mean they fail to abide by the obligation to ensure all national activities are carried out in conformity with the Outer Space Treaty as stipulated in Article VI.

[124] Jakhu and Freeland (2016), p. 9. Although the element of imputability is not so much gone than it is assumed. Once it is determined that an activity is a space activity, and once that activity has been linked to a State, then the activity is attributed, and this attribution is inescapable. The element is still there but we do not need to assess it separately.

In essence this means that while Article VI might be adequate for certain circumstances, such as narrow AI and, in limited cases, general AI, it will fail in other aspects. For such cases, the appropriate solution is to look beyond Article VI to general international law.

It would be entirely narrow-minded to argue that we should cast aside a treaty provision that is able to govern certain situations involving AI. However, this author argues to look outside the treaties when it is necessary to do so, and when the provisions are not sufficiently able to address certain issues. For Article VI this means, we need to assess each element carefully vis-à-vis the type of AI involved.

In cases where Article VI can be applied, the analysis is, like it is in general international law, objective and does likewise not require fault. The activities must only qualify objectively as national activities in outer space.[125]

However, this author shares the view of Professors Jakhu and Freeland and thinks that the attribution rule of Article VI of the Outer Space Treaty has crystallised into customary international law. This view also means that the non-requirement of imputability is extended to general international law and applicable even to States not party to the Outer Space Treaty. For cases of AI this would mean that in a first step we only need to determine whether the activities of the AI can be classified as space activities, that is can the AI be objectively linked to the space activity, in a second step identify the appropriate State and in a third step evaluate whether a breach occurred.[126] Once these objective elements are present, the State is responsible.

4.3.3.1 State Responsibility Under Article VI OST of the State of the Software Developer

The application of Article VI of the Outer Space Treaty means that States are not only directly responsible for national activities in Outer Space but also for the continuing supervision and authorization of such space activities. With the adoption of AI and other computational software for space activities, it is not hard to imagine that a dedicated industry sector, whose focus is on the development of such dedicated software, will emerge. The question that arises in this regard is whether the development of AI intended for the use in space applications can be seen as a "national activity in outer space" as stipulated in the Outer Space Treaty and therefore directly impute the State.

To answer this question, we first need to ascertain what the Outer Space Treaty means when it speaks of "national activities in outer space" because the treaty does not further define this crucial term.

---

[125] Gerhard (2009).

[126] Art. VI, Treaty on Principles Governing the Activities of States in the Exploration and Use of Outer Space, including the Moon and Other Celestial Bodies, 27 January 1967 610 UNTS 205.

Authors seem to reach agreement that activities, even if they take place on the surface of the Earth, should be seen as activities in outer space as long as they are intentionally and primarily directed towards the outer space environment.[127] However, in the literature two divergent views emerge as to how to determine the meaning of "national". One school of thought leans towards the understanding that national activities are linked to domestic law, that is, domestic space law determines what should be considered a national activity in outer space.[128] The second, and predominant, view argues that any interpretation of the term national should be given in the context of the outer space treaty.[129] In other words, the term "national activities in outer space" should be interpreted around the outer space treaty separately from domestic space legislation. In this author's opinion, the second view is preferable, especially when Article VI is read as a whole. Article VI, amongst other things, imposes on States the responsibility for "assuring that national activities are carried out *in conformity with the provisions set forth in the present Treaty*"[emphasis added]. This is an obligation of compliance which means that the content of the States' obligations must be extracted from the treaty text itself. Further, if one were to allow domestic law to determine what the term "national" means, it would allow States to circumvent their obligations under Article VI by declaring domestically that a certain activity is not a national space activity, which would be a violation of the principle of *pacta sunt servanda*. Additionally, it is a generally accepted principle that a State cannot invoke internal law to justify the failure to perform a treaty obligation, or to escape responsibility.[130]

We therefore ought to interpret the treaty provision in accordance with the ordinary meaning of "national" in the context of the treaty and in light of the treaty's object and purpose.[131] The ordinary meaning of the term "national" is to relate to a country or a nation.[132] States ordinarily exercise jurisdiction over something that relates to them. In other words, national space activity needs to be interpreted as any activity over which a State is in a position to exercise jurisdiction or control. Thus, any activity concerned with outer space that relates to a State and over which that State is in a position to exercise jurisdiction and control should be seen as national

[127] Gerhard (2009); Cheng (1998); Wedenig S-M (2023) Artificial Intelligence in Outer Space: The Responsibility of the State of the Software Developer. https://www.mcgill.ca/iasl/article/artificial-intelligence-outer-space-responsibility-state-software-developer. Accessed 5 August 2025.

[128] See e.g. Wassenbergh, p. 336.

[129] Cheng (1990), p. 36ff; Qizhi (1990); Van Traa-Engelman (1984); Van Traa-Engelman (1993); Hermida (2004), p. 8; Hobe and Chen (2017), p. 37.

[130] Art. 27, VCLT; "Report of the International Law Commission on the work of its fifty-third session' (Un Doc A/56/10) in Yearbook of the International Law Commission 2001, vol 2, part 2 (UN Doc A/CN.4/SER.A/2001/Add.1), art. 3.

[131] Art. 31, VCLT.

[132] The Cambridge Dictionary defines national as "relating to countries or to one particular country". See Cambridge Dictionary. https://dictionary.cambridge.org/dictionary/english/national. Accessed 5 August 2025.

space activity, regardless of whether it takes place on Earth or in outer space as long as it is primarily directed towards outer space.

During the negotiation of the 1962 Principles Declaration from which Article VI Outer Space Treaty later emerged, States never directly addressed what the term "national" means and in earlier proposals the term "national" was not included.[133] However, during the discussions States seemed to be in agreement that the responsibility attached to space activities should be wide.[134]

Therefore, the development of AI applications intended for space applications should be brought under the scope of the term "national activity in outer space".[135] This could give rise to a potentially new responsible State under Article VI of the Outer Space Treaty, namely that of the State of the software developer. The development of dedicated software designed for space applications is primarily intended for the outer space environment. The "national" element is established through the jurisdiction that the State exercises over its territory on which the software developer is situated. Indeed, only the State where the software developer is located is able to effectively authorise and provide continuing supervision as mandated by Article VI of the Outer Space Treaty. For purposes of the Outer Space Treaty, the software developer would be considered a non-governmental entity. In other words, the State of the software developer, having jurisdiction and control over the territory and thus the entity developing the software, would accept direct responsibility under Article VI to comply with the Outer Space Treaty and public international law.[136] While it would go beyond the scope of this section to delve deeper into this issue, it is nevertheless important to discuss this problem and raise awareness for a potential new responsible State that could emerge.

[133] For example, the USSR proposed "[a] State undertaking activities in outer space bear international responsibility for damage done to a foreign State or to its physical or juridical persons as a result of such activities." See COPUOS, Report of the Committee on the Peaceful Uses of Outer Space, Un Doc A/5549/Add.1, p. 12.

[134] See e.g. LSC, Summary Records of the 9th meeting held at the Palais des Nations, Geneva on 12th June 1962, UNCOPUOS 1962, Un Doc A/AC.105/C.2/SR.9; LSC, Provisional Summary Record of the 29th meeting held at Headquarters, New York, on 3rd May 1963, UNCOPUOS 1963, Un Doc A/AC.105/C.2/SR.28; LSC, Summary Records of the 29th to 37th meetings held at the Palais des Nations, Geneva from 9 to 26 March 1964, UNCOPUOS 1964, Un Doc A/AC.105/C.2/SR.29-37.

[135] This is particularly important for the development of AI software. While the initial development of the software may primarily take place on Earth, the application (i.e., operation, subsequent software updates etc.) throughout the lifecycle of the space object will be in outer space. Additionally, highly advanced AI equipped with ML will make decisions on its own in outer space.

[136] Wedenig S-M (2023) Artificial Intelligence in Outer Space: The Responsibility of the State of the Software Developer. https://www.mcgill.ca/iasl/article/artificial-intelligence-outer-space-responsibility-state-software-developer. Accessed 5 August 2025.

4.3.4 Potential Conflict with Bona Fide

This research argued that the fault standard, and how we assess that standard, will be challenged by highly advanced generation AI and could cause a situation in which fault becomes impossible to prove under the current *lex lata*. This would essentially mean that a State is effectively shielded from any liability claims arising from damage in outer space.

It is not hard to imagine a scenario in which a State would use these circumstances to its advantage by purposefully deploying highly advanced AI to circumvent the Liability Convention's provisions. In this author's view, this would amount to not acting in good faith (*bona fide*) and thus potentially give rise to responsibility claims for a breach of the *bona fide* obligation.

The principle of *bona fides* in many ways permeates the international legal order.[137] It is one of the most fundamental principles, seen even as the basic foundation of the well-recognised principle *pacta sunt servanda*, that pre-dates even Roman times.[138] It "can be qualified as an equally fundamental and universal structure of any legal order regardless of its social, political, economical, development-related, or cultural particularities" and is thus a general principle of law recognised by nations.[139] The VCLT for its part codifies this principle and states that every treaty in force "is binding upon the parties to it and must be performed by them in good faith".[140] This *bona fide* obligation demands that parties to a treaty, *inter alia*, execute the treaty in accordance with its object and purpose, act reasonably and take regard of the other parties to the treaty.[141] Actions that would contravene the object and purpose of the treaty would go against this principle. This would also include situations in which a party gains an unfair advantage due to a too literal interpretation "if the mere focus on the wording would fall short of respecting the objects, purposes, and spirit of the agreement".[142]

---

[137] Schmalenbach (2018), p. 473.

[138] Hugo Grotius for example refers to Aristotle and argues that without faith "all human correspondence ceases". See Grotius (2005), p. 1638.

[139] Kotzur M (2007) Good faith (Bona Fide). Max Planck Encyclopedia of International Law.

[140] Art. 26, VCLT.

[141] Kotzur M (2007) Good faith (Bona Fide). Max Planck Encyclopedia of International Law. Cf also Article 18 of the VCLT, underpinned by the bona fides principle, which demands that a State refrains any actions that would defeat the object and purpose of the treaty after signature. This principle logically also applies to later stages of the treaty.

[142] Ibid; This is very close to the "abuse of rights" doctrine. Indeed, as Prof. Brownlie points out "[w]hen the criteria of good faith, reasonableness, normal administration, and so on are provided by an existing legal rule, reference to 'abuse of rights' adds nothing". We agree with this. For example, if a contracting party would interpret a treaty to literal and through this interpretation justify actions that go against the object and purpose of the treaty, then this lacks bona fides but can also be an abuse of rights. Therefore, a separate analysis under the abuse of rights doctrine would not add anything to it. See Brownlie (2008), p. 445.

As pointed out above, the objective of the Liability Convention is to create a system that enables access to compensation. This becomes even more important when we consider the negotiation history of the treaty. As mentioned, parties saw liability as a pressing issue, especially in regard to ground damage.

If a State would purposefully employ AI to circumvent the liability provisions of the Liability Convention for damage in outer space and argue that due to the nature of AI it cannot be held liable, then that State could arguably be seen to lack *bona fide*.[143] This would constitute a breach of a primary rule of international law which could lead to the responsibility of that State under general international law. In this regard AI plays only a small role and is irrelevant for the responsibility assessment. This is another illustration of how technological advancement is not necessarily relevant for the functioning and the application of the international legal system.

4.3.5 Conclusion

The first part of this chapter looked more closely at State responsibility under general international law, that is responsibility found in the ILC Articles, and responsibility under Article VI of the Outer Space Treaty. The book discussed that the responsibility rules of general international law can, and most likely will, be applied successfully to both narrow AI, which is currently used, and highly advanced next generation AI, which has yet to emerge. This is possible because the system of public international law only requires the breach of an international obligation and the attribution of the breach to a State to give rise to State responsibility, all of which is assessed purely objectively. While there is "a proper role of fault" in international law and it can be important in certain contexts, it is not a necessary element. This chapter attempted to show that responsibility norms under general international law can be applied to AI regardless of whether the AI is recognised as a separate legal person or not. In the former case, the AI itself can then be classified as organ or entity equipped with governmental authority and impute the State directly. The latter case would mean that the AI itself cannot be attributed to the State directly. However, the AI can be brought under the umbrella of the existing attribution rules by establishing an objective link to either a State organ or person or entity equipped with governmental authority. In this case, the actions of the AI would become the actions of the organ or person or entity equipped with governmental authority, and the State can be imputed that way.

Regarding space activities this author argued that Article VI of the Outer Space Treaty can be successfully applied to all forms of AI since Article VI only needs (1) a national activity in outer space, and (2) a State this activity can be linked to. In the

[143] This argument is meant to illustrate that international responsibility can arise from a lack of bona fide and responsibility could be based on a breach of that principle.

scope of Article VI imputability does not need to be assessed separately, it is prescribed and cannot be escaped.

The author also mentioned, and agreed, with the view in the literature that sees the attribution rule of Article VI of the Outer Space Treaty of having crystallised into customary law which means that these rules would leave the confines of treaty law and apply to all States, even those that have not signed the Outer Space Treaty. Consequently, the attribution rules found in the ILC articles need not be assessed when dealing with space activities, even under general international law.

Finally, the chapter illustrated how the intentional use of highly advanced next generation AI to circumvent the liability provision for damage in outer space could constitute a breach of the *bona fide* principle and give rise to State responsibility.

This should highlight that regardless of what view is followed, i.e. whether one sees Article VI as having crystallised into customary law or not, the norms are capable of adequately governing the responsibility of States for their AI-enabled activities in outer space.

4.4 The Liability of States for Injurious Consequences Not Prohibited by Law

4.4.1 Introduction

The first part of this chapter was primarily focused on State responsibility under the norms of general international law and how it can be applied to the use of AI in space activities. The present research engaged with liability on numerous occasions. However, this was mostly in response to the liability found in the Outer Space Treaty and the Liability Convention and, as emphasised above, these liability provisions are therefore contractual obligations contained and arising primarily from treaty law. We looked at State responsibility outside of the treaties and in a similar fashion we can also look to State liability outside the Outer Space Treaty and the Liability Convention. This will allow us to determine how the liability rules of general international law can be applied to AI used in space activities and show that these rules, in this author's view, are suitable for this technology, regardless of the level of autonomy the AI possesses.

Before we can delve deeper into this inquiry, we need to briefly discuss the difference between responsibility and liability, two terms which are often used interchangeably and can lead to confusion among authors and readers of public international law.

The ILC decided to address the issue of State liability separately.[144] It seems prudent to mention here that this author is very critical of the ILC's undertaking to

[144] "Report on the International Law Commission on the work of its twenty-first session" (UN Doc A/7610/Rev.1) in Yearbook of the International Law Commission 1969, vol 2 (New York: UN,

artificially separate State responsibility from liability in general international law. Although this author does not "express total opposition to this particular enterprise"[145] as Prof. Brownlie does, he does question this undertaking, something we will discuss more in detail at the end of this section. However, the author does understand that there are other authors and States that support this view, and it seems therefore necessary for the present research to discuss State liability and explain that these rules can be applied to cases of AI successfully. However, the following section should not be misconstrued as support for this area but should rather be seen as an area developing under a shadow of doubt.

4.4.2 State Liability Distinguished

In very simple terms, international liability means to bear the consequences for activities that are lawful but breach a legal duty which is based on a duty to compensate.[146] As already mentioned, and the PCIJ made clear in the Chorzów Case, the breach of an international obligation giving rise to State responsibility also entails the obligation to make reparation, that is to bear the consequences for the breach.[147] In other words, liability is also contained within State responsibility, and they are two sides of the same coin.[148] This, and perhaps the fact that languages such as Spanish and French use the same term for both concepts, led to the practice of using these two terms interchangeably.[149]

However, the ILC and some authors draw a distinction between these two terms because State responsibility arises, in their view, from an internationally wrongful act or omission while international liability can arise even in the absence of such an act or omission.[150] While State responsibility relies on a breach of an international obligation, State liability is concerned with the consequences and is solely

1970) (A/CN.4/SER. A/1969/Add. 1), para. 83; Stubbe (2018), pp. 108–109.

[145] Brownlie (1983), p. 50.

[146] Stubbe (2018), p. 62; Cheng (1998), p. 9.

[147] Case Concerning the Factory at Chorzów (Germany v Poland), (1928) PCIJ (Ser A) No 17; see also Lee (2006), p. 359.

[148] In this case, the duty to compensate, on which liability depends, arises from secondary rules of State Responsibility. See also Kayser (2001), p. 32.

[149] "Second report on international liability for injurious consequences arising out of acts not prohibited by international law, by Mr. Julio Barboza, Special Rapporteur" (UN Doc A/CN.4/402) in Yearbook of the International Law Commission 1986, vol 2, part 1 (New York: UN, 1988) (UN Doc A/CN.4/SER.A/1986/Add.1), p. 146; Goldie (1985), p. 180. For example, the French version and the Spanish versions of the Outer Space Treaty, which are equally authentic, speak of *responsabilité* and *responsabilidad* respectively in both, Article VI and VII.

[150] Montjoie (2010); Barboza (2011), p. 23ff.

contingent on the occurrence of harm.[151] Consequently, to give rise to State liability only a causal connection between the harm and the activity must be established.[152]

As mentioned earlier, State responsibility is a secondary rule of international law. It relies on a breach of a primary obligation (i.e., treaty, customary norms etc.) and deals with the consequences of that breach.

State Liability is different insofar as it is understood to be a primary obligation of international law because "in liability, the primary norm includes the legal consequence [as] there is no breach of an international obligation".[153] Therefore, this liability needs to be differentiated from the liability flowing from State responsibility, that is the obligation to make reparation due to a breach of an international obligation attributable to the State. The latter would not arise without an internationally wrongful act or omission. In other words, according to this view, where there is no internationally wrongful act or omission, State responsibility cannot arise and thus no liability can flow from it.

State liability tries to remedy this and applies to activities that are lawful and not prohibited by international law per se but carry a certain degree of risk which could cause damage to another State (e.g., hazardous and ultra-hazardous activities) and for these activities States are required to exercise them in a way to not cause harm to others.[154] Such activities include, *inter alia*, nuclear energy, outer space activities or certain environmental activities.[155]

The ILC decided in 1997 to sub-divide the topic of international liability for injurious consequences not prohibited by international law into two parts, namely (1) the prevention of transboundary damage from hazardous activities and (2) international liability in case of loss from transboundary harm arising out of hazardous activities.

In this author's view, this sub-division adds another unnecessarily complicated layer to an already complicated topic in international law, especially because the topic of prevention of transboundary damage should be a matter of State responsibility rather than State liability.[156]

---

[151] Boyle (1990); Crawford et al. (2010); Brownlie (2008), pp. 443–445; Montjoie (2010), p. 503; Akehurst (1985).

[152] Dennerley (2018), p. 281; Barboza, supra note 250; Manzini and Masutti (2008), p. 18.

[153] Barboza (2011); Fitzmaurice (2008); Sucharitkul (1996); Horbach (1991); Stubbe (2018); Boyle (1990); Barboza (1994); Douhan A (2019) Liability for Environmental Damage. Max Planck Encyclopedia of International Law; Palmisano G (2007) Fault. Max Planck Encyclopedia of International Law; Tanzi A (2021) Liability for Lawful Acts. Max Planck Encyclopedia of International Law.

[154] Cf Byers (2002); Brunnée J (2010) Sic utere tuo ut alienum non laedas. Max Planc Encyclopedias of International Law; Tanzi A (2021) Liability for Lawful Acts. Max Planck Encyclopedia of International Law; Trial Smelter Case (United States v Canada), (1938), RIAA 1905; Stubbe (2018).

[155] Irwin et al. (2000); Jenks (1966); Barboza (2011).

[156] In this author's view, Special Rapporteur Pemmaraju confuses State responsibility and liability in this regard. To prevent transboundary harm, indeed, to prevent any conduct, is closely linked to a due diligence obligation of a State. This obligation is a primary obligation arising in international law, and its breach would lead to responsibility. It does not matter whether the activity itself, which

State liability is broadly based on the general principle of *sic utere tuo ut alienum non laedas* ("use your own property in such a way that you do not cause injury to that of another"), a principle that was expressed, amongst others, in the *Corfu Channel Case* and *Trail Smelter Arbitration*.[157] The ILC therefore concluded that State liability arises in cases of transboundary harm absent an internationally wrongful act and omission and saw it as a primary obligation of international law, as opposed to a secondary rule.

State liability is concerned with damage caused by activities within the territory or control of one State which cause harm to persons or things within the territory of another State.[158]

In other words, State liability is concerned with transboundary damage. The ILC later clarified that transboundary damage "means damage caused in the territory or in other places outside but under the jurisdiction or control of a State other than the State of origin or in other places beyond the jurisdiction or control of any State including the State of origin"[159]

Transboundary damage refers to damage caused to persons, properties or the environment and includes material damage, such as loss of life, personal injury, loss of or damage to property, loss of income or economic interest and the costs to

should have been prevented, was lawful or not. It is the failure to prevent the transboundary harm which constitutes a wrongful omission (Special Rapporteur Quentin-Baxter alluded to this problematique in his third report). See "Third report on international liability for injurious consequences arising out of acts not prohibited by international law (prevention of transboundary damage from hazardous activities), by Mr. Pemmaraju Sreenivasa Rao, Special Rapporteur" (UN Doc A/CN.4/501) in Yearbook of the International Law Commission 2000 (New York: UN, 2009) (UN Doc A/CN.4/SER.A/2000/Add.1, p. 122; see also "Third report on international liability for injurious consequences arising out of acts not prohibited by international law, by Mr. Robert Q. Quentin-Baxter, Special Rapporteur" (UN Doc A/CN.4/360) in Yearbook of the International Law Commission 1982, vol 2, part 1 (New York: UN, 1984) (UN Doc A/CN.4/SER.A/1982/Add.1), p. 55.

[157] "Preliminary report on international liability for injurious consequences arising out of acts not prohibited by international law, by Mr. Julio Barboza, Special Rapporteur" (UN Doc A/CN.4/394) in Yearbook of the International Law Commission 1985, vol 2, part 1 (New York: UN, 1987) (UN Doc A/CN.4/SER.A/1985/Add.1), p. 99; "Report of the International Law Commission on the work of its thirty-second session (5 May–25 July 1980)" (UN Doc A/35/10) in Yearbook of the International Law Commission 1980, vol 2, part 2 (New York: UN, 1981) (A/CN.4/SER.A/1980/Add.1), pp. 159–160; Corfu Channel Case (United Kingdom v Albania) [1949] ICJ Rep 4; Trial Smelter Case (United States v Canada), (1938), RIAA 1905.

[158] "Fourth report on international liability for injurious consequences arising out of acts not prohibited by international law, by Mr. Robert Q. Quentin-Baxter, Special Rapporteur" (UN Doc A/CN.4/373) in Yearbook of the International Law Commission 1983, vol 2, part 1 (New York: UN, 1985) (UN Doc A/CN.4/SER.A/1983/Add.1), p. 223.

[159] "Second report on the legal regime for allocation of loss in case of transboundary harm arising out of hazardous activities, by Mr. Pemmaraju Sreenivasa Rao, Special Rapporteur" (A/CN.4/540) in Yearbook of the International Law Commission 2004, vol 2, part 1 (New York: UN, 2010) (UN Doc A/CN.4/SER.A/2004/Add.1), p. 76.

reinstate or respond to the damage caused as well as loss or damage of the environment or natural resources.[160]

The damage has to be caused by activities that originate in the territory of one State (the injuring State) and cause damage to something or someone in the territory of another State (the injured State). Consequently, the ILC differentiates between the State of origin and the State of injury. The former referring to the State in whose territory the harmful activity takes place, the latter to the State in whose territory the damage occurs. The ILC speaks of territory "or otherwise under the jurisdiction and control" of the State.[161] In earlier drafts the ILC, when defining territory and control, spoke of maritime areas and flag States, which means that territory includes any area where the State enjoys territorial and quasi-territorial jurisdiction.[162]

State jurisdiction can generally be divided into three types, namely territorial jurisdiction, quasi-territorial jurisdiction, and personal jurisdiction.[163] Territorial jurisdiction is closely linked to the sovereignty of a State over a certain territory.[164] It constitutes the sum of powers that a State exercises over a portion of physical territory, including all persons and entities contained therein.[165] This type of jurisdiction is generally derived from the territorial sovereignty of a State but may also, *inter alia*, arise from treaties or occupation.[166]

---

[160] Ibid, p. 76.

[161] Ibid.

[162] "Third report on international liability for injurious consequences arising out of acts not prohibited by international law, by Mr. Robert Q. Quentin-Baxter, Special Rapporteur" (UN Doc A/CN.4/360) in Yearbook of the International Law Commission 1982, vol 2, part 1 (New York: UN, 1984) (UN Doc A/CN.4/SER.A/1982/Add.1), p. 60.

[163] Cheng (1997), p. 387. This tripartite division of territorial, quasi-territorial and personal jurisdiction has also been criticized by the literature as too broad. However, this author supports Cheng's view on this topic and will therefore use it in the present research.

[164] Case Concerning Sovereignty over Pedra Branca/Pulau Batu Puteh, Middle Rocks and South Ledge (Malaysia v Singapore), [2008] ICJ Rep 12, para. 122.

[165] Cheng (1997), p. 72; Brownlie (2008), p. 105.

[166] For example, Canada has sovereignty over the land mass contained within her borders and accordingly exercises territorial sovereignty over anybody or anything within. Hong Kong is a rather remarkably good example of how territorial jurisdiction was first derived from a treaty. In 1898 the UK leased the territory from China for a period of 99 years. In 1997 the lease came to an end and the UK had to hand territorial sovereignty back to China. See also Territorial and Maritime Dispute (Nicaragua v Colombia), [2012] ICJ Rep 624, para. 21; Case Concerning Sovereignty over Pulau Ligitan and Pulau Sipadan (Indonesia v Malaysia), [2002] ICJ Rep 625; Case Concerning the Frontier Dispute (Benin v Niger), [2005] ICJ Rep 90; Connected to this is the long-standing and extensive debate concerning extraterritorial jurisdiction (e.g., border crossing activities and events). Extraterritorial jurisdiction refers to the ability of a State to regulate persons, conduct or property outside its borders and it raises fundamental sovereignty issues and concerns about overlapping jurisdictions. So far, there are no widely accepted rules (e.g., treaties) to govern the application of extraterritorial jurisdiction and any rules are largely derived from customary law, which remains very ambiguous in this regard, due to different legal traditions (common and civil law), varying State responses and political concerns. This gave rise to doctrines such as "effects jurisdiction" or the "control theory". These proposals resulted in criticism and did not succeed in providing more clarity to the issue. Efforts at a codification of rules for extraterritorial jurisdiction

Personal jurisdiction describes the power of a State over individuals or entities bearing its nationality. Personal jurisdiction is linked to the nationality of the person or entity and thus continues to exist, even when the person or entity is outside the territorial or quasi-territorial jurisdiction of the State.[167]

Quasi-Territorial Jurisdiction describes a form of jurisdiction that a State exercises in regards to ships, aircraft and spacecraft having its nationality.[168] It extends not only to the ship, aircraft or spacecraft in question but also to all persons onboard of such a craft.[169] For example, the nationality of an aircraft (i.e., the quasi-territorial jurisdiction of the State of registry of the aircraft) is one of the fundamental principles in civil aviation. The nationality of an aircraft allows the aircraft to stay under the regulatory control of the State of registry, even when the aircraft is located in a foreign country.[170] The nationality of an aircraft, and the quasi-territorial jurisdiction flowing from it, are the reason why the State of registry is responsible for crimes committed on board an aircraft and usually also regulates deaths and births taking place onboard. The Soviet Union, for example, invoked the principle of quasi-territorial jurisdiction during the 1979 Godunov defection to deny American authorities access to the aircraft.[171] The US recognised that, although the plane was within its sovereign territory, thus under the territorial sovereignty of the US, the

likewise failed. For an excellent overview of these issues, see Sender and Wood (2023). In certain instances, in the space legal context, States opted to regulate these issues. For example, the International Space Station Intergovernmental Agreement (IGA), contains provisions dealing with criminal jurisdiction and intellectual property rights (Articles 21–22). It also stipulates that States retain jurisdiction and control over the elements they register (in accordance with Article VIII of the Outer Space Treaty) and over all personnel in or on the Space Station who are their nationals. See International Space Station Intergovernmental Agreement. https://www.state.gov/wp-content/uploads/2019/02/12927-Multilateral-Space-Space-Station-1.29.1998.pdf. Accessed 5 August 2025.

Additionally, the traditional conception of jurisdiction being primarily territorial is increasingly being challenged by economic globalisation, digitalisation and the emergence of new technologies. Professor Zumbansen, for example, points towards spatialized regimes of power that challenge the traditional notion by operating across borders often without clear jurisdiction or a centralised authority. This results in an accountability deficit and the multiplicity of normative orders which create regulatory complexity. He argues that traditional legal doctrines need to evolve to better regulate transnational networks and that there is a need for new legal mapping methodologies to better capture the complexity of modern power structures. See Zumbansen (2023).

With the emergence and increasing use of AI in space applications, legal scholars will have to deal with these issues in due course and more detailed research in this regard will be necessary. As this is not the main topic of the present research, the author will not delve deeper into it but directs the reader to other sources dealing with problems of extraterritorial jurisdiction, such as Parrish & Ryngaert, Research Handbook on Extraterritoriality in International Law.

[167] Cheng (1997), p. 73 The obligation for US citizens to declare and pay taxes in the US regardless of where they live, is a good example of a State exercising personal jurisdiction over its nationals.

[168] Ibid, p. 73; Brownlie (2008), p. 239.

[169] Cheng (1997), p. 73; Kindred et al. (2006), pp. 249–250.

[170] Wedenig and Hanley, p. 396.

[171] Fitzgerald (2011).

aircraft itself and any passenger on board fell under the quasi-territorial jurisdiction of the Soviet Union.[172]

Quasi-territorial jurisdiction becomes particularly important when the craft is operating outside the sovereign territory of any State (e.g., the high seas, international airspace or outer space).

As far as space objects are concerned Article VIII of the Outer Space Treaty determines that the State on whose registry a space object is carried, shall retain jurisdiction and control and as such the State of registry enjoys quasi-territorial jurisdiction.[173]

However, State liability also encompasses damage in places beyond the jurisdiction or control of any State including the State of origin.[174] This applies for example to two space objects having different States of registrations traversing though outer space or two space objects during launch traversing airspace over the high-seas.[175] However, for example in outer space, it should be argued that if the AI on the space object of State A causes damage to the space object of State B, the damage originated from territory of State A—State A has (at least quasi-territorial) jurisdiction and control over the space object on its national registry—and caused damage to the territory of State B.

4.4.3 State Liability, Fault and AI

Many commentators have employed varying terms for State liability, such as 'liability without fault', 'liability for risk', 'objective liability', 'strict liability' and 'liability sine delicto', which shows strong indication that there seems to be consensus that subjective fault is not required. Although authors seem to use these terms interchangeably, they describe something different.

---

[172] Ibid.; Dunning J (1995) Alexander Godunov, Dancer And Film Actor, Dies at 45. https://www.nytimes.com/1995/05/19/obituaries/alexander-godunov-dancer-and-film-actor-dies-at-45.html. Accessed 5 August 2025.

[173] This jurisdiction is quasi-territorial. It must be noted, however, that Article VIII uses the term "retain". This makes it clear that registration is not the only means to assert jurisdiction. Indeed, there is a great amount of unregistered space objects in outer space. Whether a State enjoys jurisdiction over a space object must therefore be determined according to principles of general international law. For example, this can be done by determining the nationality of the operator of the space object.

[174] "Second report on the legal regime for allocation of loss in case of transboundary harm arising out of hazardous activities, by Mr. Pemmaraju Sreenivasa Rao, Special Rapporteur" (A/CN.4/540) in Yearbook of the International Law Commission 2004, vol 2, part 1 (New York: UN, 2010) (UN Doc A/CN.4/SER.A/2004/Add.1), p. 76.

[175] "Third report on international liability for injurious consequences arising out of acts not prohibited by international law, by Mr. Julio Barboza, Special Rapporteur" (UN Doc A/CN.4/405) in Yearbook of the International Law Commission 1987, vol 2, part 1 (New York: UN, 1989) (UN Doc A/CN.4/SER.A/1987/Add.1), p. 53.

As mentioned earlier, 'fault' has two sides: the objective element that refers to the breach of an obligation itself (i.e. the conduct required of the State, and the actual conduct the State has followed) and the subjective element which refers to *dolus* and *culpa*. As mentioned above, liability without subjective fault refers to cases in which these mental elements are not required and as Julio Barboza correctly observes, the "double meaning of "fault" has led to confusion between cases of strict liability due to the irrelevance of culpa—i.e., the subjective element of State responsibility notwithstanding the breach of an obligation—and sine delicto liability, where the breach of an obligation is not required".[176] State liability for injurious consequences not prohibited by international law is addressing cases where no delict, i.e. an internationally wrongful act or omission, is present. Since State liability is contingent on the occurrence of harm, there is no objective fault analysis.[177] We do not need to assess whether there is an objectively different conduct from the conduct that was required—that would be in international law the objective analysis whether there has been an internationally wrongful act or omission. The pillar of State liability is that the activity is not prohibited by international law. In other words, there can be no objective fault analysis. But without an objective fault analysis, a subsequent subjective fault analysis becomes meaningless. Subjective fault cannot exist without objective fault, for there would be nothing against which we can measure *dolus* or *culpa*.

Therefore, since State liability deals with acts not prohibited by international law, the term liability *sine delicto* best reflects the character of State liability and should be employed.

Space activities would seem to fit within the framework of State liability. They are not prohibited by international law. Indeed, one might argue that space law facilitates such activities. They are, however, hazardous activities and States need to conduct them in such a way as to not cause harm to others. Should the space object of one State cause damage to the space object of another State, then the first State will be liable to pay compensation. Adding AI to this will not change the legal analysis in this regard. In the same way as for State responsibility, the question of how advanced the AI is also of less concern in the matter of State liability. This is so because the inquiry is solely concerned with whether harm objectively occurred and whether that harm can be linked to a State. An inquiry into the realm of subjective fault is not required, indeed it will not be possible since both subjective and objective fault are absent in State liability (liability *sine delicto*). Even if AI was granted legal personhood, it would still be possible to apply the rules of State liability to it. As a legal person, the AI will still have some sort of link to the State (e.g., a nationality). The State itself would enjoy jurisdiction and control over the space object (see above), and we only need to link the damage to the State.

---

176 Barboza (2011), p. 23.

177 The author will come back to this later, because he takes quite a critical stand against State liability in general.

4.4.4 A Critical View of State Liability

As mentioned at the beginning of this section, this author is critical of the ILC's approach to separate the question of State liability from State responsibility. It is the author's view that the ILC, despite its best efforts, fails to differentiate and separate State liability from State responsibility successfully.

First, as mentioned above, the ILC fundamentally places State liability on the concept of *sic utere tuo ut alienum non laedas*, which can be traced back to the first preliminary report of Special Rapporteur Quentin-Bexter and consequently influenced all subsequent Special Rapporteurs in their work.[178] This due diligence obligation to not use one's own property to cause harm to the property of another means that "[l]'ombre de l'illicéité plane d'une manière permanente sur les activités non interdites".[179] The ILC sees the principle of *utere tuo ut alienum non laedas* as an obligation arising under international law.[180] In other words, a State is under the due diligence obligation to prevent a certain conduct, namely to not let its territory be used in a way that would cause damage in the territory of another State. Consequently, should transboundary harm occur then the originating State failed in its duty of prevention and breached an obligation because it allowed its territory to be used in a way that gave rise to transboundary harm. This means that the State objectively failed to prevent the conduct, and thus committed and internationally wrongful omission which would lead to the breach of an international obligation and thus to State responsibility.

In this author's view, the ILC conflates the activity itself, which may very well be not prohibited by international law, with the obligation of the State. However, these two elements ought to be kept separate. The answerability of a State attaches to the breach of the obligation and not necessarily the activity per se. Of course, a State can engage in an illegal activity, and that activity would lead to an internationally wrongful act. This does not change the fact, however, that responsibility attaches to the breach. A State must have breached an international obligation to be responsible for it. In the present case of the liability for injurious consequences from activities not prohibited by law, the activity itself is not prohibited. However, the State is under the obligation to make sure that these 'lawful' activities do not cause harm. It is this obligation to which State responsibility would attach. It is strictly separate from the question of whether the activity itself was lawful or not. Indeed, it might

[178] "Preliminary report on international liability for injurious consequences arising out of acts not prohibited by international law, by Mr. Robert Q. Quentin-Baxter, Special Rapporteur" (A/CN.4/334) in Yearbook of the International Law Commission 1980, vol 2, part 1 (New York: UN, 1982) (UN Doc A/CN.4/SER.A/1980/Add.1), pp. 256–263.

[179] Caubet (1983), p. 107 [The shadow of doubt hangs permanently over the non-prohibited activities].

[180] "Preliminary report on international liability for injurious consequences arising out of acts not prohibited by international law, by Mr. Robert Q. Quentin-Baxter, Special Rapporteur" (A/CN.4/334) in Yearbook of the International Law Commission 1980, vol 2, part 1 (New York: UN, 1982) (UN Doc A/CN.4/SER.A/1980/Add.1), p. 263.

even be irrelevant in the inquiry. The breach of the international obligation occurs the moment transboundary harm arises because the State in that very moment committed a wrongful omission to prevent the harm from occurring. It is therefore a matter of State responsibility. Indeed as Prof. Brownlie correctly states, "[m]uch of [S]tate responsibility (…) is concerned with categories of lawful activities which have caused harm".[181]

Second, to date there is no sufficiently accepted State practice to assert that a regime of liability for injurious consequences not prohibited by law would have the character of customary law. In addition, jurisprudence does not seem to support the concept of State lability for activities not prohibited by law. Cases, such as the Corfu Channel Case, the Lac Lanoux Arbitration or the Trail Smelter Arbitration, often seen as support for a State liability regime, are in fact further examples of State responsibility.[182]

It is for the aforementioned reasons that this author counts himself among authors that place this endeavour of the ILC in doubt. This should not be seen as a denial of the existence of State liability as a separate regime. Quite the contrary, in this author's view, it does have a place in public international law, not as a customary rule or a general principle of law but rather as contained within international treaty law. Space law is a rather clear example of this. The Outer Space Treaty and the

[181] Brownlie (1983), p. 50.

[182] Montjoie (2010), p. 507; Brownlie (1983), p. 50; In the Corfu Channel case, Albania breached its obligations which according to the court consisted in "notifying for the benefit of shipping in general, the existence of a minefield in Albanian territorial waters and in warning the approaching British warships of the imminent danger to which the minefield exposed them. Such obligations are based (…) on certain general and well-recognised principles, namely: elementary considerations of humanity (…); the principle of the freedom of maritime communication; and every State's obligation not to allow knowingly its territory to be used for acts contrary to the rights of other States." Albania's failure to adhere to these obligations gave rise to its responsibility. As Prof. Brownlie remarks "the laying of mines in a territorial sea is equally lawful without more". See Corfu Channel Case (United Kingdom v Albania) [1949] ICJ Rep 4, p. 22; In the Trial Smelter Arbitration the tribunal reference the principle of *sic utere tuo ut alienum non laedas* and prescribed as follows, "no State has the right to use or permit the use of its territory in such a manner as to cause injury by fumes in or to the territory of another or the proper-ties or persons therein". In other words, Canada was under the international obligation to prevent the harmful consequences of the operation of the Trail Smelter to occur on the territory of the United States and consequently the tribunal held "that the Dominion of Canada is responsible in international law for the conduct of the Trail Smelter". In this regard the operation of the Trial Smelter in itself is a lawful activity without anything more. See Trial Smelter Case (United States v Canada), (1938), RIAA 1905, p. 22; In the Lax Lanaoux Arbitration the tribunal established that there is an international obligation of the upstream State to take into consideration in a reasonable manner the interests of the downstream State. Should a State fail to adequately take into consideration the interests of the other State, then that State would breach and obligation and accordingly be responsible under international law. See Affaire du lac Lanoux (Espagne v France) (1957) 12 RIAA 281 (Arbitrators: Sture Petrén et al), p. 317.

Liability Convention both set out an independent liability regime which is framed differently and has different elements than State responsibility.[183]

However, this does not change the fact that, should one accept the existence of an independent legal regime for liability for injurious consequences arising from activities not prohibited by law, that these principles could be applied to AI.

4.4.5 Conclusion

The preceding sub-section has talked in more detail about the liability of States for injurious consequences arising from activities not prohibited by international law. While the author is very critical of the ILC's undertaking to codify them as general rules, he does not deny its existence in international treaty law. The space law legal regime is a unique example of how State liability can be treated separately in a treaty-based regime. However, in this author's view, the ILC seems to conflate State responsibility and liability and while they try to differentiate the two legal regimes, they in fact talk about an aspect of State responsibility, namely the obligation to prevent transboundary harm.

In any case, should one follow the view of the ILC and support State liability as a separate legal regime, then we need to ask ourselves the question of whether these rules can be applied to AI. We discussed this question and answered it in the affirmative. If an AI causes damage in the space activities of one State, the rules of State liability can be applied to these accidents as long as there is transboundary harm and the harm can be linked to a State. Under international space law, the State of registration has jurisdiction and control over the space object. This jurisdiction is of quasi-territorial character. This means that should the AI located on the space object of one State, cause damage to the space object of another State, then the harm can be considered transboundary.

Since State liability is a *liability sine delicto* neither objective fault nor subjective fault is required for the liability to arise. Therefore, the autonomy of the AI, its ML component and its independence, in short everything that would challenge our traditional fault analysis, is irrelevant for the assessment whether a State is liable internationally for the actions of the AI. The inquiry is concerned with completely different aspects, namely whether transboundary harm occurred and whether that harm can be linked to a State.

---

[183] For example, the responsible State can change while the launching State, to which liability attaches, always remains the same. Once a launching State, always a launching State.

Websites and Online Sources

Cambridge Dictionary. https://dictionary.cambridge.org/dictionary/english/national. Accessed 5 August 2025.
CIMM – Question Period Note - Use of AI in Decision-Making at IRCC – November 29, 2022. https://www.canada.ca/en/immigration-refugees-citizenship/corporate/transparency/committees/cimm-nov-29-2022/question-period-note-use-ai-decision-making-ircc.html. Accessed 5 August 2025.
Dunning J (1995) Alexander Godunov, Dancer And Film Actor, Dies at 45. https://www.nytimes.com/1995/05/19/obituaries/alexander-godunov-dancer-and-film-actor-dies-at-45.html. Accessed 5 August 2025.
International Space Station Intergovernmental Agreement. https://www.state.gov/wp-content/uploads/2019/02/12927-Multilateral-Space-Space-Station-1.29.1998.pdf. Accessed 5 August 2025.
NAV CANADA: About Us - Who We Are. https://www.navcanada.ca/en/about-us/pages/who-we-are.aspx. Accessed 5 August 2025.
Wedenig S-M (2023) Artificial Intelligence in Outer Space: The Responsibility of the State of the Software Developer. https://www.mcgill.ca/iasl/article/artificial-intelligence-outer-space-responsibility-state-software-developer. Accessed 5 August 2025.

UN Documents

COPUOS, Report of the Committee on the Peaceful Uses of Outer Space, Un Doc A/5549/Add.1.
"Eight Report on responsibility on international organizations by Mr. Giorgio Gaja, Special Rapporteur" (UN Doc A/CN.4/640) in Yearbook of the International Law Commission 2018, vol 2, part 1 (New York: UN, 2010) (UN Doc A/CN.4/SER.A/2011/Add.1).
"Fourth report on international liability for injurious consequences arising out of acts not prohibited by international law, by Mr. Robert Q. Quentin-Baxter, Special Rapporteur" (UN Doc A/CN.4/373) in Yearbook of the International Law Commission 1983, vol 2, part 1 (New York: UN, 1985) (UN Doc A/CN.4/SER.A/1983/Add.1).
"Fourth report on State Responsibility by Mr. James Crawford, Special Rapporteur" (UN Doc A/CN.4/517) in Yearbook of the International Law Commission 2001, vol 2, part 1 (New York: UN, 2010) (UN Doc A/CN.4/SER.A/2001/Add.1).
Koskenniemi M (2006) Fragmentation of International Law: Difficulties arising from the Diversification and Expansion of International Law UN Doc A/CN.4/L.682.
LSC, Provisional Summary Record of the 29th meeting held at Headquarters, New York, on 3rd May 1963, UNCOPUOS 1963, Un Doc A/AC.105/C.2/SR.28.

LSC, Summary Records of the 29th to 37th meetings held at the Palais des Nations, Geneva from 9 to 26 March 1964, UNCOPUOS 1964, Un Doc A/AC.105/C.2/SR.29-37.

LSC, Summary Records of the 9th meeting held at the Palais des Nations, Geneva on 12th June 1962, UNCOPUOS 1962, Un Doc A/AC.105/C.2/SR.9.

"Preliminary report on international liability for injurious consequences arising out of acts not prohibited by international law, by Mr. Julio Barboza, Special Rapporteur" (UN Doc A/CN.4/394) in Yearbook of the International Law Commission 1985, vol 2, part 1 (New York: UN, 1987) (UN Doc A/CN.4/SER.A/1985/Add.1).

"Preliminary report on international liability for injurious consequences arising out of acts not prohibited by international law, by Mr. Robert Q. Quentin-Baxter, Special Rapporteur" (A/CN.4/334) in Yearbook of the International Law Commission 1980, vol 2, part 1 (New York: UN, 1982) (UN Doc A/CN.4/SER.A/1980/Add.1).

"Report of the International Law Commission on the work of its fifty-third session" (Un Doc A/56/10) in Yearbook of the International Law Commission 2001, vol 2, part 2 (UN Doc A/CN.4/SER.A/2001/Add.1).

"Report of the International Law Commission on the work of its thirty-second session (5 May-25 July 1980)" (UN Doc A/35/10) in Yearbook of the International Law Commission 1980, vol 2, part 2 (New York: UN, 1981) (A/CN.4/SER.A/1980/Add.1).

"Report on the International Law Commission on the work of its twenty-first session" (UN Doc A/7610/Rev.1) in Yearbook of the International Law Commission 1969, vol 2 (New York: UN, 1970) (A/CN.4/SER. A/1969/Add. 1).

"Report on the International Law Commission on the work of its twenty-first session" (UN Doc A/7610/Rev.1) in Yearbook of the International Law Commission 1969, vol 2 (New York: UN, 1970) (A/CN.4/SER. A/1969/Add. 1).

Request for the codification of the principles of international law governing State responsibility, UNGA, 8th Sess, UN Doc A/Res/798(VIII) (1953) GA Res 799(VIII).

Resolution adopted by the General Assembly: Responsibility of States for Internationally Wrongful Acts, UNGA, 56th Sess, UN Doc A/Res/56/83.

"Second report on international liability for injurious consequences arising out of acts not prohibited by international law, by Mr. Julio Barboza, Special Rapporteur" (UN Doc A/CN.4/402) in Yearbook of the International Law Commission 1986, vol 2, part 1 (New York: UN, 1988) (UN Doc A/CN.4/SER.A/1986/Add.1).

"Second report on international liability for injurious consequences arising out of acts not prohibited by international law, by Mr. Julio Barboza, Special Rapporteur" (UN Doc A/CN.4/402) in Yearbook of the International Law Commission 1986, vol 2, part 1 (New York: UN, 1988) (UN Doc A/CN.4/SER.A/1986/Add.1).

"Second report on the legal regime for allocation of loss in case of transboundary harm arising out of hazardous activities, by Mr. Pemmaraju Sreenivasa Rao,

Special Rapporteur" (A/CN.4/540) in Yearbook of the International Law Commission 2004, vol 2, part 1 (New York: UN, 2010) (UN Doc A/CN.4/SER.A/2004/Add.1).
"Third report on international liability for injurious consequences arising out of acts not prohibited by international law (prevention of transboundary damage from hazardous activities), by Mr. Pemmaraju Sreenivasa Rao, Special Rapporteur" (UN Doc A/CN.4/501) in Yearbook of the International Law Commission 2000 (New York: UN, 2009) (UN Doc A/CN.4/SER.A/2000/Add.1.
"Third report on international liability for injurious consequences arising out of acts not prohibited by international law, by Mr. Robert Q. Quentin-Baxter, Special Rapporteur" (UN Doc A/CN.4/360) in Yearbook of the International Law Commission 1982, vol 2, part 1 (New York: UN, 1984) (UN Doc A/CN.4/SER.A/1982/Add.1).
"Third report on international liability for injurious consequences arising out of acts not prohibited by international law, by Mr. Julio Barboza, Special Rapporteur" (UN Doc A/CN.4/405) in Yearbook of the International Law Commission 1987, vol 2, part 1 (New York: UN, 1989) (UN Doc A/CN.4/SER.A/1987/Add.1).
UN ILC, State Responsibility: Comments and observations received by Governments, UN Doc A/CN.4/488, March 1998.
UNCOPUOS, "Status of International Agreements relating to activities in outer space as at 1 January 2025" (2025) UN Doc A/AC.105/C.2/2025/CRP.9.

Judicature

Affaire des biens brittaniques au Maroc espagnol (Espagne contre Royaume-Uni) (1925), RIAA 615.
Affaire du lac Lanoux (Espagne v France) (1957) 12 RIAA 281 (Arbitrators: Sture Petrén et al).
Application of the Convention on the Prevention and Punishment of the Crime of Genocide in the Gaza Strip, Order of 26 January 2024 [2024].
Application of the Convention on the Prevention and Punishment of the Crime of Genocide (The Gambia v Myanmar), [2022] ICJ Rep 477.
Armed Activities on the Territory of the Congo (Democratic Republic of Congo v Rwanda) [2006] ICJ Rep 6.
Armed Activities on the Territory of the Congo (Democratic Republic of Congo v Rwanda) [2006] ICJ Rep 6.
B3 Croatian Courier Coöperatief U.A. v. Republic of Croatia (2019) ICSID Case No ARB/15/5 (International Centre for Settlement of Investment Disputes).
Case Concerning Application of the Convention on the Prevention and Punishment of the Crime of Genocide (Bosnia and Herzegovina v Serbia and Montenegro), [2007] ICJ Rep 43.
Case Concerning Military And Paramilitary Activities in and Against Nicaragua (Nicaragua v United States) [1986], ICJ Rep 14.

Case Concerning Sovereignty over Pedra Branca/Pulau Batu Puteh, Middle Rocks and South Ledge (Malaysia v Singapore), [2008] ICJ Rep 12.
Case Concerning Sovereignty over Pulau Ligitan and Pulau Sipadan (Indonesia v Malaysia), [2002] ICJ Rep 625.
Case concerning the Barcelona Traction, Light and Power Company, Limited (Belgium v Spain), [1970] ICJ Rep 3.
Case concerning the Barcelona Traction, Light and Power Company, Limited (Belgium v Spain), [1964] ICJ Rep 6.
Case concerning the difference between New Zealand and France concerning the interpretation or application of two agreements, concluded on 9 July 1986 between the two States and which related to the problems arising from the Rainbow Warrior Affair (1990), RIAA 215.
Case Concerning the Factory at Chorzów (Germany v Poland), (1928) PCIJ (Ser A) No 17; Lee (2006).
Case Concerning the Frontier Dispute (Benin v Niger), [2005] ICJ Rep 90.
Case Concerning the Frontier Dispute (Burkina Faso v Republic of Mali), [1986] ICJ Rep 554.
Case concerning the Gabčíkovo-Nagymaros Project (Hungary v Slovakia), [1997] ICJ Rep 7.
Case Concerning United States Diplomatic and Consular Staff in Tehran (United States v Iran [1980] ICJ Rep 3.
Consutel Group S.P.A. in liquidazione (Italy) v La République algérienne démocratique et populaire (2020), Case-No 2017-33 (Permanent Court of Arbitration).
Corfu Channel Case (United Kingdom v Albania) [1949] ICJ Rep 4.
Dickson Car Wheel Company (USA v United Mexican States) (1931), RIAA 669.
Gustave Caire (France) v United Mexican States, (1929), 5 RIAA 590.
Jesse Lewis (United States) v. Great Britain (David J. Adams case) (1921), 6 RIAA 85.
L. F. H. Neer and Pauline Neer (U.S.A.) v. United Mexican States (1926), 4 RIAA 60.
Laura M. B. Janes et al (USA) v United Mexican States (1925), 4 RIAA 82.
Legal Consequences of the Separation of the Chagos Archipelago from Mauritius in 1965, [2019] ICJ Rep 95.
Loizidou v Turkey, No 15318/89, [1996] ECHR.
Massey, Getrude Parker Massey (U.S.A) v United Mexican States (1927), 4 RIAA 155.
Obligation to Negotiate Access to the Pacific Ocean (Bolivia v Chile), Advisory Opinion, [2018], ICJ Rep 507.
Petrolane, Inc Eastman Whipstock Manufacturing, Inc., And Seahorse Fleet, Inc. v The Government of The Islamic Republic of Iran, Iranian Pan American Oil Company, National Iranian Oil Company, And Oil Services Company of Iran (1991) (Iran-United States Claims Tribunal), Case- No 131.
Phosphates in Morocco Case (Italy v France) (1938), PCIJ (Ser A/B) No 74.
Prosecutor v Dusko Tadic, IT-94-1-A, Judgement (15 July 1999) (International Criminal Tribunal for the former Yugoslavia, Appeals Chamber).

Question relating to Settles of German Origin in Poland (1931), Advisory Opinion, PCIJ (Ser B) No 6.
Reparation for injuries suffered in the service of the United Nations, Advisory Opinion, [1949] ICJ Rep 174.
Staur Eiedom AS, Ebo Invest AS & Rox Holding AS v Republic of Latvia (2020), ARB/16/38, ICSID.
Territorial and Maritime Dispute (Nicaragua v Colombia), [2012] ICJ Rep 624.
The Steamship Lotus (Fance v Turkey) (1927), PCIJ (Seri A) No 10.
Thomas H Youmans (USA) v United Mexican States (1926), 4 RIAA 110.
Trial Smelter Case (United States v Canada), (1938), RIAA 1905; Stubbe (2018).
Tulip Real Estate and Development Netherlands BV v Republic of Turkey (2015) Case-No ARB/11/28 (International Centre for Settlement of Investment Disputes).
Venezuela US, S.R.L. (Barbados) v The Bolivarian Republic of Venezuela (2021), Case-No 2013-34 (Permanent Court of Arbitration).

Legislation and International Treaties

Convention on the International Liability for Damage caused by Space Objects, 29 March 1972, 961 UNTS 187.
Civil Air Navigation Services Commercialization Act, SC 1996, c 20.
Treaty on Principles Governing the Activities of States in the Exploration and Use of Outer Space, including the Moon and Other Celestial Bodies, 27 January 1967 610 UNTS 205.
UN Charter, 26 June 1945, Can TS 1945 No 7.
Vienna Convention on the Law of Treaties, 23 May 1969, 1155 UNTS 331.

References

Literature

Abass A (2012) International law: text, cases, and materials. Oxford University Press, New York
Ahlborn C (2011) The rules of international organizations and the law of international responsibility. Intl Org Law Rev 8:397–482. https://doi.org/10.1163/157237411X634970
Akehurst MB (1985) International liability for injurious consequences arising out of act not prohibited by international law. Neth Yearb Int Law 16
Anzilotti D (1929) Cours de droit international. Imprimerie Cadoret, Bordeaux
Aust A (2010) Handbook of international law, 2nd edn. Cambridge University Press, Cambridge
Barboza J (1994) International liability for the injurious consequences of acts not prohibited by international law and protection of the environment. Rec des Cours 247. https://doi.org/10.1163/1875-8096_pplrdc_A9789041100795_03

Barboza J (2011) The environment, risk and liability in international law. Martinus Nijhoff Publishers, Leiden
Bedjaoui M (1987) Responsibility of states: fault and strict liability. In: Encyclopedia of public international law. Elsevier, Amsterdam
Boyle AE (1990) State responsibility and international liability for injurious consequences of acts not prohibited by international law: a necessary distinction? ICLQ 39:1–26. https://doi.org/10.1093/iclqaj/39.1.1
Brownlie I (1983) State responsibility. Oxford University Press, New York
Brownlie I (2008) Principles of public international law, 7th edn. Oxford University Press, New York
Brunnée J (2010) Sic utere tuo ut alienum non laedas. Max Planck Encyclopedias of International Law
Byers M (2002) Abuse of rights: an old principle, a new age. McGill Law J 47:389
Cassese A (2001) International law. Oxford University Press, Oxford
Castel JG (1976) International law, chiefly as interpreted and applied in Canada, 3d edn. Butterworths, Toronto
Caubet CG (1983) Le droit international en quête d'une responsabilité pour les dommages résultant d'activités qu'il n'interdit pas. AFDI 29:99–120. https://doi.org/10.3406/afdi.1983.2541
Cheng B (1990) The commercial development of space: the need for new treaties. J Space Law 19
Cheng B (1997) Studies in international space law. Oxford University Press, Oxford
Cheng B (1998) Article VI of the 1967 Space Treaty Revisited: "International Responsibility", "National Activities", and "the Appropriate State". J Space Law 26:7
Combacau J, Alland D (1985) "Primary" and "secondary" rules in the law of State responsibility categorizing international obligations. NYL 16:81. https://doi.org/10.1017/S0167676800003470
Condorelli L, Kress C (2010) The law of international responsibility. Oxford University Press, New York
Crawford J (2013) State responsibility: the general part. Cambridge University Press, New York
Crawford J, Pellet A, Olleson S, Boyle AE (eds) (2010) Liability for injurious consequences of acts not prohibited by international law. In: The law of international responsibility. Oxford University Press, New York
De Visscher C (1935) Le déni de justice en droit internationale. Receuil de Cours 52
De Wet E, Vidmar J (2012) Introduction. In: De Wet E, Vidmar J (eds) Hierarchy in international law: the place of human rights. Oxford University Press, Oxford
Dennerley JA (2018) State liability for space object collisions: the proper interpretation of 'fault' for the purposes of international space law. Eur J Int Law 29:281–301. https://doi.org/10.1093/ejil/chy003
Fitzgerald PP (2011) In defense of the nationality of aircraft. Ann Air Space Law 36:81
Fitzmaurice M (2008) International responsibility and liability. In: Bodansky D, Brunnée J, Hey E (eds) The Oxford handbook of international environmental law. Oxford University Press, Oxford
Gerhard M (2009) Article VI. In: Hobe S, Schmidt-Tedd B, Schrogl K-U (eds) Cologne commentary on space law. 1: outer space treaty. Berliner Wissenschafts-Verlag, Berlin
Goldie LFE (1985) Concepts of strict and absolute liability and the ranking of liability in terms of relative exposure to risk. Neth Yearb Int Law 16
Gourgourinis A (2011) General/particular international law and primary/secondary rules: unitary terminology of a fragmented system. Eur J Int Law 22:993–1026. https://doi.org/10.1093/ejil/chr092
Grotius H (2005) The rights of war and peace. Liberty Fund, Indianapolis
Hermida J (2004) Legal basis for a national space legislation. Kluwer Academic, Dordrecht
Hobe S, Chen K-W (2017) Legal status of outer space and celestial bodies. In: Jakhu RS, Dempsey PS (eds) Routledge handbook of space law. Routledge, New York
Horbach NLJT (1991) The confusion about state responsibility and international liability. Leiden J Int Law 4:47–74. https://doi.org/10.1017/S0922156500001837

Irwin A, Allan S, Welsh I (2000) Nuclear risks: three problematics. In: Adam B, Beck U, van Loon J (eds) The risk society and beyond: critical issues for social theory. SAGE, London
Jakhu RS, Freeland S (2016) The relationship between the outer space treaty and customary international law. In: Blount PJ et al (eds) Proceedings of the International Institute of Space Law 2016. Eleven International Publishing, The Hague
Jenks W (1966) Liability for ultra-hazardous activities in international law. Rec des Cours 117:101
Kayser V (2001) Launching space objects: issues of liability and future prospects. Springer, Netherlands, Dordrecht
Kindred HM, Saunders PM, Brunnée J (eds) (2006) International law, chiefly as interpreted and applied in Canada, 7th edn. Emond Montgomery Publications, Toronto
Kindred HM, Sounders PM, Currie RJ (eds) (2014) International law: chiefly as interpreted and applied in Canada, 8th edn. Emond Montgomery Publications, Toronto
Kolb R (2017) The international law of state responsibility: an introduction. Edward Elgar Publishing, Cheltenham
Kotzur M (2007) Good faith (Bona Fide). Max Planck Encyclopedia of International Law
Lachs M (2010) The law of outer space: an experience in contemporary law-making. Martinus Nijhoff Publishers, Leiden
Latty F (2010) In: Crawford J, Pellet A, Olleson S, Parlett K (eds) The law of international responsibility. Oxford University Press, New York
Lee RJ (2006) The Liability Convention and private space launch services. Ann Air Space Law 31
Lyall F, Larsen PB (2018) Space law: a treatise, 2nd edn. Routledge, New York
Manzini P, Masutti A (2008) An international civil liability regime for the Galileo services: a proposal. Air Space Law 33:2
Momtaz D (2010) Attribution of conduct to the State: State organs and entities empowered to exercise elements of governmental authority. In: Crawford J, Pellet A, Olleson S, Parlett K (eds) The law of international responsibility. Oxford University Press, New York
Montjoie M (2010) The concept of liability in the absence of an internationally wrongful act. In: Crawford J, Pellet A, Olleson S, Parlett K (eds) The law of international responsibility. Oxford University Press, New York
Oppenheim L (1955) In: Lauterpacht H (ed) International law, 8th edn. Longmans, London
Palkovitz N (2020) Regulating a revolution: small satellites and the law of outer space. Wolters Kluwer, Alphen aan den Rijn
Pauwelyn J (2003) Conflict of norms in public international law: how WTO law relates to other rules of international law. Cambridge University Press, Cambridge
Pellet A (2010) The definition of responsibility in international law. In: Crawford J, Pellet A, Olleson S, Parlett K (eds) The law of international responsibility. Oxford University Press, New York
Qizhi H (1990) Certain legal aspects of commercialization of space activities. Ann Air Space Law 15:11
Rousseau C (1932) De La Compatibilité des Normes Juridiques Contradictoires dans L'Ordre International. RGDIP 133
Schmalenbach K (2018) Article 26. In: Dörr O, Schmalenbach K (eds) Vienna Convention on the Law of Treaties: a commentary, 2nd edn. Springer, Berlin
Sender O, Wood M (2023) Extraterritorial jurisdiction and the limits of customary international law. In: Parrish AL, Ryngaert C (eds) Research handbook on extraterritoriality in international law. Edward Elgar Publishing, Cheltenham, UK Northampton
Shaw MN (2008) International law, 6th edn. Cambridge University Press, New York
Stern B (2010) The elements of an internationally wrongful act. In: Crawford J, Pellet A, Olleson S, Parlett K (eds) The law of international responsibility. Oxford University Press, New York
Stubbe P (2018) State accountability for space debris: a legal study of responsibility for polluting the space environment and liability for damage caused by space debris. Brill, Leiden
Sucharitkul S (1996) State responsibility and international liability under international law. Loy LA Int Comp Law J 18:20

Tanzi A (2021) Liability for lawful acts. Max Planck Encyclopedia of International Law
Van Traa-Engelman HL (1984) Problems of state responsibility in international space law. In: Proceedings of the International Institute of Space Law 1984. American Institute of Aeronautics and Astronautics, Washington D.C.
Van Traa-Engelman HL (1993) Commercial utilization of outer space: law and practice. Martinus Nijhoff, Dordrecht
Wassenbergh H International space law: a turn of the tide. Air Space Law 22:334
Wedenig S-M, Hanley DP The Russian Actions: impact on the Chicago and Cape Town Convention - an analysis. German J Air Space Law 71:387
Zumbansen P (2023) In: Parrish AL, Ryngaert C (eds) Research handbook on extraterritoriality in international law. Edward Elgar Publishing, Cheltenham, UK Northampton

Chapter 5
Conclusion

The conclusion will serve as a stepping stone to bring the arguments together and propose a viable way forward. This chapter will therefore look at our hypothesis, briefly recapitulate the essential arguments of each chapter and answer the research questions asked at the beginning of this book. This chapter will make three viable proposals for a way forward, including a solution within the current *lex lata* of public international law, which is the preferred approach, that can be sufficient to address liability and responsibility issues arising from the use of AI in space activities, and more broadly in general international law.

5.1 Hypothesis and Research Questions Answered

What the present research set out to do was to shed light on the international responsibility of States for their AI-enabled space activities. We were concerned with finding a solution primarily within the existing framework of international law to govern any responsibility and liability claims that might arise from the use of AI in space activities. While the majority of contemporary literature in space law is worried that the use AI will expand in a lawless area, and thus urgently proposes the amendment of existing or the creation of an entirely new legal framework, this book argues that, within the context of public international law and State responsibility, the existing law provides a solid framework to govern these novel issues. While the rest of the literature tries to apply the space treaties entirely to AI, even in cases where they might not work sufficiently, this research proposes to look beyond the boundaries of the treaties towards general international law when necessary.

Let us therefore briefly recapitulate the research questions stipulated at the beginning of this book, and by answering them propose a way forward.

S.-M. Wedenig, *The International Responsibility of States for AI-enabled Space Activities*, Space Regulations Library 13,
https://doi.org/10.1007/978-3-032-09506-0_5

The primary research question, which framed this book, was: how can States be held responsible under international law for AI-enabled space activities? To answer this essential question, the author divided the research into three sub-questions, namely

(1) How can a possible fault standard under international law be reconciled with the emerging nature of AI,
(2) should such a fault standard be challenged, how can States be held responsible and liable for their space activities, and
(3) could the norms of State Responsibility under general international law be the appropriate avenue to seek recourse for harm caused AI-enabled space activities?

First, albeit there is no definition to be found in public international law as to how fault is established, this research determined that negligence and intent anchor fault in public international law. The author did this by arguing that negligence and intent, as the basis of fault, are found in every legal system, and thus constitute a principle of law recognised by nations. However, this also means that negligence in the context of the use of AI in international law is subject to the same limitations as it is in domestic legal regimes and while the reasonable person test might be applicable in cases of currently available narrow AI, it will fail once highly advanced next generation AI emerges. This in turn means that fault cannot be proven anymore, and the launching State could not be held liable under the Liability Convention, and Article VII of the Outer Space Treaty, for damage caused by AI in outer space.

While for damage on the surface of the Earth or to an aircraft in flight, the Liability Convention and Article VII of the Outer Space Treaty can be applied—the liability being absolute in these cases—this will not be the case for damage in outer space. In other words, the fault standard under international law cannot be reconciled with the emerging nature of AI and once AI has matured to a point where it can be considered highly advanced and autonomous, it will fail altogether. This leads us directly to our second sub question.

Second, how can States then be held responsible for their respective AI-enabled space activities?

There are multiple possible avenues that can be found in the *lex ferenda*:

A small amendment to the Liability Convention could be considered. While the Liability Convention currently differentiates whether the damage occurred in outer space or the surface of the Earth, the absolute liability regime for surface damage could be extended to include damage in outer space. To do this, States could consider combining Articles II and III of the Liability Convention to read as follows: "A launching State shall be absolutely liable to pay compensation for damage caused by its space object on the surface of the Earth, to an aircraft in flight, or to a space object of one launching State or to persons or property on board such a space object."

Another way that would keep the two-tiered regime intact but help solve the issue of proving subjective fault, is to incorporate a reversed onus clause into the treaty text for damage in outer space. As this research mentioned in Sect. 3.3.2.2, during the negotiation of the treaties Italy proposed a system of a reversed burden of proof for damage to an aircraft and for damage in outer space between two space objects. Building upon this suggestion, an amendment to Article III of the Liability Convention can be made to read "in the event of damage being caused elsewhere than on the surface of the Earth to a space object of one launching State or to persons or property on board such a space object by a space object of another launching State, the fault of the latter shall be presumed". In the author's view this amendment is preferable to the first suggestion as it aligns more closely with what the drafters intended. They wanted to assure that third parties on the ground are protected as they do not participate in the space activity in question whereas applications in outer space generate a benefit for the respective State and thus the parties operating in outer space accept a certain risk. If an amendment to existing treaties is adopted, a reversed burden of proof approach would strike the right balance while staying closer to the legislative intent. It further also alleviates the problem of subjective fault as it will be presumed and therefore does not need to be established, but it would maintain the possibility of the defendant State to provide evidence to rebut the presumption.

Additionally, like-minded States could consider concluding an Annex to the existing treaties to govern these novel issues. This option would bear the advantage that it does not require an amendment of the existing treaty regime itself. Further, a successful negotiation between like-minded States which are politically aligned might be far easier to achieve. One only needs to look towards aviation law and the success of the Chicago Convention and its corresponding Annexes.

However, what all suggestions have in common is that they require us to change the existing legal regime, or to engage in renewed negotiations.

Proposals *de lege ferenda* in international law, while they may have merit, are, given the current political environment concerning space activities, simply too difficult to put into practise. States are showing increasing unwillingness to enter into legally binding agreements and the will to cooperate in space activities is not as prominent as it used to be in the golden age of treaty making, the post-war area of the 50s, 60s and 70s. As legal academics, we are to play the hand that we are dealt and instead of devoting resources toward the question of what the law should be, this author thinks it is more prudent to address the question of what the law is and advocate for the regulation of new and emerging fields with the means that are presently at our disposal, which leads us to our third, and in the author's view preferred, solution.

Third, could the norms of State responsibility under general international law be the appropriate avenue to seek recourse for harm caused by AI-enabled space activities of States?

We can answer the question in the affirmative. The rules of State responsibility are able to not only cover cases of currently used narrow AI but can also be applied to highly advanced next generation AI yet to emerge.

This research determined that should legal regimes start to recognise the legal personhood of AI, then there is nothing that would prevent an AI from being considered a State organ or an entity equipped with governmental authority. The attribution rule relating to entities acting under the control or instruction of the State might remain to be difficult to ascertain in cases of highly advanced next generation AI as the autonomy of such AI will make asserting control difficult to impossible. In the very least the "effective control" standard developed by the ICJ would need to be re-assessed.

This is proof that the rules of public international law will be applicable even when the law evolves, and States start to prescribe some form of legal personhood to the AI.

However, this possible development is not actually necessary for the application of the rules of State responsibility. This is so because responsibility under international law attaches to the breach of the international obligation. Any act or omission contrary to international law will be a breach of that obligation, and if it is imputed to the State, will make the State responsible for it. The analysis in international law therefore is an objective one geared towards the breach of an international obligation. How advanced technology is, or what exactly was used to breach an obligation, is not relevant in that assessment. We only assess whether the threshold of a breach was reached, and this depends on the exact content of the primary obligation in question. The question of attribution is equally an objective analysis, and it is generally accepted that fault is not required to give rise to State responsibility.

In the case of AI, the existing attribution rules can be used to also include actions undertaken by AI. This can be done by establishing an "objective link" to each category that is recognised under international law to impute the State (i.e., State organs, persons and entities equipped with governmental authority, persons and entities acting under the instruction and control of the State). This objective link exists independently from the autonomy of the AI. The AI can always be linked to one of the categories outlined in the attribution rules and whether it acts autonomously and independently is not part of the inquiry. To remind the reader of the example given in Chap. 4: If the military of State A deploys a fully autonomous surveillance drone in the territory of State B, and the drone subsequently malfunctions and destroys a government building of State B, then State A will be internationally responsible. In this regard it is not the AI that imputes the State, absent recognised legal personhood it cannot, but the behaviour of its military. The drone is objectively linked to the military of State A, and the military is attributable to the State. Should an AI be employed purely by a private person or entity, then it will be treated the same as actions of private individuals would under the existing attribution rules, namely that they generally do not impute the State unless the State is under obligation to prevent a certain conduct or the private actors act under the instruction or control of the State.[1]

Using the objective link to bring the AI under the umbrella of the existing attribution rules ensures that the norms of State responsibility can be applied to such cases. As regards space activities, the attribution rules are stricter insofar as Article VI of

[1] The objective link is also present in this case. The AI can be objectively linked to the person or entity that utilises it.

the Outer Space Treaty makes States also directly responsibility for national activities in outer space conducted by private individuals. This acceptance of direct responsibility for the activities of non-governmental entities has crystallised into customary law.

In summary, the *lex lata* provides a sufficient legal framework to govern responsibility and liability aspects for AI-enabled space activities. Of course, this means that both, the dedicated treaty regime and the norms of general international law, need to be kept in mind when dealing with the matter of AI. In some instances, the treaty regime might be sufficient, for example for narrow AI or more generally for cases of surface damage where the liability is absolute, while in other cases we need to look beyond it. Read in tandem and carefully applied on a case-by-case basis, the legal framework is sufficient.

This underpins our hypothesis, and while proposals to amend existing laws, create new legal regimes or use national legal rules and adopt them for the international legal arena are valid, they miss an essential ingredient, and neglect to take into account the currently existing rules. To remind the reader again of the words of Professor Easterbrook, "[o]nly by putting the law of the horse in the context of broader rules about commercial endeavors could one really understand the law about horses."[2] This is very much relevant today. To understand the "international law of AI" we ought to bring it into the broader context of the rules of international law pertaining to responsibility and liability. This does not only allow us to address current challenges but also the challenges yet to come. It is, in this author's view, a future proof way to continue to ensure the responsibility of States for their AI-enabled space activities even when fully autonomous next generation AI emerges.

As space lawyers and academics, it is important that we do not lose sight of the fundamentals. Often, we focus too much on the space treaty regime, try to find solutions solely within that particular framework and attempt, some more successfully than others, to apply an imperfect legal regime to new technology. We often fall into the trap of elevating the space treaties to something more than they are, and of divorcing them from the other rules of public international law.

However, the truth is that the space treaties are just that, treaties. Nothing more, and nothing less. Are they important? Certainly. But they do not constitute a *magna carta* or a constitution. We can and should look beyond them when necessary. This book is an attempt to do just that: to go back to the basic rules and to look at the bigger picture of public international law when the dedicated treaty regime is lacking. The author does not only think that this is legally important but also necessary in the case of AI which has the potential to penetrate every international legal aspect. Public international law is a complex legal arena and many problems that arise for AI in domestic legal regimes need to be assessed differently in general international law. State responsibility is anchored in the breach of an international obligation. A fault analysis, except where it is stipulated by a dedicated treaty regime, is simply

[2] Easterbrook (1996), p. 208 It is very interesting indeed that Professor Easterbrook delivered this lecture during a conference about cybersecurity in the late 90s. It is still very much relevant today.

not necessary to give rise to State responsibility. Since States are the addressee of such claims, it alleviates the problem of finding the appropriate responsible party. As long as the AI has some objective link to the State, which in this author's view it will always have irrespective of the degree of autonomy, we can determine the responsible State, and should damage occur, also the liable State. This system ensures that responsibility and liability claims for AI can be adequately addressed and solved. Adhering to the accepted *lex lata* of public international law will not only ensure legal certainty but also make it future proof. It applies to currently available narrow AI, the same way it will be applicable to a computer system like the fictitious HAL 9000. Even though highly advanced next generation autonomous AI has not emerged yet, the development in this area is rapidly progressing and as researchers we need to choose an *ex-ante* rather than *ex-post facto* approach. In the same way as the Outer Space Treaty attempted to address legal issues in outer space pre-emptively, we also must investigate these issues before the fact. Legal certainty and the safety of space operations require no less!

Reference

Easterbrook FH (1996) Cyberspace and the Law of the Horse. University Chicago Legal Forum

MIX
Papier aus verantwortungsvollen Quellen
Paper from responsible sources
FSC® C105338

If you have any concerns about our products,
you can contact us on
ProductSafety@springernature.com

In case Publisher is established outside the EU,
the EU authorized representative is:
Springer Nature Customer Service Center GmbH
Europaplatz 3, 69115 Heidelberg, Germany

Printed by Libri Plureos GmbH
in Hamburg, Germany